The Ark, the Covenant, and the Poor Men's Chest

The Ark, the Covenant, and the Poor Men's Chest

Edmund Bonner and Nicholas Ridley on Church and
Scripture in Mid-Tudor England

Mark A. Newcomb

ST. AUGUSTINE'S PRESS
South Bend, Indiana

Manufactured in the United States of America.

1 2 3 4 5 6   26 25 24 23 22 21 20

Library of Congress Cataloging in Publication Data
Newcomb, Mark A.
The ark, the covenant, and the poor men's chest : Edmund Bonner & Nicholas Ridley on church and scripture in sixteenth-century England / Mark A. Newcomb. – 1st [edition].
pages cm
Includes bibliographical references and index.
ISBN 978-1-58731-035-5 (paperbound: alk. paper) 1. England – Church history – 16th century. 2. Church – History of doctrines – 16th century. 3. Bonner, Edmund, 1500?–1569. 4. Ridley, Nicholas, 1500?–1555. I. Title.
BR756.N484 2013
274.2'06 – dc23   2013027532

Cover Illustrations: Portrait of Nicholas Ridley, used with the permission of the National Portrait Gallery, London and Portrait of Edmund Bonner, used with the permission of the Hamilton Kerr Institute, Cambridge.

∞ The paper used in this publication meets the minimum requirements of the American National Standard for Information Sciences - Permanence of Paper for Printed Materials, ANSI Z39.48-1984.

St. Augustine's Press
www.staugustine.net

This work is solemnly dedicated to the members of my immediate family who did not live to see it completed:

to my grandfather, Charles U. Baldwin,
who taught me to invest my whole, best self in every task;

to my grandmother, Ida B. Baldwin,
who taught me to look for and praise God in the small wonders of His Creation;

and to my Dad, William F. Baldwin,
who taught me the value of personal Honor, and the role of tenacity in preserving it.

"As the center of the world, [Christ] is the key to the interpretation not only of creation, but of God himself. He is so not only in and through his teaching, through the particular or universal truths which he stands for, but essentially and above all by his existence. *We cannot separate his word from his existence: it possesses his truth only in the context of his life, that is, of his giving himself for the truth and love of the Father even unto death on the Cross. Without the Cross, which means equally without the Eucharist, his word would not be true, it would not be that testimony to the Father which contains within itself the testimony of the Father as well (John 8:18)."*

"Fidelity was the content of Yahweh's covenant with Israel.... Thus in the Old Testament we have both a fides *of God towards Israel and the answering* fides *of Israel towards God; and where Israel's fidelity fails, there then arises, out of the sheer mystery of love, that baffling dialectic between the proclamation of rejection (because the unity of mutual fidelity has been broken) and the promise of fidelity on God's part reaching beyond all threats—a dialectic that plunges into the uttermost abyss of God."*

-- *Hans Urs von Balthasar,* A Theology of History

Contents

Acknowledgments ix

Preface xiii

Chapter 1: The Careers of Ridley and Bonner 1

Chapter 2: Ridley on Biblical Interpretation 69

Chapter 3: Ridley on the Nature and Role of the Church 133

Chapter 4: Bonner on Biblical Interpretation 181

Chapter 5: Bonner on the Nature and Role of the Church 235

Conclusion 280

Bibliography 292

Timeline of Major Events 314

Glossary of Key Terms and Concepts 322

Biographical Index of Main Persons 327

Acknowledgements

Over the course of two decades of reading, research, reflection, and writing on a given historical period, one gradually relinquishes the hope that, this side of eternity, he will ever be able to adequately repay his intellectual debts. That fact, however, does not absolve us of our duty to honor, by way of public thanks, those who expended great energy in attempting to teach, assist, counsel, or guide us along the way. This work's roots lie in my early intellectual formation at Hampden-Sydney College where Dr. Amos Lee Laine, first my mentor and then my friend, introduced me to the study of Tudor and Stuart Britain. As a graduate student in Divinity at Duke University, Drs. Geoffrey Wainwright, David Steinmetz, and Susan Keefe encouraged me in the study of historical theology and a better understanding of the major doctrinal disputes of the sixteenth century.

My appreciation for the historical development of Church teaching was deepened through the study of the Christian Sacraments with John Macquarrie as part of a summer studies institute hosted at Nashotah House Theological Seminary. During my doctoral studies at Fordham University, I had the great good fortune to discuss Protestant and Catholic perspectives on liturgy, scripture, worship, and ecclesiology with Avery Cardinal Dulles, S.J. It is startling to note that so many of those who inspired my love of historical theology have passed to their eternal reward. It is my hope that some part of each of them lives on in my own work and scholarship. My dissertation mentors, Dr. Susan R. Wabuda and Monsignor Thomas J. Shelley, deserve a great deal of praise for their patient work with me during the many revisions of my thesis. This study would be much the stronger had I been consistently able to encapsulate and heed their good counsel and the better advice of all of those who have helped me to grow as a Reformation scholar over the years. The defects of this work, in light of such outstanding intellectual and personal qualities in my mentors, teachers, and friends, can only be attributed to me.

I am deeply indebted to Dr. Anne Carson Daly, former Vice President for Academic Affairs at Belmont Abbey College, who not only read over the manuscript and provided a host of excellent suggestions for the text, but who also helped me to obtain a research grant in the summer of 2010. That support enabled me to visit important sites in London, Oxford, Canterbury, and Colchester connected with the key figures of this study. As a part of those travels, special thanks are due to Annie Lucas at Rochester Cathedral as well as to John and Audrey Rutherford for an expert tour and peerless hospitality. Kay Tyler, Coordinator for Non-commercial Events, and Yeoman Gaoler, Vic Lucas, took great care to ensure that my visit to the Tower of London and the cells of Sts. John Fisher and Thomas More was thoroughly informative and conducted at my own pace. John Whitehead guided me through the major sites at Oxford, including the Martyr's Monument and the remains of the entrance of Edmund Bonner's Broadgates Hall. The Reverend Christopher Garland and Mr. Warburton were very knowledgeable about the furnishings and history of Copford Church, and graciously indulged my many questions and requests during my visit there. Mr. Michael J. Wood provided invaluable aid in accessing the key passages of the London Guildhall Library volumes of Bonner and Ridley's episcopal registers (MS 9531/12, parts 1 and 2). Ms. Régine Paige of the Hamilton Kerr Institute at Cambridge was most obliging in her assistance, making it possible for the recently identified and only known sixteenth-century portrait of Edmund Bonner to be featured on the cover of this book.

The good men and women who maintain the Davidson County Sportsman's Club and Firing Range in Nashville, Tennessee were kind enough to provide me with a quiet place to write during major revisions of the manuscript. Dr. Richard Bulzacchelli of Aquinas College and the Catholic Studies Academy has been a great source of encouragement and support over the years, and provided key feedback on many of the main concepts of this study. Ms. Catherine Brandolini was invaluable as a proofreader in preparing the manuscript for publication. My students in the First-Year Thomas More Seminar at Belmont Abbey College proved most helpful in assembling sources and references for the

Biographical Index, and to encourage them as they have aided me, I would like to express my gratitude for the assistance of David Brandolini, Virginia Davison, Gioia DiBartolomeo, Jordan Killian, Daniel Korycki, Justin Kuhlman, Joseph Mack, and Jennifer Walk. I am very grateful to Andrew Chronister, my editor with St. Augustine's Press, for his very wise counsel on key portions of the text and for his gimlet eye. I am deeply grateful to Bruce and Benjamin Fingerhut of St. Augustine's Press for agreeing to publish this work and for being such kind, helpful, and patient mentors during the entire process. Finally, I would like to acknowledge the support of my family on the long road that produced this study, especially my wife, Kimberly, who has on many occasions assisted nobly in the acquisition of obscure source materials, been held captive for endless readings or discussions of its contents, and has tirelessly provided help for travel itineraries associated with it. Despite all of these travails, she has remained steadfast throughout.

— M. A. Newcomb

Preface

On April 22, 1509, Henry VII, King of England and victor of the Battle of Bosworth Field that ended the Wars of the Roses, lay dead at Richmond palace. The following day, Prince Henry was proclaimed King Henry VIII, and the seventeen-year-old heir made his way with his retinue to the Tower of London to begin preparations for his coronation. Nearly thirty-eight years elapsed from that day to Henry VIII's own death in January of 1547. Although on the calendar fewer than four decades had passed, momentous changes had occurred. England, Europe, and the Western world had been shaken by religious and philosophical transformations that still reverberate more than half a millennium later. During Henry VIII's reign, Christendom was riven, and England underwent a series of sweeping transformations that permanently altered her legal and political structures, and saw the eradication of much of her religious heritage. The scope of the destruction, most evident in the literal dismantling of England's monasteries, still resounds nearly five centuries later.

Everyone knows something about Henry VIII's England, and how the King's marriage to Catherine of Aragon (1485–1536) did not bring forth a legitimate male heir to the throne. It is common knowledge that this circumstance prompted King Henry to reconsider both the validity of his marriage, and the validity of papal authority over the Church in England. In high school, most of us studied Henry's fateful decision in our World History classes, and learned that Henry's actions set in motion a series of religious reactions as England moved from being Roman Catholic in the 1530s to becoming an English Catholic nation under Henry. We also learned that England became a Protestant nation under Henry's son, Edward VI (1537–1553), returned to Catholicism under Henry's eldest daughter, Mary I (1516–1558), and finally established a lasting Protestant religious identity under Henry's youngest daughter, Elizabeth I (1533–1603), that was not sufficiently reformed to suit the Puritans.

What most of us cannot appreciate, however, is how difficult and perilous these changes were for the talented and dedicated men and women who professed vows or were ordained in the Church prior to Henry's break with Rome. All of us have struggled with trying to determine how far we could, in good conscience, cooperate with an enterprise that raises moral scruples for us, but few of us have had to ponder this problem while facing the real possibility of legal persecution or bodily peril for defending religious views to which we had pledged eternal fidelity a few years beforehand. This was the unpleasant fate of those who became monks, nuns, priests, and bishops in England in the 1520s and early 1530s.

One such person was Stephen Gardiner (d. 1555), Bishop of Winchester under Henry VIII, who had labored to advance the King's cause in the matter of the divorce, and assisted the King in assuming the title Supreme Head of the Church of England. By the start of Edward's reign in 1547, however, Gardiner believed that the new doctrinal reforms being set forth, were beyond the pale. Gardiner was, like many of his traditionalist colleagues among the bishops, imprisoned and removed from his see or cure under Edward.

Writing from prison, Gardiner attempted to explain why he could not embrace the new changes in the Church under Edward. Interestingly, the Bishop's letters focused on the exegetical work of Desiderius Erasmus (1466–1536), the famous Humanist Scholar of Rotterdam. Gardiner was concerned about the Royal Injunctions, promulgated in July 1547, which called for the New Testament *Paraphrases* of Erasmus, to be purchased and studied by every cleric of the realm: "This booke of the Paraphrasis is not like the other expositions of Scripture, where the aucter speaketh in his owen persone; for Erasmus taketh upon him the Evangelistes persone and Christes persone, and enterpriseth to fill uppe Christes tale and his wordes. ...In his Paraphrasis, whiche he wrott in his wanton age, the wordes and termes were able to subverte, if it were possible, as

Christ saith, thelecte."[1] In a follow-up letter, Gardiner declared, "I have favored Erasmus name as much as any other, but I never studied over this booke til now, and now I aggre with them that said Erasmus laid the eggs and Luther hat[c]ed them; ...of al the monstrous opinions that have arisen, evil men had a woundrous occasion ministred to them of that booke."[2] What Gardiner noted in this pair of letters was not merely his distaste for Erasmus' *Paraphrases*, but the fact that they are written in an interpolative style which does not disclose where scriptural citations end, and where the commentator's remarks begin.

Gardiner was beginning to see that Erasmus' Humanist exegesis carried certain theological consequences that encouraged the development of Protestantism. To fully understand the relationship of Humanism to Protestantism in sixteenth-century England, however, one must weigh Gardiner's assertion carefully and from various angles, always bearing in mind that it is two-fold: that there is something different in the work of Erasmus compared with traditional scriptural commentary, and that Erasmus' ideas lie at the foundation of Protestantism. These points are today, nearly 470 after Gardiner's death, still live questions for Reformation scholarship.

In recent decades, the idea of a direct connection between Erasmian Humanism and Protestantism has been historiographically discounted. Thus, John Olin asserted in the 1960s and 1970s, "Protestantism has a theological origin and doctrinal base quite distinct from Erasmian Humanism. Therefore, to make Erasmus responsible in some way for Luther... is to imply ...that Erasmus' cry for reform necessarily led to the disruption of the Church. There was indeed an historic nexus between reform and disruption in the sixteenth century, but that link will not be found in the thought and work of Erasmus."[3]

1   Stephen Gardiner, "Letter 130 to Protector Somerset," in *The Letters of Stephen Gardiner*, ed. James A. Muller (Cambridge: University Press, 1933) [hereafter, Gardiner, Letters], pp. 384, 385.
2   Gardiner, *Letters*, p. 403.
3   See the editor's introduction to Desiderius Erasmus, *Christian Humanism and the Reformation*, ed. John C. Olin (New York: Fordham University Press, 1975), pp. 92–106.

The current study seeks to explore both Gardiner's and Olin's assessments of Erasmian Humanism through a careful review of its distinctive principles. Gardiner was certainly correct to note that an interpolative approach to explicating scripture is characteristic of Erasmian Humanism. Erasmus also sought to separate the words of Christ from the larger context of the Old Testament narrative of salvation History through the people of ancient Israel. The current work seeks to show that for many sixteenth-century Humanists, if their earliest or most substantial introduction to Humanism was via Erasmus, the step from there to Protestantism was often much shorter than for students of Italian Humanism. This thesis will be tested by exploring the writings two other men who found themselves caught up in the doctrinal whirlwind of Henry VIII's religious settlement, Edmund Bonner (c. 1498–1569), Bishop of London under both Henry VIII and Mary I, and Nicholas Ridley (c. 1500–1555), Bishop of London under Edward VI.

The results of this research suggest that insights from the sixteenth-century and modern reflection on these issues must both be modified: Gardiner's idea of a direct causal relationship between Erasmian biblical commentary and Protestantism is no more tenable than Olin's assertion that there was no "link" at all between Erasmian Humanism and Protestantism. To reprise both Gardiner's metaphor and Olin's terminology, the "disruption of the Church" in the sixteenth century is not so much a question of causation as accommodation. Luther did not hatch Erasmian eggs, but Erasmus did build a conceptual nest that could cradle a clutch of eggs laid in part by Luther, in part by Zwingli, and eventually, in part by Nicholas Ridley. Studying the contours of that nest will help us to better understand how Erasmian concepts may have held and insulated nascent Protestant ideas, particularly in England, where Humanism was nearly synonymous with the name of Erasmus for men coming to the University at Cambridge in the 1520s.

With respect to terminology, Humanism in this study is considered as a movement focused on classical ideas about education and oratory, which dominated intellectual life in early modern Europe. The different modes of classical oratory had implications for biblical exegesis, whether or not a particular sixteenth-century author was conscious of the fact. Humanist exegesis is generally characterized by a marked historical consciousness and the use of philology for discovering *the* meaning of the text. These principles distinguish Humanist exegesis from the multi-layered approach to the *meanings* of the text often encountered in the writings of patristic and medieval biblical commentators. With respect to historical consciousness, Humanist authors such as Erasmus and John Colet (1467–1519), Dean of St. Paul's Cathedral under Henry VIII, tended to treat scripture primarily as a historical record of the events these writings relate. Those who imitated Erasmus and Colet in the succeeding generation exhibit a similar focus on the sacred text as a historical chronicle. In the current study, philology is treated not in the technical sense of the specialist in this area, but primarily as etymological digressions that Erasmus, Colet, Ridley, and Bonner often undertake in their exegetical endeavors. Each of these authors is inclined to focus at points on the meanings of discrete words as vital for the historical circumstances that govern their interpretation of a given passage.

In the chapters dedicated to the Ecclesiology of a given author, this study is not conditioned by modern attitudes that attempt to separate that branch of theology from sacramental theology or Christology. The term is used here in a sense that is more in keeping with the writings of sixteenth-century theologians, where each of these topics is generally taken to be mutually interpenetrating.

A thornier problem of terminology presents itself in the matter of rival factions within Christendom from the start of the Reformation. As Peter Marshall has pointed out, describing conservatives in Henry's reign as "Catholic" is somewhat problematic, not merely because the official faith of the realm involved rejection of the Petrine ministry from 1533, but also because a number of the Reformers wished to claim this same title.[4] Even here, however, Marshall concedes that the term could not be, "comprehensively annexed from the remaining adherents of Rome."[5] Nevertheless, the current work generally refers to figures who attempted to hold to traditional Catholicism as much as they might and still

---

4 Peter Marshall, "Is the Pope a Catholic?" in *Religious Identities in Henry VIII's England* (Burlington, Vermont: Ashgate, 2006) [hereafter, Marshall, "Is the Pope a Catholic?"], pp. 169–197.

5 Marshall, "Is the Pope a Catholic?" p. 196.

conform to Henry's religious polity as "conservatives" or "traditional-ists," although occasionally referring to "Catholic" polemics or "Catholic" theological principles among these writers, where they are clearly attempting to advocate concepts that were a part of the Church's teaching prior to the rupture of Western Christianity in sixteenth-century England, but had become controversial thereafter.[6]

How best to describe the opponents of conservatives under Henry and of Catholics under Edward raises yet another set of difficulties. The now fashionable term "Evangelical" avoids appropriation of the origi-nally denigrating term "Protestant," but does not necessarily bring better precision to historical enquiry for all that. Were the Reformers the sole promoters of the Gospel in the sixteenth century? Was the effort of Re-formers to identify themselves as "Gospel men" or "Gospellers" any less controversial than their contemporaries' desire to take sole possession of the label "Catholic"? These are questions that cannot be elided in any study that devotes many thousands of words to outlining the efforts of sixteenth-century conservatives and Catholics to promote scripture. In the following pages, figures who aimed to substantially re-constitute the doctrine and shape of the church in the sixteenth century are therefore ordinarily described as "Protestants" under Edward VI, or "early Protes-tants" for those espousing reformist views in the 1530s. There is cer-tainly contemporary warrant for doing so from the middle 1550s, since Ridley himself, although not sanguine about the label, declares, "call me a protestaunt who lusteth. I pass not thereof."[7] This terminology has the advantage, whatever its shortcomings, of avoiding other anachro-nisms that result from the use of "Evangelical" or "Gospel men." For example, we are told by Andrew Pettegree that two individuals con-demned by order of Charles V in 1521 were among, "the first executions for support of the Gospel anywhere in Europe."[8] This proclamation would likely startle St. Augustine of Canterbury no less than St. Paul

6   See Marshall, "Is the Pope a Catholic?" pp. 187–191.
7   Nicholas Ridley, *A Brief Declaracion of the Lordes Supper* ([STC 21046] Emden: Egidius van der Erve, 1555) sig. A.6, *verso*.
8   Andrew Pettegree, *Marian Protestantism: Six Studies* (Brookfield, Ver-mont: Ashgate, 1996), p. 89.

himself. The idea that only Protestant reformers attempted to live by, and win souls to, the message of the Gospel in the sixteenth century must be resisted, if the efforts of conservatives and Catholics in this same period are to be fully understood. In the face of these difficulties, the best course is to recognize, *quelle surprise*, that tidy and pleasingly precise terminology for rival factions did not emerge from the very outset of the largest and most enduring schism in Western Christianity. To overlook or intentionally evade these issues will only distort what one seeks to study in this period.

Early modern spelling conventions have been altered only slightly in citations from primary sources. The thorn symbol and raised "e" ($\mathrm{þ}^{e}$) has been rendered "the" throughout, and "v" has been substituted for "u" for the sake of clarity, where, for example, that letter is employed in words such as "neuer" and "foreuer." The long s (ſ) has been regularized and implied consonants supplied, such as we find with Ridley's text: "**proteſtaūt**" in the passage cited above, is rendered here as "protestaunt." In an effort to make this study accessible to a broad English readership, citations from sixteenth-century print editions have been cross-referenced to passages in to nineteenth- and twentieth-century publications, wherever possible. Scriptural passages have been contextualized by the use of the Great Bible when explicating a biblical citation from Nicholas Ridley and his allies, and the Vulgate when exploring a point related to the ideas of Bonner and his chaplains.

The great schism that divided Western Christianity in the sixteenth century, the de-Catholicization of England, the spoliation of the monasteries, and the wrenching of a whole people away from the faith to which they had held for a millennium, is of enduring interest to all those who care about world history or Western Civilization. No one with an appreciation for drama can avoid being attracted to the intrigue and machinations of English life under the last four Tudors. No student of psychological profiles could ask for more fascinating subjects to study than Henry VIII, Edward VI, Mary I, and Elizabeth I. Theirs was an age of breaking with the Old World and exploring the New, of rending old ties and forming new alliances. The decisions the Tudors made are responsible for cultural, political, and religious alliances that perdure today five hundred years later. The effects of the religious changes they mandated continue to play out in the various groups within the Church of England and in the Anglican Church's relationship to Roman Catholicism and to other Protestant communions. Of perennial interest to scholars, humanists, and all those who study the human condition is the predicament in which men like Gardiner, Ridley, and Bonner—and their contemporaries—found themselves. Everyone in every age faces issues of conscience and compromise. Gardiner, Ridley, Bonner, and the other men and women of their period weighed their decisions under the menace of prosecution, imprisonment, torture, and death. What these men chose, how they chose, and why they chose what they did, illuminate not only the Tudor period and religious history, but the great psychomachia that is always being waged in the human soul with conscience as the untiring protagonist.

Chapter 1
The Careers of Ridley and Bonner

Two Bishops and One See

A curious drama was being played out in London on 29 September 1549, and it was scripted to show that the Protestant establishment under Edward VI had attained a new high-water mark. On that day, the sixth session of the Royal commission to deprive Edmund Bonner of his jurisdiction was convened. Bonner, then Bishop of London, opened his remarks with a charge that the commissioners had vitiated their legal authority to try him by showing bias against his case. At that, one of the commissioners, Nicholas Ridley, Bishop of Rochester (later of London), denounced Bonner with a biblical citation from John's Gospel: "He that doeth evil hateth the light." Bonner responded with another citation from John.[1] The commissioners then informed Bonner that they would pass sentence on him at the next and final session. The fact that he had been incarcerated several days earlier did not bode well for a favorable verdict, and, in fact, Bonner was officially deprived of office on 1 October 1549.

These proceedings were remarkable for a number of reasons, not least of which was that Bonner was being removed from his see for having failed to mention just one of the several articles he was commanded to preach upon at Paul's Cross on 1 September. Under the Royal Supremacy, matters of episcopal jurisdiction were firmly under state control, and Bonner's case was meant to drive that point home for anyone

---

1   For the exchange between Ridley and Bonner, see Ridley's register as Bishop of London, MS 9531/12, pt. 2, Guildhall Library Collection, London, fol. 241, *dorso*.

else inclined to resist the Protestant reforms then being openly promoted in the realm. Bonner's deprivation trial revealed that he and Ridley were now clearly on opposing sides of the new religious initiatives. Until the mid-1540s, there was little in the public career of either Bonner or Ridley that would have suggested such divergent views of scripture and ecclesiology. In fact, it was Bonner who had distinguished himself in the effort to produce an English Bible during the 1530s, and understood this work as vital to promoting the Gospel. The careers and ecclesiastical labors of Ridley and Bonner have not received the scholarly attention that they deserve. This study will explore several important intellectual currents that preceded their work, to illustrate precisely how these two men found themselves hurling rival scriptural quotations from the same Gospel at each other in late September of 1549.

Nicholas Ridley (c. 1500–1555): A Brief Introduction to His Life and Labors

Although he was undoubtedly a leading reformer of the English church during the reign of Edward VI, Ridley answered the call to Protestantism rather later in his career than did several of his close associates. The editor of *Certen Godly, Learned, and Comfortable Conferences Between . . . Nicolas Rydley and Hughe Latymer* compared the two men by saying that Latimer had come to labor for the Gospel "earlier in the morning" than Ridley, who arrived "aboute thelevnth howre."[2] Ridley was a junior

---

2 *Certen godly, learned, and comfortable conferences, betwene the two reuerende fathers, and holye martyrs of Christe, D. Nicolas Rydley late Bysshoppe of London, and M. Hughe Latymer sometyme Bysshoppe of Worcester, during the tyme of their emprysonmentes. Whereunto is added. A treatise agaynst the errour of transubstantiation, made by the sayd reuerende father D. Nicolas Rydley* ([STC 21048] Strasbourg: Heirs of W. Rihel, 1556) [hereafter: Ridley, *Comfortable Conferences*], fol. 3, *verso*. This tract was a collaborative effort on the parts of Latimer and Ridley while they were held as prisoners of the Marian regime. Another edition produced the same year offered a "Conclusion to the Reader," where the editor identifies himself merely as "J. O.", almost certainly John Olde. See *Certein godly, learned, and comfortable conferences, betwene the two reuerende fathers, and holy martyrs of Christe, D. Nicolas Rydley late Biss-*

figure to Latimer and Cranmer, both in terms of his actual years, and also with respect to the relatively late stage at which he decisively cast his lot with the English Protestant cause.

Perhaps this is why he has received so much less scholarly attention than his career and ideas merit, but this lack of scholarly attention may result in part from the fact that historians of Reformation England, especially since the early part of the twentieth century, have generally focused on the political intrigues of the period. Therefore, Thomas Cranmer's long and often precarious relationships with kings and councils have won him the lion's share of attention. Historical theologians, many of whom today are often concerned with tracing the roots of high Anglicanism, find no friend in Ridley, who had altars removed from the churches of London and destroyed.[3] Since the poetics of liturgical language have left more room for ambiguity and reinterpretation, Anglican scholars have also chiefly focused on Cranmer, hoping to locate material to open a theological *rapprochement* with Catholicism in his orders of worship.[4]

Since the close of the sixteenth century, only a handful of scholars have concentrated explicitly on the thought and work of Ridley. Nicholas' distant kinsman, Gloucester Ridley, published a brief biography of the bishop in the mid-eighteenth century,[5] while another of the

---

hoppe of London, and M. Hughe Latimer, sometyme Bisshop of Worcester, *during the tyme of their emprisonmentes* ([STC 21047.3] Emden: Egidius van der Erve, 1556), sigs. f.3–f.5. For Olde's career as a religious controversialist and manuscript editor for Protestant prisoners of Marian England, see C. Bradshaw, "Old, John (d. 1557)," Oxford Dictionary of National Biography, Oxford University Press, 2004 [http://www.oxforddnb.com/view/article/20673, accessed 23 Feb 2006].

3   See, e.g., Ridley's visitation injunctions as Bishop of London ([STC 10247] London: Reynolde Wolfe, *Cum privilegio ad imprimendum solum*, 1550).

4   See, e.g., Francis Clark, S.J., *Eucharistic Sacrifice and the Reformation* (Oxford: Basil Blackwell, 1967). Cf. Diarmaid MacCulloch's wry comment on Stephen Gardiner's approach to the 1549 *Book of Common Prayer* providing "theological fool's gold" for Anglo-Catholic elements within the English Church. Diarmaid MacCulloch, *Thomas Cranmer: A Life* (New Haven: Yale University Press, 1996) [hereafter: MacCulloch, *Cranmer*], p. 485.

5   Gloucester Ridley, *Life of Dr. Nicolas Ridley* (London, 1763).

bishop's kinsmen, Jasper Ridley, produced the biography *Nicholas Ridley* which appeared in 1957.[6] This latter work is not an original study and is mostly a corrected and expanded edition of Gloucester's earlier work. Both these volumes draw quite heavily on the extant tracts, treatises, and letters of Nicholas, which were finally collated by the Parker Society in the mid-nineteenth century.[7]

The bulk of modern Ridley scholarship has also narrowly focused on select events in his life or isolated themes in his writings with little effort to systematically analyze or critique his ideas. Thus, David Loades discusses Ridley's fate as a prisoner of conscience in Marian England,[8] and Diarmaid MacCulloch touches on Ridley's career only tangentially, noting that the Bishop of London was an influence upon and ally of Thomas Cranmer during the reign of Edward VI.[9] Efforts to present a better understanding of Ridley's personality and thought include Patrick Collinson's comments on Ridley in the former's work on Edmund Grindal,[10] Susan Wabuda's fine entry in the new *Oxford Dictionary of National Biography*,[11] and the article "We Understand His Benefits to be Greatest in the Sacrament."[12]

To understand what Ridley was hoping to achieve with Thomas

---

6   Jasper Ridley, *Nicholas Ridley.* (London: Longmans, Green & Co. LTD, 1957).

7   Nicholas Ridley, *The Works of Bishop Ridley,* ed. Henry Christmas, for the Parker Society (Cambridge: University Press, 1841) [hereafter: Ridley, *Works*].

8   David Loades, *The Oxford Martyrs* (Batsford, 1970). Cf. Andrew Pettegree, *Marian Protestantism: Six Studies* (Brookfield, Vermont: Scholar Press, 1996).

9   MacCulloch, *Cranmer, passim.*

10 Patrick Collinson, *Archbishop Grindal 1519–1583: The Struggle for a Reformed Church* (London: Jonathan Cape, 1979) [hereafter: Collinson, *Grindal*], esp. p. 43ff.

11 Susan Wabuda, "Ridley, Nicholas (c.1502–1555)," *Oxford Dictionary of National Biography,* Oxford University Press, 2004 [http://www.oxforddnb.com/view/article/23631, accessed 23 Feb 2006], [hereafter: Wabuda, "Ridley, Nicholas"].

12 Mark A. Newcomb, "We Understand His Benefits to be Greatest in the Sacrament," in *The Anglican,* vol. 26, no. 2, pp. 9–14.

Cranmer, Hugh Latimer, and other Edwardine prelates, one must acknowledge that the leading English reformers were all, to a greater or lesser extent, engaged in some deliberate theological ambiguity. As a group, they were all concerned that the various fracturing groups within the nascent Protestant movement would serve to discredit each other by their very divisions. Under the influence of Martin Bucer (1491–1551), early Protestant ecumenist, the English Reformers sought in their various opinions and formulae to establish some accord between Lutheran and Zwinglian theological emphases. While Ridley applied his talents to this conciliatory effort at sacramental theology, his work did not consist of liturgical and devotional poetics, but took the form of tracts and treatises. His ideas and writings are therefore valuable for historians and theologians because of their more direct presentation of essential concepts at the heart of early English Protestantism. It is in the relative straightforwardness of Ridley's writings that we are able to recapture and comprehend much of the *animus* of Cranmer's liturgical work. Ridley merits study because his ideas played so great a role in shaping the Edwardine church, both directly through his own labors, and indirectly through his decisive influence on Cranmer, and upon a number of younger but quite prominent Protestant divines and martyrs, including Edmund Grindal, John Bradford, and John Philpot.

Since Ridley's thought is key to understanding early English Protestantism, it is essential to give some account of his ecclesiastical work and early life. Ridley's enemies acknowledged his role in the establishment of English Protestantism, so much so that Dr. James Brooks, the Edwardine Bishop of Glouchester, once remarked: "For what a weake and feeble stay in religion is this I pray you? Latimer leaneth to Cranmer, Cranmer to Ridley, & Ridley to the singularitie of his owne witte: so that if you ouerthrowe the singularitie of Ridleyes wit, then must needes the Religion of Cranmer and Latimer fall also."[13]

13   The pointed statement of the Marian Bishop of Glouchester, Dr. James Brooks, as quoted by John Foxe, *Actes and Monuments of matters most speciall and memorable, happenyng in the Church, with an Universal history of the same, wherein is set forth at large the whole race and course of the Church, from the primitive age to these latter tymes of ours, with the bloudy times, horrible troubles, and great persecutions agaynst the true*

Yet far from commending Ridley for self-reliant wisdom, Brooks suggests that Ridley believed in and promulgated little more than intellectual idiosyncrasies. To be described as "leaning to the singularity" of personal wit in the sixteenth century was to be considered as someone guided by nothing less arbitrary and unstable than one's own everchanging lights. Brooks' intimation that Ridley was one of the leading promulgators of Protestant doctrine was no mere rhetorical device: Thomas Cranmer himself attributed his final position on the Eucharist to the instruction of his close friend, Nicholas Ridley.[14] For Cranmer and Ridley, their Eucharistic doctrine did not belong to an *adiaphora* category of Protestant teaching;[15] their conception of the Eucharist was the issue which defined the choice between turning or burning.[16] Both

Martyrs of Christ, sought and wrought as well by Heathen Emperours, and now lately practised by Romish Prelates, especially in this Realme of England and Scotland ([STC 11225] London: John Daye, 1583) [hereafter: Foxe, *Actes and Monuments*], p. 1765. Cf. Ridley, *Works*, p. 283.

14   Thomas Cranmer, *Miscellaneous Writings and Letters of Thomas Cranmer, Archbishop of Canterbury*, ed. John Edmund Cox, for the Parker Society (Cambridge: Cambridge University Press, 1846) [hereafter: Cranmer, *Miscellaneous Writings*], p. 218. See also Diarmaid MacCulloch's lucid discussion of this topic in MacCulloch, *Cranmer*, pp. 354–55.

15   *Adiaphora* is the English equivalent of the Greek word ἀδιάφορα, meaning "indifferent things." Matters of Church teaching which were not considered crucial were referred to as "adiaphora," i.e., "non-essential," in the sixteenth century. Since both Cranmer and Ridley went to the stake affirming their Protestant conceptions of the sacrament of the altar, it is apparent that they did not consider their Eucharistic theology as an "indifferent thing." See, e.g., Collinson, *Grindal*, p. 43ff.

16   See, e.g., the articles for disputation at Oxford in Foxe, *Actes and Monuments*, p. 1483 and Ridley, *Works*, p. 192. Cf. Ridley's closing remarks to Cranmer, "Letter XII" in Ridley, *Works*, p. 363. The editors of the Parker Society volume indicate that they have taken this letter from Coverdale, but it does not appear in Miles Coverdale, *Certain most godly, fruitful, and comfortable letters of such true saintes and holy martyrs of God, as in the late bloodye persecution here within this realme, gaue their lyues for the defence of Christes holy gospel written in the tyme of their affliction and cruell imprysonment* ([STC 5886] London: John Day, 1564) [hereafter: Coverdale, *Comfortable Letters*].

Ridley and Cranmer would go to the stake professing Eucharistic views that were deemed heretical by the Catholic Church.

Ridley was accorded high status among the early English ecclesiastical Reformers because he was one of the best-educated divines of his day. A member of the gentry, he was born into a Northumberland family, near Willimontswick.[17] Though he grew up in the wild country of Tynedale in Northern England, where Scottish and English marauders traded blows back and forth across the borderlands,[18] Nicholas was a nephew of Robert Ridley, a prominent Catholic, Humanist scholar. According to William Turner, a friend and pupil of Nicholas Ridley, it was this uncle who provided the funds that procured Nicholas' impressive educational opportunities.[19]

Robert Ridley's money was not wasted on his nephew. Nicholas applied himself to his studies, entered Pembroke Hall, Cambridge about 1518, and took his B.A. in 1522. Young Nicholas Ridley continued at Pembroke Hall, was elected Fellow in 1524, and took his M.A. in 1525. Between 1527 and 1530, he studied at Louvain and the Sorbonne. When he returned to England in 1530, he assumed the position of Junior Treasurer of Pembroke Hall. Resuming his studies at Cambridge, Ridley took his B.D. in 1534, his D.D. in 1540, and was made Master of Pembroke Hall the same year.[20] Nicholas Ridley's broad learning would, in time, lead him to conclude that the Catholic tradition was less monolithic than

17 Wabuda, "Ridley, Nicholas."
18 For a graphic description of sixteenth century life in far North England, see Ridley's "Farewell," in Coverdale, *Comfortable Letters*, pp. 80–91 and Ridley, *Works*, pp. 398–408. See also William Turner's letter to John Foxe, in Ridley, *Works*, pp. 433–37. Turner's original letter is in Harleian MS no. 416, fol. 132, British Library Collection, London.
19 Nicholas Ridley also benefited from his uncle's University connections, as Robert Ridley was a Cambridge-educated doctor of divinity. On this subject, see William Turner's letter to John Foxe, in Ridley, *Works*, p. 434. For more on Robert Ridley, see Richard Rex, "Ridley, Robert (d. 1536?)," *Oxford Dictionary of National Biography*, Oxford University Press, 2004 [http://www.oxforddnb.com/view/article/68881, accessed 23 Feb 2006].
20 For a description of difficulties in dating the salient events of Ridley's early life, see J. Ridley, *Ridley*, pp. 7–42. I have mainly followed the chronology of the Parker Society's preface to Ridley, *Works*, pp. i–xvi.

his adversaries maintained. Years later, when his Catholic dinner companions insisted that the Scholastic teaching of transubstantiation was in line with apostolic belief on the Eucharist, Ridley could cite obscure sources from Church tradition as late as the ninth century which questioned the notion that the eucharistic elements were substantially transformed.[21] Similarly, when his examiners denounced Ridley's eucharistic theology as unchristian because it differed from Roman tradition, Ridley, referring to the tumultuous events of the Council of Florence, alleged that the Eastern Church had also refused to countenance the Roman doctrine of transubstantiation.[22]

Ridley's intellectual labors and laurels were but one aspect of the man. In addition to his broad learning, Ridley's friendship with Thomas Cranmer, coupled with Ridley's pastoral appointments and duties, served to encourage his Protestant formation. Following his appointment as chaplain to Archbishop Cranmer in 1537, Ridley received a series of swift promotions. He was made Vicar of Herne, Kent, in 1538, and Chaplain to Henry VIII in 1540. He successively held prebendaries at Canterbury and Westminster in 1541 and 1545, respectively. Made Vicar of Soham in 1547, Ridley was installed as the Bishop of Rochester later that same year.[23] He was translated to the bishopric of London in 1550, and was still serving the Church in that capacity when in 1553 he was nominated Bishop of Durham. Before Ridley succeeded to this position, Edward VI died and Mary Tudor came to power. With the accession of a Catholic queen, Ridley's further appointments came to an abrupt end. Mary's dislike of Ridley's religious principles had certainly not been moderated by his staunch efforts to have the royal succession diverted to Lady Jane Grey, Mary's Protestant cousin.[24] Rather than being translated to the see of Durham,

---

21 See Foxe, *Actes and Monuments*, pp. 1426–27. Cf. Ridley, *Works*, pp. 155-160.

22 Foxe, *Actes and Monuments*, p. 1454. See also, Ridley, *Works*, p. 237 and ff. The Council of Florence was convened from 1439–442.

23 On Ridley's appointments, see the Parker Society's preface to Ridley, *Works*, pp. i–iii. Cf. Coverdale, *Comfortable Letters*, pp. 80–103 and Ridley, *Works*, pp. 395–427.

24 See J. Ridley, *Ridley*, pp. 303–05.

Ridley was committed to the Tower in July of 1553, and sent to the stake in October of 1555.

If Cranmer's confession is accurate, and we have the testimony of Sir John Cheke to confirm his statements, it would be hard to overestimate Ridley's importance for the English Reformed tradition.[25] According to Cheke and Cranmer, Ridley converted the Archbishop to a symbolic view of the Eucharist sometime between 1546 and 1548, during the fateful period of the drafting and editing of the 1549 *Book of Common Prayer*.[26]

25 Collinson, *Grindal*, p. 43. Cf. Cranmer, *Miscellaneous Writings*, p. 218.
26 Collinson, *Grindal*, p. 43 and Cranmer, *Miscellaneous Writings*, p. 218. See also MacCulloch, *Cranmer*, pp. 354–55. It is just possible that William Peryn's *Thre Godly Sermons* serve to validate Cranmer's statement that he was converted by Ridley to a symbolic view of the Eucharist in 1546. In the text, Peryn refers repeatedly to those resurrecting the errors of Oecolampadius "with the ashes of Frythe." His frequent statement that he is challenging only uneducated persons in these remarks makes it hard to resist the idea that he was aware of others with more learning who were following this same course. Peryn's sermons were modeled on Fisher's *De Veritate*, wherein the latter attacked Oecolampadius with references to Ratramnus, whom Ridley credited with "opening his eyes" on the subject of a symbolic view of the sacrament of the altar. On Peryn's assertions about "unlearned" people embracing the ideas of Frith, see William Peryn, *Thre godly and notable Sermons of the moost honorable and blessed sacrament of the Aulter* ([STC 19785.5] London: John Hereforde for Robert Toye, 1546) [hereafter: Peryn, *Thre godly sermons]*, sig. iii, *recto*. Cf. sigs. ii, *recto*; B.7, *recto*; D.3, *recto*; H.7, *verso*; H.7, *verso*, and M.6, *verso*. On Ridley's debt to Ratramnus, see, e.g., Foxe, *Actes and Monuments*, p. 1427 and Ridley, *Works*, p. 159. On Peryn's use of Fisher's *De Veritate*, see L. E. C. Wooding, "Pendleton, Henry (d. 1557)," *Oxford Dictionary of National Biography,* Oxford University Press, 2004 [http://www. oxforddnb.com/view/article/21863, accessed 1 Feb 2007]. On Fisher's use of Ratramnus, see Richard Rex, *The Theology of John Fisher* (Cambridge: University Press, 2003), pp. 129–48. Ridley certainly knew of the exchange between Fisher and Oecolampadius long before it was briefly rehearsed to him by the Bishop of Chichester during the Lords' debate on Cranmer's first Prayer Book in 1548. See Abbot Francis Aidan Gasquet and Edmund Bishop, *Edward the Sixth and the Book of Common Prayer-An Examination of its Origin and Early History: With an Appendix of Unpublished Do-*

Ridley persuaded Cranmer to forsake what might be called a broadly Lutheran conception of the Eucharist in favor of Ridley's own view of the sacrament, a position which admits of no easy characterizations. Ridley's Eucharistic theology combines an affirmation of the power and high mystery of the sacrament through Christ's spiritual presence, with a systematic repudiation of the notion that the substantial materials of Christ's body and blood are encountered in the consecrated elements. With the Eastern Fathers, in whom he delighted, Ridley maintained that the Eucharist was an efficacious mystery wherein bread and wine, which are normally food for the body, are, through the power of Christ, made to be food for the soul.[27] Ridley explored the relationship between the Nicene-Constantinopolitan Creed and Church dogma. He argued that Christ could not be substantially present in the Eucharist if He has truly "ascended into heaven, and sitteth on the right hand of the Father," with the Church awaiting His coming "again with glory, to judge both the quick and the dead."[28]

Although he knew several continental reformers both personally and through their writings, Ridley's surviving literary corpus does not include a single positive appraisal of any sixteenth-century continental theologian.[29] A great part of his written legacy comes to us in the form

cuments, third edition (London: Burns and Oates, 1891) [hereafter: Gasquet and Bishop, Edward the Sixth], p. 435. The fact that Fisher's tract was written in 1526 undermines J. N. Bakhuizen van den Brink's surmise that Ratramnus was unknown in England prior to the arrival of Peter Martyr in the realm, several months after the death of Henry VIII. See J. N. Bachuizen van den Brink, "Ratramn's Eucharistic Doctrine and its Influence in 16th Century England," in vol. 2 of Studies in Church History, ed. G. J. Cuming (London: Thomas Nelson, 1965), pp. 54–77.

27 See, e.g., Foxe, Actes and Monuments, p. 1452. Cf. Ridley, Works, pp. 241–43.

28 Ridley's quotations from the Nicene-Constantinopolitan Creed, in Foxe, Actes and Monuments, p. 1443. Cf. Ridley, Works, p. 199. See also Creeds of the Churches, ed. John Leith, third edition (Louisville: John Knox Press, 1982) [hereafter: Leith, Creeds] pp. 28–33; and The First and Second Prayer Books of Edward VI, ed. E. C. S. Gibson (London: J. M. Dent & Sons Ltd., 1910) [hereafter: The Prayer Books of Edward VI], pp. 214, 379–80.

29 See Ridley, Works.

of his own transcripts of Eucharistic disputations, and indeed, in this context, references to other Protestant thinkers would have been imprudent. Still, even when he was not directly engaged in a defensive enterprise, Ridley nowhere declares himself the disciple of another Protestant theologian.[30]

Rather than taking his cue from contemporary Protestant thinkers, Ridley claimed to be inspired by the writings of Bertramus (Ratramnus), a relatively obscure, ninth-century French monk of the Abbey of Corbie.[31] Ratramnus' treatise *De corpore et sanguine domini* asserted that the substance of the bread and the wine remained after the consecration of the eucharistic elements. After reading Ratramnus' work, Ridley reexamined the writings of the Church Fathers in the light of this relatively late contention against the doctrine of the Real Presence. The dual influence of the Eastern Fathers and a Western repudiator of the foundational concepts of transubstantiation gave rise to Ridley's singular combination of a high estimation of the sacramental mystery with a low estimation of literal language about Christ's body and blood in Eucharistic theology. Ridley's understanding of the Eucharist lies at the heart of his ecclesiology, so it is particularly important to analyze how he tried to harmonize the seemingly contradictory impulses in his eucharistic thought.

A careful consideration of Ridley's eucharistic theology and its influence upon Cranmer also helps to tease the meaning out of certain enigmatic passages contained in the 1549 and 1552 *Books of Common Prayer*. Portions of the Eucharistic prayers in these orders of worship have long been thought to affirm or permit an almost transubstantiationist view of the sacrament, beseeching God that "whosoever shalbe partakers of thys holy Communion, maye worthely receive the most precious body and bloude of thy sonne Jesus Christ."[32] Yet, such a statement is wholly compatible with Ridley's view of the sacrament as a

---

30 See Ridley's *A Brief Declaracion of the Lordes Supper* ([STC 21046] Emden: Egidius van der Erve, 1555) [hereafter: Ridley, *Brief Declaration*] and *Comfortable Conferences*. Cf. Ridley, *Works*, pp. 1–45, 97–151.
31 See Foxe, *Actes and Monuments*, pp. 1387, 1427, 1443, and 1768. Cf. Ridley, *Works*, pp. 158–60 and Collinson, *Grindal*, p. 43.
32 *The Prayer Books of Edward VI*, p. 223; cf. p.389.

spiritual communion with Christ's natural body and blood.[33] Intriguingly, after the communicants have received the sacrament, they more precisely confess the manner in which they have communed with Christ: "Almightye and everlyvyng God, we most hartely thanke thee, for that thou hast vouchsafed to feed us in these holy Misteries, with the spirituall foode of the most precious body and blood of thy sonne, our saviour Jesus Christ . . . ."[34] The early prayer books bear witness to Ridley's influence in that they extol the high mystery of the Eucharist, while repudiating the notion that the efficacy of the sacrament results from the substantial presence of Christ's physical body and blood.

Apart from Ridley's direct influence upon Cranmer, it is not surprising that the early English orders of worship bear traces of his thought, since he assisted with the compilation of the first *Book of Common Prayer* and wrote certain sections of the *Catechism of King Edward VI*.[35] As Bishop of London, Ridley was a member of the upper echelons of the mid-sixteenth-century English Church and was therefore a major force in the ecclesiastic intrigues and politics of the realm. His chaplaincies to Cranmer and Henry VIII spanned the turbulent years between the Pilgrimage of Grace (1536) and the final spoliation and dissolution of the monasteries (1541). As a minister to the King and an ally of Archbishop Cranmer, Ridley was well-placed to lend his talents to ecclesiastical reform.

As with many of the leading English reformers, several of whom had supported the cause of Lady Jane, Ridley was excepted from Mary's "general amnesty" and spent the last years of his life in prison. John Foxe, never a disinterested chronicler, recounts an exchange between Mary and Ridley that preadumbrated the official repudiation of Edwardine ecclesiastical reforms. Some eight months before her accession, Ridley paid Mary a visit at Hunsden. Mary indicated that she remembered both him and one of the sermons he had preached at Court as chaplain to Henry VIII.[36] Ridley asked if she would likewise allow him to preach

---

33 See Foxe, *Actes and Monuments*, p. 1448. Cf. Ridley, *Works*, pp. 222–28.
34 *The Prayer Books of Edward VI*, p. 227; cf. p. 390.
35 See the Parker Society's preface to Ridley, *Works*, p. xii; cf. pp. 226–27.
36 Foxe, *Actes and Monuments*, p. 1396.

before her and her household, which request she staunchly refused, despite his persistence. Mary declared, "You durst not for your eares, have advouched that for Gods worde in my fathers dayes, that now you doe. And as for your new bookes, I thanke God I never read none of them: never did, nor never will doe."[37]

Ridley upbraided himself for staying to have a drink after his conversation with Mary: "Surely I have done amisse. . . . For I have dronke . . . in that place where Gods word offred, hath bene refused: Whereas if I had remembred my duetie, I ought to have departed immediately, and to have shaken of the dust of my shoes for a testimonie agaynst this house."[38] This would not be the only time that Ridley would confront his failures of steadfast resolve.[39] It is uncertain what prompted Ridley to visit Mary, but it was perhaps apparent to him even by September 1552 that the health of Mary's brother, King Edward VI, was failing. Ridley may have undertaken his visitation of Mary in an effort to preclude the destruction of his own Protestant labors, by attempting either to convert her or to temper her Catholic sentiments. In any event, genuine anxiety for what changes Mary might bring to the realm as queen distressed the reforming prelates throughout the reign of Edward VI. Edwardine statesmen, many of whom had supported Protestant reforms for personal and political gain, were well aware of their peril should the staunchly Roman Catholic Mary succeed to the throne. Certainly by the opening months of 1553, the Duke of Northumberland was becoming increasingly alarmed at Edward's deteriorating health.[40]

---

37 Foxe, *Actes and Monuments*, p. 1396. Cf. The Parker Society's preface to Ridley, *Works*, pp. x–xi, note 1.

38 Foxe, *Actes and Monuments*, p. 1396. Cf. The Parker Society's preface to Ridley, *Works*, pp. x–xi, note 1.

39 In the closing paragraph of a letter to Bradford, Ridley described himself as the weakest among the Protestant prisoners. See Coverdale, *Comfortable Letters*, p. 69 and Ridley, *Works* p. 378. Ridley wept at his official degradation while speaking of his sister. He then composed himself and said, "This is nature that mooveth mee. But I have now done." See Foxe, *Actes and Monuments*, p. 1768 and Ridley *Works*, p. 291.

40 Roger Lockyer, *Tudor and Stuart Britain: 1471–1714* (Essex: Longman, 1985), pp. 96–97.

Following Edward's death on 6 July of 1553, Ridley preached his final sermon from that most celebrated pulpit of the realm, Paul's Cross. Echoing Henry VIII's succession settlement, Ridley declared that both Mary and Elizabeth were bastards and stated that their advent to the throne would cause England to be subdued by a foreign Prince.[41] The sermon, coupled with his active and vocal support of the plot to divert the royal succession to Lady Jane Grey, did nothing to insulate him from the wrath of the Marian régime. Ridley was seized at Ipswich while *en route* to speak with Mary at Framlington, and committed to the Tower on 26 July 1553. Despite his imprisonment, Ridley continued to labor for Protestant ecclesiastical reform by clarifying and setting forth his theological formulations in English.

Several of the tracts produced by Ridley during this period were covertly transferred out of the country by friends, published by the exiled English Protestants on the continent, and secretly redistributed in England while Mary yet reigned. Ridley's most concise and explicit statements of reformed theology appear in his prison writings, composed as they were for wide distribution and Protestant evangelization. These prison tracts are the key to understanding the teaching that Thomas Cranmer found so persuasive.

Salient Points on Ridley's Approach to Ecclesiology, Sacraments, and Scripture

Ridley's ideas about the proper form and function of the Church begin and end with his eucharistic thought. While his understanding of these

---

41 For a discussion of the controversy surrounding the date of Ridley's final sermon at Paul's Cross, see J. Ridley, *Ridley* pp. 303–05 and notes. Contemporary chronicles indicate conflicting dates for the sermon's delivery. Allegedly, the difference in dates would alter the significance of Ridley's statements. According to Jasper Ridley, the *Greyfriars Chronicle* reports that Ridley's final sermon was delivered at Paul's Cross on Sunday, 9 July 1553, while Wriothesley's *Chronicle* suggests that Ridley preached on Sunday, 16 July 1553. Cf. Millar Maclure, *Register of Sermons Preached at Paul's Cross, 1534–1642* (Toronto: University Press, 1958), p. 195, which supports the 9 July date of Ridley's sermon.

matters is fully displayed in his eucharistic writings, which form the bulk of his surviving literary and theological corpus, Ridley's extant works do not include any single treatise devoted solely and directly to the subject of ecclesiology. For him, the Church and the Eucharist are theologically inextricable, and, in Ridley's writings, they are therefore characterized by such interrelatedness that to consider one is to contemplate the other.

The English Reformers were keenly aware that the various divisions between Protestant factions threatened to undermine their efforts to reform the Church according to competing views of scriptural provision. The doubts that such internecine strife raised against Protestant concerns could hardly escape notice, since they were already being rather pointedly highlighted by Thomas More in 1532: "if every man that can finde out a new fonde phantasie upon a texte of holy Scripture, may have hys owne mynde taken and hys owne exposition beleved agaynst the expositions of the olde cunnynge Doctors and Saintes," then, More asserted: "may you surely see that no article of the christen faith, can stand and endure long. . . . [If] every man might be beleved that could bryng some textes of Scripture, for hym expounded as it pleaseth hym selfe, then could I bryng a new sect also, and say by Scripture, that no man were a true Christen man nor a member of the Church, that kepeth two coates." The heart of More's argument was that, logically, scripture "alone" could not govern ecclesiology without some external structure that placed the precepts of holy writ into some ordered hierarchy of concerns. Otherwise: "in good faith . . . I were able my selfe to find out fifteen new sectes in one fore noone."[42] Ridley himself decried Protestant doctrinal

---

42 Thomas More, quoted in John Frith, *An Answere to the Treatise that M. More Made*, ed. John Foxe ([STC 24436] London: John Daye, 1573), pp. 121–22. For an analysis of historical and modern meanings of sola scriptura, see Anthony N. S. Lane, "*Sola Scriptura?* Making Sense of a Post-Reformation Slogan," in *A Pathway into the Holy Scriptures*, eds. Philip E. Satterwhite and David F. Wright (Grand Rapids: Eerdmans, 1994) [hereafter: Lane, "Sola Scriptura?"], pp. 297–327. Lane concludes his article noting that the "price to be paid" for Protestant rejection of a normative interpretation of scripture is a multitude of churches in conflict about the meaning of the Bible. See especially pages 326–27.

divisions resulting from rival interpretations of scripture: "Thou knowest, (O heavenly father), that the controversie about the Sacrament of the blessed bodye and blood of thy deare sonne, our saveour Jesu Christ, hathe troubled, not of late only, thy church of Englande, Fraunce, Germanye, and Italie, but also many yeares agoo."[43]

In fact, eucharistic controversies erupted in Europe almost from the very inception of Protestantism. In the mid 1520s, first Carlstadt and then Zwingli began to teach that Christ was not substantially present in the sacrament, but was there in a spiritual sense only. For Zwingli, in saying "this is my Body," Jesus had meant that the blessed bread "signified" his body. Zwingli supported his view by interpreting the texts relating to the Last Supper in light of John 6:63, "the flesh profiteth nothing."[44] Luther was characteristically strident in his attacks on the Thomistic teaching of transubstantiation prior to this point, but had always stood firm in the profession of Christ's real presence in the sacrament. He blasted the formulations of Carlstadt and Zwingli, whom he described as "sacramentarians," or sacramental fanatics: "Before I would have sheer wine with the fanatics, I would have sheer blood with the pope."[45] Luther and his disciples viewed any notion that refuted Christ's real presence as unfaithful to the plain words of the gospels' institution narratives.[46]

The Protestant Reformers firmly rejected the conception of a sacerdotal priesthood with its attendant focus on sacrifice and offerings to God on behalf of the faithful. Their various eucharistic formulations were therefore poised to strike fatal blows at these sacrificial themes associated with the traditional priesthood and the sacrament of the altar. Their eucharistic controversies are best seen as disputes over the means

43 Ridley, *Brief Declaracion*, sigs. A.2, *recto*-A.3, *verso*. Cf. *Works*, p. 5.
44 See Huldrych Zwingli, excerpts from *Commentary on True and False Religion*, in *The Protestant Reformation*, ed. Hans J. Hillerbrand (New York: Harper & Row, 1968) [hereafter: Zwingli, *Commentary*], pp. 108–21. Cf. Heiko A. Oberman, *Luther: Man Between God and the Devil*, trans. Eileen Walliser-Schwarzbart (New York: Doubleday, 1992) [hereafter: Oberman, *Luther*], pp. 241–43.
45 Luther, as quoted in Oberman, *Luther*, p. 232.
46 For more information on the controversy between Luther and Zwingli, see Oberman, *Luther*, pp. 232–45.

to be employed in re-casting the role and purpose of ministerial functions within the church. For Luther, it was enough to state that ministers were to be first and foremost ministers of the Word. He left the doctrine of the real presence intact, even if he eschewed philosophical investigations into the manner in which Christ was understood to be truly present in the sacrament. For Zwingli and those who held sympathies with his views, the roots of sacerdotal priesthood were inextricably bound up with Christ's presence in the sacrament. According to this line of argument, the repeal of an oblational form of ministry required the total eradication of the concept of Christ's Real Presence in the Eucharist.

A last-ditch effort to ford the widening gulf between Luther and Zwingli was attempted in a series of meetings at Marburg organized by Philip of Hesse in early October of 1529. Although they were able to reach accord on every other major issue of doctrine, the eucharistic chasm between Luther and Zwingli was never bridged. It therefore fell to succeeding groups of Reformers to seek a mediating conception of the sacrament that would harmonize the various emphases of Lutheran and Zwinglian concerns.

The generation of Reformers just after Luther and Zwingli offered several compromise solutions, each of which met with mixed results. Melanchthon advanced the doctrine of consubstantiation, asserting that there were two substances present in the sacramental elements, bread and flesh, wine and blood. This was an attempt at compromise by saying everything rather than too little, and so tended to draw critics from all sides. Nevertheless, in time this position won favor among later generations of Lutherans, while remaining repugnant to most early Swiss Protestants because it still maintained a view of Christ's substantial presence in the sacrament. From Geneva, Calvin offered his own compromise formula, a position sometimes described as the doctrine of "a real spiritual presence." In Calvin's view, the communicants received the life-giving benefits of Christ's flesh by the work of the Holy Spirit, which operated to connect the consecrated elements with the ascended body of Christ in Heaven.[47]

---

47   John Calvin, *The Institutes of Christian Religion, 1559*, trans. Ford Lewis Battles, ed. John T. McNeil (Philadelphia: Westminster John Knox Press, 1960) [hereafter: Calvin, *Institutes*], IV.xvii.9, pp. 1369–70.

Calvin's formulation won approval from the Swiss party, but was not embraced by the greater part of Luther's followers.

The lukewarm reception of Calvin's eucharistic doctrine among German Protestants was the result of two interrelated aspects of his teaching. In the first place, Calvin denied Christ's personal presence in the consecrated elements, and attributed whatever efficacy the sacrament held primarily to the power of the Holy Spirit.[48] Here, as elsewhere in his theological thinking, Calvin tends to allege the Holy Spirit alone to be the agent of operation if there is a theological mystery to be solved. This general tendency of Calvin's thought is even more pronounced in his eucharistic considerations, where he claims that Christ's material body and blood could have no efficacy at all apart from the power of the Holy Spirit acting through them: "The flesh of Christ does not of itself have a power so great as to quicken us, for in its first condition, it was subject to mortality; and now endowed with immortality, it does not live of itself."[49] These ideas failed to capture many adherents among early German Protestants because, for Luther and his followers, Christ was present in the sacrament precisely because the Word of God gave His personal pledge to be there in the declaration, "This is my body." The centerpiece of Luther's real presence doctrine was faith and trust in the promise of Christ to be present in the sacrament. Luther maintained that Christ could not and would not deceive ordinary believers, and that the second person of the Trinity had both the power and desire to accomplish whatever he pledged to do for his faithful followers.[50]

48 See B. A. Gerrish, *Grace and Gratitude: The Eucharistic Theology of John Calvin* (Minneapolis: Fortress Press, 1993) [hereafter: Gerrish, *Grace and Gratitude*], pp. 142–45. Gerrish's main aim is to promote Calvin's theology as essentially eucharistic in nature, which the author admits is and has often been obscured by Calvin's heavy emphasis on double Predestination, his often ambiguous language, and the fact that he does not hold that the sacrament brings any power or virtue to the believer that has not already been given through faith by the Word. Ridley's debt to early Swiss Protestantism will be more closely considered in Chapter II.

49 Calvin, 1559 *Institutes*, IV.xvii.9, pp. 1369–70. Cf. e.g., Foxe, *Actes and Monuments*, p. 1452 and Ridley, *Works*, pp. 239–40.

50 Martin Luther, *The Pagan Servitude of the Church,* in *Martin Luther: Selections From His Writings*, ed. John Dillenberger (New York: Anchor

It is in this context of deep Protestant divisions and efforts to develop a mediating conception of the Eucharist that the English Reformers lived and wrote. When the eucharistic doctrine of English Protestants is viewed against this background of controversy and successive compromise formulae, the various pieces of their sacramental reflections fall into place. The writings of Ridley, who was possessed of a more analytical mind than either Cranmer or Latimer, give a clearer picture of early reformed English eucharistic propositions.

Ridley advances a view of the Eucharist that attempts to mediate between early German and Swiss Protestant concerns, placing more emphasis on the direct power and presence of Christ in the sacrament and less on the work of the Holy Spirit than is often the case with Calvin. Ridley's expression of these themes is most clearly and concisely stated in his treatise *A Brief Declaration of the Lord's Supper*. After critiquing and denying the Thomistic doctrine of transubstantiation, Ridley goes on to declare his opinion of those who deny a corporeal presence of Christ in the Eucharist: "Bryefly, they denie the presence of Christes body in the naturall substaunce of his humane and assumed nature, and graunt the presence of the same by grace. . . . The same natural substaunce of . . . Christ, bycause it is united in the divine nature in Christ, the second person of the Trinitie, . . . hathe not onley lyfe in it selfe, but is also hable to geve, and dothe geve life unto so many as be, or shalbe partakers thereof." Ridley asserts that this is true despite the fact that "the selfe same substaunce [of Christ] abyde styll in heaven."[51] He further explicates his view of the relationship between Christ's divinity and his humanity through a solar metaphor: "We saye, the same Sunne which (in substaunce), never removeth his place out of the heavens, is yet present here by his beames, light, and naturall influence, where it shyneth upon the earthe. For Goddes worde and his Sacramentes be (as it were), the beames of Christ, which is *Sol justitiae*, Sunne of ryghteousnes."[52]

Books, 1962) [hereafter: Luther, *Selections*], pp. 268–70. Cf. Oberman, *Luther*, pp. 232–45.

51 Ridley, *Brief Declaracion*, sig. B.2, *recto*. Cf. *Works*, pp. 12–13.

52 Ridley, *Brief Declaracion*, sig. B.3, *verso*. Cf. *Works*, pp. 12–13. At first blush, Ridley's likening Christ's eucharistic presence to the sun would seem

A scholarly consensus on the eucharistic views of the early English Reformers has never been established. For some reviewers, the books of *Common Prayer* and Cranmer's writings on the sacrament advocate a "real spiritual presence" akin to the teachings of Calvin. These appraisals are often supported by reference to the known contacts between Cranmer, Latimer, and Ridley with Peter Martyr Vermigli and Martin Bucer, the Strasbourg Reformers who had close personal and conceptual ties to Geneva, but who eventually took up residence in Edwardine England.[53] Certainly the affinity between Ridley's eucharistic thought and that of Calvin cannot be denied, but neither can the fact that there are key differences of emphasis between them.

First and foremost, in a manner consistent with the concerns of the German Reformers, Ridley connects Christ's personal presence in the

to recall Martin Bucer's analogy; however, Bucer specifically employs this concept as a caution against the idea that Christ's human nature can be said to be circumscribed in Heaven: "For, though we should grant you, that He is circumscribed even in heaven by a physical place, how is that inconsistent with His being now truly present to us by faith; even as the sun, in whatever part of the world we behold him, is truly present to us by sight. Certainly all errors which can possibly arise from the name 'Presence,' may be altogether excluded by such words. . . . I have never felt disposed, nor am I up to this moment disposed, to come forward in that controversy. Whether Christ is circumscribed by any Physical place in the heavens, He sits at the right hand of God; He has left the world. . . ." Martin Bucer, quoted in Constantin Hopf, *Martin Bucer and the English Reformation* (Oxford: Basil Blackwell, 1946), p.48. Bucer reasserted this admonition to Cranmer when plans were being made to revamp the first Book of Common Prayer: "Therefore in company with those most holy Fathers we say willingly, as we ought, that in his human nature the Lord Christ has left this world and is in heaven: and let us say also with the same holy Fathers, even as the Book says, that we receive Him in the mysteries of the holy Supper, we receive him as man, we receive his body and blood, but by faith alone." Martin Bucer, quoted in *Martin Bucer and the Book of Common Prayer*, ed. E. C. Whitaker for the Alcuin Club (Great Wakering: Mayhew-McCrimmon, 1974), p. 74.

53 For a brief overview of some of the more influential opinions, see Collinson, *Grindal*. Ridley's relationship with Peter Martyr will be more closely considered in Chapter II.

sacrament with his institution of the rite: "Do [they] take awaye symplie and absolutly the presence of Christes body and blood from the Sacrament, ordayned by Christ, and duely ministred according to his holy ordinaunce and institucion of the same. Undoubtedly, they doo denye that utterlye, either so to saye, or so to meane."[54] Secondly, Ridley attributes to Christ's flesh and blood the ability to confer life: "it hathe not onley lyfe in it selfe, but is also hable to geve, and dothe geve life unto so many as be, or shalbe partakers thereof."[55] However, Ridley's most significant departure from Calvinist eucharistic thought lies in his attributing the manner of Christ's presence in the sacrament to Christ himself, and not primarily to the work of the Holy Spirit.

Whereas Calvin declares that the presence of the ascended Christ in the sacrament is made possible by virtue of the Holy Spirit connecting the body and blood of the Lord with the consecrated bread and wine as a channel, Ridley proposes that Christ's divine nature is present in the sacrament, while his body remains in Heaven.[56] Ridley approaches this theological mystery through Christology, grounding his view of the sacrament in the hypostatic union[57] of Jesus' divine and human natures: "The same natural substaunce of the very bodye and blood cf Christ, bycause it is united in the divine nature in Christ, the second person of the Trinitie, . . . though the selfe same substaunce abyde styll in heaven. . . . By grace (I saye), that is, by the gyfte of thys lyfe (mencioned in John) and the properties of the same mete for our pilgrimage here upon

54   Ridley, *Brief Declaracion*, sig. B.2, *verso*. Cf. Ridley, *Works*, p. 13.
55   Ridley, *Brief Declaracion*, sig. B.2, *recto*. Cf. Ridley, *Works*, p. 13.
56   See Gerrish, *Grace and Gratitude*, pp. 142–43. Ridley, *Brief Declaracion*, B.2, *recto*-B.3, *verso*. Cf. Ridley, *Works*, p. 13 and Calvin, 1559 *Institutes*, IV.xvii.9, pp. 1369–70.
57   The dogmatic proposition that the divine and human natures of Christ form a hypostatic union in a single, truly human person was officially promulgated in 451 A.D. by the Council of Chalcedon. Ridley and the other early Protestant reformers who cited this Definition for a defense of their eucharistic views and interpretations of scripture, did not rehearse the sections of it that expressly declare that as a result of a true union of Christ's divine and human natures, they could not be contrasted with respect to efficacy or location. See Leith, *Creeds*, pp. 34–36, "without contrasting [these two natures] according to area or function."

earth, the same bodye of Christ is here present with us."[58] Ridley also clearly displays his sympathies for the Swiss party in this formulation, concentrating on the properties of a human body in a manner consistent with their concerns.

Zwingli and his followers invariably repudiated any characterization of Christ's flesh that ignored the physical and spatial limitations of a natural human body.[59] Zwingli's own primary concern was that any presence of Christ associated with the Eucharist should be referred to a transformation of the believer, not of the consecrated elements: "For Christ everywhere emphasizes these two things, namely, redemption through Himself, and the obligation of those redeemed through Him to live according to His example." Citing Jesus' counsel that those who would have life must eat his flesh, Zwingli declared: "We ought, then, to be as eagerly bent upon a change of life as we trust in redemption through Him."[60] Zwingli derided any notion of the flesh of Christ as present in the Eucharist as "monstrous" and "senseless."[61]

Because he attempts to base his understanding of the Eucharist on the hypostatic union of Christ's two natures, however, Ridley's position appears as something of a "hypostatical" sacramentalism. The dynamic force of this "hypostatical" conception of the Eucharist rests upon an attempt to yoke two paradoxical postulates: Christ is physically absent from the sacrament according to his human nature, but he is spiritually present there according to his divine nature. For Ridley and the other English Reformers, this doctrine proved quite flexible, since, by emphasizing one premise or the other, they could alternately claim more or less veneration for the sacrament, as circumstances required.

This felicitous ambiguity concerning the proper reverence due to the Eucharist is readily evident in Ridley's writings. When pressed by Mary's Catholic examiners, he could declare: "We adore and worship Christ in the Eucharist. And if you meane the externall sacrament, I say,

---

58 Ridley, *Brief Declaracion*, B.2, *recto*-B.3, *verso*. Cf. Ridley, *Works*, p. 13.
59 See Zwingli, *Commentary*, pp. 108–21. Cf. Oberman, *Luther*, pp. 241–43.
60 Zwingli, *Commentary*, pp. 119–20. Cf. John 6:57.
61 Zwingli, *Commentary*, p. 112.

that also is to be worshipped as a Sacrament."[62] Alternatively, when writing to clarify and promulgate his eucharistic views for other Protestants, Ridley could assert: ". . . the natural substaunce of Christes humane nature, which he toke of the Virgine Mary is in heaven, where it reigneth nowe in glorie, and [is] not here inclosed under the fourme of bread. Than that godly honour, which is only due unto God the creatour, may not be done unto the creature without idolatrie and sacrilege, is not to be done unto the holy Sacrament."[63] This eucharistic doctrine also enabled the English Reformers to believe that there was a plain method for distinguishing their sacramental views from those of the Anabaptists, since, according to Ridley the members of this "secte" posit: "no difference between the Lordes table and the lordes meat, and their owne."[64] Against such stark anti-sacramentalism, Ridley could assert that there was a real change in the consecrated elements, in that they were transformed not into the actual body and blood of Christ, but into a sacramental communion with his flesh, through his divine nature: "Yes, there is a miracle, good sir, Christ is not idle in his sacraments. Is not the miracle great (trow you) when bread, which is wont to susteine the body, becommeth food to the soule? He that understandeth not that miracle, hee understandeth not the force of that misterye."[65]

Although Ridley and his fellow reformers in England could assert that an actual change occurred in the consecrated eucharistic elements, they took their tenet concerning the absence of Christ's physical substance in the sacrament as sufficient grounds to repudiate the oblational nature of the priesthood. Ridley personally set about to literally dismantle the intercessory and sacrificial dimensions of the English presbyterate, ordering the removal and destruction of altars from London churches.[66] First and

---

62 Foxe, *Actes and Monuments*, p. 1451. Cf. Ridley, *Works*, p. 236.
63 Ridley, *Brief Declaracion*, sig. B.1, *recto*. Ridley, *Works*, p. 12.
64 Ridley, *Brief Declaracion*, sig. A.7, *verso* and Ridley, *Comfortable Confernces*, fol. 17, *recto*. Cf. Ridley, *Works*, pp. 9, 119–20.
65 Foxe, *Actes and Monuments*, p. 1448 and Ridley, *Works*, p. 223.
66 See *Iniunctions geven in the visitation of the reverende father in God, Nycolas byshoppe of London for an vniformitie in the Diocesse of London...* ([STC 10247] London: Reynolde Wolfe, *Cum priuilegio ad imprimendum solum*, 1550), article v, sig. ii, and Ridley, *Works*, p. 319–21.

foremost in his list of reasons for removing altars and replacing them with moveable tables was his doctrine of a purely spiritual presence of Christ in the Eucharist: "For the use of an altare is to make sacrifice upon it: the use of a table is to serve for men to eate upon. Nowe when we come unto the Lordes boorde, what do we come for? To sacrifice Christe agayne, and to crucifie hym againe?" Denying this possibility, Ridley asserted: "If wee come to feede uppon him, spiritually to eate his body, and spiritually to drinke his bloud, which is the true use of the Lordes supper, then no man can denie, but the forme of a table is more meete for the Lordes boorde, then the forme of an aultare."[67] These and many other aspects of Ridley's thought merit thorough study, for the revelations they yield on the nature and causes of early English Protestantism.

In addition to tracing the main outlines of Ridley's exegetical and ecclesiological thought for its own sake in the following chapters, the current study will consider his personal struggles to address Protestantism's "lack of visible roots," as Alec Ryrie describes the early Protestant crisis of historical legitimacy.[68] Ryrie has identified four types of apologetic motifs that Protestants developed to fashion an historical past for their movement: appeals to Lollardy and other heretical movements of the recent past; attempts to claim more mainstream figures in Catholic history as crypto-Protestants; the development of Church and Anti-church schema of history that united all past heretical movements in ecclesiastical history; and apocalypticism.[69]

---

67 Foxe, *Actes and Monuments*, p. 1331 and Ridley, *Works*, p. 322. As Ridley's quote discloses, his ideas about the corporal absence of Christ from the sacrament are closely related to general early Protestant claims that the sacrifice of the Mass derogated from Christ's once and for all self-sacrifice on Calvary. See Francis Clark, S.J., *Eucharistic Sacrifice and the Reformation* (Oxford: Basil Blackwell, 1967).

68 Alec Ryrie, "The Problems of Legitimacy and Precedent in English Protestantism, 1539–1547," in *Protestant History and Identity in Sixteenth-Century Europe*, vol. 1, The Medieval Inheritance, ed. Bruce Gordon (Brookfield, Vermont: Scholar's Press, 1996) [hereafter: Ryrie, "Problems of Legitimacy in English Protestantism"], pp. 78–92.

69 Ryrie maintains that the mercurial nature of Henry's ambitions and religious legislation greatly complicated and compromised the utility of the

Interestingly, each of these strategies appears in Ridley's extant writings.[70]

Edmund Bonner (c. 1498–1569): Twice Bishop of London

For the scholar of sixteenth-century England, Edmund Bonner represents an equal, if often opposite, force to Nicholas Ridley in the course of the Reformation. Bonner's career spanned such a large portion of the period, and his work was central to so many of the pivotal moments of it, that he merits close study for those reasons alone. His early service to the Church and the king under Wolsey in the 1520s began during the last complacent days of the old Church. Despite his religious conservatism in the late 1540s, Bonner was, in the early 1530s, directly responsible for conducting much of the thornier negotiations at the papal court for Henry's divorce suit. When the final break with Rome did come in the mid-1530s, Bonner's preface to Gardiner's *De Vera Obedientia* established him much more decisively than Ridley as an anti-papal propagandist at the time. In the latter 1530s, it was Bonner who steered the text of the *Great Bible* through the presses of Paris. In 1540, when Thomas Cranmer was testing the waters for official doctrinal reform, Bonner was one of the divines consulted on a number of theological questions. As the spiritual head of the most populous diocese in England, Bonner was the first target of the Protestant initiative to deprive conservative bishops under Edward VI. Thus, well before the accession of Mary Tudor and the production of his seminal dogmatic and homiletic works, Bonner had already played a leading role in the major religious controversies of the realm for nearly three decades.

It was under Mary that Bonner came into his own and was finally afforded the opportunity to directly affect the shape of religion throughout

first three strategies outlined above. See Ryrie, "Problems of Legitimacy in English Protestantism."

70 Including apocalyptic predictions, which are common in some of Ridley's prison tracts. This aspect of Ridley's writings has received very little scholarly attention.

the whole of England. Bonner's *Profitable and Necessarye Doctryne*[71] and *Homelies*[72] were published in July and September of 1555, respectively. The *Profitable and Necessarye Doctryne* was an effort at lay faith formation that treated a series of biblical, theological, and devotional topics, including the Ten Commandments, the Nicene-Constantinopolitan Creed, the Lord's Prayer, and the Ave Maria. It quickly attained the status of a semi-official statement of doctrine in Marian England when Cardinal Pole ordered it to be purchased and used by all the parish clergy within his jurisdiction. In 1556, the wardens of Morebath are mentioned as having obtained a copy for the sum of 2s 9d.[73] Bonner's *Homelies* had an even wider influence in the realm, being translated even into Cornish for the preachers of Wales.[74]

Yet the historical significance of Bonner's *Profitable and Necessarye Doctryne* and *Homelies* far transcends their contemporary use and official endorsement in Marian England. Their contents and the circumstances of their publication are remarkable for a number of reasons that disclose much about episcopal authority and the state of belief in

71 Edmund Bonner, *A profitable and necessarye doctryne with certayne homelies adioyned thervnto set forth by the reuerende father in God, Edmonde byshop of London, for the instruction and enformation of the people beynge within his diocesse of London, [and] of his cure and charge* ([STC 3281.5] London: John Cawood, 1555) [hereafter: Bonner, *Necessary and Profitable Doctrine*]. I have worked from this edition primarily because three copies of it have been preserved, allowing for the greatest comparisons where certain signatures have been damaged, poorly printed, or lost in any one copy. See STC Reel Positions 176:7A; 655:07; and 1829:05.

72 *Homelies sette forth by the righte reuerende father in God, Edmunde Byshop of London, not onely promised before in his booke, intituled, A necessary doctrine, but also now of late adioyned, and added therevnto, to be read within his diocese of London, of all persons, vycars, and curates, vnto theyr parishioners, vpon sondayes, [and] holydayes* ([STC 3285.4] London: In Poules churcheyarde, at the sygne of the holy Ghost, by Ihon Cawodde, 1555) [hereafter: Bonner, *Homelies*].

73 See Eamon Duffy, *The Stripping of the Altars* (New Haven: Yale, 1992) [hereafter: Duffy, *Stripping of the Altars*], p. 537.

74 See Diarmaid MacCulloch, *The Reformation* (New York: Viking, 2004) [hereafter: MacCulloch, *The Reformation*], p. 276.

the wake of the Edwardine religious reforms. Both productions were published in London under Bonner's name and title, revealing the authority and influence that sixteenth-century bishops could exert upon the presses of the realm. Since these writings were not prepared by Bonner alone— he was assisted throughout by a circle of conservative Humanists and clerics under his patronage—they also reflect the consensus of a host of Marian divines working towards the re-establishment of Catholicism in the mid-1550s. Bonner's *Profitable and Necessarye Doctryne* and *Homelies* reveal just how deeply committed leading Marian religious authorities were to a number of Henrician and Edwardine religious initiatives. It was no accident that the *Profitable and Necessarye Doctryne* was modeled on the *King's Book*, and Bonner's *Homelies* actually reissued two selections from Cranmer's 1547 *Book of Homilies* with only minor emendations. Both of these facts suggest that Bonner and his allies sought to retain whatever was of value in the reforms begun under both Henry and Edward, especially in the way of providing clear statements of belief for the laity and sound standards of preaching for clergy.[75]

Bonner's *Profitable and Necessarye Doctryne* and *Homelies* also provide many unparalleled insights into Protestant ideas and arguments from the period. These were not abstract treatises prepared by an absentee bishop and his associates. Instead, many of the central arguments of both works were drafted as direct responses to the lead concepts that Bonner and his *confrères* encountered in their day-to-day examinations of accused heretics. The *Profitable and Necessarye Doctryne* and *Homelies* are therefore focused squarely on biblical and patristic sources, and are calculated to persuade the reader on a number of doctrinal points, often as incisive refutations of mainstays of early English Protestant apologetics. Both works reveal one of the two primary directions that Humanist biblical exegesis took in England in the wake of Erasmus' and John Colet's pioneering work in New Testament studies a generation earlier. For all of these reasons, close study of Bonner's career and publications is invaluable for anyone attempting to fully comprehend the major themes of the English Reformation.

75 Duffy, *Stripping of the Altars*, pp. 533–37.

The Character and Thought of Edmund Bonner

Bonner's intellectual accomplishments and interests extended well beyond his formal studies in Law and Philosophy. He had a keen mind and, over the course of his career, proved impressively adroit as a linguist. He was capable of delivering long Latin orations to the Senate of Hamburg, but was also fluent in both French and Italian. In the early 1540s, he commenced the study of Spanish, acquiring sufficient skill for both conversation and translation of diplomatic documents into English.[76] Bonner's study of French would have been natural for a young man endeavoring to prepare for a diplomatic career, but he did not let those skills lapse in later life: during his imprisonment in the Marshalsea, he regularly read a French chronicle for relaxation.[77] In April of 1530, we find Bonner writing to Cromwell to ask for the *Triumphs* of Petrarch and Castiglione's *The Courtier* in Italian. These readings would have acquainted Bonner with two major exponents of the Italian Renaissance. He continued to cultivate an interest in this language in later life, quoting Italian proverbs in a letter to his servant, Richard Lechmere, in 1549.[78] As befitted an eminent prelate, Bonner also displayed some knowledge of the Church Fathers, including St. John Chrysostom, St. Jerome, and St. Augustine of Hippo, and actually owned an edition of Eusebius' *Church History*, edited by Rhenanus, the Humanist publisher and friend of Erasmus.[79]

---

76 Gina Mary Vere Alexander, "The Life and Career of Edmund Bonner, Bishop of London, Until His Deprivation in 1549," unpublished doctoral dissertation (University of London: 1960) [hereafter: Alexander, "Bonner Until His Deprivation"], p. 244.

77 Alexander, "Bonner Until His Deprivation," p. 53. Bonner also wrote to the French constable in French while Ambassador in that country for Henry VIII. See Alexander, "Bonner Until His Deprivation," p. 53, note 25.

78 Alexander, "Bonner Until His Deprivation," pp. 53–54. Bonner was also fluent with spoken Italian, and, as Ambassador to the Pope, was able to understand Clement VII's asides in Italian on the subject of Henry VIII's divorce suit.

79 Alexander, "Bonner Until His Deprivation," pp. 51–52 and note 22. It appears that Bonner owned the 1528 re-issue of this volume, published at Basel.

Perhaps the most surprising and consistent theme in Bonner's writings and labors, given his generally conservative outlook on ecclesiology, was his desire to have scripture readily available to the laity in the vernacular. While this aim took various forms at different points in his career, it was a conceptual thread that connected the two halves of his London episcopate. In fact, Bonner's leading effort in seeing the English scriptures through the presses of Paris in the late 1530s was so prominent that his later detractors felt compelled to explain away his work as a ruse. John Foxe recounts at length Bonner's "great friendship to the merchants that were imprinters of [the Bible]," and that he "moreover did divers and sundrie times call and commande the said persons, to be in maner daily at his table both dinner and supper . . . and to his cost, which, as it seemed, he little wayed," but he is careful to describe Bonner's generosity as only "outwardly shewed." Foxe also notes that Bonner "was so frevent that he caused the said Englishmen [Grafton and Whitchurch] to put in print a new testament in english and latine, and himselfe took, a great many of them and payd for them and gave them to his friends."[80] Despite Foxe's commentary, it is unlikely that Bonner would have commissioned and presented copies of this New Testament to those whom he favored if he was indeed inwardly opposed to the setting forth of an English Bible.

Although Foxe was dubious of Bonner's intentions, it is clear from one of Bonner's surviving letters to Grafton that the Bishop was sincere in promoting vernacular scriptures in the London Diocese. Bonner asserted of his predecessor, John Stokesley, that, "the greatest fault that I ever found in [him] was for vexing and troubling of poor men . . . for having the scripture in English; and God willing he did not so much hinder it but I will as much further it."[81] Bonner's initial plan to "further the scripture in English" was an ambitious program that provided six complete volumes of the new Bibles to be set up in St. Paul's Cathedral. This scheme far exceeded Henry's proclamation that two copies should

---

80 Foxe, *Actes and Monuments*, p. 1191.
81 See *Records of the English Bible: The Documents Relating to the Translation and Publication of the Bible in English: 1521–1611*, ed. A. F. Pollard (London: Oxford University Press, 1911), p. 225.

be set up in every church, hardly suggesting the actions of a man with serious misgivings. Even in this early experimentation with the English scriptures, however, Bonner attempted to establish some balance between the reading of them and due reverence for Church rites. Each of the Bible copies in St. Paul's had an admonition posted directly above them, charging the reader not to recite from them aloud during any Church service or sermon.[82]

To comprehend why Bonner would have been so "frevent" in setting forth the English Bible, it is important to understand that his predecessor, Bishop John Stokesley, initiated and led a campaign to extirpate vernacular scriptures from the London Diocese. Stokesley, firmly persuaded that lay consumption of scripture would lead only to strife among the common people, had a clear strategy for subverting efforts to market unauthorized Bibles within his see. He would regularly enquire where such books were sold, and then buy up all the available copies. These efforts yielded mixed results, however, since the monies thus expended often wound up in the hands of the original printers, enabling them to produce another edition of their work. The details of Stokesley's actions were well enough known to Bonner that he could name many of the booksellers who had been harassed by his predecessor.[83] It is quite likely that the worldly and practical Bonner viewed Stokesley's efforts in this arena as a losing battle. He resolved that the laity would be far better served, if they were reading unauthorized vernacular scriptures anyway, to have an official version made available to them, and to have it regularly expounded by orthodox preachers.

82 On Bonner's "Admonicion" and the Bibles chained to reading desks in St. Paul's, see Margaret Aston, "Lap Books and Lectern Books: The Revelatory Book in the Reformation," in *The Church and the Book*, ed. R. N. Swanson, vol. 56 of *The Ecclesiastical History Society* (Rochester, New York: Boydell Press, 2004) [hereafter: Aston, "Lap Books and Lectern Books"], pp. 163–88, esp. p. 180ff. Figure 5 on p. 181 presents the full text of Bonner's original "Admonicion."

83 He in fact indicates the very location of some of their shops within the city of London. See Andrew A. Chibi, *Henry VIII's Conservative Scholar: Bishop John Stokesley and the Divorce, Royal Supremacy and Doctrinal Reform* (Bern: Lang, 1997), pp. 98–101.

Whatever Bonner's hopes for his early efforts to bring the English scriptures to the lay people of London, it is clear that Stokesley's warnings were largely confirmed in the controversies that Bible reading engendered in the realm.[84] When Bonner returned from another diplomatic mission to France in 1540, he was obliged to strengthen his original "friendly" admonition to the parishioners of St. Paul's, threatening to take down all of the Bibles if they were not read reverently and quietly during Mass and other celebrations within the cathedral.[85] At least one person was eventually prosecuted for violating the terms of Bonner's admonition: John Porter was charged with assembling many people to him "to make tumultes" as he read the Bible in the Cathedral. He was imprisoned in Newgate, where he died not long after.[86] These troubles led John Bale to claim that Bonner's intention in setting up the St. Paul's Bibles had been malicious from the outset, and that they were put forward solely "as snares" to catch the people.[87] Bale's judgment notwithstanding, it does not appear that Bonner engaged in any deliberate program of harassment towards those who came to read the Bible reverently in his Cathedral.

Nevertheless, Bonner was certainly chastened by his early efforts to promote the English scriptures under Henry, and we might therefore expect that he would not have resumed this initiative when he was pardoned by Mary Tudor and released from prison in the summer of 1553. However, nearly all of Bonner's writings from this second period of his episcopate are replete with lengthy citations of scripture in English, even his short catechism for children, published in January of 1556.[88] He often

---

84 See Susan Wabuda, *Preaching During the English Reformation* (Cambridge: University Press, 2002) [hereafter: Wabuda, *Preaching*], pp. 99–106.
85 See Aston, "Lap Books and Lectern Books," p. 180.
86 See Foxe, *Actes and Monuments*, p. 1207.
87 See Susan Brigden, *London and the Reformation* (Oxford: Clarendon Press, 1989) [hereafter: Brigden, *London and the Reformation*], p. 1207.
88 See Edmund Bonner, *An Honest Godly Instruction, and information for the tradying, and bringinge up of Children, set furth by the Bishoppe of London.* . . ([STC 3281] London: 1556) [hereafter: Bonner, *An Honest Godly Instruction*].

reveals a careful concern for the translation of the biblical text, even noting that a very old Lollard text that he has in his possession renders certain parts of the Ten Commandments more accurately into English than many of the late "false and ungodly translations."[89]

Similarly, Bonner rants that Protestants have lately corrupted both common speech and passages of scripture in offering "The Lorde" in place of "Our Lorde" at many points in the text.[90] True to his concern, we find that he employs "Our Lorde" exclusively throughout his catechism for children.[91] In his latter efforts for the promotion of scripture, Bonner discovered a formula for ensuring that the text is closely associated with expositions that are not inimical to the Church, exploring the meanings of passages alongside details about liturgy, worship, and doctrine. To fully appreciate what Bonner accomplished in the production of his *Homelies* and *Profitable and Necessarye Doctryne*, they must be seen as the culmination of a long-held desire to place scripture in the hands of the people, in a form that would inculcate faith and trust in the Church.

Edmund Bonner: A Brief Biographical Sketch

As with Ridley, many of the details of Bonner's youth and early education are unknown. He was probably born in Hanley, Worcestershire. Since the days of John Foxe and his circle, stories have circulated widely that Bonner was the bastard son of a Worcestershire priest. The only twentieth-century scholar to devote a lengthy study solely to Bonner, Gina M. V. Alexander, determined that these claims are not fully substantiable. Nevertheless, the existence of several credible pedigrees of the Bishop drawn up near the end of his life or shortly thereafter, coupled with his close connections with the Savage family, make the claims of Bonner's bastardy rather plausible.[92]

89 See Edmund Bonner, *Necessary and Profitable Doctrine*, sig. II.4ff.
90 See Edmund Bonner, *Necessary and Profitable Doctrine*, sig. D.3, *verso*.
91 See Bonner, *An Honest Godly Instruction*.
92 Alexander, "Bonner Until His Deprivation," pp. 13–42 and appendices i and ii, pp. 457 and 458, respectively. Throughout this section on Bonner's life and work, I am heavily indebted to Alexander. While laboring through

Bonner's early education was most likely at Worcester, where there is some strong evidence to connect him with the chapel school.[93] Bonner's primary education commenced when he was about fourteen years old, in 1512, when he entered Broadgates Hall, later Pembroke College, Oxford. He took both a bachelor of civil and canon law in July 1519, and doctor of civil law in 1525.[94] It may also have been from his early Worcester connections that Bonner first made the acquaintance of John Bell, the Worcestershire-born Archdeacon of Gloucester. Bell became vicar-general and chancellor of Worcester in 1518, and was one of Wolsey's commissaries in 1526. That same year, Bell and Bonner are recorded as investigating heresy together in the Worcester Diocese.[95]

We do not know when Bonner was ordained to the priesthood, nor by whom, although it may have occurred as early as 1519. There is also no source that describes and dates Bonner's first contact with Wolsey, although by 1529 he was Wolsey's chaplain, and was serving the Cardinal as commissary of dispensations or "faculties" by 1530.[96] We also know that Bonner had established himself as a competent legal advisor both to Wolsey and Cromwell by 1529, since another of Wolsey's commissaries,

the thorny problem of Bonner's family heritage, Alexander provides useful contextual information on the Savages, the great northern family who entered into peerage through service to Henry, Duke of Richmond, at Bosworth. See Alexander, "Bonner Until His Deprivation," pp. 19–23.

93 Alexander, "Bonner Until His Deprivation," pp. 45–46. In 1525, Bonner received 42 shillings to pursue his doctoral studies from the then prior, William More. One of Bonner's close friends, Dr. Thomas Bagarde, was also a beneficiary of William More and the chapel school of Worcester. In 1521 and 1523 More noted in his journal that he had rewarded money to "our ii scholars at Oxforde," and continued to donate small sums of money to Bonner after 1525.

94 Alexander, "Bonner Until His Deprivation," p. 48. For an outline of what Bonner's studies would have entailed, see pp. 49–51.

95 Bell was also consecrated bishop of Worcester in 1539 when Hugh Latimer resigned his cure. On Bell's association with Bonner and his episcopate, see Susan Wabuda, "Bell, John (d. 1556)," *Oxford Dictionary of National Biography*, Oxford University Press, 2004 [http://www.oxforddnb.com/view/article/2010, accessed 24 Feb 2006].

96 Alexander, "Bonner Until His Deprivation," pp. 54–55.

Edward Jones, suggested to the Lord Privy Seal that an inhibition against the Bishop of Bangor should be pursued according to the counsel of Bonner and Rowland Lee.[97] Evidence from one of Bonner's early law cases shows not only his impressive legal skill, but also his contact with the spiritual courts in a case of matrimonial law, and of Star Chamber proceedings in the early 1530s. Intriguingly, Bonner declared in this case, just as he would at his own trial nearly twenty years later, that he was not bound to answer court interrogatories orally since he had already filed written answers with the notaries.[98] By all appearances, Bonner rightly merited the respect of his peers and superiors as a potent advocate and legal advisor, progressively establishing his reputation in this direction from the mid-1520s to the early 1530s. He had, in fact, already become a member of the Doctors' Commons association of Canterbury by October of 1526, just one year after proceeding doctor of civil law from Oxford.[99]

In Wolsey's final months, it appears that he increasingly relied upon Bonner as his personal emissary to the king. Once it became clear to Henry that Wolsey could not obtain the divorce he sought from Catherine of Aragon, the Chancellor's position was most perilous. In the late summer and early fall of 1529, Wolsey sent Bonner on numerous visits to Henry in an effort to restore himself to the king's favor. Henry had banished the Chancellor from court, but still needed Wolsey's advice on how next to proceed with the matter of the divorce, and on the treaty of Cambrai, recently concluded between the Holy Roman Emperor and the King of France. On many of these missions to the king, Bonner was accompanied by Edward Carne, a Welshman from Glamorganshire, who had proceeded doctor of civil law from Oxford in 1524. He had been

---

97 Alexander, "Bonner Until His Deprivation," p. 56.
98 See Alexander, "Bonner Until His Deprivation," p. 58, and cf. Foxe, *Actes and Monuments*, p. 1320.
99 "The 'Association of doctors of law and of advocates of the church of Christ at Canterbury' had probably been founded before 1509. An unofficial body, it was comprised of those licensed to practice as advocates before the courts whose procedure was linked with the civil law. . . . At all events [Bonner's] membership of the college was an indication that he was establishing himself as a civilian advocate." Alexander, "Bonner Until His Deprivation," pp. 58–59.

one of Wolsey's commissaries for the suppression of monasteries, and had worked from that time forward with Bonner in several capacities. They were both sent in the English delegation to the Pope in 1532 and 1533, served together in various diplomatic negotiations, and also sat as joint commissioners to determine Admiralty cases. Bonner appears to have been on good terms with Carne until at least 1538.[100]

Wolsey seems to have been generally pleased with Bonner's handling of his affairs throughout most of the difficult and dangerous negotiations carried out on his behalf in the last eighteen months of his life. Only on one occasion is there any indication to the contrary, when Wolsey wrote to Cromwell concerning an abortive effort to obtain a pardon for himself. Wolsey pleaded with Cromwell that if Bonner "for lake of wyte and experyence hath not, as I fere me, done well let nat (me) peryshe for the same."[101] Whether Bonner had truly botched these negotiations is far from certain; Cromwell himself would in time discover that pardon for a high official was not easily wrested from the hand of Henry VIII. Despite Bonner's failure to obtain a pardon for Wolsey, the Cardinal retained his protégé in his service. Bonner traveled with Wolsey when he was banished into his province of York and, according to Wolsey's biographer, was the subject of a famous scene at Cawood Castle on All Saints Day, 1530. While at dinner that evening, Wolsey's great silver processional cross is said to have fallen on Bonner's head, drawing blood. Wolsey reputedly took the incident as a harbinger of his own death.[102] When Wolsey did die, less than one month after his fateful supper at Cawood, Bonner passed into the service of the king.

As Bonner rose in prominence and influence, he certainly did not forget his early friends. In 1532, Bonner procured Cromwell's favor for Thomas Bagarde, opening the way for his friend to become chancellor of the Diocese of Worcester.[103] In turn, Bonner's friends did not hesitate to ask their

---

100 On Bonner's working relationship with Carne, see Alexander, "Bonner Until His Deprivation," p. 60–61.

101 Alexander, "Bonner Until His Deprivation," p. 64.

102 George Cavendish, *The Life and Death of Cardinal Wolsey*, ed. R. S. Sylvester, *Early English Text Society*, no. 243 (1959), pp. 151–52.

103 On Bonner's friendship with Bagarde, see Alexander, "Bonner Until His Deprivation," pp. 47–48.

well-placed friend for political and ecclesiastical favors. When Bonner was Ambassador to Rome, John Bell prompted him to "further the matter" of the Charterhouse at Sheen, an issue that involved an exchange of lands between the monks of the Charterhouse and the King in 1531.[104]

Bonner's introduction to legal and diplomatic issues through Wolsey bore full fruit under Cromwell and Henry VIII, and he would grow in favor and preferments throughout the 1530s. In 1532, Bonner was dispatched to Rome to obstruct the proceedings of the papal curia against the king. Bonner pressed Henry's interests with vigor, informing Clement VII personally that the king had resolved to appeal the annulment suit from the pope's authority to that of a General Council.[105] Throughout 1535 and 1536, when Henry and Cromwell committed themselves to a policy of frustrating Imperial designs on northern Germany, Bonner was dispatched by the king in an effort to win the throne of Denmark for England.[106] Henry and Cromwell's selection of Bonner for this commission indicates that they firmly trusted and valued his talents since, although they had chosen him as their senior agent for the delegation, he had had no previous experience in English-German relations.[107] The complete failure of Bonner and his fellow commissioners to fulfill any of Henry's wishes in their mission to Denmark and Hamburg[108] did not result in any loss of the king's or Cromwell's confidence in Bonner. He was chosen thereafter for other important diplomatic appointments, including an embassy to the Court of Charles V in 1538,[109] and the post of Resident Ambassador to the Court of Francis I from 1538–1540.[110] It was not until 1540 that Henry had cause to withdraw his support of Bonner as a diplomat, recalling him to England at the insistence of Francis I.

104 For Bonner's association with Bell, see Alexander, "Bonner Until His Deprivation," pp. 46–47.

105 Bonner made these remarks in November of 1533, while both he and Clement were guests at the court of Francis I in Marseilles. See Alexander, "Bonner Until His Deprivation," p. 109ff.

106 Alexander, "Bonner Until His Deprivation," pp. 114–69.

107 See Alexander, "Bonner Until His Deprivation," p. 126ff.

108 Alexander, "Bonner Until His Deprivation," pp. 166–68.

109 Alexander, "Bonner Until His Deprivation," pp. 169–86.

110 Alexander, "Bonner Until His Deprivation," pp. 188–236.

Despite Henry and Cromwell's regular reliance on Bonner as an ambassador, however, it does not appear that they considered him a very tactful or diplomatic personality. Instead, they seem to have employed him mainly for thornier work where blunt directness was required.[111] Early in 1540, Bonner's plain-spoken and impetuous nature led directly to his being recalled as England's Ambassador to France. Bonner and another of Henry's agents in France, Thomas Wyatt, endeavored to capture and extradite the English rebel, Robert Brancetour. Brancetour had been at the Emperor's court since 1529, and was serving Cardinal Pole by March of 1539. Standing treaties stipulated that English traitors in France were to be delivered over to Henry VIII. Bonner and Wyatt managed to confront Brancetour in early January 1540, but since he stated that he was a servant of the Emperor, the French authorities would permit neither his arrest nor detainment. Under instructions from Henry, Wyatt pressed the case on the Emperor's side, meeting with Charles V's minister, Granvelle.[112] Bonner took up the matter with the French king, but it is uncertain whether he acted on his own initiative, or in compliance with instructions from Henry VIII.[113] Whatever the impetus, these

---

111 Such was the nature of Bonner's declaration to Clement VII in November of 1533. Henry's conflicted attitude towards Bonner was clearly indicated in his instructions to Thomas Wyatt in late November 1539. Henry dispatched Wyatt to France, having determined that Bonner and his associates were insufficient to the task of disrupting the nascent amity between the Emperor and the king of France. While Henry considered Bonner a competent advisor to Wyatt, he requested that audiences with the French king be had without Bonner present, whenever possible. See Alexander, "Bonner Until His Deprivation," p. 228ff. Cf. pp. 66–78, 230–37. This same pattern held in Bonner's final foreign envoy, when Henry sent him to the continent to serve as Resident Ambassador to Charles V. Henry made certain that the most substantial negotiations with the Emperor were conducted through a diplomatic team in London working with Chapuys, the Imperial Ambassador to England. See Alexander, "Bonner Until His Deprivation," pp. 238–273, esp. pp. 258, and 272ff.

112 Alexander, "Bonner Until His Deprivation," pp. 231–32.

113 Bonner's account of his interview with Francis concerning Brancetour has not survived, but it is unlikely that he proceeded entirely without instructions from Henry or Cromwell. Bonner's fellow Ambassador, Giovanni Baptista de Gambera of Mantua, firmly believed that Bonner had been

negotiations collapsed when Francis reported that Bonner had, in an audience with him on 23 January, declared that the French king's actions were, "totallement contre Dieu, raison et devoir, chose infâme, injuste et contre les traictez qui estoient entre sondict maistre et le roi de France."[114]

Francis demanded that England recall the ambassador at once, and Henry apologized for Bonner's remarks. An extant letter from de Montmorency, minister to the French king, suggests that this episode was probably not the sole source of Francis' "gran coler" towards Bonner. Writing on 7 February, Montmorency declared that Bonner, "n'a pas seulement en toutes les autres qu'il a eu charge de conduire par deçà, feust avec la personne du roy, moindres erreurs, sans avoir aucun respect ne considération aux choses requises en ung bon ministre et ambassadeur."[115] In the wake of this incident,Henry asked the French Ambassador in London to communicate to Francis that the English king was furious with Bonner. Henry also indicated that he would have Bonner recalled at once, but Henry was more forgiving of his agent after speaking with Cromwell about the whole affair. Thereafter, Henry attempted to console Francis while requesting that Bonner not be revoked, "comme par ignominye."[116] Francis would not be placated, however, and again insisted that Bonner be recalled to England. After much tarrying along the way, Bonner arrived in London on 16 March. Some observers doubted whether Henry was truly angry with Bonner and speculated that the king merely wanted to give this impression to French observers.[117]

If Bonner did escape the earnest wrath of Henry VIII, it was largely due to the unswerving allegiance of Thomas Cromwell to Bonner. Even during the final diplomatic debacle with Francis, Cromwell's defense of

made the scapegoat when Francis angrily refused Henry's request that Brancetour be handed over to English authorities. See Alexander, "Bonner Until His Deprivation," pp. 232–33.

114 See Alexander, "Bonner Until His Deprivation," p. 232.

115 Alexander, "Bonner Until His Deprivation," p. 233. Cf. p. 236.

116 Alexander, "Bonner Until His Deprivation," p. 234.

117 This was the opinion of the French Ambassador in London. See Alexander, "Bonner Until His Deprivation," p. 235–36.

Bonner was so well known that the French ambassador in London made note of the fact. Since both Bonner and Cromwell had served Wolsey, they may have met quite early in their careers, although their first recorded meeting was in the early months of 1530. As Wolsey's messenger to the king, Bonner came to know Cromwell rather well during the Cardinal's continuous entreaties for a pardon. By April of 1530, Bonner was on familiar enough terms with the Lord Privy Seal to ask about borrowing some of his books. Whatever the circumstances of their earliest acquaintance, there is no denying that Bonner's ecclesiastical and diplomatic preferments were the direct result of Cromwell's patronage. It was likely that Bonner's profound loyalty was what Cromwell most valued in his constant envoy. For his part, Bonner labored diligently to cultivate both the trust and true friendship of his patron. Bonner declared himself ready to inform Cromwell of all things, "though it were against my own brother."[118] In his reports to the Lord Privy Seal, Bonner constantly described himself as "moost bounden" to Cromwell, asserting, "I committe all, and my self to, unto the good order and dexteritie of your honourable good lordeship."[119] Bonner's extant correspondence strongly suggests that his obsequious comments to Cromwell were not mere flattery. During Bonner's term as Resident Ambassador to France, he submitted seven reports to Henry VIII, but wrote twenty times to Cromwell over the same period. During Bonner's various missions abroad, he was scrupulous in remembering to send small tokens of friendship to Cromwell, including a dialogue from Rabelais, Italian cheeses, and outright gifts of cash.[120]

For these kindnesses and his unflagging diligence in executing Cromwell's wishes, Bonner was repeatedly rewarded with the incomes of several smaller ecclesiastical posts and was eventually promoted to the episcopate. In December 1532, Bonner expressed his thanks to Cromwell for intervening on his behalf for the benefice of Cheriburton. Throughout the 1530s, Bonner similarly acquired the benefices of at least twelve ecclesiastical appointments, was made archdeacon of

118 Alexander, "Bonner Until His Deprivation," pp. 66–68.
119 Alexander, "Bonner Until His Deprivation," p. 68.
120 Alexander, "Bonner Until His Deprivation," pp. 68–69.

Leicester in October of 1535, and bishop of Hereford in 1538.[121] Bonner was abroad so much for diplomatic purposes that he had still not been consecrated as a Bishop of Hereford when Stokesley died. Only after Bonner was elected to the Diocese of London, in October of 1539, was he officially raised to the episcopate.[122] Some measure of how much Bonner benefited from Cromwell's patronage may be gleaned from the fact that after Cromwell's fall in the summer of 1540, Bonner was only sent on one other diplomatic mission, and from that time forward, his ecclesiastical preferments were not greatly augmented. Although Bonner vigorously pursued his debtors within his scattered holdings, he was not diligent in the payment of his own debts, and the wide geographical distribution of his curacies and his frequent embassies abroad resulted in his being a mostly absentee prelate under Henry VIII.[123]

At some point between his return to England in the winter of 1540 and his dispatch to the continent as resident Ambassador to Charles V in 1542, Bonner was reconciled to Stephen Gardiner, the Bishop of Winchester. In 1538, Bonner was specifically sent by Cromwell to replace Gardiner at the court of Francis I. As the protégé of Gardiner's archrival, the Bishop of Winchester was ill-disposed towards Bonner from their first conversations in France. Despite having worked with Bonner on previous diplomatic missions, Gardiner initially refused to hand over his linen, mules, and plate to the new ambassador, as was customary when one delegation succeeded another. After exchanging hard words with Bonner, he later repented his rashness and cooperated with his successor in the transfer of furnishings and supplies. Gardiner's change of heart may have been rooted in a suspicion that Bonner would make an unfavorable report to Cromwell of his behavior. If so, this intuition proved sound, for Bonner, in his regular correspondence with

---

121 Alexander, "Bonner Until His Deprivation," pp. 67–74.

122 See Kenneth Carleton, "Bonner, Edmund (d. 1569)," *Oxford Dictionary of National Biography*, Oxford University Press, 2004 [http://www.oxforddnb.com/view/article/2850, accessed 23 Feb 2006] [hereafter: Carleton, "Bonner, Edmund"].

123 Alexander, "Bonner Until His Deprivation," p. 75–78.

the Lord Privy Seal, denounced at length both Gardiner and the company he kept.[124] Bonner's intentional efforts to disassociate himself from Cromwell after the latter's fall in the summer of 1540[125] perhaps paved the way for a *rapprochement* with Gardiner. In any event, the two of them were on much closer terms by the winter of 1542.[126]

As with his previous envoys, Bonner did not distinguish himself as a diplomat during his embassy to Charles V from 1542 to 1543. Perhaps mindful of past experiences with Bonner, Henry insisted that the most delicate negotiations with the Holy Roman Emperor be conducted by a domestic team in England working with Charles' Ambassador, Chapuys. Although Bonner's function as Resident Ambassador to Charles V was mostly that of a courier and ceremonial observer, he did not much please either Henry or the Imperial Court even in this capacity. Greatly restricted in his role, Bonner returned home in 1543 with little to show for his diplomatic labors.[127]

Intriguingly, it is at about the same time that he reconciled with Gardiner that Bonner's theological conservatism begins to be clearly evident. Along with several of his fellow bishops, Bonner was chosen for a number of commissions convened sporadically from 1540–1547 for strengthening and enforcing the Act of Six Articles. The first of these commissions met in 1540 to weigh several points of doctrine. At that time, the commissioners' views were solicited on various scriptural and sacramental questions. Although many of Bonner's replies were vague or equivocal, his appeal to precedent and tradition, a line of reasoning wholly congruent with his legal and diplomatic training, was distinctly clear in his response on the number of sacraments. Here Bonner asserted that, "the seven have been specially of very long and ancient season received, continued, and taken for things of such

---

124 On the quarrel between Gardiner and Bonner in 1538, see Glyn Redworth, *In Defence of the Church Catholic: The Life of Stephen Gardiner* (Oxford: Basil Blackwell, 1990) [hereafter: Redworth, *Gardiner*], pp. 83ff.
125 Alexander, "Bonner Until His Deprivation," pp. 276–77.
126 Alexander, "Bonner Until His Deprivation," pp. 242–43.
127 See Alexander, "Bonner Until His Deprivation," pp. 238–273, esp. pp. 258, and 272ff.

sort."[128] Similarly, in reply to a question about whether a man was obligated "to confess his secret deadly sins to a priest," Bonner denied that sin could ever be a strictly private matter, declaring not only that a sinner should "confess his open sins," but also, "all sins as touching God are open, and in no wise secret or hid."[129]

In his 1542 injunctions to clergy, Bonner was even more forthright on the value of custom and theological tradition, charging his preachers not to deliver homilies composed "by other men within these CC or CCC years . . . every preacher shall declare the same Gospel or Epistle . . . not after his own mind, but after the mind of some catholic doctor allowed in this church of England, and in no wise affirm any thing but that which he shall always be ready to shew in some ancient writer."[130] When Bonner was commissioned to examine Anne Askew for heresy in 1545, he was then in a position not only to answer doctrinal questions, but to ask them as well. His aim to preserve traditional eucharistic doctrine was clearly revealed in his lengthy interrogations of the accused woman.[131]

Despite serving alongside Nicholas Ridley in examining Askew, Bonner's profession of orthodox eucharistic views in the final years of Henry's life placed him almost ineluctably on a collision course with the doctrinally reformist program of Cranmer and his colleagues. The eucharistic views of Ridley and the Archbishop became more radical in this same period,[132] and their new convictions shaped religious policy under Edward as surely as Bonner and Gardiner had influenced it in the twilight of Henry's reign. Despite later recanting his behavior, Bonner was committed to the Fleet prison in September of 1547 after stipulating that he would only accept the Council's visitation injunctions and the new *Book of Homilies* provided "they be not contrary and repugnant to

128 Alexander, "Bonner Until His Deprivation," p. 429.
129 Alexander, "Bonner Until His Deprivation," p. 429.
130 Alexander, "Bonner Until His Deprivation," p. 430.
131 Alexander, "Bonner Until His Deprivation," p. 431. On Ridley's part in Askew's interrogations, and Protestant reluctance to refer to her by her married surname, Kime, see MacCulloch, *Cranmer*, pp. 352–54. On Bonner's role in examining Askew, see also Redworth, *Gardiner*, p. 235.
132 See MacCulloch, *Cranmer*, pp. 354–55.

God's law and the statutes and ordinances of the church."[133] He was imprisoned briefly. Released on bail by late September, Bonner's incarceration was nonetheless certainly a warning both to him and to his conservative colleagues of what would follow if they continued to resist the Protestant Council's program of religious innovation.[134] That Bonner, in his official capacity as Bishop of London, denounced the eucharistic teaching of the first *Book of Common Prayer* in the Lords' debate in December 1548 on the grounds that it had already been condemned as heresy, is wholly in keeping with his public words and deeds beginning from the early 1540s.[135] Such comments were the cause of his renewed troubles in September of 1549.

Bonner took to heart the lesson of his imprisonment in the Fleet and acquiesced to the demands of the new government with respect to religious reform for nearly two full years. During that time, he showed himself to be outwardly compliant with the new order of religion imposed by the Council, despite their repeated efforts to provoke him into another act of open resistance. In June of 1549 he was expressly commanded to abolish private masses at St. Paul's Cathedral, and to celebrate the new Communion service at the high altar only. Two days later, Bonner forwarded this demand to his diocesan officers, ordering them to conform. In July, the king and Council wrote to Bonner again, urging him to be more diligent in the use and promotion of the new *Book of Common Prayer*. Again, just three days later, he informed his archdeacons that they were to see to it that the Council's order was enforced.[136]

These repeated admonitions to Bonner probably reveal his passive resistance to the new religious order, and the Council probably feared his grudging compliance would embolden other conservatives. They decided to force the issue directly in August of 1549, ordering the bishop himself not to travel outside London proper, "untill ye shall be otherwise

133 Alexander, "Bonner Until His Deprivation," pp. 436–37.
134 Alexander, "Bonner Until His Deprivation," pp. 437–38.
135 See Bonner's remarks in Gasquet and Bishop, *Edward the Sixth*, p. 406.
136 On Bonner's tepid conformity to the Council's new religious program from September 1547–1549, see Alexander, "Bonner Until His Deprivation," pp. 438–440.

licensed by us."[137] Meanwhile the Council authorized such radicals as John Hooper to speak at length in Bonner's own diocese on matters of eucharistic doctrine.[138] Bonner was also commanded to preach a set-piece sermon at St. Paul's on 1 September, in accord with an officially scripted outline.[139] His original instructions directed Bonner to address three principal points: first, that rebellion against the king would result in damnation; second, that God required the sacrifice of humility and obedience to powers of authority, even in the establishment of new religious rites; and third, that young King Edward's authority as a minor was no less than if he were thirty or forty years old.[140] On 29 August, Bonner was instructed to add one other item to his forthcoming sermon: he was to inform the crowd that the government had been victorious over the rebels in Norfolk, Devon, and Cornwall.[141]

The list of topics that Bonner was required to address in this sermon were likely crafted with multiple purposes in mind. Certainly in the wake of widespread rebellions throughout the realm over the new religious order, it was useful politically to have the ecclesial head of the government's central and most populous diocese call for an end to the uprisings, while announcing the lawful authority of the king and

---

137 Alexander, "Bonner Until His Deprivation," p. 441.
138 On Hooper's "lecture," curiously delivered earlier on the same day that Bonner was set to preach at St. Paul's, see MacCulloch, *Cranmer*, p. 441,
139 On the Privy Council's instructions to Bonner concerning this sermon, see Alexander, "Bonner Until His Deprivation," pp. 438–440. Diarmaid MacCulloch astutely notes that it was probably no coincidence that Bonner was hauled before the Council and charged with this task on the very day that Cranmer seized St. Paul's to preach on the subject of obedience. See MacCulloch, *Cranmer*, pp. 440–41 on Cranmer's sermon and Bonner's efforts to subvert the Protestant spirit of the Communion service in the Cathedral.
140 Alexander, "Bonner Until His Deprivation," pp. 441–42. Alexander's rehearsal of the points that Bonner was to address in his official sermon are drawn from Foxe, who in turn is citing material from Bonner's episcopal register. See MS 9531/12, pt. 1, Guildhall Library Collection, London.
141 Alexander, "Bonner Until His Deprivation," p. 442. Cf. MacCulloch, *Cranmer*, p. 440. On the rebellions that flared up when the new Prayer Book was initially enforced, and Cranmer's penned assaults on the rebels' articles, see MacCulloch, *Cranmer* pp. 429–440.

his Privy Council. On a more personal note, these same items were probably selected to underscore Bonner's own laggard and half-hearted compliance with the Council's new religious directives, especially his desultory and subversive use of the first *Book of Common Prayer.* Even more to the point, Bonner had been an enthusiastic champion of the Royal Supremacy over the church in the 1530s under Henry, and was now ostensibly being asked to maintain under Edward precisely what he had so vigorously promoted in the previous reign.[142] The article on Edward's minority was a skillfully aimed blow against Bonner, since he and Gardiner had entertained a theory that the Royal Supremacy was in abeyance until a monarch reached full maturity of years.[143] Tellingly, this item did not appear in the first draft of sermon

142 Certainly Cranmer and Ridley themselves, still advocates of the Royal Supremacy at this stage, would have seen the obedience demanded by Edward of Bonner as wholly congruent with the Erastian policies forcefully advanced in the 1536 preface to *De Vera Obedentia.* On Bonner's authorship of the famous forward to Gardiner's work, see Alexander, "Bonner Until His Deprivation," pp. 411–13, 416–19. If certain of Bonner's Protestant adversaries on the Council sought to turn the tables on him in this fashion, they would turn twice more before any lasting religious settlement was established in England. Writing from prison under Mary, Ridley and Latimer devoted more space to the question of their disobedience to the monarch than to any explicitly doctrinal question in their *Comfortable Conferences*: see fols. 31–34 and Ridley, *Works*, pp. 141–48. Caught on the horns of the same dilemma and singling out Gardiner as "the Antonian," Ridley could only declare, "A man oughte to obei his prince, but in the Lorde, and never against the Lorde." When circumstances shifted again at the death of Mary, Bonner had already learned that a Royal Supremacy was much less a guarantee of liberty than the pope's primacy. He refused to sign the oath when tendered to him twice, and remained in the Marshalsea until his death in 1569. His steadfastness here was very consistent with the position outlined in the *Homelies*, where the papal primacy was the only subject to be the focus of two complete sermons in the collection. See Bonner, *Homelies*, fols. 43–54.

143 This notion was not, however, an invention of Gardiner and Bonner, but was rather a key proviso of Henry VIII's will. Somerset expressly reassured Gardiner on this point about the time of Edward's coronation, stating that there would be no religious innovations during the period of Edward's minority. See C. D. C. Armstrong, "Gardiner, Stephen (c. 1498x8–1555),"

articles for Bonner to address, but was later added by the Council in a subsequent revision.[144] This was also the only topic given to Bonner by the Council that he completely failed to touch when he ascended to the pulpit at St. Paul's on 1 September 1549.

As a result of this omission, Bonner's enemies immediately moved to have him deprived of his ecclesial office as bishop of London. By 8 September, a commission that included both Cranmer and Ridley had already been chosen and charged with examining Bonner on the subject of his sermon and the topic list previously presented to him by the Council. Bonner's explanation for his behavior was that his notes had fallen away from him during the sermon, and that he had been distracted with trying to remember the various subjects he had been directed to address.[145] Feeble as his excuse was, a trial for deprivation on such grounds was without precedent. The fact that Bonner had been imprisoned well before sentence had been pronounced against him indicated that there was only ever one verdict to be returned by his appointed examiners.[146] During the course of the trial, which lasted three weeks, Bonner conceded the point on Edward's authority several times, acknowledging "with harte and mowthe the kings majestie auctorytie and regall power in his minorytie aswell and full as in his majorytie."[147] Nevertheless, precisely one month after the trial began, Bonner was found guilty of failing to uphold the king's authority in his youth, and formally deprived of office as Bishop of London on 1 October 1549. He had already been in jail for ten days, and was never

Oxford Dictionary of National Biography, Oxford University Press, 2004 [http://www.oxforddnb.com/view/article/10364, accessed 1 March 2006].

144 Alexander, "Bonner Until His Deprivation," p. 442, note 26.

145 Alexander, "Bonner Until His Deprivation," p. 449.

146 On the rather irregular legal proceedings against Bonner, see Alexander, "Bonner Until His Deprivation," p. 451.

147 Alexander, "Bonner Until His Deprivation," p. 449. Bonner exhibited considerable legal skill at his trial, managing to so successfully question the legitimacy of the original royal commission that a new one had to be issued for the proceedings a week into the trial. See MacCulloch, *Cranmer*, pp. 442ff. Much of the trial proceedings, taken from Bonner's episcopal register, can be found in Foxe, *Actes and Monuments*, pp. 1309–30.

again at liberty in the reign of Edward. Instead, Ridley, having served as one of Bonner's examiners, was translated from Bishop of Rochester to Bishop of London in April of 1550.[148]

Little is known about Bonner's activities during his imprisonment under Edward VI, although we know that his confinement was quite strict. The author of the *Grey Friars' Chronicle* relates an incident of 8 January 1550, when Bonner refused to pay the keeper of the Marshalsea prison a sum of £10, and was subsequently punished by having his bed removed. For eight days, he had only straw and a coverlet to sleep upon in his chamber. On 6 February 1550 he was taken from prison to Star Chamber at Westminster to be informed that his appeal had been heard and refused by eight Privy Councilors. While many prisoners of conscience in Reformation England, Protestant and Catholic alike, directed their energies to theological polemics during their incarceration, Bonner seems to have written nothing for public consumption from October of 1549 until his release in August of 1553.

Bonner's delivery from the Marshalsea followed close upon the death of Edward VI on 6 July 1553. Queen Mary sent him pardon on Saturday, 5 August, under the Great Seal of England, and he returned to his livings at St. Paul's that same evening. Popular reaction in the London Diocese to his reinstatement was mixed: although the people pealed the bells of St. Paul's at his release, on 13 August a dagger was thrown at Gilbert Bourne when he preached at Paul's Cross that Bonner had been wrongfully imprisoned. The blade missed its intended target and lodged in the pulpit post, but Bonner, present for the sermon, was escorted to safety within the Cathedral amidst the ensuing uproar. Bonner was officially restored to his cure on 22 August, but there remained a curious impediment to his singing Mass straightaway in St. Paul's. Ridley's destruction of the Cathedral's altars in 1550 delayed Bonner's triumphal celebration until 17 September, and it was only on 7 October, at the opening of Convocation, that he was able to conduct a proper ceremony in full episcopal regalia at the newly restored high altar.

Bonner was accorded a place of honor in the new reign and he was

---

148 See MacCulloch, *Cranmer*, p. 455. Cf. Alexander, "Bonner Until His Deprivation," pp. 238–74.

a central figure in the main proceedings of government. In January of 1554, he was dispatched as one of the queen's ambassadors to receive Philip of Spain at Portsmouth. By mid-March, the tables had fully turned and he was appointed as a commissioner for the examination of bishops who had themselves gotten married in the previous reign. Several were deprived of their episcopal jurisdiction as a result of this inquest, and on 1 April, Bonner assisted Stephen Gardiner in the consecration of six bishops to occupy the newly vacant posts. In late July, he was present at Winchester Cathedral for the marriage of Mary and Philip, with Gardiner presiding.

By autumn, Bonner was focusing much of his attention on faith and morals in his own diocese, launching a sweeping episcopal visitation of the Diocese of London on 3 September 1554. During this same period, he was engaged in preparing and publishing his *Profitable and Necessarye Doctryne* and *Homelies*. Despite his active involvement in official business for the crown, and his catechetical projects, Bonner's investigation of the beliefs and practices of the clergy and laity of his cure was not left to his commissaries and other administrators. He visited the parishes of his jurisdiction in person, preaching in each locale. The entire process has been described by Kenneth Carleton as "a model of thoroughness."[149] Indeed, Bonner did not rush through his responsibilities, but rather devoted more than a year to the task, bringing his visitation to a close on 8 October 1555, one month after the *Homelies* were published in London. If imitation is high flattery, Bonner's labors were greatly esteemed: several other bishops, and Cardinal Pole himself, used Bonner's Visitation Articles as a model for examination of their own jurisdictions. Bonner and Gardiner together officially received Pole at St. Paul's on Advent Sunday, 2 December 1555. Gardiner, however, would not survive the year, and Bonner conducted the Bishop of Winchester's funeral rites on 13 November 1556.[150]

Despite Bonner's position and prestige, he still had differences with

---

149 See Carleton, "Bonner, Edmund."
150 The foregoing details on Bonner's imprisonment under Edward VI and the early portion of his restoration under Mary are drawn from Carleton, "Bonner, Edmund."

Mary's Council as well as with Cardinal Pole. Gina Alexander, Bonner's only modern biographer, has, in fact, described Bonner as being "caught between the upper and nether millstone" as Bishop of London under Mary.[151] The chronicle of his activities in the second portion of his episcopate is also the story of the government's action to extirpate Protestantism in the Diocese of London. Suspected heretics were referred to Bonner for examination directly by the Council,[152] by specially appointed royal commissioners,[153] and by justices of the peace.[154] This multi-layered system for deposing suspects was made even more convoluted by Bonner's own appointment to serve on several royal commissions for heresy inquests.[155] He found himself ensnared in terrible tangles between the Council and the Cardinal-legate: Bonner examined thirteen suspects and excommunicated them on 13 June 1556. All of them were absolved by Pole, who procured a royal pardon for each. Hoping to avoid further trouble in the wake of this episode, Bonner consulted Pole before proceeding against another twenty-two alleged heretics in August. The Bishop of London dutifully presented these suspects with a gentler, shortened oath of submission, which each felt he or she could sign, and so all were released. Nevertheless, by November, the Council reprimanded Bonner for such leniency, and ordered him to re-commence proceedings against two of the August suspects.[156]

The epithet "Bloody Bonner" was bestowed on the Bishop by John Foxe, whose fondness for alliterative slights against the Catholic

---

151 Gina Alexander, "Bonner and the Marian Persecutions," in *The English Reformation Revised,* ed. Christopher Haigh (Cambridge: University Press, 1987) [hereafter: Alexander, "Marian Persecutions"], p. 166.

152 Council members ordered the arrest of John Rough and Cuthbert Simpson while directing Bonner to examine them. See Alexander, "Marian Persecutions," pp. 161–62.

153 Royal commissioners conducted many preliminary examinations for heresy before referring several on to Bonner. See Alexander, "Marian Persecutions," pp. 162–63.

154 Suspects referred by the justices were often reconciled or absolved: none of the three suspects sent to Bonner by Essex justices in early March 1556 were executed. See Alexander, "Marian Persecutions," pp. 164–67.

155 Alexander, "Marian Persecutions," pp. 164–65.

156 See Alexander, "Marian Persecutions," pp. 161–62.

divines of the Reformation is equally apparent in his soubriquet for Stephen Gardiner: "Wily Winchester."[157] Of Bonner's central role in the prosecution of Protestants there can be no doubt: of 282 burnings recorded in Marian episcopal registers, 116 were conducted within Bonner's own see.[158] Despite this fact, however, we should not be too swift to embrace Foxe's assessment of Bonner. In the first place, Bonner was reluctant to see Protestants executed at the outset of Mary's reign. In fact, he was reprimanded by the Council in 1555 for months of delay in proceeding against known heretics within his cure. It was only after late May of 1555 that Bonner seems to have pursued such persecutions with much vigor.[159] Some additional notes of caution must also be sounded on this score, in that London had a long history of Lollardy, and it was there that the Edwardine religious reforms had rooted most firmly within the realm, due in large part to the labors of Ridley. London's history of heresy inquests and executions was centuries old, and the victims were often Anabaptists or other radical non-conformists. As an urban center, it was dense with inhabitants, and non-conformity was therefore more readily detected there than in a rural backwater.[160] In such a setting, there would likely have been a number of heresy trials in the Diocese quite apart from the Council's efforts to discover and execute professing Protestants under Mary Tudor.

Once goaded by the government, however, Bonner was diligent in the destruction of unrepentant Protestants through the end of Mary's reign. One individual who could not be saved even by full recantation, of course, was Thomas Cranmer. In February of 1556, Bonner assisted Thirlby, then Bishop of Ely, in the ritual degradation of Cranmer, prior to the former Archbishop's execution by burning on 21 March. Cardinal

157 See C. D. C Armstrong, "Gardiner, Stephen (c. 1498x8–1555)," *Oxford Dictionary of National Biography*, Oxford University Press, 2004 [http://www.oxforddnb.com/view/article/10364, accessed 1 March 2006]. Armstrong's article concludes with the assertion that Foxe's title was not really very appropriate to Gardiner, whose strident willfulness was all too evident throughout his career.

158 See Carleton, "Bonner, Edmund."

159 See Carleton, "Bonner, Edmund."

160 See Carleton, "Bonner, Edmund."

Pole was consecrated Archbishop the very next day, and Bonner assisted in the rite. He continued to play a public role in all manner of official proceedings and religious services until Mary's death. He was one of the commissioners selected to establish new regulations for solemn processions in June of 1556, and was also chosen to conduct another heresy inquest in February of 1557. In late summer of that year, he presided at a number of state funerals, including those of Anne of Cleves (fourth of the six wives of Henry VIII), the Duchess of Norfolk, and the Countess of Arundel. In March of 1558, he examined and condemned three more heretics from London Diocese.[161]

Another key funeral also saw Bonner's good fortunes expire: Mary Tudor's life slipped quietly away in the early morning hours of 17 November 1558 as she lay in the royal palace of St. James. With her passing and that of Pole just a few hours later at Lambeth, Bonner would find himself in dramatically changed circumstances in the next reign. Reputedly, he was the sole bishop to whom Elizabeth Tudor would not extend her hand to be kissed at her accession, an omen of what was in store for Bonner in the coming months.[162]

The first signs of real trouble for Bonner surfaced during the rancorous debates of Elizabeth's first Parliament, which was convened from 25 January to 8 May 1559.[163] The unenviable task of attempting to sort out the legal labyrinth of property rights for confiscated or relinquished church estates fell to this body. The controversy centered on a number of competing claims from tenants of church-owned lands and estates who had been displaced first under Edward VI and then again under Mary I. Such lands were often leased to the families and friends of prominent clergy, and the double volte-face in religion in England in the middle decades of the sixteenth century meant that the disputes embodied a great deal of religious controversy.

Bonner's own holdings were a central part of this dispute, in that

---

161 See Carleton, "Bonner, Edmund."
162 See Carleton, "Bonner, Edmund."
163 See Gina Alexander, "Bishop Bonner and the Parliament of 1559," in *The Bulletin of the Institute of Historical Research*, vol. 56 no. 134 (November 1983) [hereafter: Alexander, "Bonner and the Parliament of 1559"].

after he was deprived of his see in 1549, Nicholas Ridley, Bonner's Protestant successor, leased a handful of titular manors that belonged to London Diocese to several of his own kinsmen, including his sister, Alice, and her husband, George Shipside. After Bonner's restoration in 1553, he had evicted Ridley's tenants, including the Shipsides, from their livings. Bonner, keen to preserve the interests of his own lessees, many of whom were among his closest friends, proved totally recalcitrant in the parliamentary proceedings.[164] On at least one occasion he came in person to argue his case before the Commons. There is some evidence that Bonner's pertinacity on this question served to divide the powerful spiritual peers and erode popular confidence in their stance on religious matters. If so, Bonner ironically helped pave the way for a Protestant settlement in religion by stirring up popular sympathy for the surviving relatives of Ridley.[165] Whatever the cause, the spiritual peers' opposition to religious change collapsed in the wake of Bonner's protracted maneuvers to retain his estates and leases. This turn of events paved the way for the bills for the Royal Supremacy and the Act for Uniformity in Religion to eventually pass both houses and become law under Elizabeth.

Not long after the conclusion of Parliament, Bonner was directly confronted with the Oath of Supremacy. Despite her personal dislike of him, Elizabeth and her advisors recognized that Bonner's long diplomatic service could still be of some use to the government. Accordingly, he was charged with entertaining the French ambassadors in the spring of 1559. The delegation departed Bonner's palace on 28 May, and he was offered the Oath on 30 May, which he refused to sign.[166] He cannot have been in doubt as to the consequences of his decision. He was again deprived of his see, but not imprisoned until 20 April 1560, when he

164 For Bonner's attitude and the legal implications of his position, see Alexander, "Bonner and the Parliament of 1559," pp. 170–79. Cf. Norman Jones, "A Bill Confirming Bishop Bonner's Deprivation and Reinstating Bishop Ridley as the Legal Bishop of London, from the Parliament of 1559," in *The Journal of Ecclesiastical History*, vol. 33 no. 4 (October 1982), pp. 580–85.
165 Alexander, "Bonner and the Parliament of 1559," pp. 178–79.
166 See Carleton, "Bonner, Edmund."

was seized and placed once more in the Marshalsea. For the rest of his life, Bonner would never again be at liberty. In April of 1564, the Elizabethan Bishop of Winchester, Robert Horne, hauled him from the Marshalsea to again offer Bonner the opportunity to take the Oath of Supremacy. The penalty for a second refusal was death. The episode clearly revealed that Bonner's legal skill had not diminished with age and confinement. Predictably, Bonner again declined the Oath, and the certificate of his refusal was presented by Horne to the queen's bench. When confronted by Elizabeth's examiners, Bonner declared that the certificate did not carry legal force, because it named Horne as the bishop of Winchester, whose consecration was invalid because it had been performed by Matthew Parker, whose own consecration in 1559 had not been conducted according to the statutes then in force. The strength of his argument may be measured by three remarkable events: Bonner was never prosecuted for refusing the Oath a second time; it was never tendered to him again; and in 1567, Parliament passed an act retroactively validating all of the consecrations carried out from the start of Elizabeth's reign.[167]

In the last dozen years of his life, September was to be a momentous month for Bonner. In September of 1547, the Edwardine Council had briefly imprisoned him in the Fleet. In September of 1549, he was charged to preach at Paul's Cross and deprived of his see. In September 1553, he sang Mass again for the first time at St. Paul's after his restoration; and in September of 1554, he launched his episcopal visitation of London Diocese. His *Homelies* were published in September of 1555. In 1569, September was once more a fateful month for Bonner: he died of natural causes in the Marshalsea. The final irony was that Edmund Grindal (c. 1519–1583), Nicholas Ridley's protégé and *fidus Achates,* was the Bishop of London at the time and issued Bonner's burial order. For fear of hostile riots, Grindal had Bonner interred at midnight in the churchyard of St. George's Southwark.[168] At some point, Bonner's body was removed to Copford Church in Essex, near

---

167 Carleton, "Bonner, Edmund."
168 See Carleton, "Bonner, Edmund." For Grindal as Ridley's *fidus Achates,* see William Turner's letter to Foxe, in Ridley, *Works*, pp. 489, 493.

Colchester, where, in 1809, a workman found Bonner's coffin under the floor by the altar.[169]

Despite a long and distinguished career in service to the Church, Bonner is mostly known today as "Bloody Bonner," Archfiend of John Foxe's martyrs. Foxe's depiction of Bonner parallels the martyrologist's presentation of Stephen Gardiner as "Wily Winchester" in the *Actes and Monuments*.[170] Foxe developed his portrait of Bonner by degrees, altering his assessment of the Bishop with successive editions of his book of Protestant martyrs, to depict the Bishop more effectively as inconstant in both belief and action. Foxe clearly combined his own apologetic skills and his knowledge of Bonner's involvement with heresy prosecutions in the capitol diocese, to distort the Bishop's role in the repression of Protestantism in the reign of Mary. To fully appreciate Bonner's gifts and accomplishments, it is essential that we evaluate his theological writings in their own right, along with a reappraisal of his character and works by exploring the motive and means of Foxe's deliberate mischaracterizations of Bonner in the *Actes and Monuments*, commonly known as *Foxe's Book of Martyrs*.

169 It is fascinating to speculate about those who might have had a hand in relocating Bonner's body from London to Copford. John Morren or Morwen, chaplain and secretary to Bonner, is certainly a person of interest in the case. Morren was rector of Copford from 1558–1559, and was arrested in 1561 for distributing a text condemning a sermon by James Pilkington (1520–1576), Bishop of Durham under Elizabeth I. Morren's imprisonment seems to have been brief, since the records of the Second Ecclesiastical Commission under Elizabeth reported in 1562 that he was abroad and supposedly spreading sedition in Staffordshire and Lancashire. Morren was ordained and appointed rector of Copford by Bonner and worked closely with the Bishop in heresy cases for London. Like his bishop, Morren was also imprisoned by Elizabethan authorities for his faith. Curiously, the first divine appointed to be rector of Copford under Elizabeth was the Marian Exile, John Pullain, who died in 1565. The rectorate of Copford stood vacant from that time until 1572, a circumstance which would have made it much easier to re-inter Bonner's remains following his first burial in London in September 1569.

170 Michael Riordan and Alec Ryrie, "Stephen Gardiner and the Making of a Protestant Villain," *Sixteenth Century Journal*, vol. 34 (2003) [hereafter: Riordan and Ryrie, "Making of a Protestant Villain"], pp. 1039–65.

Conflict and Continuity

From everything that has been said, it is apparent that Ridley and Bonner were central figures in the progress of the Reformation in England, and that their lives were closely intertwined. For both men, their Henrician past complicated the roles they played and the labors they performed during the reigns of Edward VI and Mary I. In the middle of the sixteenth century, Ridley and Bonner strove against each other, attempting to win the people of London to strongly opposing conceptions of the Church. Given their rival stances on ecclesiology by the 1540s, it would be easy to imagine that the two men held no common principles when it came to scriptural exegesis, but, in fact, their biblical explications exhibit key shared characteristics, especially in the Humanist concern for historical consciousness in biblical interpretation and the application of philology for textual exposition.

In order to understand the similarities and differences between the exegetical work of Ridley and Bonner, however, one must first consider their writings in the context of both late medieval scriptural exegesis and the revolution in New Testament studies opened by John Colet and Desiderius Erasmus at the very start of the sixteenth century. These evaluations must start with a survey of the traditional conception of the relationship between the Old and New Testaments as this idea was captured in late medieval sermons and art. The liturgical and exegetical writings of Thomas Aquinas are an excellent starting place to see how the Church understood the relationship between the Old Covenant and the New, prior to the Renaissance and the advent of the "New Learning" of Protestantism.

Church and Synagogue: the Medieval Heritage

In the early 1260s, Thomas Aquinas sought to collect the exegetical insights of several previous biblical expositors into a single running commentary on the four Gospels. The fruit of his labors, the *Catena Aurea in Quatuor Evangelia,* draws heavily on the writings of Jerome, Ambrose, Cyprian, Chrysostom, and Augustine, and remains a useful compendium of patristic thought on the biblical books of Matthew, Mark,

Luke, and John even today. Although never intended to be a very original work, the *Catena* nevertheless bears the traces of Thomas' key preoccupation on the subject of salvation: the relationship of the covenant history of ancient Israel to the Church.[171]

The portions of the *Catena Aurea* that relate to the Eucharistic institution narrative found in Matthew are a case in point, and are comprised of excerpts from the Church Fathers, Chrysostom and Jerome, among several others. One key passage from Chrysostom cited there focuses on the subject of the Old Testament's similitude to the New: "'This is my blood of the new covenant.' This statement pertains to the proclamation of the new law. Indeed, the old covenant promised that which the new covenant contains; whereas the Old Testament had the blood of sheep and goats, the New has the Lord's Blood."[172] Chrysostom's remark is a clear assertion of the inter-relatedness of the Old and New Covenants. However, the links in Thomas' *Golden Chain* were not all of the same form. Patristic citations that argue for the mutual co-inherence of the Old and New Covenants rest side by side in the work with passages that deplore the unbelief of the Jews. A passage from Jerome on the very next verse in Matthew (26:29) makes this point plain: "Holy Scripture bears witness that the people of Israel are the vine brought out of Egypt. It is therefore of this vine that the Lord says he will not drink except in his Father's kingdom. The kingdom of his Father I hold to be the faith of believers. When the Jews shall receive his Father's kingdom, the Lord will then drink of their vine."[173] These attitudes were part of

---

171 See Matthew Levering, *Christ's Fulfillment of Torah and Temple: Salvation According to Thomas Aquinas* (South Bend: University of Notre Dame Press, 2002), [hereafter, Levering, *Salvation According to Aquinas*].

172 "'Hic est sanguis meus novi testamenti,' hoc est annuntiationis legis novae: hoc enim promittebat vetus testamentum quod continet novum: sicut enim vetus testamentum habuit sanguinem vitulorum et ovium, ita novum habet sanguinem dominicum." St. John Chrysostom, Homily 83 on Matthew (26:28). In Thomas Aquinas, *Catena Aurea in Quatuor Evangelia*, vol. 1, *Expositio in Mattheum et Marcum* (Rome: Marietti Editori Ltd., 1953), [hereafter, Aquinas, *Catena Aurea*], p. 385, translation mine.

173 "Quod vinea de Aegypto transplantata populus sit Israel, sacra Scriptura testatur. Dicit ergo Dominus se de hac vinea nequaquam esse bibiturum,

the patrimony of the Fathers that Thomas collected and handed on to the latter Middle Ages. This patrimony of biblical commentary consisted of two distinct but intertwined strands of thought on the subject of Israel's relationship to holy mother Church, one triumphal, and the other concerned to highlight the similitudes between Judaism and Christianity.

In his most celebrated production, the *Summa Theologica*, Thomas again focused his attention on the points of connection between the Old and New Covenants. In his reflections on the consecration of the eucharistic elements, he is naturally led by the subject matter to an analysis of the institution narratives: "The blood of Christ's Passion has its efficacy not merely in the elect among the Jews, to whom the blood of the Old Testament was exhibited, but also in the Gentiles; nor only in the priests who consecrate this sacrament, and in those others who partake of it; but likewise in those for whom it is offered."[174] Thomas continues: ". . . Therefore He says expressly, *for you*, the Jews, *and for many*, namely the Gentiles; or *for you* who eat of it, *and for many*, for whom it is offered."[175] Thomas' interpolations on the Jews and the Gentiles not only underscore the inter-relatedness of the Old and New Covenants, but also emphasize the fact that the Apostles were Jews, and that the New Covenant came first to them before being transmitted to the Gentiles. Although criticized by post-Renaissance biblical commentators as historically naive, Thomas' Scholastic biblical commentary proved more contextually astute than the models of interpretation that immediately succeeded it. Thomas' positive estimation of the Jewish religious heritage of Jesus and the Apostles stands in sharp contrast to the views of Erasmus and his disciples. The loss of Old and New Testament inter-textuality in exegesis was one of the major casualties

---

nisi in regno Patris. Regnum Patris fidem puto esse credentium. Ergo cum Iudaei regnum receperint Patris, tunc de vino eorum Dominus bibet." Jerome in Aquinas, *Catena Aurea*, p. 386, translation mine.

174 Thomas Aquinas, *Summa Theologica*, trans. and eds. the Fathers of the English Dominican Province, vol 2. (New York: Benziger Brothers, Inc., 1947) [hereafter, Aquinas, *Summa Theologica*], Pt. III, Q. 78,Art. 3, Reply to Objection 8, p. 2476.

175 Aquinas, *Summa Theologica*, Pt. III, Q. 78, Art. 3, Reply to Objection 8, p. 2476.

of the Renaissance and deserves a great deal more scholarly attention than it has received to date.

From various angles, Thomas rehearses the point that the New Covenant is grounded directly upon the Old. An explication of the two testaments found in the *Summa*, for example, asserts that Christ's blood was exhibited to humanity in two chief ways: "First of all in figure, and this belongs to the Old Testament; consequently the Apostle (Hebrews 9:16) concludes: *Whereupon neither was the first indeed dedicated without blood*, which is evident from this, that as related in Exodus 24:7–8, when every commandment of the law *had been read* by Moses, *he sprinkled all the people* saying: *This is the blood of the testament which the Lord hath enjoined unto you.*"[176] Thomas' references to Exodus 24 and the blood covenant between the people of Israel and the Lord are natural in this context, not only because the author of Hebrews, generally presumed to be St. Paul in Thomas' day, makes this connection, but also because Christ himself alludes to the very same portion of the Pentateuch in the institution of the Eucharist: "This is my blood of the [new] covenant, which is poured out for many for the forgiveness of sins" (Matt. 26:28).[177] Jesus' use of the defining language and imagery of Jewish religious identity in the deliverance and acceptance of the Decalogue on Mt. Sinai would not have been lost on his audience, and Thomas has followed this same line of explication in many places where he labors to illuminate Jesus' dual messianic role, as both priest and victim.[178]

The view that the Old and New Covenants are mutually interdependent is by no means unique to Aquinas, as his own patristic and biblical researches reveal. Exposure to this concept was not limited to those who studied theology with him at Paris and across Italy. However, preoccupied

176 Aquinas, *Summa Theologica*. Pt. III, Q. 78,Art. 3, Reply to Objection 3, p. 2475.
177 The Revised Standard Version of the Bible indicates that several ancient authorities include the word "new" in this verse. In any event, Jesus' express allusion to Exodus 26:8 remains indisputable: "And Moses took the blood and threw it upon the people, and said, 'Behold the blood of the covenant which the Lord has made with you in accordance with all these words.'"
178 See Levering, *Salvation According to Aquinas*.

with the idea as he was, and being one of the only premier theologians in the history of the West to compose an office for a major liturgical rite, Thomas was especially well-placed to promote this notion according to his own formulations. Celebrations of the Feast of *Corpus Christi* had been growing steadily for nearly twenty years prior to Urban IV's request to Thomas to compose an official rite, or office, for *Corpus Christi*, in 1264. The rubrics for the celebration of *Corpus Christi* down through the Middle Ages had little cohesive form prior to Thomas' labors. Thomas' *Corpus Christi* compositions eventually ensured a broad dissemination of his insights concerning both the Eucharist and the blood covenants of Sinai and Golgotha. Observed in England from 1318, this feast and its attendant liturgical devotions rapidly won a strong lay allegiance throughout the realm that remained vital on the eve of the Reformation.[179]

Thomas' Office for the Feast of *Corpus Christi* recapitulates the idea that Christian salvation is anchored in the substantial harmony between the Old and New Covenants. The *Pange Lingua* is just one of the hymns Thomas composed for the celebration of *Corpus Christi*, and it is replete with Old and New Testament interconnections: "That last night at supper lying mid the twelve, his chosen band,/ Jesus with the Law complying, keeps the feast its rites demand;/ then more precious food supplying, gives himself with his own hand."[180] In observing that Jesus fully complied with the Law in the Passover meal that was the setting for the institution of the Eucharist, Thomas highlights Jesus' Jewish religious heritage, and then links it with Christian ritual practice in the very next verse of the *Pange Lingua*: "Word made flesh, the bread he taketh, by his word his Flesh to be;/ wine his sacred Blood he maketh, though the senses fail to see;/ faith alone the true heart waketh to behold the mystery."[181] The same motif is

---

179 Duffy, *Stripping of the Altars*, pp. 43–44. Cf. pp. 35, 460, 566, and 580.
180 "In suprema nocte coenae recumbens cum fratribus observata lege plene cibis in legalibus, cibum turbae duodenae se dat suis manibus." Latin text from Thomas Aquinas, *Devoutly I Adore Thee: The Prayers and Hymns of St. Thomas Aquinas*, trans. Robert Anderson, ed. Johann Moser (Manchester, N.H.: Sophia Press, 1993), pp. 88–89. The English translation of this excerpt from the *Pange Lingua* is from *The Hymnal 1982, According to the Use of the Episcopal Church* (New York: Church Hymnal Corporation, 1982), selection no. 329.

found in Thomas' *Sacris Solemnis*, his vesper hymn for the *Corpus Christi* feast: "Recall that final evening meal/ When Christ did offer lamb and bread/ according to the ancient Law/ from Patriarchs inherited. The feast of the Paschal Lamb now over/ the body of the Lord was shared/ Thus everything to all and to each/ from his own hands was then declared."[182] Thus, Thomas not only emphasizes that Jesus was a Paschal victim himself, but also that the Messiah personally performed the Jewish rites associated with the Passover meal even as he blessed and distributed the first Eucharist. Unless one recognizes that medieval theologians and biblical commentators saw much to praise in the ancient Jewish religion, and that they were not timid in highlighting Jesus' adherence to it, one risks misunderstanding much of the art and literature of the period.

Eamon Duffy, Catholic ecclesiastical historian, has perhaps done more than any other modern scholar to cogently challenge what was the received opinion about the religious life of Christians in late medieval England. In *The Stripping of the Altars*, he gives ample play to the devotional literature and ecclesial art from the period, demonstrating the vigor of medieval piety just prior to and during the English Reformation. Among the many topics Duffy explores surrounding the cult of the Eucharist in Medieval England is the role of unbelieving Jews in miracle stories associated with the consecrated host.[183] In these narratives, the antagonist beholds the eucharistic miracle in an aspect of its ultimate reality—as flesh and blood—rather than under the forms of bread and wine. What appears as a normal communion to the Christian

181 "Verbum caro, panem verum verbo carnem efficit: fitque sanguis Christi merum, et si sensus deficit, ad firmandum cor sincerum sola fides sufficit." English translation of this excerpt is from *The Hymnal 1982, According to the Use of the Episcopal Church* (New York: Church Hymnal Corporation, 1982), selection no. 329.

182 "Noctis recolitur cena novissima/ Qua Christus creditur agnum et azyma Dedisse fratribus, iuxta legitima/ Priscis indulta patribus. Post agnum typicum, expletis epulis, corpus Dominicum datum discipulis, sic totum omnibus, quod totum singulis, eius fatemur manibus." Latin text and translation from Thomas Aquinas, *Devoutly I Adore Thee: The Prayers and Hymns of St. Thomas Aquinas*, trans. Robert Anderson, ed. Johann Moser (Manchester, N.H.: Sophia Press, 1993), p. 93.

183 Duffy, *Stripping of the Altars*, pp. 105–08.

protagonist is witnessed as an act of cannibalism by the Jew who has accompanied his friend to mass: "If I had eeten as moche as thy hast eten I wolde not be a hungred as I trowe in thre days. . . . I saw ye ete a childe the which the preest helde up at the awter."[184] In these plays, the Christian often replies that the frightful vision of a child or the bleeding flesh of Christ in the Eucharist is the direct consequence of the Jews having crucified Christ.[185] In Duffy's estimation, Jews feature prominently in these medieval miracle stories because they serve as "outsiders," or representatives of "culpable unbelief."[186]

Why such unbelief should appear culpable to medieval Christians can often be unclear to modern readers, who are usually steeped in cultural and religious pluralism. This medieval perspective proceeded from the view that there was a substantive harmony and overlap between the Old and New Covenants. It is hard to overestimate how much Old Testament themes and piety shaped medieval Christianity. In fact, two major feasts of the medieval Church calendar directly celebrated specific ritual practices of the Law: the Purification of the Virgin (Candlemas), and the Circumcision of the Lord. Rosary devotions urged reflection on Jesus' presentation in the temple, his teaching in the Synagogue, and also his Transfiguration, where according to scripture, Moses and Elijah appeared at his sides. It was nearly inevitable that medieval Christians, like their Patristic forebears, would believe that committed reflection on the Old Covenant led almost ineluctably to acceptance of the New. In Paul and the other authors of the New Testament, they had Jewish authorities who espoused this very concept, citing the Psalms, Prophets, and other Old Testament writings at every turn for supporting evidence. For medieval Christians, Jesus' Passion appeared to be such a perfect embodiment of messianic themes in the Old Testament, that they simply could not comprehend Jewish unbelief with respect to Christ. Given the angle from which medieval Christians were taught to view the Hebrew Bible,

---

184 John Mirk, *The Festial*, (1403? [STC 17975]), fol. 53, *recto*.
185 E.g. Duffy, *Stripping of the Altars*, pp. 105. Cf. p. 107 where Duffy also speculates that many of these stories were aimed to strike at not only unbelievers, but the well-known heresies of the Lollards as well.
186 Duffy, *Stripping of the Altars*, p. 105.

such a perspective was nearly inescapable. The two Covenants were so intertwined in the medieval religious landscape that individuals or communities maintaining a sharp separation between them appeared to be engaged in a willful act of contrariety.

The extent to which Old and New Covenant themes were wedded together in late medieval devotional life confronts the reader time and again in the art and literature of the period. Duffy's study bears witness to this fact even in passing, as he describes early sixteenth-century primers that depict Old Testament analogues to the Church's sacraments in block illustrations, and that feature woodcuts of Moses and Aaron adorning the text of the Ten Commandments.[187] Popular hagiographical materials that included substantial collections of Old Testament stories went through several different editions in the late medieval period.[188] Similarly, a catechetical guide to the Mass, produced for the Duchess of Suffolk in the mid-fifteenth century "moralizes the priest's departure at the end of Mass as recalling Moses' leading of Israel through the Red Sea."[189] Nor were such themes limited to print productions, since one of the most remarkable commonplace books (a personal manuscript collection of prayers and meditations) to survive to us, the so-called Brome commonplace, includes a play of Abraham and Isaac alongside a verse life of St. Catherine of Alexandria.[190]

These Old Testament allusions, both as texts and images, were a focus of devotion in sanctuaries that often featured an imposing mural to aid in the examination of one's conscience. Frequently, they are com-

187 See Duffy's description of *The Arte or Crafte to Lyve Well* in *Stripping of the Altars*, p. 81. In the illustration on Christian marriage, the accompanying Old Testament vignette shows God joining the hands of Adam and Eve together in Eden, while the Mass illustration features the corresponding image of Melchizedek offering bread and wine (this latter illustration can be viewed in plate 43 of *Stripping of the Altars*). As Duffy indicates on p. 81, the catechetical device of using a Moses and Aaron woodcut to adorn the text of the Ten Commandments was also common to the *The Floure of the Commanundements of God* (Winken de Worde 1505, [RSTC 23875.1]). Other editions of this work followed in 1510 and 1512.

188 See the description of Caxton's translation of *The Golden Legend* in Duffy, *Stripping of the Altars*, p. 79.

189 Duffy, *Stripping of the Altars*, pp. 118–19.

190 Duffy, *Stripping of the Altars*, p. 74.

plete with portraits of Moses holding the tablets of the Commandments as Christ stands in judgment over the wicked and the righteous.[191] The sermons delivered in such late medieval sanctuaries frequently reinforced the similitude of Moses to Christ: "Thus was Moyses a fygure and a token of Cryst. Moyses came before and gave the lawe, and Cryste came after and gave his grace and mercye."[192] For such parishioners, Renaissance and Reformation notions about the major divide that separated Law and Gospel would doubtless have seemed somewhat puzzling: "For in the same maner as Moyses sette the people out of Egypte thrughe the reed see to the hylle of Synay in the same wyse Cryste whan he come by his prechynge and myracles doynge, he sette the people out of derkenes of synne and of all euyll lyuynge thrughe the water of baptysme to the hyll of vertuous lyuynge."[193]

Such casual intermingling of Old and New Testament religious themes in their devotions indicates that medieval Christians found much of value in the religion of ancient Israel. Sermon cycles from the late Middle Ages, even those Duffy does not discuss in *The Stripping of the Altars*, also promote a fluid view of the two Covenants. In the *Speculum Sacerdotale*, a fifteenth-century collection of sermons akin to Mirk's *Festial*, the lay faithful who assemble for the Feast of the Purification are reminded of Mary's dutiful compliance with the Law: "In this day oure lady Marie and alle hire frendus that was with hure brought Ihesu in-to Jerusalem that he schuld be offred as the olde lawe commaundide. And the law commaundid that tyme that who-so-ever were firste conceyved, born and brought forthe, were it of man, were it of beste, it shulde be offred to God."[194] The author continues at some length on the subject of Levitical prescriptions for thank offerings, explaining that the temple priest, "Be-felle for to take for iche man and womman that were so offred v sycle. . . . Hit was also commanundid be the lawe that iche woman shuld offure for hure sone in the xl day after his birthe and for hure doughter in the lxxx day after hure burthe

---

191 Duffy, *Stripping of the Altars*, p. 63.
192 Mirk, *Festial*, fol. 24, *recto*.
193 Mirk, *Festial*, fol. 24, *recto*.
194 *Speculum Sacerdotale*, Edward H. Weatherly, ed., unaltered reprint of the original 1936 edition, (Oxford: Early English Text Society, 1988) [hereafter *Speculum Sacerdotale*], p. 24.

a clene lombe that shuld be unfiled and a turtyl or ellis a dowue. And hif that sche were pore and noght in power for to offre a lambe, hit was ordeyned that sche schuld gheve two turtuls or ellis two dowuys."[195] Although somewhat confused in the case of turtledoves, the author is at pains to relate the Hebrew religious customs that shaped Jesus and Mary's devotional life, and their adherence to the same.[196]

The congruence of Old and New Covenant religious themes was probably nowhere made more evident to medieval laity than during the Passion liturgies and sermons, where sincere devotion was earnestly enjoined upon them: "Sires, cometh in that holy weke to youre chirche in the moste deuocion, and maketh youre confession, ye that ben noyt yit confessid."[197] It was here also that the incongruity and scandal of the Crucifixion was felt most deeply: "And when ye schal here rehersid the voyce of the Jewys in tyme of his passion when they seid to Pylat: 'Crucifige, crucifige eum'; *scilicet*, they badde hym deme hym to be crucified; then let your hertes sorowe and take compunccion you oweth to be conuerted unto hym that vochidsafe for us wrecchis for to be yeven and betrayed to the power of syche wyckyd peple and to suffre the turment of the crosse unto deth."[198] If one does not grasp that many Old Testament religious themes were readily incorporated into medieval Christian devotion, one misses a major cause of the animosity that they directed against those whom they judged responsible for the death of Christ. The scandal of the Crucifixion was heightened precisely because the Church shared and valued so much of the patrimony of Israel. Nevertheless, that ire itself was tempered with the confession that Christians themselves were "wrecchis" in need of conversion.

Errant Christians were, in fact, negatively compared to the Jews of the Crucifixion reenactments of medieval English liturgies. Thus John Mirk upbraided parishioners at the Passion Sunday Mass: "I fere gretely leste there ben moche fals people that be chrystened that pursuen (per-

---

195 *Speculum Sacerdotale*, p. 24.
196 The section on The Feast of the Circumcision of the Lord similarly discusses the procedure itself and the precepts of the Law governing it in great detail. See *Speculum Sacerdotale*, p. 16. Cf. Mirk, *Festial*, fol. 82.
197 *Speculum Sacerdotale*, p. 101.
198 *Speculum Sacerdotale*, p. 101.

secute) Cryst in heuen now. Saynt Austyn sayeth that they synne more greuously that pursue hym in heuen than the Jewes dyde that pursueden hym here in erthe."[199] Such confessions about the wounding effect of sinful behavior could even be extended to include the entire parish community: "Thus ben we worse than the Jewes, thus we be unkynde to hym that shewed to us all kindness."[200] Yet even in the midst of liturgical recollections of the Crucifixion, medieval Christians celebrated and embraced what they held in common with Israel: "Creeme is made of the clennyst bawme and clennest oyle. . . . Creem has his begynnyng in the Olde Testament when God bade Moyses that he schuld make creeme where-through the temple myght be enoynted in his dedicacion, and also the archa of the testament, and Aaron and other prestes and kyngis myght be enoynted there-with."[201]

In the Good Friday liturgy, medieval parishioners were reminded that the Apostles themselves were Jews: "He was crucified and slayn of hem the whome he come for to delyuere. And this day he ghafe his body to his disiples; and therefore ghif we wolle worthily take his body, let vs do as the Jewis dide. For thei cutte oute a stone fro a roche and wele polischid it and made it and put the lord in that monument. Sires, this wele polischide sepulcre is the herte of man, the whiche moste be clensid and polischid with penaunce and contricion."[202] The author goes further to develop the analogy: "And they brought forth as offyrnge myrre and annoyntid hym. And both they ben byttre. And so offre we bitterness of penaunce, *scilicit* in fastynge and absteynyng fro swete metis and drynkis, the whiche is bitter to the body, that we mowe then with the body so sauorede put the body of Crist and worthely receyve it. Amen."[203] Even the Easter Vigil liturgy revealed several vital links between the Church and Israel: "On Ester euen the pascall is made the chyef tapre in the chyrche, soo is Cryste chyef above all the sayntes in heuen. The pascall also betokenth the pyler of lyghte fyre that wente before Moyses and the

199 Mirk, *Festial*, fol. 26, *verso*.
200 Mirk, *Festial*, fol. 27, *verso*.
201 *Speculum Sacerdotale*, pp. 102–03, excerpt from Shere Thursday (Maundy Thursday) sermon.
202 *Speculum Sacerdotale*, p. 108.
203 *Speculum Sacerdotale*, p. 108.

chyldern of Israel whan Moses ladde theym out of Egypte in to the londe of byhest, that is Jherusalem and soo they passed saue and sounde."[204] Mirk proceeds immediately to liken the baptismal font to the Red Sea, and then to associate the water that flowed from Christ's side at Calvary to both baptism and the Exodus flight of the Israelites.[205]

Since a major portion of the religious imagery, symbolism, catechetical instruction, and liturgical action within Medieval sanctuaries urged the identity of the Church with Israel, the art adorning the exterior of these structures is best viewed from a similar perspective. The well-known medieval depictions of *Ecclesia* and *Synagoga* are a case in point. Examples of this motif have survived from the fourteenth century at the cathedrals of Cologne, Strasbourg, and Rochester. It is tempting to view them as mere artifacts of medieval Christian hostility to Jews: the triumphal figure of *Ecclesia* is shown standing proud, often holding a ciborium, the vessel for storing the consecrated host. *Synagoga* is depicted with a blindfold in place, clutching a broken staff. The precise intent of the patrons who commissioned these pieces is not wholly recoverable at this remove, and it is clear that the figures are not meant to form a flattering comparison of *Synagoga* to *Ecclesia*. Nevertheless the figures also do not portray *Ecclesia* as embattled with *Synagoga*. Like *Ecclesia*, *Synagoga* is portrayed as a woman, and the blindfold on the figure is perhaps to suggest that her inability to see is unnatural or even willful. The figures of *Ecclesia* and *Synagoga*, apart from their paraphernalia, are remarkably similar in proportion as well as in dress.

If the artists who carved the figures wished to portray *Ecclesia*'s total eclipse of *Synagoga*, the normal method to express this theme in the West would be to place the latter under the feet of the former.[206] It is far more likely though that these pieces are a pictorial representation of the conflicted self-understanding of the medieval Church with respect to Israel: a sort of indebted triumphalism, the same themes en-

204 Mirk, *Festial*, fol. 32, *verso*.
205 Mirk, *Festial*, fol. 32, *verso*. Cf. Hebrews 11.
206 A good example of this ancient figure form can still be found on the state flag of the Commonwealth of Virginia, where the male tyrant is supine under the feet of a rather muscular female protagonist, who proclaims: *Sic Semper Tyrannis* (Thus Ever Unto Tyranny).

countered time and again in much of medieval theology, liturgy, and catechesis. At Rochester, cure of St. John Fisher from 1504–1535 and Nicholas Ridley from 1547–1550, the artist's purpose is even more difficult to discern, since the figures were decapitated by Protestant iconoclasts during the Reformation. However, the circumstances surrounding the construction of the chapel door provide some vital clues as to the meaning of the art that still adorns it. Bishop Haymo had the door tracery carved and erected in the fourteenth century, as part of a new passageway for monks coming into the cathedral to sing the morning office. Haymo likely meant to put the brothers in mind of both the contrasts and similarities between Church and Synagogue, as they entered the cathedral with the express intention of chanting the hymns of Israel, the Psalms. The later years of Haymo's episcopacy at Rochester also coincided with the most virulent outbreak of the Black Death in Kent. One of Haymo's monks, William Dene, reported in 1348 that labor shortages had compelled the few remaining religious to grind their own grain for bread, or go hungry.[207] Under such circumstances, the Church's resemblance to Israel, in the latter's biblical trials and persecutions, may well have been at the forefront of both Haymo's thoughts and those of the monks entering Rochester Cathedral by the new chapel door. The chanting of Psalm 80 must have carried a heightened significance for them: "Give ear O Shepherd of Israel,/ thou who leadest Joseph like a flock!/ . . . Restore us, O God;/ let thy face shine, that we may be saved!/ O Lord God of hosts,/ how long wilt thou be angry with thy people's prayers?/ Thou hast fed them with the bread of tears, and given them tears to drink in full measure" (verses 1a, 3–5).

Positive comparisons of the religion of Israel to Christianity showed

---

207 See the first-hand account of William Dene, monk of Rochester, in Ian Coulson, *The History of Health and Medicine in Kent* (Kent: West Kent Health Authority, 1998), p. 15. Dene paints a somber portrait of the events of 1348: "A plague of a kind which had never been met with before ravaged our land of England. The Bishop Haymo of Rochester, who maintained only a small household, lost four priests, five esquires, ten attendants, seven young clerics and six pages, so that nobody was left to serve him in any capacity. At Malling he consecrated two Abbesses but both died almost immediately, leaving only four established nuns and four novices."

no signs of abating in England down to the Reformation, and they feature prominently in Thomas à Kempis' *De Imitatio Christi*, which went through eleven known editions in two separate English translations from 1504 through the mid-1530s.[208] Book four of the work opens with an extended and detailed comparison of the covenant history of Israel with the Eucharist: "Your great servant and special friend, Moses, made an ark of imperishable wood, overlaying it with purest gold, to place the Tables of the Law in it; then how shall I, a corrupt and perishable creature, dare so lightly to receive the Maker of the Law and the Giver of Life?" The "vast difference" between the Ark and the New Covenant in the sacrament of the altar is a matter of degree, not kind: "For those sacrifices of the Law prefigured what was to come; while the sacrifice of Your Body is the fulfillment of those ancient sacrifices." In addition to the works of Moses, à Kempis compares preparation for Eucharistic reception to the deeds of Noah, David, and Solomon's building of the Temple in Jerusalem.[209] Throughout this portion of the work, à Kempis draws his readers' attention to the similitude between the Ark and the New Covenant.

It is fascinating that the late medieval focus on Old Testament themes or "types" as a method for understanding the words and actions of Christ in the New Testament, are almost non-existent in some strands of Renaissance biblical interpretation. For Erasmus and his disciples in particular, there was to be no positive appraisal of the Old Testament patrimony for the Church. What motivated the abrupt departure from so much of the Church's tradition of biblical commentary, liturgy, and art? This rupture results from deeply embedded themes in the writings and thought of Erasmus that have yet to be properly explored in contemporary scholarship.

---

208 See the entry for *De Imitatione Christi* in *The Short Title Catalogue of English Books*, pp. 393–94.

209 Thomas à Kempis, *The Imitation of Christ in Four Books*, ed. and trans. Clare L. Fitzpatrick (New York: Catholic Book Publishing Co., 1977), pp. 239–240.

Chapter 2
Ridley on Biblical Interpretation

In the whole of his extant writings, Nicholas Ridley bestowed praise on only two contemporary figures for their exegetical acumen: Thomas Cranmer and Erasmus of Rotterdam.[1] Of Cranmer, Ridley declared, "He passeth me no lesse, then the learned mayster his yong scholer." Ridley's assessment of Erasmus is also quite revealing: "Erasmus . . . was a man that coulde understande the wordes and the sense of the wrytor."[2] Here Ridley offers a general endorsement of Erasmus' explication of biblical and patristic texts. Given that such enthusiasm for the work of another scholar is extremely rare in Ridley's tracts and treatises, it is worthwhile to ponder the salient features of Erasmus' exegetical method. Ridley's uncommonly high praise of Erasmus suggests that discovering the nature of Erasmus' exegesis is very likely to illuminate Ridley's own principles of scriptural interpretation. The thematic analysis of Erasmus' exegetical writings will not only show what an original thinker in the field of biblical interpretation

---

1 See John Foxe, *Actes and Monuments of matters most speciall and memorable, happenyng in the Church, with an Universal history of the same, wherein is set forth at large the whole race and course of the Church, from the primitive age to these latter tymes of ours, with the bloudy times, horrible troubles, and great persecutions agaynst the true Martyrs of Christ, sought and wrought as well by Heathen Emperours, and now lately practised by Romish Prelates, especially in this Realme of England and Scotland* ([STC 11225] London: John Daye, 1583) [hereafter: Foxe, *Actes and Monuments*], p. 1427 and Nicholas Ridley, *The Works of Bishop Ridley*, ed. Henry Christmas, for the Parker Society (Cambridge: Cambridge University Press, 1841) [hereafter: Ridley, *Works*], pp. 160–61.
2 This commendation of Erasmus is in Nicholas Ridley, *A Brief Declaracion of the Lordes Supper* ([STC 21046] Emden: Egidius van der Erve, 1555) [hereafter: Ridley, *Brief Declaration*], sig. D.6, *verso-recto*, and *Works*, p. 33.

he was, but will also reveal how strikingly similar some of Ridley's hermeneutical principles are to those of Erasmus.

John O'Malley, one of the best modern students of Erasmus and an expert on Humanist exegesis, observes that Erasmus' focus on deliberative rhetoric predisposes him to concentrate on Jesus' words in an oracular fashion, abstracting Christ's sayings from the narrative and setting of the Gospel text.[3] Whereas advocates of demonstrative or epideictic rhetoric tended to read scripture inter-textually, praising God for his great deeds throughout salvation history as recounted in both the Old and New Testaments,[4] Erasmus was inclined to view the Old and New Testaments as fundamentally different in content. While Erasmus was very interested in the historical context of the New Testament books, he rarely related New Testament narratives to Old Testament events and rites. Erasmus also frequently interpolated a number of his own ideas or words directly into the biblical text, especially when paraphrasing Paul.[5] The

3   John W. O'Malley, "Grammar and Rhetoric in the Pietas of Erasmus," The Journal of Medieval and Renaissance Studies 18.1 (1988) [hereafter: O'Malley, "Grammar and Rhetoric"]: pp. 89, 94, 99.

4   John W. O'Malley, Praise and Blame in Renaissance Rome: Rhetoric, Doctrine and Reform in the Sacred Orators of the Papal Court, c. 1450–1521, vol. 3 of Duke Monographs in Medieval and Renaissance Studies (Durham, NC: Duke University Press, 1979) [hereafter: O'Malley, Praise and Blame], p. 49. Compared to Erasmus' deliberative emphasis in exegesis, the author states that the epideictic rhetoric typical of the Papal Court sermons of the late fifteenth and early sixteenth centuries "evince a tendency to look upon scripture more as a history of God's actions and less as a manual for doctrinal proof-texts or a book of artfully disguised philosophical principles." Cf. ibid., pp. 38–49 and O'Malley, "Grammar and Rhetoric," pp. 89, 94, 99.

5   See, e.g., Robert D. Sider, "Historical Imagination and the Representation of Paul in Erasmus' Paraphrases on the Pauline Epistles," in Holy Scripture Speaks: the Production and Reception of Erasmus' Paraphrases on the New Testament, eds. Hilmar M. Pabel and Mark Vessey (Toronto: University of Toronto Press, 2006) [hereafter: Sider, "Historical Imagination and the Representation of Paul"]. Sider notes that Erasmus' interpolative comments are encountered with such frequency in the Paraphrases that the result is a portrait of Paul that rather closely resembles Erasmus himself. See especially pp. 88, 89, 92, and 101.

nature, abundance, and length of these interpolations suggest that they are the keys to unlocking Erasmus' understanding of the relationship between the Old and New Testaments, the work and writings of Paul, and the nature and role of Christ in salvation history.

Closely related themes are so frequently encountered throughout Ridley's biblical explications that there can be little doubt that he appropriated much of Erasmus' exegetical method along with substantial elements of his Christology. Exploring the parallels between the thought of Erasmus and Ridley reveals that both men held exegetical views that were clearly distinct, not only from several key patristic and medieval approaches to biblical explication, but also from the Roman Humanist school of scriptural interpretation. At this point, however, we will merely survey Erasmus' and Ridley's primary exegetical principles by paying special attention to passages in Erasmus' *Paraphrases* and *Paraclesis*,[6] on the one hand, and to Ridley's *Certen Godly, Learned, and Comfortable Conferences Between . . . Nicolas Rydley and Hughe Latymer*[7] and *Brief Declaracion of the Lordes Supper*, on the other.[8]

The Rebirth of Exegesis: Valla, Erasmus, and Colet on Scriptural Interpretation

About 1489, Desiderius Erasmus wrote to his friend Cornelius Gerard extolling the virtues of Laurentius Valla. Erasmus urged his friend to make himself as familiar with the work of Valla as Gerard was with his

6 This text is Erasmus' preface to his 1516 *Novum Instrumentum*, later printed separately. A modern English translation of the *Paraclesis* can be found in Desiderius Erasmus, *Christian Humanism and the Reformation*, ed. John C. Olin (New York: Fordham University Press, 1975) [hereafter: Erasmus, *Paraclesis*], pp. 92–106.

7 Ridley, *Brief Declaracion*, and Ridley, *Works*, pp. 5–45.

8 *Certen godly, learned, and comfortable conferences, betwene the two reuerende fathers, and holye martyrs of Christe, D. Nicolas Rydley late Bysshoppe of London, and M. Hughe Latymer sometyme Bysshoppe of Worcester, during the tyme of their emprysonmentes. Whereunto is added. A treatise agaynst the errour of transubstantiation, made by the sayd reuerende father D. Nicolas Rydley* ([STC 21048] Strasbourg: Heirs of W. Rihel, 1556) and Ridley, *Works*, pp. 5–45.

own fingers and toes. Erasmus was so taken with the work of Valla that he resolved to become the personal defender and vindicator of Valla and his controversial scholarship.[9] Valla (1407–1457) had been an object of both praise and scorn in Europe since the printing of his 1440 treatise on the *Donatio Constantini*, which exposed that document as a forgery.[10] Valla fashioned cogent arguments concerning the origins of the *Donation* through the consistent application of philological principles. By carefully weighing the style and diction of the Latin employed in it, Valla demonstrated that the *Donation* was not an authentic production of Constantine's era.[11] Valla's focus on the historical and cultural development of language was groundbreaking for the tremendous possibilities it opened up for understanding and assessing the origins of important texts.

Valla's work, on the *Donation of Constantine* and elsewhere, concerned itself with the historical milieu of a text's composition.[12] He investigated the time and place of a document's origin through a disciplined consideration of the historical development of language. The young Erasmus saw in Valla's philological method a way to assail the presumptions of scholastic biblical scholarship, which both he and Valla viewed as a betrayal of the scriptural heritage of the early Church Fathers. Erasmus

---

9   Desiderius Erasmus, "To Cornelius Gerard," Letter 29 in *The Correspondence of Erasmus, Letters 1–141, 1484–1500*, trans. and eds. R. A. B. Mynors and D. F. S. Thomson, The Complete Works of Erasmus 1 (Toronto: University of Toronto Press, 1974), p. 54.

10 For Valla's treatment of the *Donatio Constantini*, in both Latin and English, see Lorenzo Valla, *The Treatise of Lorenzo Valla on the Donation of Constantine*, trans. and ed. Christopher B. Coleman (Buffalo, New York: Renaissance Society of America, 1993) [hereafter: Valla, *Donatio Constantini*]. This is a reprint of the sole complete extant text.

11 See Valla, *Donatio Constantini*, p. 21–183.

12 See for example his response to the section of the *Donatio Constantini* that refers to the granting of lands for the maintaining of temple lights for the churches of Saints Peter and Paul: "Were there in Rome churches, that is, temples, dedicated to Peter and Paul? Who had constructed them? Who would have dared to build them, when, as history tells us, the Christians had never had anything but secret and secluded meeting-places? . . . There was no need to care for the temple lights, before the temples themselves were provided," Valla, *Donatio Constantini*, p. 97.

was firmly convinced of the merit of Valla's method for the confutation of scholastic scholarship even prior to his great discovery in 1504, of Valla's unprinted manuscript *In Novum Testamentum ex diversorum utriusque linguae codicum collatione adnotationes*, in a monastery library near Louvain. This work, completed by Valla in the 1450s, was the first critical study of the text of the New Testament. Through a close analysis of the language and narrative form of the text, Valla was able to make several incisive conjectures about the authors of the various books that comprise the New Testament canon.[13] Valla's commentary on the New Testament lay hidden until Erasmus discovered it and had it printed with a foreword defending the method and character of the author.[14]

The emergent Valla-Erasmus axis in biblical scholarship formed, in the late fifteenth and early sixteenth centuries, the intellectual germ of modern historical criticism. While it would be erroneous to consider Erasmus or any of his contemporaries as historical critics in the modern sense of the term, it is certainly true that they were the first to commit themselves consistently to weighing the historical setting of the text as the only sure method for constructing a proper translation.[15] With respect

13 As early as his declamation of the *Donatio Constantini*, Valla applies historical-critical commentary to sacred texts; of the Book of Job, he notes that if it was indeed written by Job himself, it is remarkable that he managed to mention his own death. See Valla, *Donatio Constantini*, p. 133.

14 Erasmus' critical edition of Valla's *In Novum Testamentum ex diversorum utriusque linguae codicum collatione adnotationes* was published in 1505. Throughout this discussion of Erasmus' admiration for Valla, and Valla's interpretive method, I am indebted to J. B. Trapp's lucid synopsis of these concepts in *Erasmus, Colet and More: The Early Tudor Humanists and Their Books* (London: The British Library, 1991) [hereafter: Trapp, *Erasmus, Colet and More*], pp. 3–7.

15 This observation is not to suggest that either Valla or Erasmus was exclusively concerned with the historical context of holy scripture, but that historical concerns were their first concern in reconstructing what the biblical authors actually intended to convey in a passage or book of the Bible. Thus J. B. Payne, in "Toward the Hermeneutics of Erasmus," *Scrinum Erasmianum* II (Leiden: Brill, 1969), pp. 13–49 takes J. W. Aldridge, *The Hermeneutic of Erasmus* (Zurich-Richmond: John Knox Press, 1966), to task for describing Erasmus as the "forerunner of historical criticism." However, even if we can show, as Payne has, that Erasmus speaks often of the "letter"

to biblical studies, the new Humanist exegesis was characterized by the pursuit of a single, historically contextualized meaning for individual scriptural texts.[16] In John Colet (1467?–1519), a fellow Humanist, Dean of St. Paul's Cathedral, and a pioneer in education, Erasmus had a like-minded friend to spur on his new-found interest in biblical exegesis. Already in 1497, a strong sense of historical consciousness governed Colet's own lectures on the Epistles of St. Paul.[17] At the time, Colet's treatment of Paul as a concrete historical figure was perceived by his students to be a dramatic and abrupt departure from the methods of biblical study to which they had been previously accustomed in the course of their studies.[18]

and "spirit" of a text, and of the role of allegory and tropology in mediating between the two, it still must be acknowledged that Erasmus' research into the meaning of the particular books of the Bible begins with a great effort at reconstructing the historical setting of the text in question. Erasmus' historicist tendencies were clearly revealed in debates with his contemporaries. When, for example, Erasmus was confronted in the matter of his translating "λόγος" as "*sermo*" rather than "*verbum*" in the prologue to John's Gospel in the second edition of his *Novum Instrumentum*, Erasmus merely asserted that his opponents were historically ignorant. See Margery O'Rourke Boyle, *Erasmus on Language and Method in Theology* (Toronto: University of Toronto Press, 1977) [hereafter: Boyle, *Erasmus on Language and Method*], esp. pp. 5–29.

16 See Brian Cummings, *The Literary Culture of the Reformation: Grammar and Grace* (Oxford: University Press, 2002) [hereafter: Cummings, *Literary Culture of the Reformation*], p. 113, where the author notes that Erasmus' pursuit of a single, simple meaning for scriptural texts proved a fractious notion, especially in Protestants' disagreements with Erasmus about the meaning of the Bible. Cf. his observations that Calvin, despite rejection of Erasmus' theology, retains Erasmus' method of exegesis in seeking a single meaning for Scripture, *ibid.*, p. 225.

17 See Jean-Claude Margolin, "The Epistle to the Romans (Chapter 11) According to the Versions and/or Commentaries of Valla, Colet, Lefevre, and Erasmus," in *The Bible in the Sixteenth Century*, trans. John L. Farthing, vol. 11 of *Duke Monographs in Medieval and Renaissance Studies*, ed. David Steinmetz (Durham: Duke University Press, 1990), p. 137.

18 See Leland Miles, *John Colet and the Platonic Tradition* (London: Allen and Unwin, 1962), pp. 17–40. See also, John Colet, *Commentary on First Corinthians*, trans. and eds. Bernard O'Kelly and Catharine Jarrott, Me-

The new exegetical method differed from the traditional approach to scripture not just in a vigorous emphasis on the historical context of the scriptures, but also in an insistence upon a single unitive meaning for sacred texts. In a letter to Erasmus, Colet exemplified the new attitude in biblical studies by employing the unlikely analogy of the breeding habits of various species of winged creatures. He notes that the lowest orders of flying animals, flies and the like, breed in swarms. As one ascends the chain of being, the number of offspring declines; the most exalted of all winged creatures, the eagle, nurtures a brood of one. Similarly, the true meaning of scripture, as opposed to lower forms of literature, bears a single and vital primary sense.[19] Nevertheless, at least as far back as Origen, Christian biblical commentary allowed that there were various layers of meaning within a single biblical text. Origen himself identified three such striations in scripture, which he likened to the body, soul, and spirit of the human person. John Cassian extended Origen's three-fold sense of scripture, identifying a fourth layer of meaning which he thought corresponded with the collective spiritual progress and evangelical mission of the Church. By the Middle Ages, clergy were encouraged to focus primarily on any of the three layers beyond the "literal" or historical sense to explicate the moral of a biblical pericope.[20]

dieval and Renaissance Texts & Studies 21 (Binghamton, New York: Medieval & Renaissance Texts & Studies, 1985) [hereafter: Colet, *Commentary on First Corinthians*].

19   Colet, "Reply to Erasmus on the Agony in the Garden," in Erasmus, *Lucubratiunculae*, 1518, vol. V of *Desiderii Erasmi Roterdami Opera Omnia*, ed. Jean Leclerc (Leiden: Lugduni Batavorum, 1703–1706), col. 1291. Cf. John Colet, "Introduction to Orders," in *Ecclesiastical Hierarchy*, vol. I of *Super Opera Dionys*, trans. and ed. J. H. Lupton (London: Bell and Daldy, 1869), pp. 232–42. Colet's idea of a single meaning for scripture did not represent a complete break with the tradition of Medieval exegesis, but rather goes just a step beyond the observations of biblical commentators of the Middle Ages, that the four meanings of scripture were unified or in harmony with each other. See, e.g., the comment of Richard of St. Victor as related by G. R. Evans, *The Language and Logic of the Bible: The Earlier Middle Ages* (Cambridge: Cambridge University Press, 1984), p. 121, "*scriptura multa nobis in unum loquitur*."

20   See, e.g., the advice of Guibert de Nogent, as cited by H. Caplan, "The

Advocates of the Humanist approach to biblical studies gradually es-chewed this broad approach to scriptural interpretation, valuing instead depth and precision in biblical explication.

The new Humanist method made great contributions to exegesis, especially in the way of deepening our understanding of the historical nature of biblical texts. Yet it also gave rise, immediately and almost in-eluctably, to interpretive discord. By insisting that biblical texts had a single meaning, it became much more difficult to reconcile different points of view on a given pericope. Humanists' insistence on a single layer of meaning for sacred scripture meant that rival interpretations of a given text were more likely to result in outright conflict.[21] The first sparks of this unstable admixture of interpretive exclusivity and histor-ical consciousness were to erupt not a generation later, but within Eras-mus' own circle of friends in 1499, well before he began work on the *Novum Instrumentum.* That year, in one of his early sojourns in England, Erasmus was embroiled in lengthy and pointed debates with none other than John Colet himself on the proper interpretation of key passages of scripture. The nature of their quarrels and the positions they assumed in these controversies reveal a great deal about their contrasting approaches to scriptural interpretation.

The first disagreement between them centered on the nature of Cain and Abel's offerings to God, as recounted in Genesis. Erasmus argued the traditional position, urging that Cain had brought forth what he wished to offer God, rather than what God had commanded. Colet in-sisted that Cain earned God's disfavor because he was a cultivator: not content with what God had provided naturally, he set about to refine the

Four Senses of Scriptural Interpretation and the Medieval Theory of Prea-ching," in *Of Eloquence: Studies in Ancient and Mediaeval Rhetoric* (Ithaca, New York: Cornell University Press, 1970), p. 93.

21 Cummings, *Literary Culture of the Reformation,* p. 104. According to Cummings, Erasmus' entrée into New Testament studies "marks Erasmus' ultimate failure" for the dissention that ensued. While he wished to quell the contentious nature of theology as practiced by the Scholastics, Erasmus' *Novum Instrumentum* simply transported these controversies onto the grounds of biblical interpretation. Cf. his rehearsal of Erasmus' clash with Luther over the bondage or freedom of the will, pp. 118–75.

quality of his own food. Erasmus responded with a facetious account of how Cain had garnered such substantial horticultural skills.[22] The second dispute between Colet and Erasmus concerned the precise exposition of Christ's agony at Gethsemane as related by the synoptic Gospels. The medieval and patristic consensus was that, in this instance, Jesus' human nature was asserting itself in the face of his impending suffering. Consonant with this view, Erasmus argued that at Gethsemane, Jesus was revealing his kinship with all humanity in his fear of death. Colet asserted that this view did not do proper justice to Jesus' divinity. Perhaps influenced by a passing notion expressed once only by St. Jerome, Colet argued that Jesus' sweat and tears resulted from his being aware of the guilt that the Jews were to bring upon themselves in ordering and obtaining his execution. It is in the course of their debate on the Agony in the Garden that Colet offers Erasmus his analogy of winged creatures to the single, unitive sense to be sought in explicating the scriptures.[23] Despite these early conflicts, Erasmus set out to examine the text of the New Testament itself, beginning work on his amended text of the Vulgate in 1505. Erasmus completed this project in 1516, and entitled it the *Novum Instrumentum*. A second edition followed in 1519, and he continued to write critical studies on various books of the Bible, along with paraphrases of them, until his death.

Any assessment of Erasmus' contributions to biblical studies must begin with an earnest acknowledgement of the remarkable scope and range of his scholarship. In general, Erasmus' formidable endeavors dedicated to New Testament studies consists of four basic strata: his *Novum Instrumentum*, intended to present an accurate text of the Greek original with a Latin parallel translation; the *Paraphrases*, which recount the text of a biblical book in Latin; his *Annotations*, which explore philological issues relating to particular phrases or expressions in a sacred text; and finally, prescriptive works on how exegesis should be conceived, approached, and executed, like the *Ratio verae theologiae* and *Ecclesiastes sive De ratione concionandi*. In his *Paraphrases* alone, Erasmus' interpretive sources range from ancient pagan works to direct citations of the

---

22   See Trapp, *Erasmus, Colet and More*, pp. 118–19.
23   See Trapp, *Erasmus, Colet and More*, p. 119.

early Church Fathers and excerpts of Medieval commentators from the *Glossa Ordinaria*, to the work of the early Scholastics.[24] Despite his vociferous denunciation of Scholastic scriptural exegesis, he often took his interpretive cues from the biblical commentary of Thomas Aquinas.[25] Erasmus' skills in classical Greek and Latin syntax are conspicuous in each of the different types of his New Testament writings. This range of sources and his linguistic skills earned for Erasmus the well-deserved praise of his contemporaries across the continent as well as in England.

In addition to his considerable erudition, however, Erasmus also wove a number of idiosyncratic notions into his Paraphrases. His work on First Corinthians is a case in point. In his paraphrase of the seventh chapter of the epistle, he places an intriguing assemblage of words into the mouth of Paul on the subject of celibacy: "Truly, that thing that Christ demanded not of his, I dare not demand of you."[26] The idea that Church doctrine should be referred to the verbal pronouncements of Christ, in this matter or any other relating to Christian praxis, is not to be found in the text of First Corinthians. Erasmus reprises this interpolative method, complete with references to what Christ did or did not say, when he turns to consider Paul's injunctions on avoiding meat sacrificed to idols, in 1 Corinthians 10: "In this, Christ would have us exercise the greatest liberty, who neither enjoined nor forbade any kind of food."[27] Once more, on a point of doctrine we are referred to what

24 See, e.g., Erasmus, *Paraphrases on Romans and Galatians,* trans. and eds. John B. Payne, Albert Rabil Jr., and Warren Smith Jr., The Collected Works of Erasmus 42 (Toronto: University of Toronto Press, 1984), and Desiderius Erasmus, *Annotations on Romans,* trans. and eds. John B. Payne, Albert Rabil Jr., and Warren Smith Jr., The Collected Works of Erasmus 56 (Toronto: University of Toronto Press, 1994) [hereafter: Erasmus, *Annotations on Romans*].

25 See, e.g., Erasmus, *Paraphrase on Hebrews,* trans. and ed. John Bateman, The Collected Works of Erasmus 44 (Toronto: University of Toronto Press, 1993) [hereafter: Erasmus, *Paraphrase on Hebrews*], p. 215 and corresponding notes.

26 Erasmus, *Paraphrasis in Epist. Pauli ad Cor. 1,* Cap. VII, in vol. VII of *Desiderii Erasmi Roterdami Opera Omnia,* ed. Jean Leclerc (Leiden: Lugduni Batavorum, 1706), p.880, col. C: "*Verum, quod Christus non exegit à suis, non ausim à vobis exigere.*"

Jesus did not say on the subject. Paul himself does not raise this question throughout the whole of First Corinthians. By means of such insertions, Erasmus attributes to Paul himself a concern for historical matters, by submitting questions of doctrine to the prevenient words of Christ.

Text & Context:
Historical Consciousness in Erasmian Exegesis

Since the late 1960s, secondary scholarship on Erasmus' biblical writings has been focused less on the historical consciousness of his work, and more on the theme of allegory and rhetorical mediation that exercised him so thoroughly in the *Ratio verae theologiae* and *Ecclesiastes sive de ratione concionandi*. The authors of two seminal revisionist monographs on Erasmus' contributions to biblical studies concentrate their attention almost exclusively on the *Ratio* and *Ecclesiastes,* largely overlooking the actual content of Erasmus' paraphrases of the books of the Bible.[28] Valuable as these studies are for indicating and emphasizing the inner consistency of Erasmus' theological thought, they tend to a certain distortion with respect to his views of symbolic language. For all of the ink Erasmus devoted to allegory in works in which he describes what should constitute good exegetical method, in practice, he believed that too frequent recourse to it corrupts the true meaning of biblical texts: "I always put forward in all honesty what seemed to me

27 Erasmus, *Paraphrasis in Epist. Pauli ad Cor. 1*, Cap. X, in vol. VII of *Desiderii Erasmi Roterdami Opera Omnia*, ed. Jean Leclerc (Leiden: Lugduni Batavorum, 1706), p.894, col. C: *"Christus in his summam libertatem nobis esse voluit, qui nullam cibi genus aut indixit, aut interdixit."*
28 See Boyle, *Erasmus on Language and Method* and Manfred Hoffman, *Rhetoric and Theology: The Hermeneutic of Erasmus* (Toronto: University of Toronto Press, 1994) [hereafter: Hoffman, *Rhetoric and Theology*]. The tendency among modern scholars to ignore the biblical commentaries of sixteenth-century theologians is described and cogently challenged by David Steinmetz in his editorial introduction to *The Bible in the Sixteenth Century*, Duke Monographs in Medieval and Renaissance Studies 11, ed. David Steinmetz (Durham: Duke University Press, 1990), pp. 1–2.

to be the true meaning, although I could clearly see that ancient authorities engaging in fighting the views of heretics distort the sense in places
with some force. . . . Allegorical interpretations, to which I find some of
the ancients devoted so much space that it became a superstition, I have
touched on sparingly."[29]

Occasionally, even revisionist authors are forced to concede that establishing the true and literal meaning of the text, by way of an historical
reconstruction, is fundamental to Erasmus' exegetical method.[30] Erasmus' little-studied direct application of allegory in his biblical paraphrases almost always assumes one of two forms: either a Christological
explication of Old Testament precepts and rites, or a neo-Platonic *leit-
motif* wherein believers are urged to raise their minds to heavenly things,
leaving behind all concern for flesh and matter. In fact, he often fastens
these two themes together in a single bundle. Following a negative assessment of the juridical content of the Old Testament, Erasmus declares,
"but care was being taken in this way to make the crude minds of humans gradually become accustomed to move from the things of the
senses to the things of the mind."[31]

Throughout his biblical writings, Erasmus expends a considerable
portion of his gifts and energies reconstructing the historical settings of
the biblical texts he explicates. He is at pains to focus the reader's attention on the historical context of biblical books, presenting first and
foremost an extended *argumentum* on the time period and circumstances
of the author for each of his paraphrases. Even in a dedicatory epistle to
Archduke Ferdinand, brother of Charles V, he cannot resist the urge to

---

29 Desiderius Erasmus, dedicatory letter to *Paraphrase on John,* trans. and
    ed. Jane E. Phillips, The Collected Works of Erasmus 46 (Toronto: Uni-
    versity of Toronto Press, 1991) [hereafter: Erasmus, *Paraphrase on John*],
    p. 12.
30 See, e.g., Hoffman, *Rhetoric and Theology,* pp. 104–05, 214. Cf. Boyle's
    admission that Erasmus was the forerunner to modern scriptural criticism
    in terms of method and approach, Boyle, *Erasmus on Language and Me-
    thod,* p. 62–63.
31 Erasmus, *Paraphrase on Hebrews,* p. 231. The neo-Platonist orientation
    of the *philosophia Christi* and the consequences of this ideal for Erasmus'
    biblical reflections will be more fully considered in Chapter III.

instruct his patron at length concerning the historical milieu of a biblical book: "When our Lord Jesus Christ's life and teaching had already been spread widely through the world by the preaching of the apostles and the writings of the other evangelists, John, well known as he whom Jesus loved, took in hand last of them all the writing of this Gospel, not so much to put together a gospel-history as to supply certain things that the other evangelists had passed over, since they seemed not unworthy of record." Rather, according to Erasmus, "The chief reason for his writing this Gospel is thought to be the desire to assert the divinity of Christ against the heresies which were already like evil tares sprouting up in the good crop; in particular those of the Cerinthians and Ebionites, who apart from other errors taught that Christ had been nothing more than a man and had not existed at all before he was born of Mary."[32] Here again Erasmus remains in pursuit of Colet's single unitive textual meaning— and increasingly suggests that the single meaning has to do with a specific historical event or setting. Each of his biblical paraphrases is conditioned by the historical preface that Erasmus insists the reader absorb and ponder before the text itself is even to be considered.

Erasmus' focus on the historical period and setting of the scriptural text is commendable for helping readers to understand the human setting of the narrative. Nevertheless, Erasmus is often so preoccupied with historical concerns in exegesis that he either does not attend sufficiently to the spiritual realities that a more allegorical approach might reveal, or he situates the biblical narrative in the wrong historical and cultural context. Philology regularly drives such historical digressions in Erasmus' exegetical writings: the explication of a term provides an occasion for a history lesson about the background of a biblical text.[33] This two-part dynamic is often displayed in his *Annotations*. His observations on the names Saul and Paul, as he ponders the Epistle to the Romans, are a case in point: "Chrysostom thinks his name was changed by the divine will, like that of the chief of the apostles who was called Cephas or Peter instead of Simon. There are those who think he had two names; and this

---

32 Erasmus, *Paraphrase on John*, p. 11.
33 Cummings, *Literary Culture of the Reformation*, p. 108. The author asserts here that philology is central to Erasmus' theology.

in my opinion is closer to the truth, though I believe that the Hebraic name Saul was originally given to Paul, who was first a Hebrew." Erasmus then presses the biblical narrative into a classical mould: "Since for the most part by that time Egypt, Cilicia, and the part of Syria that bordered it spoke Greek—a result of Alexander the Great's empire and the later Roman administration—the Hebrew word was changed to a Greek form. . . . Since the name Paul was equally familiar to Greeks and Romans, Saulus was further changed to Paulus, so that they . . . would with even greater pleasure recognize his name, and in this, too, he would be all things to all men."[34]

For Erasmus then, the change of Saul's name to Paul was the result of the historical and cultural forces in play following the conquests of Alexander's armies. In the context of the New Testament, we should expect that Erasmus' historical consciousness would lead him to relate key events in the lives of Jesus and the Apostles to the history of ancient Israel, especially as recounted in the Old Testament. However, we repeatedly discover Erasmus referring the work and deeds of the Apostles to Greek and Roman political and philosophical currents, rather than to Old Testament analogues to key New Testament events.[35] His many textual interpolations follow this pattern of explicating a biblical theme by way of an insight drawn from antique culture, which unfortunately connects the text with historical and cultural forces that would have been quite foreign to Jesus and the Apostles. Such digressions reveal the neo-Platonic cast of Erasmus' thought, which sometimes carries the appearance of an Anti-Semitic attitude.

This salient feature of Erasmus' writings is closely related to the stark polarity he regularly posits between the Mosaic Law and the Gospel of Christ. Thus, we read in his *Paraphrase on Luke* that the purity of Christianity is to be measured precisely in its distance from "the Judaic manner,"[36] while in his *Enchiridion Militis Christiani*, he worries

34 Erasmus, *Annotations on Romans*, p. 3.
35 See Sider, "Historical Imagination and the Representation of Paul," p. 89, where the author notes that this same theme is found in Erasmus' *Paraphrase on Romans*, and that it constitutes a "virtual renunciation of ethnicity" in Paul.
36 Shimon Markish, *Erasmus and the Jews*, trans. Anthony Oliver (Chicago:

that the great majority who promote the veneration of relics and the observance of saints' days are engaged in a "revolt against the spirit of the Gospel" that is nothing less than "a reversion to the superstitions of Judaism."[37] In his *Ecclesiastes* of 1535, Erasmus asserts that verse 22:10 of Deuteronomy, which prohibits plowing with an ox and ass yoked together, indicates that Christianity and Judaism are not to be mixed.[38] In the *Hyperaspistes II*, his list of total contrasts between Law and Gospel sprawls the full length of a folio page.[39]

Erasmus' etiology of Paul's new name is telling in this regard, because the exegete works to bind the New Testament narrative to events in Greek and Roman history. In this passage, Erasmus discounts even the authority of Chrysostom, who points out the historical and cultural proximity of Peter and Paul's circumstances with respect to a change of name in the face of their being called to a special ministry by the Lord. Christ's changing Peter's name at Caesarea Philippi is at least as contextually important as any ancient Greek military conquests for understanding how Saul of Tarsus became Paul. Whenever possible, Erasmus weaves classical motifs into his explication of New Testament texts, while only rarely making references to Hebrew words or Old Testament events and customs. Erasmus' historical focus is not disinterested. In fact, he wants to situate Paul, the other Apostles, and even Jesus in the world of Greek and Roman culture as much as possible.[40] Erasmus' historical consciousness is, in part, another manifestation of his desire to

University of Chicago Press, 1986), [hereafter, Markish, *Erasmus and the Jews*] p. 8 and n. 9.

37 Desiderius Erasmus, *The Handbook of the Militant Christian*, in *The Essential Erasmus*, trans. and ed. John P. Dolan (New York: Penguin Books, 1993) [hereafter, Erasmus, *Enchiridion*], p. 68.

38 Markish, *Erasmus and the Jews*, p. 8 and n. 11.

39 Markish, *Erasmus and the Jews*, p. 8 and n. 12.

40 See editor's note 13 on this passage. Cf. Erasmus, *Paraphrase on First Timothy*, trans. and ed. John Bateman, The Collected Works of Erasmus 44 (Toronto: University of Toronto Press, 1993) [hereafter: Erasmus, *Paraphrase on First Timothy*], p. 22 where the author relates each office of the Church to levels and titles within Roman governmental structures. See editor's note 11 on this same passage. Erasmus' classicizing of New Testament events and figures will be more carefully examined in Chapter III.

Platonize Christianity. Many of Erasmus' secular works on the virtues of pagan philosophy and rhetoric urged their enduring value and universal validity, especially when compared to the alleged barbarism of his own era. These themes were his stock in trade for such productions as the *Adagia* and *Antibarberi Liber*.[41] When Erasmus turned his attention from the study of the classics to the New Testament, his efforts to return biblical exegesis "to the sources" often seem more bent toward ancient Greece and Rome than to Israel.

From the completion of his *Novum Instrumentum* in 1516 and throughout his subsequent biblical work, Erasmus made it quite clear that he perceived of scripture as a font. In the *Paraclesis*, he speaks frequently of the New Testament as the "source" from which "all the conversations of every Christian" should "be drawn."[42] Similarly, he is persuaded that true wisdom "may be drawn" from the "few books" of the New Testament "as from the most limpid springs."[43]

Erasmus held that the biblical scholarship of scholastic commentators had tainted the pure stream of Christ's true wisdom. The source of Christ's philosophy is, he says, "derided by some . . . neglected by many,

41 O'Malley, "Grammar and Rhetoric," p. 89.

42 Erasmus, *Paraclesis*, p. 97. The *Paraclesis* or *Adhortatio ad christianae philosophiae studium* was first translated into English in 1525, probably by William Roye. See Desiderius Erasmus, *An Exhortation to the Diligent Studye of Scripture*, ([STC 10493] Antwerp, 1529). The manner of Roye's handling of this text tends to confirm the idea that early English Protestants aimed, in a bid for greater legitimacy, to connect their enterprise to the name of Erasmus. See Susan Wabuda, *Preaching During the English Reformation* (Cambridge: Cambridge University Press, 2002) [hereafter: Wabuda, *Preaching*], pp. 90–93. Erasmus' *Paraclesis* holds three points of interest for our current enquiry: here again, Erasmus advocates for a *philosophia Christi*; the New Testament is described as a font of that philosophy; and the biblical text is described as a truer communion with Christ than a direct physical encounter with the Lord. Similar assertions can be readily drawn from the *Enchiridion*, or any of Erasmus' *Paraphrases*, given his thoroughly Platonic orientation. For other instances of Erasmus' "font" imagery, cf. Boyle's catalogue of such references in Erasmus' writings, *Language and Method in Theology*, p. 132.

43 Erasmus, *Paraclesis*, p. 96. On Erasmus' application of the Humanist credo *ad fontes* to scripture itself, see O'Malley, *Praise and Blame*.

and is discussed by a few, but in a cold manner."[44] Rather, Erasmus asserts, "he is truly a theologian who teaches not by skill with intricate syllogisms but by a disposition of mind," shaped by reading the "literature of Christ."[45] In contrast to his model of the true, pious theologian, Erasmus singles out a number of medieval scholastics as "learned" and "subtle," including Albert the Great, Alexander of Hales, Thomas Aquinas, Egidio of Rome, Richard of St. Victor, and William of Occam.[46] Here as elsewhere throughout the *Paraclesis*, Erasmus describes the New Testament as the undiluted font of Christ's teaching: "I think . . . that the pure and genuine philosophy of Christ is not to be drawn from any source more abundantly than from the evangelical books and from the Apostolic Letters."[47]

To extend Erasmus' metaphor, he conceives of scholastic biblical commentators as having trodden through and muddied the pure stream of Christ's "philosophy." Erasmus therefore intends to conduct Christian laymen upstream, by the use of historical research and philology, so that they may drink from purer waters. Although this exercise necessarily requires Erasmus to proceed against the current of time and history, he is certain of his goal. Those who follow him to the "pure and genuine" source of Christ's philosophy will be rewarded not with just a truer likeness of Christ, but with an encounter greater even than a direct meeting with the Lord himself: "[the New Testament] brings Christ to us so much more effectively than any paltry image. . . . These writings bring you the living image of His holy mind and the speaking, healing, dying,

---

44 Erasmus, *Paraclesis*, p.94.
45 Erasmus, *Paraclesis*, pp. 98, 99.
46 Erasmus, *Paraclesis*, p. 103. On Erasmus' anti-scholastic ideal of "practical divinity" rooted in the Aristotelian concept of virtue as reflected in Plutarchean biographical models, see Patrick Collinson, "'A Magazine of Religious Patterns': An Erasmian Topic Transposed in English Protestantism," in *Godly People: Essays in English Protestantism and Puritanism* (London: Hambledon Press, 1983) [hereafter: Collinson, *An Erasmian Topic*], pp. 499–526. We will consider Collinson's insights in greater detail in Chapter IV, as we discuss Foxe's editorial contrasts between Ridley and Bonner in *Actes and Monuments*.
47 Erasmus, *Paraclesis*, p.102. See also the determination of Boyle, *Erasmus on Language and Method*, p. 132.

rising Christ himself, and thus render Him so fully present that you would see less if you gazed upon Him with your very eyes."[48] Erasmus' belief that the biblical text has the ability to make Christ even more directly accessible to us than to his earthly contemporaries is a regular feature of his thought: "in this literature, . . . He lives for us even at this time, breathes and speaks, I should say almost more effectively than when He dwelt among men. The Jews saw and heard less than you see and hear in the books of the Gospels, to the extent that you make use of your eyes and ears, whereby this can be perceived and heard."[49] According to the Erasmian principle of scripture as a vibrant textual communion with Christ, the sacred text is a font of biblical history.

Erasmus regularly employs an intriguing ocular metaphor to describe his own purpose in explicating the scriptures: Christ is the "*scopus*" or "prefixed sign" upon which Erasmus' theological and exegetical gaze is riveted.[50] He prescribes the same method for his readers, declaring in the *Enchiridion* that the goal of Christian life "is set before you as the only *scopus* of your whole life and direct all your efforts, all your activities, all your leisure, all your business in [Christ's] direction."[51] Erasmus warns that those who do not similarly train their eye on Christ do no less than risk shipwreck of their own faith. Perhaps taking a cue from St. Athanasius, Erasmus eventually develops this metaphor into a full-blown nautical analogy for spiritually steering by reference to a sure and reliable point of orientation.[52] Such comments remind us that, in a Christian context, exegesis is never undertaken merely for its own sake, but to introduce or promote a particular image of Jesus Christ himself.

---

48 Erasmus, *Paraclesis*, p.102. Cf. Cummings, *Literary Culture of the Reformation*, pp. 105–110.

49 Erasmus, *Paraclesis*, p.106.

50 See the lucid discussion of this theme and its development in Erasmus' thought as recounted by Boyle, *Erasmus on Language and Method*, pp. 7281. Cf. the observations of D. F. S. Thompson, *The Latinity of Erasmus*, ed. T. A. Dorey (Albuquerque: University of New Mexico, 1970) [hereafter: Thompson, *The Latinity of Erasmus*], pp. 117, 119.

51 Erasmus, quoted by Boyle, *Erasmus on Language and Method*, p. 75.

52 See Boyle, *Erasmus on Language and Method*, p. 76–82.

Erasmus' navigation towards the *scopus* of his theological vision requires several distinct maneuvers. These include a concentration on the biblical text as chiefly historical in nature, and a focus on Christ's words as abstracted from the Gospel narrative and from related Old Testament themes.[53] Also characteristic of Erasmus' exegetical approach is the interpolation of words and concepts into the text that cannot be derived from the verses themselves.[54] Not accidentally, these same traits are found in the exegetical work of Nicholas Ridley. A review of key passages in Ridley's prison tracts, *Certen Godly, Learned, and Comfortable Conferences Between . . . Nicolas Rydley and Hughe Latymer* [55] and the *Brief Declaracion of the Lordes Supper*,[56] shows that he too relies on heavy interpolation to present a Jesus that is an abstraction from the narrative context of the Old and New Testaments. The similarities between his and Erasmus' exegetical methods reveal Ridley's deliberate appropriation of Erasmian concepts for interpreting the Christian scriptures.

Traditio and *Scriptura*

In Ridley's ecclesiological vision, no church doctrine should be considered necessary for salvation that is not expressly enjoined upon believers in scripture. Like most of his Protestant allies, Ridley explicitly promoted the idea that scriptural exegesis should govern ecclesiology, rather than the reverse. Restricting ecclesiology by reference solely or principally to scripture, first launched by Martin Luther, was plainly articulated later in the tenet of *sola scriptura*.[57] The ironic difficulty this

---

53 See O'Malley, *Praise and Blame*, p. 49. Cf. O'Malley, "Grammar and Rhetoric," pp. 89, 94, and 99.
54 Sider, "Historical Imagination and the Representation of Paul," pp. 88, 89, 92, and 101.
55 Ridley, *Comfortable Conferences* and *Works*, pp. 97–151.
56 Ridley, *Brief Declaracion* and *Works*, pp. 1–45.
57 For a useful analysis of the history and meanings associated with the term *sola scriptura*, see Anthony N. S. Lane, *"Sola Scriptura?* Making Sense of a Post-Reformation Slogan," in *A Pathway into the Holy Scriptures*, eds. Philip E. Satterwhite and David F. Wright (Grand Rapids: Eerdmans, 1994) [hereafter: Lane, "Sola Scriptura?"], pp. 297–327. Lane helpfully dispels

concept posed for the Reformers in general and for Ridley in particular was that such a principle is not self-evidently expressed within the canon of *scriptura*. Several of the Reformers themselves were aware of this problem, and attempted various solutions to ensure the advancement of the keystone concept of Protestant dogma. Sometimes these solutions required altering or amending the text of scripture. Luther himself inserted the word "alone" in several passages of scripture, both in his German and Latin editions of the text.[58]

Although proponents of the movement claimed to rely solely or chiefly on the authority of scripture, Alec Ryrie has noted that early English Protestantism suffered from a crisis of historical legitimacy

> common misunderstandings of the term, but ends with the anachronistic suggestion that scripture does not need a normative interpretation; the catechetical, exegetical, and ecclesiological efforts of the early reformers make plain, however, that they did not hold this view themselves. At Marburg, for example, both Luther and Zwingli felt that they had discovered normative interpretations of the sixth chapter of John that should govern theological understanding of the Eucharist. Their disagreements resulted in a rupture, not a common assertion that scripture needs no authoritative explication. The principle of *sola scriptura* had as its forerunner Erasmus' notion that scripture is self-interpreting, and that the sense of it is both plain and simple. See, Cummings, *Literary Culture of the Reformation*, p. 105. Cummings notes, however, that both the Erasmian and Protestant concepts of Scripture as, "self-explicating . . . is a claim not borne out by the need for a thousand folio pages of Erasmian paraphrase along side [the *Great Bible*]," p. 235. See *The Byble in Englyshe of the largest and greatest volume. . . .* ([STC 2073] London: Edwarde Whitchurch [or Rycharde Grafton] *cum priuilegio ad imprimendum solum*, 1541)] [hereafter: *The Great Bible*].

58 Luther defended these insertions by claiming that this was the "sense" of scripture in general, and that, for the German edition, the vernacular language required such interpolations to be comprehensible for German readers. To ensure that no doctrine was alleged from scripture that was not in keeping with his own ecclesiological vision, Luther separated the Deuterocanonical books into an *Apochrypha* for his translations of the Bible. This move excluded a biblical appeal to traditional church teachings such as Purgatory, based on the verses of 2 Maccabees 12:40–45. See Diarmaid MacCulloch, *The Reformation* (New York: Viking, 2004) [hereafter: MacCulloch, *The Reformation*], pp. 129–30.

throughout the early decades of the sixteenth century. Ryrie maintains that various problematic strategies were devised in this period in an effort to explain "Protestantism's lack of visible historical roots." He outlines at least four basic tacks taken by Protestant apologists in their writings to address this major concern.[59] This central problem of Protestant identity certainly concerned Ridley, since his prison tracts feature each of the strategies that Ryrie identifies. Ridley's blend of all four of these stratagems accounts for several historical and theological incongruities to be found in his Protestant apologetical writings.

Like Luther, Ridley was aware of the tensions at the heart of Protestant conceptions of scripture and the church, and his efforts to promote these ideas shed light on the English Reformers' concern with the writings of the Church Fathers in matters of ecclesiology, a subject that occupied them more than most of their reforming continental *confrères*. The effort to restrict ecclesiology to the express directives of scripture required Ridley and his fellow Reformers to promote scripture as the highest form of authority in church polity.[60] This initiative

59 Alec Ryrie, "The Problems of Legitimacy and Precedent in English Protestantism, 1539–1547," in *The Medieval Inheritance*, vol. 1 of *Protestant History and Identity in Sixteenth-Century Europe*, ed. Bruce Gordon (Brookfield, Vermont: Scholar's Press, 1996) [hereafter: Ryrie, "Problems of Legitimacy in English Protestantism"], pp. 78–92. The four types of Protestant apologetic employed can be summarized as: an appeal to Lollardy and other heretical movements of the recent past; attempts to claim more mainstream figures in Catholic history as crypto-Protestants; the development of Church and Anti-church schema of history that united all past heretical movements in ecclesiastical history; and apocalypticism.

60 It is in this limited sense that Ridley may be said to promote the concept of *sola scriptura*, although he does not use the term itself. See Lane, "Sola Scriptura?" for a lucid consideration of whether the early Reformers conceived of scripture as the sole source or resource for Christian theology, or simply the highest authority for establishing matters of dogma. Nevertheless, approaching scripture as the chief doctrinal authority still raises hard questions about whether this concept itself can be explicitly located within scripture, and how such a principle might be a recovery of the Apostolic age when there were no written Gospels or New Testament canon in that period of Church history.

coalesced in part under force of attack by Catholic commentators on Protestant conceptions of the church. Of Ridley's extant writings, such conceptual thrust and parry is most evident in his *Certen Godly, Learned, and Comfortable Conferences Between . . . Nicolas Rydley and Hughe Latymer.* In their second *Conference*, Ridley and Latimer wrestle in tag-team fashion with objections to Protestant dogma penned by Stephen Gardiner under his pseudonym of Marcus Aurelius Constantius.[61] Gardiner was the Henrician Bishop of Winchester as well as a friend and leading counselor of the king. A conservative in matters of sacramental theology, at least by the standards of early English Protestants, Gardiner was therefore a favorite target of reform-minded clergy in the reign of Henry VIII.

The research of Michael Riordan and Alec Ryrie helps us to better understand precisely why Gardiner was the target of Ridley and Latimer's attack in their *Conferences*. Since they dared not to attack Henry VIII for his religious conservatism, English Protestants fostered the legend of "Wily Winchester" starting in the 1530s.[62] Following the first period of reformist hopes in the wake of Henry VIII's break with Rome, early Protestants grew increasingly frustrated with the slow progress of their movement. The religiously conservative beliefs and laws of the king checked the progress of the Gospel, in their estimation, but Henry's regular execution of his critics meant that they could not safely mount a direct challenge to him.[63] Gardiner, as the leading conservative figure near the king by the late 1530s, served as a scapegoat for the king's conservatism, and consequently the Bishop of Winchester became an object of scorn. Gardiner's willingness to meet Protestant arguments on their own ground in the form of several strong polemical treatises and books also meant that he was a real threat to nascent Protestantism, especially when these activities were connected

---

61 See Ridley, *Comfortable Conferences* and *Works*, pp. 97–151. For the identification of Gardiner with Marcus Aurelius Constantius, see *Comfortable Conferences*, fols. 35, *recto*-36, *verso*, and *Works*, p. 147.

62 Michael Riordan and Alec Ryrie, "Stephen Gardiner and the Making of a Protestant Villain," *Sixteenth Century Journal* 34 (2003) [hereafter: Riordan and Ryrie, "Making of a Protestant Villain"]: pp. 1039–65.

63 Riordan and Ryrie, "Making of a Protestant Villain," pp. 1044–45.

with both his real and alleged involvement in the discovery and prosecution of heretics.[64]

By the 1550s, reforming polemicists were charging Gardiner with being an inconstant intellectual changeling. These claims gained credence in light of Gardiner's efforts to promote and secure Roman jurisdiction during the reign of Mary, after he and Edmund Bonner had publicly rejected papal primacy in the 1530s in their *De Vera Obedentia*.[65] We must bear in mind, however, that Ridley himself understood that targeting Gardiner's change of heart on papal primacy also raised questions against his and Latimer's disobedience to the reigning monarch, Mary I. Gardiner's charge of inconstancy against them for not conforming to the religious settlement of the Marian régime forms one of the longest sections of the *Comfortable Conferences*, and is preceded by an earnest prayer from Ridley for grace to "understande how this pestilent and deadly dart is to be borne of, and with what answere it is to be beaten backe." He concludes this section with, "a man oughte to obeie his prince, but in the Lorde, and never against the Lorde."[66] Under Mary, Ridley and Latimer were therefore reconsidering the notion of the Royal Supremacy no less earnestly than Gardiner.

Ridley makes a significant contribution to the early English Protestant legend of "Wily Winchester" by portraying Gardiner in the *Conferences* as both inconstant and malicious, referring to Gardiner/Constantius as "the Antonian," alluding to a cruel Arian bishop who persecuted Catholic Christians in North Africa when those Roman provinces were overrun by barbarian invaders in the late fourth and early fifth centuries.[67] In what he styles "the ninth objection of the Antonian," Ridley summarizes Gardiner's arguments concerning issues of

64 Riordan and Ryrie, "Making of a Protestant Villain," pp. 1042, 1047–51, 1060–65.

65 Riordan and Ryrie, "Making of a Protestant Villain," pp. 1055–60.

66 Ridley, *Comfortable Conferences*, fols. 32, *verso* and 33, *recto*. Cf. Ridley, *Works*, pp. 142 and 144. Despite this assertion, it is clear that Cranmer, Latimer, and Ridley were often circumspect with respect to what teachings were "in the Lorde" during Henry's reign.

67 See Ridley, *Comfortable Conferences*, fols. 34, *recto*-35, *verso*, and *Works*, pp. 147–48.

ecclesiastical authority and scripture: "Yf the matter shoulde go thus, that in generall counsails menne shoulde not stande to the more numbre of the whole multitude, I meane of them whiche ought to geve voices, then shoulde no certaine rule bee left unto the churche, by the whiche controversies in waightie matters might bee determined, but it is not to be beleved, that Christe woulde leave his churche destitute of so necessarie a helpe and saveguarde."[68]

In his response to this objection, Ridley replies with the classic Protestant principle of restricting ecclesiology to the express limits of scripture: "Christe, who is the moste lovinge spouse of his espoused the church, who also gave himselfe for it, that he mighte sanctifie it unto himselfe, did give unto it abundauntlye all things which are necessarie to salvacion, but yet so, that the churche shoulde declare it selfe obediente unto him in all thinges, and kepe it selfe within the boundes of his commaundementes, and further not to seke any thing, whiche he teacheth not, as necessarie unto salvacion."[69] Ridley goes on to explain how doctrinal disputes ought to be resolved: "For determination of all controversies in Christes religion, Christe himselfe hath left unto the church not only Moses and the Prophetes, whome he willeth his church in all doubtes to go unto and aske counsell at; but also the gospelles and the reste of the bodie of the newe testamente. In the whiche, whatsoever is harde in Moses and the prophetes, whatsoever is necessarie to be knowen unto salvation, is reveled and opened."[70] Ridley's basic assertion is that it is not for ecclesiastical councils to determine the substance of

68 Gardiner, as quoted in Ridley, *Comfortable Conferences*, fol. 25, *verso, and Ridley, *Works*, p. 131.

69 Ridley, *Comfortable Conferences*, fol. 25, *verso*, and *Works*, p. 131.

70 Ridley, *Comfortable Conferences*, fol. 25, *verso*, and *Works*, p. 131. It should be noted here that Ridley assumes that the Gospel will illumine what is "harde in Moses and the prophetes," but does not entertain the possibility that the Old Covenant may throw light on key passages of the New Testament. This idea is in keeping with Erasmus' portrayal of the Old Testament as "darkness," and the New Testament as "light." See Hoffman, *Rhetoric and Theology*, p. 160. Neither Erasmus nor Ridley seem concerned with the possibility that the Old Testament might be the primary and natural context for interpreting or explicating the words of Jesus in the New Testament.

Christian faith, but that all things necessary to salvation are already to be found explicitly in scripture. Ridley implicitly claims that Christ himself advocated the idea that scripture is the chief authority in Church doctrine, in the assertion that Jesus "himselfe hath left unto the church not only Moses and the Prophetes, . . . but also the gospelles and the reste of the bodie of the newe testamente." The assertion calls for clear scriptural evidence of this foundational principle of Protestantism. Ridley's opening argument necessitates an appeal to the Gospels themselves to indicate that Christ "willeth his church in all doubtes to go unto and aske counsell at" scripture alone.

Logically and theologically, the advancement of the idea that scripture is the governing authority in Church dogma, a staple of Protestant ecclesiology, should proceed from an abundance of scriptural support for the concept. If it is indeed Christ's will that the church should consult the Old and New Testaments "in all doubtes," then this principle is itself a necessary matter of faith, since by its very nature any teaching of Christ that reflects his eternal will for the entire church would not be an *adiaphora* matter of ecclesial polity. Since the church is "not to seke any thing, whiche [Christ] teacheth not, as necessarie unto salvacion," it should therefore be a relatively straightforward matter for Ridley to cite the relevant passages of scripture wherein Christ proclaims that his will is for the Church to consider only the canon of sacred writings "[f]or determination of all controversies in [his] religion." In application, however, this endeavor proves rather thorny. Ridley continues his response to the objection of "the Antonian" by paraphrasing Paul from the tenth chapter of Romans: "Now wee have no neede to saie, Who shall clime into heaven . . . to tell us what is needful to be done? Christ hath . . . commended unto us the worde of faith, whiche also is aboundantly declared unto us in his worde written; so that hereafter, if wee walke earnestly in this waie, to the serching out of the trueth, it is not to be doubted but throughe the certaine benefite of Christes spirite, which he hath promised unto his, we may find it, and obtaine everlasting life."[71]

71 Ridley, *Comfortable Conferences*, sig. 25, *verso-recto*, and *Works*, p. 132. Ridley's Pauline allusion is to Romans 10:6–8.

At first blush, Ridley's mention of Christ's promise of his Spirit would appear to be a reference to John 16:13: "When the Spirit of truth comes, he will guide you into all truth; for he will not speak on his own authority, but whatever he hears he will speak, and he will declare to you the things that are to come." However, in the context of trying to establish that everything necessary to salvation is already "declared unto us in [Christ's] worde written," biblical passages that alluded to the future arrival of a "Spirit of truth" that would teach the Apostles "the things that are to come" following Jesus' Ascension, were of little purpose. Rather than broach the subject of the Apostles being led unto the fullness of truth over time, Ridley refers here to Luke 11:9–10, assuming the immediacy of what is there promised: "And I tell you, ask, and it will be given you; seek, and you will find; knock, and it will be opened unto you. For everyone who asks receives, and he who seeks finds, and to him who knocks, it will be opened."[72]

Ridley continues his response to "the Antonian" by linking citations from Isaiah 8:19, John 5:39, and the writings of St. Jerome: "'Shoulde menne aske counsell of the dead for the living?' saieth Esaie; 'Let them go rather to the law and to the testimonie,' &c. Christe sendeth them that bee desirouse to knowe the trueth unto the scriptures, saiyeng: search the scriptures. I remember a like thing well spoken by Hierome: 'Ignoraunce of the scriptures is the mother and cause of al erroures.' And in another place: 'The knoweledge of the scripturs is the fode of everlasting life.'"[73] In this context, it is possible that Ridley intends a sort of covert word play, referring "the Antonian" to the "counsell" of scripture rather than the Councils of the Church. The biblical passage

---

72 The marginal notes for this passage indicate merely Chapter 11 of Luke's Gospel, but verses 9–10 seem to be those applicable to Ridley's point quoted above. The *Great Bible* renders these verses: "And I say unto you: 'aske and it shal be geven you. Seke, and ye shall fynde. Knocke, and it shalbe opened to you. For every one that asketh receaveth: and he that seketh, fyndeth: and unto hym that knocketh, sall it bee opened.'" See *Great Bible*, New Testament, fol. xxvii, *verso*. Acts 15:1–35 recounts the proceedings of the Council of Jerusalem. Both traditional and modern commentators hold that Luke and Acts were likely written by the same author.
73 Ridley, *Comfortable Conferences* sig. 25, *recto*, and *Works*, p. 132.

does claim superiority for the revelation contained in scripture, over against various forms of ancient magic, but not in denunciation of a synod of Hebrew elders. The scriptural context of "shoulde menne aske counsell of the dead for the living?" indicates that it is a firm prohibitive statement regarding necromancy.[74] The full verse, as rendered by the *Great Bible*, reads, "And yf they saye unto you: ask counsel at the Soth-sayers, Wytches, charmers, and conjurers, then make them this answere. Is there a people any where that asketh not counsel at hys God? Shulde men runne unto the dead for the lyvynge?"

The most direct biblical evidence that Ridley offers in support of the claim that it is the will of Christ that the Church should consult only the scriptures in "all controversies," lies in his use of John 5:39. Here, he also moves immediately to couple this verse with a pair of pithy excerpts from Jerome. Evident throughout this passage of the *Conferences* is Ridley's interpolative method of scriptural exegesis in a fashion that recalls the approach of Erasmus, especially in Ridley's use of Jesus' words from the Gospels in a sense that is rather abstracted from the narrative of the text or the religious context of the Old Testament.

In John 5:39, Jesus declares his messianic legitimacy to those who do not believe in him: "Serche the scriptures, for in them ye thynke ye have eternall lyfe and they are they whiche testifye of me. And yet ye wyl not come to me that ye might have lyfe."[75] In Greek, John 5:39 begins with verb (ἐραυνᾶτε, from ἐραυνάω, a late form of ἐρευνάω) that can be parsed in two different ways.[76] First, ἐραυνᾶτε could be read as a second person plural *imperative*, meaning "search!" Alternately, ἐραυνᾶτε could be taken as a second person plural *indicative*, which would translate to "you search" or "you are searching." While

---

74 *Great Bible*, Old Testament, fol. xxxix, *verso*.

75 *Great Bible*, New Testament, fol. xxxv, *recto. The Jerusalem Bible* offers: "You study" for ἐραυνᾶτε, with a note for the alternate translation of simply "study," while *The New King James Bible* and the *Revised Standard Version* employ "you search." The Revised Challoner-Rheims translation of the *Vulgate* (1941) renders the verb as "you are searching."

76 See *The Greek New Testament*, eds. Kurt Aland, Matthew Black, Carlo M. Martini, Bruce M. Metzger, and Allen Wikgren (Münster/Westphalia: United Bible Societies, 1983).

Ridley and the *Great Bible* offer "search the scriptures" for ἐραυνᾶτε τὰς γραφάς (reading the verb as an imperative), most modern editions of the Bible read ἐραυνᾶτε as an indicative and render the phrase as "you are searching the scriptures" or "you search the scriptures." Following this form, the Greek verses 39 and 40 would read: "You are searching the scriptures, because you think that by means of them you will have everlasting life; and these are the very ones that bear witness to me. And yet you do not want to come to me that you may have life."

Readers of the *Conferences* may be forgiven for not being fully persuaded that John 5:39 clearly establishes that Jesus both willed and taught that the Church should consult only the Old and New Testaments in all matters of doctrinal controversy. In context, the verse suggests that reading the scriptures alone has not or will not, by itself, persuade Jesus' audience that he is indeed the promised Messiah of Old Testament prophecy. The passage does not appear to speak to the utility—or permissibility—of Church councils. Just as often happens in Erasmus' work, Ridley marshals the words of Jesus and applies them to an argument quite apart from their original and essential setting. In this "oracular" view of Jesus' words from the Gospels, their original context is of little importance to Ridley, who borrows them rather freely here to question both the need of, and biblical sanction for, Church councils. Ridley's citations from Jerome are useful because they suggest the general utility of studying the scriptures for the formation of faith. Their strong wording gives ballast to his use of John 5:39, shading the meaning of the biblical passage in a way that is consonant with Ridley's view of scripture and ecclesiology.

Curiously, in one passage of the *Conferences* Ridley seems to acknowledge the difficulty of the exegetical mark he has set for himself, if only for a fleeting instant: "But nowe methinketh I enter into a verie broade sea, in that I beginne to shewe, either oute of the scriptures them selves, or oute of the aunciente writers, how muche the holy scripture is of force to teache the trueth of oure religion. But this is it that I am nowe aboute, that Christe wold have the church, his spouse, in all doubtes to aske counsell at the word of his father written, and faithfully lefte and commended unto it in bodth testaments the old and the newe."[77] If Christ "willeth" the church to have recourse only to "the word of his father written" in "all doubtes" of doctrinal controversy, then locating the source of this intention in scripture is not necessarily to "enter into a verie broad sea." Ridley's insistence that Christ "left and commended ...both Testaments" to the church is, historically speaking, somewhat puzzling. We should note that in this portion of his answer to Gardiner's objection, although Ridley began by asserting that it is Christ's will that the Church consult the scriptures in all doctrinal controversies, he has suddenly expanded his sources of evidence to include "the aunciente writers." He has decided to rely on *traditio*, in the testimony of the Fathers, to promote his understanding of the role of scripture in ecclesiology. Supplied with a pair of passages from Jerome, he suggests that the early Church subscribed to the position that scripture alone contained all things necessary to salvation. In this move, Ridley displays one of the apologetic strategies Ryrie has identified, the effort to claim Catholic historical figures as advocates of Protestant ideals, in this case, one of the leading Fathers of the Church.[78]

Ridley concludes his answer to "the Antonian" with an argument about what he cannot find in scripture, citing two additional passages from Paul: "Neither do we reede that Christ in any place hath laied soo greate a burthen upon the members of his spouse, that he hath commaunded them to go to the universall churche. 'Whatsoever thinges are written' (saith Paul), 'are written for our learninge.'" Ridley continues: "And it is true that 'Christ gave unto his churche some Apostels, some Prophetes, some Evangelistes, some shepherds and teachers, to the edifynge of the sainctes, till wee all come to the unitie of faithe,' &c. But that all menne should meete together, oute of all partes of the worlde, to define of the articles of our faith, I neither finde it commaunded of Christe, nor written in the worde of God."[79]

---

77 Ridley, *Comfortable Conferences,* sig. 25, *recto*, and *Works*, p. 132.
78 See Ryrie, "Problems of Legitimacy in English Protestantism," p. 85, where the author notes that John Bale in the *Image of both churches,* attempts to claim Dante, Savonarola, and Eneo Sylvia as crypto-Protestants.
79 Ridley, *Comfortable Conferences,* fols. 25, *recto*-26, *verso,* and *Works,* p. 132. The Pauline passages are from Romans 15:4 and Ephesians 4:11–13, respectively. Ridley is certainly right to state that he can find no

Ridley understood that granting any room to "the Antonian" on the issue of Church councils would greatly complicate his task of promoting scripture as the highest dogmatic authority. On those grounds, his answer to Gardiner in this section of *Comfortable Conferences* is logical. We should also note that in this passage, Ridley couples verses from Paul with an appeal to what Christ does not say in the Gospels, an exegetical method that is identical to Erasmus' interpolative use of First Corinthians in the *Paraphrases*.[80]

It is interesting that Ridley's response here stands in tension with the views of ecclesiastical history and church polity he expresses in his other writings. His argument concerning what he cannot locate in scripture contrasts sharply with his statements to Hooper on the Edwardine vestments controversy. In that treatise, Ridley cautions against the use of a negative hermeneutic of scripture. He asserts that the charge of illegitimacy against Church practices for which there is no express biblical warrant is tantamount to altering scripture: "To forbid that for a thing of itself unlawful which God's word doth not forbid, this is to add unto God's word."[81] As with all the early English efforts to label Gardiner and his allies as "wily"

> commandment of Christ requiring Church councils, but there is certainly scriptural and apostolic precedent for such ecclesiastical gatherings. Acts 15:1–35 recounts the convening, deliberations, and decrees of the Council of Jerusalem. Circa A.D. 50, the missionaries and remaining Apostles met to determine whether or not Gentiles must subscribe to the Mosaic Law in order to become Christians. Peter's final determination that it was not necessary for Gentile believers to be circumcised confirmed the position of Paul and Barnabas. Nevertheless, the assembled Fathers did urge observation of some aspects of the Law for Gentiles, requiring them to refrain from things sacrificed to idols, from blood, from the meat of strangled animals, and from sexual immorality (15:28–29).

80 *"Verum, quod Christus non exegit à suis, non ausim à vobis exigere."* Erasmus, *Paraphrasis in Epist. Pauli ad Cor. 1*, Cap. VII, in vol. VII of *Desiderii Erasmi Roterdami Opera Omnia*, ed. Jean Leclerc (Leiden: Lugduni Batavorum, 1706), p.880, col. C. See also *ibid.* Cap. X, p.894, col. C: *"Christus in his summam libertatem nobis esse voluit, qui nullam cibi genus aut indixit, aut interdixit."*

81 John Bradford, *The Writings of John Bradford*, vol. 2, ed. Aubrey Townsend, for the Parker Society (Cambridge: Cambridge University Press, 1840) [hereafter: *Bradford*, vol. 2], p. 382.

and inconstant, the same charge redounded to the Reformers themselves, given the shifting religious policies under Henry VIII, Edward VI, and Mary I, in turn.

Ironically, many of Ridley's theological principles, despite his explicit aim to base them on scripture alone, are grounded directly upon dogmas that were determined and promulgated in Church councils. For example, he refers to the hypostatic union of Christ's two natures to assert that Jesus is present in the Eucharist by virtue of his divinity only, while his body remains in heaven.[82] The proposition that a hypostatic union exists between the divine and human natures of Christ does not appear in express form within the canon of scripture, but was promulgated by the Council of Chalcedon in A.D. 451 to safeguard the coherence of the biblical witness to the person and salvific work of Christ. Similarly, Ridley maintains that portions of the Nicene-Constantinopolitan Creed refute the notion of Christ's real presence in the Eucharist. He was fond of arguing that Christ could not be corporally present in the Eucharist if "[h]e ascended into heaven, and sitteth on the right hande of God the Father. From whence (and not from any other place, sayeth S. Augustine), he shall come to judge both the quicke and the deade."[83] The Councils of Nicea (A.D. 325) and Constantinople (A.D. 481) were instrumental in developing and promulgating this Creed in the form that it has been known and used in the Church ever since.[84]

The various meanings that the term "faith" may indicate within the canon of scripture also present obstacles to locating biblical warrant for the principle of *scriptura* as the chief authority for ecclesial polity. Ridley noted this problem himself when he wrote to Hooper: "It is not true, that what cannot be proved by the word of God is not of faith so taken— that is to say, is contrary to the persuasion of my faith. For then to take up a straw were a deadly sin; for, that thou shouldest so do, it is not

---

82 See, e.g., Ridley, *Brief Declaracion*, sig. B.2, *recto,* and *Works*, p. 13.

83 Foxe, *Actes and Mounments*, p. 1443 and Ridley, *Works*, p. 199. Cf. *Creeds of the Churches*, ed. John Leith, third edition (Louisville: John Knox Press, 1982) [hereafter: Leith, *Creeds*], pp. 28–33.

84 Similar issues are raised by Ridley's references to Jesus as the second person of the Trinity. See Ridley, *Brief Declaracion*, sig. B.2, *recto,* and *Works*, p. 13.

found in the word of God. But if thou understand 'not to be of faith,' for not to be taken as an article of faith, then it is true, that what cannot be proved by the word of God is not of faith."[85] In contrasting the "persuasion" of faith with what is to be considered "an article of faith," Ridley probably has in mind the medieval distinction between *fides quae creditur*, or the faith which is believed, and *fides qua creditur*, the faith by which we believe. This observation rests on the principle that there is a substantial difference between the content of the Christian faith which the Church seeks to defend and promote, and the personal assent, enabled by the aid of grace, that a believer makes to what the Church teaches about the role and person of Christ.

Given the differences between "articles of faith" and the "persuasion" of faith, it is difficult to know which of these Jerome refers to in the statements cited by Ridley in the *Conferences*. The assertion, "Ignoraunce of the scriptures is the mother and cause of al errours," may more likely be aimed to address the particular errors of heretical individuals in their faulty teachings than what the Church maintains corporately about the person and role of Christ. Again, that "[t]he knoweledge of the scripturs is the fode of everlasting life," in terms of a personal faith formation that better enables one to assent to what the Church teaches about Christ, has never been in dispute.

While the paucity of biblical evidence drove Ridley to locate patristic prooftexts for the principle of *sola scriptura*, this enterprise itself was not without historical difficulties. For Jesus and his Apostles, scripture was the Old Testament canon and its Apocrypha. In a more profound way than Ridley's age could have known, we are aware today that the canon of scripture in the post-apostolic period was quite fluid in nature. The development of the New Testament canon was therefore a gradual metamorphosis that did not take decisive form until the late third and early fourth centuries. It is therefore unlikely that the early Fathers would advance the notion that "scripture contains all things necessary to salvation," since the nature of "scripture" was not yet

---

85 Ridley, *Bradford* vol. 2, pp. 376–77. See also Peter Marshall, *Religious Identities in Henry VIII's England* (Aldershot: Ashgate, 2006) [hereafter: Marshall, *Henry VIII's England*], pp. 98–99.

firmly fixed. These historical aspects of the emergence of a canon of sacred texts explains why Ridley's patristic sources date from the latter portion of the period and are comprised chiefly of citations from Jerome and Chrysostom.

In his *Conferences* with Latimer, Ridley also quoted John Chrysostom, in response to the fifth objection of "the Antonian." In this portion of Ridley's work, he interpolated patristic sources or his own ideas into scriptural passages to strengthen his arguments. Gardiner's assertion, which Ridley sought to refute, is that the Catholic Church is the ark of salvation: "Consider into what daungers you caste your selfe, yf you forsake the Churche. . . . Withoute the Arke ther is no salvation. The Churche is the Arke, and Peters shyppe. Ye knowe thys saying well inoughe: 'He shall not have godde to be his father, which acknowlegeth not the Churche to be his mother.' Moreover, 'Withoute the Church (sayeth S. Augustine), be the lyfe never so well spente, it shal not enheritte the kyngdome of heaven.'"[86] Ridley opens his response with a defense of the orthodoxy of Protestant views of the church. He brings forward the ecclesiastical sections of the Nicene-Constantinopolitan Creed to support this claim: "The holie Catholique or universalle Churche, which is the communion of sayntes, the howse of godde, the Citee of godde, the spowse of Christe, the bodie of Christe, the pyller and staye off the truth; This Church I beleve, according to the Creede: Thys Church I doo reverence and honour in the Lorde."[87]

Next Ridley develops his argument by characteristically invoking the principle of *scriptura* as the chief authority in dogma: "But the rewle off this church is the wordde of godde, accordyng to which rewle we goo forward unto lyffe. And as many as walke accordyng to thys rewle, I saye with S. Paule, peace be apon them and apon Israel, which perteyneth unto godde.'"[88] Ridley's declaration, "I saye with S. Paule," couples his own use of "rewle" with Paul's in Galatians 6:16. By yoking

---

86 Gardiner, in Ridley, *Comfortable Conferences*, fol. 19, *verso*, and *Works*, p. 122.

87 Ridley, *Comfortable Conferences*, fol. 19, *verso-recto*, and *Works*, pp. 122–23.

88 Ridley, *Comfortable Conferences*, fol. 19, *recto*, and Ridley, *Works*, p. 123.

the idea of the authority *scriptura* to this verse and the word "rule," Ridley gives the reader the impression that Paul states that scripture is to be the governing rule of the church. However, the rule that Paul would have the Galatians observe is clearly stated in the previous verse (15): "In Christ Jesu nether cyrcumcision avayleth anythynge at all, nor uncyrcumcision but a newe creature."[89] Paul's rule relates to his missionary work and the inutility of Gentile subscription to the Mosaic Law in order for them to be accepted as Christians. Paul's mention of Israel in verse 16 indicates that the issue has to do with differing Hebrew and Gentile religious rites. Once again, we find Ridley freely interpolating his own ideas into the words of Paul in a way that is reminiscent of Erasmus' *Paraphrases* on the Pauline epistles. Paul's "rule" is not that every article of faith is explicitly contained within the written scriptures.

In the succeeding portion of Ridley's response, he indicates what characteristics and signs of the true Church serve to distinguish it from any other communion. Here he applies his apologetic strategy in reverse, using his own words to complete a point raised in a passage of scripture: "The markes wherby this Churche is knowen unto me in this darke worlde, and in the myddes of this Crooked and frowarde generation, are these: The syncere preachinge of goddes worde; The due administration off the sacramentes; Charity, and faythfull observynge off Ecclesiasticall discipline accordyng to the worde off godde."[90] Ridley goes on to declare: "That Church or congregation which is garnisshed with these markes, is in verie dede that heavenly Hierusalem, which consisteth of those that be borne frome above. Thys is the mother of us all: And, by goddes grace, I will Live and dye the Chylde of thys Churche. Forth off thys (I graunte) ther is no salvation, and, I suppose, the residew of the places objected are rightly to be understanded of thys churche only."[91] Here, Ridley couples his references to the "markes" of the Church with Philippians 2:15, which does mention a crooked generation. However,

---

89 *Great Bible*, New Testament, fol. lxviii, *recto*. This rendering is very close to that of the Douay-Rheims: "For in Christ Jesus neither circumcision availeth any thing, nor uncircumcision, but a new creature."

90 Ridley, *Comfortable Conferences*, fol. 19, *recto*, and Ridley, *Works*, p. 123.

91 Ridley, *Comfortable Conferences*, fol. 19, *recto*, and Ridley, *Works*, p. 123.

Ridley does not indicate where his biblical citation ends; his readers are led to believe that the passage in Philippians relates the specific marks of the Church. The passage is actually a general exhortation to faithfulness: "Do all thynges without murmuring, and dysputyng, that ye maye bee such as no man complayne on: and unfayned sonnes of God without rebuke, in the myddes of a croked and perverse nacion: emong whom se that ye shyne as lyghtes in the world."[92]

Finally, Ridley concludes this part of his *Conferences* with an authoritative text that explicitly addresses the relationship between scripture and the Church. For this end, he cites a patristic source: "In tymes paste (sayeth Chrysostome) ther wer many waies to knowe the Churche of Christe, . . . by chastitee, by doctrine, by mynistringe the sacraments. But frome that tyme that heresies dyd take holde off the churches, it is onlye knowen by the scriptures which is the true church. They have all thinges in outwarde shewe, which the true church hath in truthe. They have temples lyke unto ours, &c. . . . Wherefore only by the scriptures doo we knowe which is the true churche."[93] The greater context of Ridley's argument is that a church whose doctrine is restricted to the express commands of scripture is the true body of Christ, but the manner of discernment is not explicitly addressed by the passage he quotes. Since the patristic author refers to the material property of various ecclesial bodies, he may be attempting to contrast such possessions with the spiritual and moral asceticism a true Christian body ought to possess, but this is not clear.

The precise meaning of "only by the scriptures doo we knowe which is the true churche" remains obscure, but we do know that the citation is not from one of St. John Chrysostom's authentic writings. Unfortunately for Ridley, the passage is from a work entitled *Opus Imperfectum in Matthaeum*, the production of a fifth-century Arian author.[94] Erasmus

92 *The Great Bible,* New Testament, fol. lxx, *recto.*
93 Ridley, *Comfortable Conferences*, fols. 19, *recto*-20, *verso*, and Ridley, *Works*, p. 123.
94 See, e.g., the *Catholic Encyclopedia* entry for St. John Chrysostom. For Erasmus' rejection of Chrysostom's authorship of *Opus Imperfectum in Matthaeum,* and his thesis that the piece was the work of an Arian author, see *The Dictionary of Early Christian Literature,* trans. Matthew

himself expressed suspicions about the authenticity of this piece in the course of his patristic studies. Although Ridley is silent on this point in his *Conferences* with Latimer, the former also seems, surprisingly, to have been aware that there were good reasons for doubting that the work was written by Chrysostom. Ridley's reference to *Opus Imperfectum in Matthaeum* in another of his prison writings is followed by the remark: "Whether the autor was John Chrisostome him self, the Archebishop of Constantinople, or no: that is not the mater. For of all it is graunted, that he was a writour of that age, and a man of great learnyng."[95] The great irony of Ridley's crossing swords with Gardiner is that he relied in part upon an Arian text to build a case against "the Antonian." To understand Ridley's reliance upon the *Opus Imperfectum in Matthaeum*, despite his misgivings about its authenticity, we must view his efforts from the angle of Protestant anxiety about their teaching being derided as the "new learning" or "new pater noster."[96] In this context, such a move is less puzzling than it might at first appear. Ridley wished to make the best of the evidence available to him, and patristic proof texts for the idea that scripture should govern ecclesiology were few and vague.[97]

O'Connell, eds. Siegmar Döpp and Wilhelm Geerlings (New York: Herder and Herder, 2000), p. 443. The editors of the Parker Society volume of Ridley's collected writings, while attempting to adduce some evidence to the contrary, discreetly note that this passage is not authentic. Note B on this subject appears at the back of the volume, and addresses the subject by comparing several sixteenth-century editions of the source text. See Ridley, *Works*, pp. 509–10. The same problem of inauthenticity besets Ridley's use of *Ad Caesarium Monachum*, as noted by the Parker Society editors in the same passage.

95 Ridley, *Brief Declaracion*, sig. D.5, *recto*, and Ridley, *Works*, p. 33.
96 Ryrie, "Problems of Legitimacy in English Protestantism," p. 79.
97 We must also bear in mind that the Marian prisoners had few books at their disposal when composing their polemical tracts. Ridley complained frequently about this fact. See Foxe, *Actes and Monuments*, p. 1428, Ridley, *Comfortable Conferences*, fols. 22, *recto*-23, *verso*, and *Works*, pp. 127–28. Ridley was also forced to improvise writing materials on some occasions, as we are told by Foxe that: "Bishop Ridley lying . . . in prison, having ther the . . . booke of Marcus Antonius, for lack of penne and paper with a lead of a window in the margent of the booke wrote annotations, Notes of D. Ridley agaynst Marcus Anthonius, as strayghtnesse of time

Here as elsewhere, Alec Ryrie's analysis of the strategies employed by early English Protestants in their efforts to legitimize their secession from Catholicism helps to explain a number of ideas to be found in Ridley's writings.[98] One common tactic was to claim unity among all past factions of dissent against the Church as having promoted Protestant principles. John Bale's *Image of both churches*[99] takes this tack as a way to address the question of where Protestantism was prior to the early years of the sixteenth century, while Ridley often advances a similar view of Church history, commending the "learning" and "godliness" of the Waldensian Brethren to one of his former chaplains, for example.[100] Intriguingly, Ridley also lauds the work of Laurentius Valla, the personal hero of Erasmus, in this same letter.[101] Another early English Protestant stratagem involved extending the idea of crypto-Protestantism to revered figures of the Catholic past, which seems to be Ridley's aim in citing the authority of figures like St. John Chrysostom. Ridley's reconstruction of Church history mirrors his borrowing of biblical passages in debate: it is not necessary for him to locate self-evident precedents for a doctrinal point so long as the source introduces similar themes or vocabulary. The

would serve him, in refutation of the same booke," *Actes and Monuments*, p. 1870.

98 Ryrie, "Problems of Legitimacy in English Protestantism," pp. 78–92.

99 John Bale, *The image of both churches* ([STC 1297] Antwerp, 1546?).

100 See Miles Coverdale, *Certain most godly, fruitful, and comfortable letters of such true saintes and holy martyrs of God, as in the late bloodye persecution here within this realme, gaue their lyues for the defence of Christes holy gospel written in the tyme of their affliction and cruell imprysonment.*, ([STC 5886] London: John Day, 1564) [hereafter: Coverdale, *Comfortable Letters*], p. 72, and *Works*, p. 374. The letter is addressed to Augustine Berneher, Hugh Latimer's servant, but contains information that Ridley wished to have conveyed to one Mr. Grimbold, who reverted to Catholicism under Mary. Nicholas Grimbold or Grimald betrayed Ridley and his brother-in-law, George Shipside, in December 1554 or January 1555 by turning over manuscripts of some of Ridley's prison tracts to the Marian authorities. See Michael G. Brennan, "Grimald, Nicholas (*b.* 1519/20, *d.* in or before 1562)," *Oxford Dictionary of National Biography*, Oxford University Press, 2004 [http://www.oxforddnb.com/view/article/11629, accessed 13 August 2007].

101 See Coverdale, *Comfortable Letters*, fol. 71, and Ridley, *Works*, p. 374.

use of related terminology by another source is ample occasion for the grafting of a tangentially related idea onto the original text. Ridley and Erasmus' use of history are therefore very similar as a result of their free borrowing and re-appropriation of texts and terminology. Ridley's effort to locate the principle of *sola scriptura* in patristic writings and the gospels fares as well as Erasmus' attempt to recast New Testament themes into classical categories, as in his explication of the transformation of Saul of Tarsus into Paul the Apostle, for example.[102]

Four Evangelists and One Gospel

In other tracts, Ridley's use of scripture is somewhat more instructional than polemical. His *Brief Declaracion of the Lordes Supper* is one such work, fashioned to furnish its readers with a compact yet incisive set of tools for dissecting the essentials of the English eucharistic debates. However, the same pattern of movement from biblical text to patristic material that is evident in his polemical writings emerges here as well, especially at key exegetical junctures. This particular treatise commences with a detailed Gospel parallel presentation.[103] Noting the harmony of both the events described and the language employed by New Testament authors in their descriptions of Christ's institution of the Eucharist, Ridley declares: "As Matthewe and Marke doo agree muche in wordes, so do likewise Luke and S. Paule; but al iiii, no doubt, as they were all taught in one schole, and inspired with one spirite, so taught they all one truthe."[104]

Ridley's insistence on the essential unity between biblical authors is characteristic of his thought. In the course of an examination of his views by the queen's commissioners, he stated: "Where is a multitude of affirmations in scripture, and where is one affirmation, all is one concerning the treueth of the matter: for that any one of the Evangelistes

---

102 See Erasmus, *Annotations on Romans*, p. 3. Cf. Collinson, *An Erasmian Topic*.
103 See Ridley, *Brief Declaracion*, sigs. A.4, *recto*-A.5, *verso*, and *Works*, pp. 6–9.
104 Ridley, *Brief Declaracion*, sig. A.4, *verso*, and *Works*, p. 7.

spake inspired by the holy ghost, was as true as that which is spoken of them all."[105] As he makes plain here and elsewhere, Ridley holds that the essential and formal unity of the ideas expressed by biblical writers is a result of their guidance by the one Spirit of Truth, the Holy Ghost. Since he is discussing the unity of the Evangelists' witness to Jesus in the context of the eucharist, one might expect Ridley to next consider passages from the sixth chapter of John's Gospel, even if no institution of the rite is explicitly described therein: "Then Jesus sayde unto them: 'Verely, verily, I say unto you: except ye eate the fleshe of the sonne of man and drinke his bloud, ye have no life in you. Who so eatheth my fleshe and drynketh my bloode, hath eternal lyfe, and I wil raise him up at the last daye. For my fleshe is meat in dede, and my bloude is drynke in dede. He that eatheth my fleshe and drynketh my bloude dwelleth in me, and I in hym.'"[106] However, in his examination in the Tower, Ridley simply sets forth a metaphorical passage from John: "It is as true as John sayth of Christ: *Ego sum ostium ovium*, I am the dore of the sheepe, as if all [the Evangelists] had sayde it."[107]

Instead of citing one of Jesus' many metaphors to intimate that the language of the sixth chapter of John is merely symbolic, Ridley pursues an alternate strategy in the *Brief Declaration*. Following his exposition of Paul and the Synoptic Gospels, he makes two brief allusions to John 6, but defers an examination of the text until some 13 folio pages later in his exegetical endeavor, where he introduces them through the writings of St. Augustine.[108] There Ridley labors to make a case that the eucharistic allusions in John 6 are simply figurative forms of speech: "The rules, wherby the speche is knowen, whan it is figurative, and wherby it is none, S. Augustine, in . . . *De doctrina christiana*, geveth diverse

---

105 Foxe, *Actes and Monuments*, p. 1427 and Ridley, *Works*, p. 156.
106 John 6:52–56 in the *Great Bible*, New Testament, fol. xxxvi, *verso*.
107 Foxe, *Actes and Monuments*, p. 1427, and Ridley, *Works*, p. 156–57.
108 See Ridley, *Brief Declaracion*, sig. A.6, *recto*, and *Works*, p. 8, where he completes his close comparison of parallel biblical passages on the Eucharist, as found in Matthew, Mark, Luke, and Paul. See *Brief Declaracion*, sig. B.2, *recto*, and *Works*, p.13 for two fleeting references to John 6; cf. *Brief Declaracion*, sig. C.2, *recto*, and *Works*, p. 21 where half of verse 53 is finally quoted.

learned lessons, very necessarie to be knownen of the studentes in God-des worde. Of the which, one I will rehearse, which is this: If (sayeth he) the scripture dothe seme to commaunde a thing, which is wicked or ungodlye; or to forbidde a thing that charitie dothe require, than knowe thou (sayeth he) that the speche is figurative."[109] Ridley then turns his attention to John 6: "For example, [St. Augustine] bringeth the sayeng of Christ in the 6 chap. of S. Jo. Except ye eate the fleshe of the sonne of man, and drinke his blood, ye can not have lyfe in you; it semeth to commaunde a wicked or an ungodly thing. Wherfore it is a figurative speche, commaunding to have communion and fellowship with Christes passion, and devoutly and holesomlye to laye up in memorie, that his fleshe was crucified and wounded for us."[110] Here Ridley seems to have found a genuine patristic confirmation of one of his own ideas with re-spect to the Church and the Eucharist. Unlike the *Opus Imperfectum in Matthaeum*, the authorship of *De Doctrina Christiana* has never been in dispute; these are indeed St. Augustine's very words from book three, chapter sixteen of that work. Augustine clearly states here that John 6:53 is to be taken figuratively. As Ryrie notes, however, Protestant efforts to enlist past figures in Church history as allies in their cause were not with-out difficulties.[111]

No Protestant explication of the Lord's Supper, brief or otherwise, was written in Ridley's day that did not take aim at the Catholic doctrine of transubstantiation. Indeed, the title given to Ridley's *Brief Declara-cion of the Lordes Supper* was already "*A Treatise Against the Error of Transubstantiation*" when a second edition of it was printed in 1556.[112] Ridley offers his readers a typically forthright statement of his goals in writing the piece: "yf, after the truthe shalbe truly tryed out, it shalbe founde, that the substaunce of bread is the naturall substaunce of the Sacrament . . . than . . . that godly honour, which is only due unto God

---

109 Ridley, *Brief Declaracion*, sig. C.2, *recto*, and *Works*, p. 21. Cf. St. Augus-tine of Hippo, *De Doctrina Christiana*, trans. and ed. Edmund Hill, O.P. (New York: New City Press, 1996) [hereafter: St. Augustine, *De Doctrina Christiana*], p. 180

110 Ridley, *Brief Declaracion*, sig. C.2, *recto*, and *Works*, p. 21.

111 Ryrie, "Problems of Legitimacy in English Protestantism," p. 79–80.

112 See Ridley, *Comfortable Conferences*, fol. 37, *verso*.

the creator, may not be done unto the creature without idolatrie and sacrilege, is not to be done unto the holy Sacrament."[113] For Ridley then, the "wicked or an ungodly thing" that necessitates a figurative interpretation of John 6:53 is that a literal reading of the passage ultimately leads to the "idolatrie and sacrilege" of eucharistic adoration. Augustine does not declare, however, that the "idolatrie" of eucharistic adoration is the "wicked or ungodly" thing suggested by a literal rendering of John 6:53.

It is in fact through Augustine's own testimony that we have historical evidence that eucharistic adoration was already a long-established practice by the early fifth century. Augustine addresses the subject clearly in his *Expositions of the Psalms*, where he notes that the fifth verse of Psalm 99 urges the faithful to "fall down before His footstool."[114] Since Isaiah 66:1 and Acts 7:49 declare that the earth itself is the footstool of the Lord, Augustine is a bit perplexed by the meaning of the passage in Psalm 99: "I fear to worship the earth, lest He who made the heaven and the earth condemn me; again, I fear not to worship the footstool of my Lord, because the Psalm biddeth me, 'fall down before His footstool.' . . . The Scripture telleth me, 'the earth is My footstool.' In hesitation I turn unto Christ, since I am herein seeking Himself: and I discover how the earth may be worshipped without impiety, how His footstool may be worshipped without impiety."[115] Augustine then offers his solution to this paradox: "For He took upon Him earth from earth; because flesh is from earth, and He received flesh from the flesh of Mary. And because He walked here in very flesh, and gave that very flesh to us to eat for our salvation; and no one eateth that flesh, unless he hath first worshipped: we have found out in what sense such a footstool of our Lord's may be worshipped, and not only that we sin not in worshipping it, but that we sin in not worshipping."[116] Augustine denies

113 Ridley, *Brief Declaracion*, sig. B.1, *recto*, and *Works*, p. 12.
114 The *Great Bible*, Old Testament, fol. xvii, *verso*: "O Magnifye the Lorde oure God, and fall downe before hys footestole, for he is holye."
115 St. Augustine of Hippo, *Expositions of the Psalms*, trans. and ed. A. Cleveland Coxe, series II, vol. viii of *Nicene and Post Nicene Fathers* (Edinburgh: T & T Clark, 1888) [hereafter: St. Augustine, *Expositions of the Psalms*], p. 486.
116 St. Augustine, *Expositions of the Psalms*, p. 486.

that worshipping Christ in the Eucharist is an act of "idolatrie and sacrilege." The "wicked and ungodly" thing that he thinks is asserted by a
literal reading of John 6:53 must then refer to some other aspect of the
passage.

There is certainly nothing distinctively modern in the idea that Augustine's explication of Psalm 99 promotes eucharistic adoration. Ridley made this point himself in the first debate on the sacrament at
Cambridge in 1549. When one of his opponents cited this portion of
Augustine's writings against a merely symbolic view of the Eucharist,
Ridley's reply was quite sharp: "Master Vavisor, you are in a wrong
boxe, for the place maketh altogether for the maintenance of adoration,
if it make for any thynge."[117] Ridley's retort indicates that he was already familiar with this passage from the *Expositions of the Psalms*,
that he believes it "altogether" tends to support eucharistic adoration,
and that he had little enthusiasm for this strand of Augustine's thought.
When his opponent returned to the passage, Ridley concluded this portion of the debate with a rare show of irritation: "It is no illusion, good
Master Vavisor; but surely you would move a Saint with your imperti-
nent reasons."[118]

Perhaps it was the lingering memory of these exchanges that compelled Ridley to take up the *Expositions of the Psalms* in the pages of
his *Brief Declaration of the Lordes Supper*.[119] There Ridley says that St.
Augustine is "speaking of the sacrament of the Lordess body and blood;
and rehearsing (as it were) Christes words to his disciples, after this

117 This portion of Ridley's exchange with Master Vavasour is found in Foxe,
   Actes and Monuments, p. 1386 (misnumbered as p. 1374 in STC 11225,
   but nevertheless falls between pp. 1385 and 1387). Dr. Glyn also quotes
   from the same text from Augustine earlier in that same debate, p. 1378.
   The transcript of this disputation was not selected by the members of the
   Parker Society for inclusion in Ridley, *Works*. Thomas Vavasour, educated
   at St. John's College, Cambridge, was later to be a physician and prominent
   recusant under Elizabeth. See Richard Rex, "Vavasour, Thomas (d. 1585),"
   Oxford Dictionary of National Biography, Oxford University Press, 2004
   [http://www.oxforddnb.com/view/article/53524, accessed 5 August 2007].
118 Foxe, *Actes and Monuments*, p. 1386 (misnumbered as p. 1374 in STC
   11225).
119 Ridley, *Brief Declaracion*, sig. E.3ff, and *Works*, p. 39.

maner: It is not this body, which ye doo see, that ye shall eate, nother shall ye drinke this blood, which the souldyours, that crucifie me, shall spill or sheade: I doo commende unto you a mysterie, or a sacrament, which spiritually understanded shall geve you life."[120] The key lines from Augustine's original text immediately precede the excerpt found in the *Brief Declaration*, and give us an actual glimpse of the "wicked and ungodly" thing that Augustine eschews in a literal reading of John 6:53: "It seemed unto them hard that He said, 'Except ye eat the flesh of the Son of Man, ye have no life in you:' . . . they thought of it carnally, and imagined that the Lord would cut off parts from His body, and give unto them; and they said, 'This is a hard saying.' It was they who were hard, . . . for unless they had been hard, and not meek, they would have said unto themselves, He saith not this without reason, but there must be some latent mystery herein."[121]

For St. Augustine then, a literal interpretation of these words raised the specter in the minds of Jesus' disciples of a gruesome act of cannibalism, because they "imagined that the Lord would cut off parts from His body and give unto them." By contrast, when Ridley states that the sacrament is to be understood "spiritually," he means that Christ is substantially absent from the consecrated elements such that any act of adoration is equally an act of "idolatrie and sacrilege."[122] For St. Augustine,

---

120 Ridley, *Brief Declaracion*, sig. E.3, *verso*, and *Works*, p. 39.
121 St. Augustine, *Expositions of the Psalms*, p. 486.
122 Ridley was not reluctant to employ the most graphic scriptural language to describe the "idolatrie" implicit in affirming Christ's real presence in the sacrament. Decrying the restoration of Catholic ritual under Mary, he exclaimed: "Of late all that were endued with the light and grace of understanding of goddes holye mysteries, did blesse god, which had broughte them out of that horible blyndenesse and ignoraunce, whereby in times paste beinge seduced by Satans subtletyes, they beleved that the sacrament was not the sacrament, but the thyng whereof it is a sacramente; that the creature was the creatour; and that the thynge whichs hathe neyther lyfe nor sense (alas, suche was the horryble blyndnes) was the Lorde him selfe; whiche made the eye to see, and hath gyven al senses and understandynge unto man. But nowe alas, Englande is returned agayn lyke a dogge to her owne vomyt and spuynge, and is in a worse case then ever she was," Ridley, *A Pituous Lamentation of the miserable estate of the church.* . . . ([STC

a "spiritual" view of the sacrament excludes a "wicked" act of cannibalism, while Christ is so profoundly present in the Eucharist that he
can declare: "He walked here in very flesh, and gave that very flesh to
us to eat for our salvation. . . . We have found out . . . that we sin not in
worshipping it, but that we sin in not worshipping."[123] To understand
why Ridley is attempting to use Augustine as an ally, even though he
was aware that there are strands in the Bishop of Hippo's thought that
cannot be readily reconciled to his own, one must recollect Ryrie's insight into the crisis of historical legitimacy that plagued English Protestantism in its early decades. Ridley must claim Catholic figures of the
past as advocates of Protestant concepts, lest his movement be discounted as a sixteenth-century novelty.[124]

Ridley labors to employ the *Expositions of the Psalms* for the advancement of a Protestant view of the Eucharist in his *Brief Declaration*, yet some tensions between his and Augustine's divergent uses of
the term "figurative" remain in this work. Ridley opens his argument
by first stating that Augustine must hold a "figurative" view of the institution of the Eucharist, given his comments on John 6: "This lesson
of S. Augustine . . . teacheth us to understande that place in John figuratively. Even so surely the same lesson with the example of S. Au-
gustines exposiciones thereof, teacheth us not only by the same, to
understande Christes wordes in the institucion of the Sacrament, bothe
of his body and of his blood, figuratyvely, but also the very true
meanyng and understanding of the same."[125] Ridley's next step is to
link his and Augustine's use of "spiritual" with their views of the Eucharist itself. Perhaps recalling his earlier broadsides with Vavasour,
the next portion of his argument commences with an ungainly sentence
that occupies some thirteen full lines in the collected edition of his writings:

21052] London: Willyam Powell, dwelling in Fletestrete, at the signe of
the George, nere to Sainct Dunstons Church, 1566) [hereafter: Ridley, *Pituous Lamentation*], sigs A.4, *verso*-A.5, *recto*, and *Works*, p. 51. Cf. Proverbs 26:11 and 2 Peter 2:22.
123 St. Augustine, *Expositions of the Psalms*, p. 486.
124 Ryrie, "Problems of Legitimacy in English Protestantism," pp. 78–85.
125 Ridley, *Brief Declaracion*, sig. C.3, *verso*, and Ridley, *Works*, p. 22.

For if to commaunde to eate the fleshe of the sonne of man, and to drinke his blood semeth to commaunde an inconvenience and an ungodlynesse, and is even so indeed, if it be understanded as the wordes doo stande in their propre significacion; and therefore must be understanden figuratyvley and spiritually, as S. Augustine dothe godly and learnedly interprete them; than surely Christ commaunding in his last supper to eate his body, and to drinke his blood, semeth to commaunde in sounde of wordes, as great and even the same inconvenience and ungodlinesse, as did his wordes in the 6 chap. of S. John; and therefore must even by the same reason, be lykewise understanden and expounded figuratively and spiritually, as S. Augustine did the other.[126]

Ridley continues: "Whereunto that exposicion of S. Augustine may seme to be the more mete, for that Christ in his supper, to the commaundement of eating and drinking of his body and blood addeth, Do this in remembrance of me, which words surely were the keye, that opened and revealed the spirituall and godly exposicion unto S. Augustine."[127] Yet neither in *De Doctrina Christiana* nor his *Expositions of the Psalms* does Augustine indicate that the institution of the Eucharist or the sacrament itself is "figurative" in the sense that worship of it is idolatrous. As frequently with his use of scripture, Ridley has interpolated his own sense of the term "spirituall" into St. Augustine's explications of the sacrament of the altar.

Close reading of Ridley and Augustine indicates that they employ the same term "figurative" in rather different senses. Their divergent interpretations of John 6 result from distinctly different starting points for biblical exegesis. Ridley clearly commends Augustine's exegetical pedagogy: "S. Augustine, in his boke *De doctrina christiana*, geveth diverse learned lessons, very necessarie to be knownen of the studentes in Goddes worde."[128] Yet in his *Brief Declaration*, Ridley resolves to consider

126 Ridley, *Brief Declaracion*, sig. C.3, *verso-recto*, and *Works*, p. 21.
127 Ridley, *Brief Declaracion*, sig. C.3, *recto*, and *Works*, p.21.
128 Ridley, *Brief Declaracion*, sig. C.2, *recto*, and *Works*, p. 21.

the matter of Christ's real presence in the Eucharist with respect to "the most playne places" of scripture alone.[129] Augustine, however, asserts ecclesial authority as a guiding principle for biblical interpretation: "you should refer it to the rule of faith, which you have received from the plainer passages of scripture *and from the authority of the Church.*"[130] For the Bishop of Hippo, the interpretation of scripture is rooted firmly in the teachings of the Church: "If people's minds are already in thrall to some erroneous opinion, whatever scripture may assert that differs from it will be reckoned by them to be said in a figurative way. The only thing, though, it ever asserts is Catholic faith, with reference to things in the past and in the future and in the present."[131]

The Typology of the Testaments

Throughout the *Brief Declaration of the Lord's Supper* and elsewhere, Ridley approaches scripture as an historical source text to be applied to contemporary church practice. Ecclesial controversy undoubtedly shaped Ridley's historical concerns, but his polemical setting does not by itself explain why Ridley's scriptural arguments are almost never drawn primarily from any spiritual reflection on, or extended analysis of, ritual themes in Old Testament narratives. Traditionally, scriptural exegesis was rooted in the idea of typology, where New Testament concepts were explicated by drawing out cultic allusions to the Old Testament, particularly with respect to the Christian sacraments.[132] Thus Thomas Aquinas refers to Melchizedek and the Aaronic high priest as "types" or figures of Christ when discussing the Passion.[133]

---

129 Ridley, *Brief Declaracion*, sig. A.6, *recto*, and *Works*, p. 17.
130 St. Augustine, *De Doctrina Christiana*, p. 169 (emphasis added).
131 St. Augustine, *De Doctrina Christiana*, p. 176.
132 We will consider these aspects of patristic and medieval scriptural commentary more fully in Chapters IV and V below.
133 Matthew Levering, *Christ's Fulfillment of Torah and Temple: Salvation According to Thomas Aquinas* (Notre Dame: University Press, 2002) [hereafter: Levering, *Salvation According to Aquinas*], pp. 66–79. As Thomas' *Catena Aurea* makes plain, this method was a staple of patristic exegesis. See, e.g., Thomas Aquinas, *Catena Aurea in Quatuor Evangelia*, vol. 1,

He also understands Moses to have prefigured Christ. In an explication of the two testaments found in the *Summa*, for example, Thomas asserts that Christ's blood was exhibited to humanity in two chief ways: "First of all in figure, and this belongs to the Old Testament; consequently the Apostle (Hebrews 9:16) concludes: *Whereupon neither was the first indeed dedicated without blood*, which is evident from this, that as related in Exodus 24:7–8, when every commandment of the law *had been read* by Moses, *he sprinkled all the people* saying: *This is the blood of the testament which the Lord hath enjoined unto you*."[134] Thomas' references to Exodus 24 and the blood covenant between the people of Israel and the Lord are natural in this context, given that the author of Hebrews, generally presumed to be St. Paul in Thomas' day, makes this connection.[135] Thomas followed this same line of explication in many places where he labors to illuminate Jesus' dual messianic role, as both priest and victim.[136] Similarly, in the *Imitatio Christi*, Thomas à Kempis presented a typological model for preparing to receive the Eucharist, likening the process of spiritual examination to the deeds of Noah, David, and Solomon's building of the Temple in Jerusalem.[137] John Fisher, commenting on the High Priests and rites of the Temple, declared Christ "entered into the *sancta sanctorum*, that is to say, into heaven, where he showed before his Father's throne the most precious blood, the blood he shed for all sinners."[138]

Ridley's writings are simply not characterized by typological interpenetration between the Old and New Testaments. Rather, when he

Expositio in Mattheum et Marcum (Rome: Marietti Editori Ltd., 1953).

134 St. Thomas Aquinas, *Summa Theologica*, trans. and eds. the Fathers of the English Dominican Province, vol 2. (New York: Benziger Brothers, Inc., 1947) Pt. III, Q. 78, Art. 3, Reply to Objection 3, p. 2475. Cf. *Great Bible*, Book II., fol. 13, *recto* [Matt 26:28]: "For this is my bloud (which is of the new testament) that is shed for many, for the remyssyon of synnes."

135 See, e.g., Hebrews 9.

136 See Levering, *Salvation According to Aquinas*.

137 Thomas à Kempis, *The Imitation of Christ in Four Books*, ed. Clare L. Fitzpatrick (New York: Catholic Book Publishing Co., 1977), pp. 239–40.

138 St. John Fisher, *Exposition of the Seven Penitential Psalms*, ed. Anne Barbeau Gardiner (San Francisco: Ignatius Press, 1998), p. 223. Cf. Hebrews 9.

139 A thorough comparative analysis of the thought of Zwingli and his intel-

concentrates his attention on the Gospels and Apostolic Letters, he takes them as the plain and full record of the thoughts and words of Jesus and his earliest disciples. In each case, Ridley attempts to reconstruct the historical setting of Jesus' statements, in order to extend that context to any contemporary use of such language in devotional and ritual practice. As with Erasmus, Ridley either remains silent about or eschews Old Testament analogues and "types" in explicating the historical setting of Jesus' words.

Ridley's reluctance to apply Old Testament typology to New Testament themes, especially in connection with the Eucharist, is all the more remarkable for his unacknowledged theological debt to early Swiss Protestantism, where such exegetical themes are not uncommon.[139] A casual survey of Ridley's extant writings reveals his major theological emphases to be congruent with many ideas found in the work of John Calvin and Heinrich Bullinger. Like these continental reformers, Ridley followed Huldrych Zwingli in declaring that the consecrated bread and wine of the Eucharist were symbols, on the grounds that Christ's body, after the Ascension, was physically present only in heaven.[140] Ridley also wished to assert that he did not conceive of the Eucharist as a "bare signe or a figure,"[141] and this aim is likewise harmonious with the aims of Calvin and Bullinger.[142] Moreover, Ridley worked closely with Peter

lectual heirs and Ridley lies beyond the scope of this study. The remarks that follow will therefore, because of their brevity, be more suggestive than probative, since Ridley does not explicitly indicate enthusiasm for the work of Calvin, Bullinger, Bucer, or Peter Martyr in his extant writings.

140 See, e.g., Huldrych Zwingli, *Commentary on True and False Religion*, in *The Protestant Reformation*, ed. Hans J. Hillerbrand (New York: Harper & Row, 1968) [hereafter: Zwingli, *Commentary*], pp. 108–21, esp. pp. 108–16. By contrast, Martin Bucer did not embrace Ridley, Calvin, and Bullinger's notion of a local presence of Christ's body in heaven alone. See Chapter I, note 52 above.

141 Ridley, *Brief Declaracion*, sig. A.7, *recto*, and *Works*, p. 10.

142 B. A. Gerrish, *Grace and Gratitude: The Eucharistic Theology of John Calvin* (Minneapolis: Fortress Press, 1993) [hereafter: Gerrish, *Grace and Gratitude*], pp. 142–45. On Calvin and Bullinger and the dissemination of their ideas in Edwardine England, see *Two Epystles, one of Henry Bullinger, with the consent of all the learned men of the Churche of Tigury, an*

Martyr Vermigli, friend and ally to Bullinger and Calvin, during the reign of Edward VI.[143] The similarities between the theological tenets of Ridley and Martyr are striking: both men advanced a hypostatic understanding of the Eucharist, asserting that it is Christ's divinity rather than his human nature that is present in the consecrated elements. Both men laid heavy stress on the Eucharist as an anamnetic ritual,[144] which primarily focuses the believer's mind on the Crucifixion and Passion of Christ, while both also promoted the ideas of Ratramnus by name in their writings. They also both relied on the spurious *Opus Imperfectum in Matthaeum* to allege that Chrysostom asserted a symbolic view of the Eucharist.[145]

other of John Calvyne, chefe Precher of the church of Geneve ([STC 4080] London: Robert Stoughton, 1548).

143 For Martyr's correspondence and contacts with Calvin and Bullinger, see Marvin W. Anderson, "Peter Martyr, Reformed Theologian (1542–1562): His Letters to Heinrich Bullinger and John Calvin," *Sixteenth Century Journal* 4 (1973): pp. 41–64. For Martyr's activities in Edwardine England and his association with Ridley and Cranmer, see Diarmaid MacCulloch, *Thomas Cranmer: A Life* (New Haven: Yale University Press, 1996) [hereafter: MacCulloch, *Cranmer*], pp. 382–83. For an overview of Martyr's sacramental thought, see Joseph C. McLelland, *The Visible Words of God: An Exposition of the Sacramental Theology of Peter Martyr Vermigli* (London: Oliver and Boyd, 1957). For a brief overview of Martyr's life and ideas, see Mark Taplin, "Vermigli, Pietro Martire [Peter Martyr] (1499–1562)," *Oxford Dictionary of National Biography,* Oxford University Press, 2004 [http://www.oxforddnb.com/view/article/28225, accessed 23 July 2007].

144 Even here, however, Erasmus' didactic exegetical method may have predisposed Ridley towards an eventual embrace of an anamnetic explanation of the Eucharist. The key passages in John 6 on the eating of Christ's flesh and blood are rendered by Erasmus as: "By my flesh and my blood I mean my teaching, if you take it eagerly through belief and pass it into the bowels of your mind." See Erasmus, *Paraphrase on John*, p. 88 and accompanying editorial notes.

145 On their shared idea of a hypostatical eucharistic theory, see Pietro Martire Vermigli, *A discourse or traictise of Petur Martyr Vermilla Flore[n]tine, the publyque reader of diuinitee in the Universitee of Oxford wherein he openly declared his whole and determinate judgemente concernynge the sacrament of the Lordes supper in the sayde Universitee (*[STC 24665]

Yet despite such concord between Ridley and Martyr on both general and particular points of their theology, we find that there is a great difference between them on the idea of Old Testament "types" in application to Christ and the Eucharist. Martyr frankly declares that the "sacraments of the old Lawe . . . dyd conteyne a significacion of Christe too. Yea and if a man have respect to the outwarde lykenesse or semblaunce, the sayd old Sacramentes wente muche more nerer to the livelye signifying or fyguryng of Christe, then dooeth breade and wyne. For their brute beastes were kylled, and the bloud of the same washed forth, whereas in bread and wine dooeth no manier suche thing happen."[146] In the course of his *Judgemente concernynge the sacrament of the Lordes supper*, Martyr discusses both Melchizedek's offering of bread and wine and the Paschal Lamb as prefiguring the Eucharist.[147] Ridley, however, is much less inclined to see something "more nere to the liveley signifying of Christ" in the "olde Sacramentes." This theme is simply not a major part of his thought.

Not only does Ridley not treat often of Old Testament "signs" or "types" in his extant writings,[148] but he tends to reject the idea of Old Testament and New Testament parallels when presented with them. For

London: Robert Stoughton [i.e. Whitchurch], 1550) [hereafter: Martyr, *Judgemente concernynge the sacrament of the Lordes supper*], fol. lxxxi, xcv. Cf. Ridley, *Brief Declaracion*, sigs. B.2 *recto*-B.3 *verso*. On their anamnetic orientation to Christ's presence in the Eucharist, see Martyr, *Judgemente concernynge the sacrament of the Lordes supper*, fol. xxvi. Cf. Ridley, *Works*, p. 211. On their joint promotion of Ratramnus as a doctrinal authority, see Martyr, *Judgemente concernynge the sacrament of the Lordes supper*, fol. xiii. Cf. Foxe, *Actes and Monuments*, p. 1427 and Ridley, *Works*, p. 159. On their use of the *Opus Imperfectum in Matthaeum*, see Martyr, *Judgemente concernynge the sacrament of the Lordes supper*, fol. xxxiii; cf. Ridley, *Brief Declaracion*, sig. D.5, *recto*.

146 Martyr, *Judgemente concernynge the sacrament of the Lordes supper*, fol. viii, *verso*.

147 Martyr, *Judgemente concernynge the sacrament of the Lordes supper*, fols. xx, xxvi, xxxiii, xxxiiii.

148 In his *Brief Declaracion,* for example, Old Testament allusions to specific figures or rites in application to the Eucharist are almost non-existent.

149 Ridley, *Comfortable Conferences*, sig. E.i, *verso-recto*.

example, Ridley attempts to refute Stephen Gardiner's comparison of Catholic worship in the Mass with the Temple worship of the Old Testament. Whereas Gardiner notes that Christ and the Apostles were not schismatics, and that they did not forsake prayer, worship, and sacrifice in the Temple, Ridley denies the applicability of the comparison, declaring that Gardiner must instead prove that "Christ or his apostles dyd in the temple, communicate with the people, in any kynde of worshippyng which is forbidden by the lawe of God, or repugnant to the word of God."[149] Ridley then goes on to note the examples of Tobit fleeing the worship of golden calves as prescribed by Jeroboam, and decrying the fact that "the people went a whoringe with their hill aulters" and were rebuked by the Prophets "for theyr false worshipping of god after their owen mindes."[150]

Perhaps Ridley was simply more at home in the writings of the Prophets than with the Levitical code, but there is a tantalizing hint about the real source of his tendency to resist Old and New Testament parallels in his interpretation of the scriptures and the Fathers: explicating a passage from Chrysostom, Ridley insists that the author cannot be speaking "of the vesselles of the old lawe," because the writer refers to "the mystery of Christes bodye." He then introduces an interesting twist on the idea of Old Testament "types" in application to the Eucharist. He insists that, in the Old Testament, "Christ was not but in shadowes and figures, and not by the sacrament of his body revealed," and the Old Testament writers "doo use no suche maner of phrase" as "Christ's body." Ridley therefore believes that Chrysostom is speaking of the Eucharist plainly and simply. Ridley suggests that if Christ was only represented in those rites as a figure, then examples of them do not refer directly to the mystery of the Eucharist. Ridley's authority for the interpretation he advances is none other than "Erasmus which was a man that coulde understande the wordes and the sense of the wrytor" who "declareth playnely that this saying of this wrytour is non otherwise to be understanden."[151] Ridley even concedes that he is following Erasmus' reading

---

150 Ridley, *Comfortable Conferences*, sig. E.ii, *verso*.
151 Ridley, *Brief Declaracion*, sig. D.6, *verso*.
152 Ridley, *Brief Declaracion*, sig. D.6, *verso*.

of this passage from Chrysostom despite the fact that the Humanist scholar "woulde not be sene to speake against this errour of transubstanciacion."[152] In short, Ridley aims to conform to Erasmus' interpretation of this passage of Chrysostom, denying that it is to be taken as a typological description of the Eucharist as presented through the vessels of the Temple.

Here Ridley displayed a firm grasp of Erasmus' normative understanding of Old and New Testament typology. In general, Erasmus tended to denigrate Old Testament analogues to New Testament concepts as "enigmas" and "superstition" when he encountered a likely parallel: "The temple at Jerusalem in the past had its own veneration, it had its own priests, its rites and sacrificial victims. Our temple is much holier than that one. It does not hide its mysteries in shadows and figures. Instead of cherubim, pomegranates, bells, the ark, and similar enigmas, it displays to us solid and genuinely evangelical truth."[153] If this contrast were not enough, Erasmus goes on to declare of the Church: "It is beyond controversy that the mystery of evangelical godliness, that mystery which frees us once for all from every superstition is far and away the greatest thing in this temple that stands open throughout the whole world. It is not a table or an ark or a sacrificed animal that is displayed, but it is Christ himself who is displayed and preached."[154] Ridley took a similar line in outlining his reasons for the removal of altars from Edwardine churches: "the forme of an aultar was ordained for the Sacrifices of the Lawe. . . . But nowe bothe the lawe and the Sacrifices thereof doe cease: Wherefore the fourme of the aultare vsed in the Lawe, ought to cease wythall."[155]

---

153 Erasmus, *Paraphrase on First Timothy*, p. 22. See editor's note 13 on this passage.

154 Erasmus, *Paraphrase on First Timothy*, p. 23. These denigrations of the temple and its rites are wholly interpolative and are not found, even in part, in Paul's First Epistle to Timothy.

155 Foxe, *Actes and Mounments*, p. 1331, and Ridley, *Works*, p. 323. Cf. Ridley's remarks to the Marian Bishop of Lincoln: "As for the taking downe of the Alters, it was done upon just considerations, for that they seemed to come to nigh to the Jewes usage." Foxe, *Actes and Monuments*, p. 1765.

156 Ridley, *Brief Declaracion*, sig. C.3, *recto*, and Ridley, *Works*, p. 22.

History and Hermeneutics

As is the case with Erasmus, Ridley's historical focus is a dominant feature of his exegetical method. Historical concerns govern even his portrayal of Augustine's view of the Eucharist: "surely Christ commaunding in his last supper to eate his body, and to drinke his blood, semeth to commaunde in sounde of wordes, as great and even the same inconvenience and ungodlinesse, as did his wordes in the 6 chap. of S. John; and therefore must even by the same reason, be lykewise understanden and expounded figuratively and spiritually. . . ."[156] In other words, if Jesus' original statements concerning his flesh and blood were meant figuratively, and Augustine had this same understanding, then our use of this language is ever after to be considered only metaphorical, even in the contemporary celebration of the Eucharist itself.

Ridley's concerns with the historical and propositional facts related by a biblical passage are displayed most fully in his exposition of texts that touch upon the Eucharist: "Christes wordes are these: after the wordes said upon the cup: I saie unto you (saieth Christ), I wil not drinke hencefurthe of this fruite of the vyne tree, until I shall drinke that newe in my fathers kingdome. Here note, how Christ calleth playnlie his cuppe the frute of the vyne tree. But the frute of the vyne tree is very natural wyne. Wherfore the natural substaunce of the wyne dothe remayne still in the Sacrament of Christes blood."[157] Again, Ridley moves freely and immediately from the institution narratives, to Jesus' oath not to drink wine again until the heavenly banquet of the Eschaton, to the contemporary celebration of the Eucharist. His mode of reasoning, in keeping with his formal training in university disputation, is syllogistic: if a biblical passage employs the words "wine" or "bread," it is taken to be a definitive proposition for current theological debate.

Ridley's pattern of searching out the historical context of biblical passages in order to telescope that context into the present is applied not only to the words of Jesus, but to those of St. Paul as well. Reflecting

---

157 Ridley, *Brief Declaracion*, sig. A.6, *recto*, and *Works*, p. 17. The biblical reference is to Matthew 26:29.

158 Ridley, *Brief Declaracion*, sig. A.6, *verso*, and *Works*, pp. 16–17. The bi-

on several biblical references to the sacramental bread, Ridley observes: "S. Paul which setteth furth most fully in his wryting bothe the doctrine and the right use of the Lordes supper, and the sacramental eating and drinking of Christes body and blood, calleth it fyve times bread, bread, bread, bread, bread."[158] Such arguments form the heart of Ridley's *Brief Declaration*: biblical references to any of the consecrated elements or the Eucharist itself as "bread" or "wine" are normative and governing for all contemporary understanding of the sacrament. Ridley states that his aim is to determine the "material substance" of the Eucharist by weighing the most plain portions of scripture: "I intende to search out and set furth by the Scriptures . . . whether the true sense and meaning of Christes wordes in the institucion of his holy supper do requyre any Transubstanciacion . . . or that the very substaunce of bread and wyne do remayne still in the Lordes supper and be the material substaunce of the holy Sacrament of Christ our saveours blessed body and blood."[159]

For anyone who would explicate the portions of scripture that relate to the Eucharist, a dilemma exists between the terms "bread" and "flesh," "wine" and "blood." All such biblical passages are bound by Christ's institution of the rite, but in the Gospels, Jesus does not indicate just how bread is his flesh or wine is his blood; he merely states that it is so. Any exegetical effort to understand Jesus here must contain, implicitly or explicitly, some method for resolving the linguistic tension between "flesh" and "bread," "blood" and "wine." Ridley's solution to the terminological paradox is to assert that "bread" and "wine" are primary and literal, and that "flesh" and "blood" are secondary or metaphorical terms in such passages. Ridley's exegetical method is aimed therefore to contravene the work of medieval scriptural commentators, who viewed "bread" and "wine" as secondary and metaphorical, and "flesh" and "blood" as primary and literal terms in the institution narratives.

blical references are to 1 Corinthians 10:16, 17 and 11:23, 26.
159 Ridley, *Brief Declaracion*, sig. C.5, *verso*, and *Works*, p. 24. Here as elsewhere, Ridley's repeated references to the "material substaunce" of the Eucharist strongly suggest that he understands the traditional sacramental language of "substance" to indicate physical matter.
160 "Yf, after the truthe shalbe truly tryed out, it shalbe founde, that the subs-

To demonstrate that his views are consonant with those of patristic authors, Ridley points primarily to Augustine's use of "figurative" in application to the Eucharistic passages in John. However, Ridley's use of "figurative" is tightly constrained: in his thought, the term always indicates that Christ is substantially absent from the consecrated eucharistic elements. The result of Ridley's tightly delineated use of "figurative" is that he tends to represent the linguistic tension in the institution narratives as a sheer dilemma: he specifically asks his readers to choose between august eucharistic adoration, or a commemoration wherein Jesus' divinity is present, but his flesh and blood are absent.[160] That such a divide could be more apparent than real is, simply, as Diarmaid MacCulloch says of Cranmer, "not part of his mental furniture."[161]

In his *Brief Declaration of the Lord's Supper*, Ridley expresses no doubts concerning his ability to reconstruct the historical facts and circumstances of the scriptural passages he ponders. He is certain that all biblical references to the Eucharist that employ the terms "bread" and "wine" speak directly to his immediate concern with "the material substaunce of the holy Sacrament." He therefore never doubts that the phrase "breaking bread" in the Acts of the Apostles is anything more than a direct indication of the Apostles' understanding of the physical content of the consecrated elements: "How often, in the Actes of the apostles, is the Lordes supper signified by breaking of bread? They did persevere (sayeth S. Luke), in the Apostles doctrine, communion, and breaking of bread. And they brake bread in every house. And

taunce of bread is the naturall substaunce of the Sacrament . . . than also the natural substaunce of Christes humane nature, which he toke of the virgine Mary is in heavenm where it reigneth now in glorie, and noe here inclosed under the forme of bread, than that godly honour, which is only due unto God the creatour, may not be done unto the creature without idolatrie and sacrilege, is not to be done unto the holy Sacrament," Ridley, *Brief Declaracion*, sig. B.1, *recto*, and *Works*, p. 12.
161 MacCulloch, *Cranmer*, p. 491. Much of what MacCulloch says about Gardiner more fully allowing for the historical and doctrinal context of patristic passages than Cranmer (pp. 490–92) could be equally said of Bonner against Ridley.
162 Ridley, *Brief Declaracion*, sig. A.6, *verso*, and *Works*, p. 16. See Acts 2:42,

again, in an other place, when they were come together to break bread, &c."[162]

Ridley's two-fold exegetical method then is "telescopic" in nature. He begins by projecting his philological skills back into history, in an effort to see past the chaotic foreground of present controversy. So that images revealed by the telescope of interpretation may be applied to the present, it is then retracted, often collapsing linguistic and liturgical categories such that they are often conflated. The image that Ridley "discovers" so completely coincides with his own view of the subject that, in the end, it is difficult to know whether he has properly employed a spy glass, or a looking glass. This overview of Ridley's exegetical method helps to account for the divergent realities that he and the Evangelists face when speaking of "scripture," and the dissimilarities between his and Augustine's use of the term "spiritual." Ridley's aim would require a much surer foundation than an attempted reconstruction of originating events sketchily recorded in the New Testament.[163]

Exegesis and the Eschaton

Exegetically then, Ridley's work is characterized by unfettered leaps from the present to the ancient past, and then back again to the present. Modern interpreters might be tempted to view such exegetical maneuvers as facile. However, Ridley's sense that the contexts of biblical texts were readily accessible from his historical standpoint is partially rooted in a far-reaching and little studied key aspect of his thought. In his later prison tracts, in which Ridley reads ancient biblical texts with such a heightened sense of immediacy, he is convinced that the Eschaton is at hand.[164] This belief made an indelible

46; and 20:7.

163 See, e.g., Cummings, *Literary Culture of the Reformation*, p. 110.

164 This apocalyptic strain in Ridley's exegetical and polemical writings relates to the fourth model Ryrie identifies by early English Protestants to legitimate their interpretations of history and ecclesiology. See Ryrie, "Problems of Legitimacy in English Protestantism." It is precisely here that Ridley betrays a sense of deep indebtedness to the Old Testament. Whereas he generally eschews the application of Old Testament types in explicating the

impression upon his view of the scriptures: their content could especially be applied to the present, because, despite their having been written well in the past, their culmination and fulfillment were upon him and his age.

Ridley appears to have grasped more firmly than some of his colleagues that the Protestant denunciation of the Pope as Antichrist was, perforce, an eschatological claim. While Ridley's prison writings contain regular apocalyptic allusions, this side of his personality is candidly revealed in his *Pituous Lamentation of the Miserable Estate of the Churche of Christ in Englande*, the very title of which announces that the work is a jeremiad. In the opening pages of this tract, Ridley repeatedly refers to the Pope as "Antechryst" and "the beast of Babylon,"[165] comparing the condition of the Church under Protestant leadership with Edward VI to the Catholic restoration then well underway with Queen Mary. Ridley is clearly and understandably embittered by all that is transpiring with respect to religion within the realm. Concerning the resurrection of eucharistic adoration, Ridley rails, "Of late all that were endued with the light and grace of understanding of goddes holye mysteries, did blesse god, which had broughte them out of that horible blyndenesse and ignoraunce, whereby in times paste beinge seduced by Satans subtletyes, they beleved that the sacrament was not the sacrament, but the thyng whereof it is a sacramente; that the creature was the creatour; and that the thynge whichs hathe neyther lyfe nor sense (alas, suche was the horryble blyndnes) was the Lorde him selfe; whiche made the eye to see, and hath gyven al senses and understandynge unto man. But nowe alas, Englande is returned agayn lyke a dogge to her owne vomyt and spuynge, and is in a worse case then ever she was."[166] Throughout the piece, Ridley's wrath falls upon the Marian repeal of the Edwardine religious statutes,

person and work of Christ in the New Testament, his prison works reveal that he is quite conversant with the writings of Old Testament prophets.

165 See, e.g., Ridley, *Pituous Lamentation*, sigs. A.3, *verso*, A.3, *recto*, and A.7, *verso*. Cf. Ridley, *Works*, pp. 49, 50, 53.

166 Ridley, *Pituous Lamentation*, sigs. A.4, *verso*-A.5, *recto. Cf.* Ridley, *Works*, p. 50–51. Cf. Proverbs 26:11 and 2 Peter 2:22.

167 Ridley, *Pituous Lamentation*, sigs. A.5, *recto*-A.7, *verso*. Cf. Ridley, *Works*,

and the repression of the *Book of Common Prayer* and the *Catechism* of 1552.[167]

In the face of these reversals of fortune for the Protestant establishment in England, Ridley advises the godly to flee the realm. Citing the prophecies of Daniel and John concerning the last days, Ridley declares that the righteous in England can only expect to meet a violent end: "Therefore if thou O man of God, doe purpose to abide in this realme, prepare and arme thy self to die, for bothe by antechistes accustomable lawes, and these prophecies, ther is no appearance or likely hode of any other thinge, excepte thou wylte deny thy master Christ, which is the losse at the laste both of body and soule unto everlasting death."[168] Not only does Ridley intimate that the last days are now at hand by the use of biblical prophecies, he explicitly states that he is living in the last age: "The world without doubt (this I do believe, and therefore I saye) draweth to an end."[169] Ridley was so earnest in Protestant fervor that the undoing of his labors in England signaled to him that the end of the world was at hand. Following the typology of the Book of Revelation, Ridley viewed the increased influence of "Antechryst" as a sure harbinger of the last judgment.

The greater portion of Ridley's *Pituous Lamentation* is a series of apocalyptic scriptures applied to his own moment in history. The mark of the righteous (Ezekiel 9:4ff) refers to those who have been stout in promoting the Gospel and resisting popery;[170] those who have sworn allegiance to the bishop of Rome are thereby marked by the sign of the beast (Revelation 13:16ff);[171] and the "women with child or who give

pp. 49–52.

168 Ridley, *Pituous Lamentation*, sig. C.1, *verso-recto*, A.5, *recto*. Cf. Ridley, *Works*, p. 62. Ridley's coupling of violence to "antechristes accustomable lawes" is a veiled reference to the reinstatement of the medieval heresy laws under which he, Cranmer, Latimer, and the other Edwardine reformers were to eventually be tried and executed.

169 Ridley, *Pituous Lamentation*, sig. D.9, *recto*-E.1, *verso*. Cf. Ridley, *Works*, p. 75.

170 Ridley, *Pituous Lamentation*, sig. D.2, *verso-recto*. Cf. Ridley, *Works*, p. 69–70.

171 Ridley, *Pituous Lamentation*, sig. D.2, *verso*. Cf. Ridley, *Works*, pp. 53–55, 69–70.

172 Ridley, *Pituous Lamentation*, sigs. C.3–C.4; D.5. Cf. Ridley, *Works*, p. 72–

suck," mentioned in Matthew 24:19, are actually English Protestants who are infirm, aged, or already prisoners of the Marian Regime.[172] Above and beyond all the other "parallels" that Ridley detected between his own time and that described in scripture as the final age, the decisive matter for him had to do with the reinstitution of Catholic worship in England: "For truly before god, I thinck that the abbomination that Daniel prophecied of so long before, is now set up in the holy place. For al antichrists doctrine, lawes, rytes, and religion, contrary to Christe and to the true servynge and worshypping of god, I understande to be that abbomination."[173]

As Ridley points out, the "abomination in the temple" is mentioned in the Book of Daniel, but only in rather obscure terms: "Forces . . . shall appear and profane the temple and fortress. . . . And from the time that the continual burnt offering is taken away, and the abomination that makes desolate is set up, there shall be a thousand two hundred and ninety days. Blessed is he who waits and comes to the thousand three hundred and thirty-five days. But go your way till the end; and you shall rest, and shall stand in your allotted place at the end of the days."[174] In the twenty-fourth chapter of Matthew's Gospel, Jesus himself refers to these prophetic passages as sure indicators that the Eschaton is at hand: "So when you see the desolating sacrilege spoken of by the prophet Daniel, standing in the holy place (let the reader understand), then let those who are in Judea flee to the mountains."[175] Here, as so often in Ridley's thought, the central issue was the Eucharist. He not only refers to these passages himself, but strongly urges his readers to review them at length.[176] For Ridley, the restoration of eucharistic adoration could be nothing other than idolatry. To his mind, the Marian religious reforms provided substantial proof that the Pope was indeed Antichrist, and that the beast of Babylon was now fortifying his kingdom upon the earth:

79.
173 Ridley, *Pituous Lamentation*, sig. C.2, *recto*. Cf. Ridley, *Works*, p. 63.
174 Daniel 11:31, 12:11–13, RSV.
175 Matthew 24:15ff, RSV.
176 Ridley, *Pituous Lamentation*, sig. B.4, *recto*. Cf. Ridley, *Works*, pp. 63 and 64.
177 Ridley, *Pituous Lamentation*, sig. A.5, *recto*. Cf. Ridley, *Works*, p. 52.

"But nowe, alas . . . is set uppe a new blasphemous kind of sacrifice, to satisfye and paie the pryce of synnes, bothe of the deade and of the quicke, to the great and intolerable contumely of Christ our saviour his death and passion."[177]

It is intriguing that Ridley did not work out the implications of his insights about the identity of Antichrist with his remarks elsewhere that eucharistic adoration is part of the doctrinal legacy of Innocent III and the "usurpacion" of the bishop of Rome dating from the pontificates of Gregory and Boniface.[178] Since Gregory I became Pope in 590, such a reckoning means that Antichrist had already ruled the Church for nearly a millennium by Ridley's day, while the "idolatry" of formal or ceremonial eucharistic adoration had been a staple of the church for well over three full centuries, since the pontificate of Innocent III. Themes of eucharistic adoration dating to the fourth century in the writings of Ambrose and Augustine were clearly known to Ridley. That he should view the *restoration* of Roman ritual practice as "a *new* blasphemous kind of sacrifice," when even he himself acknowledged the long history behind such devotions, is fascinating.

Nevertheless, the effect of Ridley's apocalypticism on his understanding of the scriptures cannot be overemphasized. Under such an apprehension, the books of the Bible appear not so much as texts from the ancient past, but as contemporary and relevant commentary. The age of the writings themselves is of little consequence in such a view, because they are seemingly written about things coming to pass in the present age. The congruence that Ridley sees between biblical history and his own time is readily apparent in his remarks on the city of Rome as the whore of Babylon: "Nowe what citie is there in al the whole world that when John wrote, ruled over the the kynges of the earthe? Or what Citie can be redde of in any tyme, that of the citie it selfe, challenged the empire

178 E.g.: "Gelasius . . . was a bishop of Rome, but one of that sea, before the wicked usurpacion and tyrannye thereof spredde and burst abrode in to all the worlde. For this man was before Bonifacious, yea and Gregorie the furst, in whose dayes bothe corruption of doctrine and tirannical usurpacion did chiefly growe, and hade the upper hande," Ridley, *Brief Declaration*, sig. E.6, *recto*. Cf. Ridley *Works*, pp. 44.

179 Ridley, *Pituous Lamentation*, sig. A.7. Cf. Ridley, *Works*, p. 53, and Rev-

over the kings of the earth, but onely the citie of Rome, and that sence the usurpation of that see hath growen to her full strengthe?"[179] Ridley assumes that the same city that dominated world affairs in St. John's age will be the Babylon of the end times. Such observations indicate that even his apocalypticism is characterized by a deep sense of the historicity of the scriptures.

Ridley, Erasmus, and the *Scopus* of the New Covenant

The characteristic features of Erasmus' exegetical method include a consistent historical approach to understanding the text, and a focus on Christ as the "prefixed sign" or "*scopus*" of biblical study.[180] This ocular metaphor governs Erasmus' own process of turning immediately from biblical history to contemporary concerns.[181] In the *Enchiridion*, he prescribes this same method for his readers, urging that in their current struggles, Christ is to be "set before you as the only *scopus* of your whole life and direct all your efforts, all your activities, all your leisure, all your business in his direction."[182] However, Erasmus also relies on heavy interpolation in order to direct the reader's historical attention away from obvious Old Testament concepts and typology. Erasmus thereby appropriates the words of Paul or Christ for purposes far removed from that of the biblical author's original narrative context, so that Erasmus can raise an issue he believes to be of contemporary concern.

Ridley's exegetical method resembles that of Erasmus not simply in fixed attentiveness to Christ, but also in the same tendency to abstract those very precious words of Jesus recounted in the Gospels from their

elation 18:9: "And the kings of the earth, who committed fornication and were wanton with her, will weep and wail over her, and lament for her, when they shall see the smoke of her burning," RSV.
180 See above, pp. 86–87.
181 See the lucid discussion of this theme and its development in Erasmus' thought as recounted by Boyle, *Erasmus on Language and Method*, pp. 72–81. Cf. the observations of Thompson, *The Latinity of Erasmus*, pp. 117, 119.
182 Erasmus, as quoted by Boyle, *Erasmus on Language and Method*, p. 75.
183 24:1–8. Cf. Matthew 26:26–29; Mark 14:22–25; and Luke 22:19–20.

narrative setting, or from inter-textual explications rooted in Old Testament themes. While the Synoptic gospels present Christ's institution of the Eucharist in clear allusions to the blood covenant recounted in Exodus,[183] neither Erasmus in the *Paraphrase on Hebrews* nor Ridley in the *Brief Declaration of the Lordes Supper*, make a single mention of this Old Testament context. Ridley's stated aim in his tract is to discover the true meaning and intent behind Jesus' words of eucharistic institution.[184] His reluctance to explore the Old Testament scriptural references relevant to the Last Supper strongly suggests that he is following Erasmus' method of exegesis, abstracting the sayings of Jesus found in the Gospels from applicable Old Testament "types" or themes.

Ridley also shared with Erasmus an instinctual aversion to the term "covenant." For all of his assaults on linguistic corruptions in the source texts of the scriptures, there was at least one such neologism that did not much trouble Erasmus: the Latin rendering of the Greek word διαθήκη as "testamentum." The Latin legal concept of a last will and testament was a poor substitute for διαθήκη, so frequently encountered in Erasmus' Greek manuscripts of the New Testament. The term actually indicates a pact or covenant between two or more parties. Nevertheless, Erasmus does not rectify this textual corruption in his *Paraphrase of Hebrews*, even with the full knowledge that St. Jerome had pointed out this conceptual error several centuries beforehand.[185] Similarly, Ridley preferred the word "testament," even in reciting biblical passages about the Passion and Last Supper of Christ: "'This cup is the New Testament in my blood; this do as often as ye shall drink it in the remembrance of me.'"[186] Here Ridley emulated the example of Erasmus in distancing

---

184 See Ridley's introduction to this treatise, in *Brief Declaracion*, sigs. A.2–A.6, and *Works*, pp. 5–10.

185 See Erasmus, *Paraphrase on Hebrews*, p. 235, where he substitutes "ark of the testament" for "ark of the covenant," even with full knowledge of Jerome's express prohibition against such an interpretation in this context (see editor's note 8).

186 Ridley, *Works*, p. 19. Ridley does not have in mind here the general concept of covenant, but the New Testament scriptures themselves: "If Christes wordes which are spoken upon the cuppe . . . be of the same might and power, bothe in working and signifieng, than must this worde (is) when

Jesus from the religion of Israel, since the original Hebrew concept of a blood covenant is the foundation of Jesus' own understanding of his Passion, not the legal concept of a will or final "testament."[187]

The result of Ridley's silence about Old Testament themes and rites in connection with Christ's institution of the Eucharist is a biblical commentary that treats the Old Testament or Covenant as something foreign

Christ sayeth: This cuppe is the newe testament, etc., turne the substaunce of the cuppe into the substaunce of the newe testament," Ridley, *Brief Declaracion*, sig. C.1, *verso*. With Ridley, placing a reference to the New Testament in the mouth of Christ at the Last Supper precludes any discussion of the Old Covenant, or Law, ratified on Sinai in a blood ritual, as recounted in Exodus 24:3–8.

187 See Exodus 26:8: "And Moses took the blood and threw it upon the people, and said, 'Behold the blood of the covenant which the Lord has made with you in accordance with all these words.'" Despite the determination of Diarmaid MacCulloch that Cranmer's likening the institution to an actual last will and testament is a "remarkable analogy," it appears that the Archbishop merely carried the neoteristic "testamentum" to its logical end (see *Cranmer*, pp. 405–06). MacCulloch does not seem to be aware that this stratagem was employed to preclude recourse to Old Testament blood rite allusions in discussing the intent of Christ in establishing the sacrament, as well as the manner of His presence within it. What truly is "remarkable" is that Thomas Aquinas, without benefit of a Greek manuscript or the erudition of Erasmus refers "testamentum" to its authentic meaning in his own reflections of the institution narrative: "Christ's blood was exhibited to men in two ways. First of all in figure, and this belongs to the Old Testament; consequently the Apostle concludes (Hebrews 9:16): 'Whereupon neither was the first indeed dedicated without blood,' which is evident from this, that as related in Exodus 24:7–8, 'when every,' commandment of the law 'had been read' by Moses, 'he sprinkled all the people' saying: 'This is the blood of the testament which the Lord hath enjoined upon you.'" *Summa*, III.78.3, Reply to Objection 3, p. 2415. Here Thomas arrives at a solid interpretation of the New Testament text because he does not shun, but rather embraces, the Old Testament scriptures in understanding the life and work of Jesus. Because he has not posited a divide between the Gospel and the religion of Israel, he does not confuse a blood covenant with a last will and testament, despite the limits of acculturation and linguistic precision in the thirteenth century.

to Christian sacramental theology. In this view, the New Testament or Covenant stands apart from its roots in the Old Covenant. For Ridley, a clear separation of the Old and New Covenants would have been necessary for him to avoid the traditional understanding of Christ's real presence in the Eucharist. By eliding the narrative background of the Sinai Covenant, Ridley does not have to wrestle—as did many of the Church Fathers—with the relationship between the New Covenant in Christ's blood and the Old Covenant blood rites and altar worship.

A generation prior to Ridley, Erasmus pioneered a method for explicating the Gospels and Apostolic Epistles that did not include positive recourse to the Old Testament scriptures, even when such comparisons might bear direct import for key New Testament pericopes. Erasmus sought to sever Old and New Testament intertextuality in exegesis for three primary reasons: he was firmly devoted to the neo-Platonic school of philosophy, which posited a gulf of separation between matter and the eternal; he had a predilection for deliberative rhetoric in his writing; and he wished to discredit aspects of late medieval ecclesiastical piety and practice which, for their formulaic nature, he often described as "theological Judaism." It is likely the latter element in Erasmus' thought that first won Ridley's admiration. Understanding how Ridley's interpretive principles came to bear so many resemblances to the *scopus* of Erasmus' exegetical endeavors, however, also requires a comprehension of biblical studies at Cambridge from the 1520s through the 1540s. For, despite close personal and intellectual affinities with such figures as Peter Martyr in the 1540s, Ridley was still prepared to follow Erasmus with respect to the idea of Old Testament "types" in exegesis. However much Ridley held in common theologically with Martyr, his allegiance to and intellectual formation from the mind of the "man that coulde understande the wordes and sense of the wrytor" was much longer and surer, stretching back to the 1520s and the patronage Nicholas Ridley enjoyed as an intellectual protégé of his uncle, Robert Ridley. The preeminence of Erasmus and Erasmian learning at Cambridge in the early sixteenth century decisively shaped the intellectual life of young Nicholas Ridley.

Chapter 3
Ridley on the Nature and Role of the Church

Erasmus' exegetical program was characterized by a deliberate separation of Old and New Testament religious themes, which resulted from several causes, including what John O'Malley outlines as Erasmus' predilection for deliberative oratory versus the demonstrative rhetoric typical of Italian Humanism.[1] Ridley displays no enthusiasm for Italian Humanism in his work, but rather follows Erasmus' model of biblical exegesis. For Ridley, the Erasmian method of starkly contrasting Old and New Testament religion seemed the surest way to advance the theological and liturgical reforms that he sought as a means to an authentic Christian society. Erasmus' approach to exegesis profoundly influenced not only Ridley's view of scripture, but his ecclesiology as well.

Ridley contrasted Old and New Testament rites and themes in a manner fully congruent with Erasmus' exegetical program. Ridley's cast of mind with respect to the relationship between the Old and New Testaments is clearly revealed in his efforts to illustrate the discrepancies between contemporary Catholic beliefs and what he felt to be genuine Christianity. While there is no record of Ridley ever meeting Erasmus in person, the former's contact with the thought and work of the Humanist scholar of Rotterdam was both early and substantial in

1   John W. O'Malley, "Grammar and Rhetoric in the Pietas of Erasmus," *The Journal of Medieval and Renaissance Studies* 18.1 (1988) [hereafter: O'Malley, "Grammar and Rhetoric"]: pp. 94–95. Cf. John W. O'Malley, *Praise and Blame in Renaissance Rome: Rhetoric, Doctrine and Reform in the Sacred Orators of the Papal Court, c. 1450–1521*, vol. 3 of *Duke Monographs in Medieval and Renaissance Studies* (Duke: University Press, 1979) [hereafter: O'Malley, *Praise and Blame*], pp. 39–49.

his intellectual formation, leaving a lasting impression on Ridley's ideas and attitudes towards both exegesis and ecclesiology.

Speech Made Flesh:
Erasmus' Conception of Christ as Sacred Rhetor

In light of Erasmus' idea of the "scopus" of authentic biblical scholarship and true theology, what was Erasmus' view of Christ? If the neo-Platonic analysis of his thought suggested thus far is sound, one would not expect Erasmus to locate Christ's chief redemptive qualities in any physical or "sensible" aspect of Jesus' being or salvific work. Nor would we expect Erasmus to describe Jesus primarily as a high priest of the Temple or Paschal victim, given Erasmus' repeated invective against the "carnal" Old Testament and its observances. Rather, the pronounced neo-Platonic dualism that runs through his thought should lead him to esteem most in Jesus some non-material quality—and this is indeed what a close consideration of Erasmus' portrayal of Jesus reveals. It is, in fact, according to Erasmus, Jesus' speech that ought to be the *scopus* of human devotion and reflection: "If our Father in Heaven finds His perfect reflection in His divine Son, so the words of His Son are the closest image of his divine personality."[2] To better understand why Erasmus singled out speech to be venerated among Jesus' various attributes, it is helpful to examine briefly the nature of both his anthropology and his soteriology.

The concept of speech is in fact the motive force that drove Erasmus' theological reflections even in the order of anthropology. He

---

2 Desiderius Erasmus, *The Handbook of the Militant Christian (Enchiridion Militis Christiani)*, in *The Essential Erasmus*, trans. and ed. John P. Dolan (New York: Meridian, 1993) [hereafter: Erasmus, *Enchiridion*], p. 67. A Hellenic notion of trance-like oracular inspiration is almost certainly at the back of Erasmus' conjectures on how Jesus is the speech or *sermo* of the Father. See, e.g. Socrates' references to being guided to right action and speech by his δαίμων, in Plato, *Euthyphro, Apology, and Crito*, trans. and ed. J. F. Church (New York: Macmillan Library of Classics, 1985). See also, Robert K. Gnuse, *The Authority of the Bible: Theories of Inspiration, Revelation, and the Canon of Scripture* (New York, Paulist Press: 1985), p. 17.

viewed this key human faculty as the main one separating man from the animals, while he described the great Scholastics and his contemporary critics as capable only of mooing like cows, barking like dogs, or grunting like pigs.[3] Speech takes pride of place in Erasmus' anthropology because it is a method for instruction. Erasmus recognized that it is mainly by speech that one man teaches another, and in the case of Christ, speech is the direct means by which God teaches man.[4] Moreover, in keeping with Erasmus' notion of a *philosophia Christi*, speech is the method employed by the classical philosophers and rhetoricians for training their students in the ancient academies. Erasmus' *sanctus Socrate* employed this method himself, if Plato's *Dialogues* are reliable as a guide. In fact, Jesus' role as oracle of the mind of the Father generally eclipses many incarnational themes in Erasmus' exegesis of scripture. For example, in the *Paraphrase on John*, Jesus' assertions on the necessity of eating his flesh and drinking his blood to have true life are elided with interpolations from classical pedagogy: "By my flesh and my blood I mean my teaching, if you take it eagerly through belief and pass it into the bowels of your mind."[5] In short, the object or *scopus* of his exegetical efforts appears to bear a striking resemblance to Erasmus himself, the man of texts: both Jesus and the sage of Rotterdam have their vocations as teachers of men through sacred

3   For a catalogue of such references drawn from Erasmus' *Dialogus de recta latini graecique sermonis pronunciatione*, see Margery O'Rourke Boyle, *Erasmus on Language and Method in Theology*, (Toronto: University of Toronto Press, 1977) [hereafter: Boyle, *Erasmus on Language and Method*], pp. 40, 42–47. One of Erasmus' earliest treatises, *De ratione studii*, includes the following assertion: "For things are only intelligible to us through vocal signs; he who is unversed in the signification of speech is blind also in the discernment of things; necessarily he hallucinates, he is delirious," *ibid.* p. 38.
4   See Manfred Hoffman, *Rhetoric and Theology: The Hermeneutic of Erasmus* (Toronto: University of Toronto Press, 1994) [hereafter: Hoffman, *Rhetoric and Theology*], esp. pp. 169–210.
5   See Desiderius Erasmus, *Paraphrase on John, trans.* and ed. Jane Phillips, The Collected Works of Erasmus 46 (Toronto: University of Toronto Press, 1991) [hereafter: Erasmus, *Paraphrase on John*], pp. 88 and accompanying editors' notes.

rhetoric.[6] Erasmus' portrayal of Jesus as a pedagogue carries both positive and negative potential, however. Just as this motif bars the door against the notion that the *scopus* of theology is to be considered a high priest or paschal victim according to the "carnal" Old Testament, it also opens up the possibility of representing Jesus as a holy sage or philosopher. Indeed, it is in this vein that Erasmus most commonly speaks of Jesus' teaching, or *philosophia Christi*.[7]

Along with the neo-Platonic dualism and preoccupation with speech that flows from Erasmus' *philosophia Christi*, there is a third component operative in his conception of Jesus as a sacred pedagogue. Such a portrayal of Jesus followed quite naturally from Erasmus' educational formation and interests prior to his New Testament scholarship. Although he had labored to become a consummate master of classical Greek and Latin in the years leading up to the production of his *Novum Instrumentum*, Erasmus had acquired very little knowledge of the languages and cultures of the ancient Near East. He was himself quite candid about his need to enlist the aid of others, notably John Oecolampadius, in investigating the meaning of Hebrew words and idioms in the course of his work.[8] Rather than sharpening his grasp of this original biblical lan-

6   O'Malley, *Grammar and Rhetoric*, p. 98: "The correspondence, between Erasmus' Christ and the style of Erasmus' own life and culture is consistent."

7   As noted above, Erasmus intends his doctrine of a *philosophia Christi* as a point of contact between classical rhetoric and philosophy and Christian faith: "The purpose of studying the basic disciplines, of studying philosophy, of studying eloquence, [is] to know Christ, to celebrate the glory of Christ." See Hoffman, *Rhetoric and Theology*, p. 26. Cf. the citation from Erasmus' correspondence on the adjoining page: "Christ is the author and originator of all branches of knowledge."

8   For Erasmus' confession of Oecolampadius' assistance and his own scant knowledge of Hebrew, see the editor's introduction and accompanying note 4 in *Annotations on Romans*, trans. and eds. John B. Payne, Albert Rabil Jr., Robert D. Sider, and Warren S. Smith Jr., The Collected Works of Erasmus 56 (Toronto: University of Toronto Press, 1991) [hereafter: *Annotations on Romans*], pp. i, xvii. On Erasmus' dictum that ignorance of syntax leads to chaos and delirium in the discernment of things, see Boyle, *Erasmus on Language and Method*, pp. 40, 42–47.

guage, Erasmus appears to have turned away from such an effort, since a significant portion of the few references to Hebrew terms that appeared in the first versions of his *Novum Instrumentum* and *Annotations* were simply abandoned in subsequent editions. This was no small matter according to Erasmus' own standards, because he persistently urged that any true theologian should be steeped in Hebrew as well as Latin and Greek, if he was to understand scripture aright.[9]

Prompted by Valla and Colet, Erasmus' signal contribution to the field of biblical studies was the insight that accurate textual translation could not take place apart from a measured consideration of the history, culture, and native languages that gave shape to the texts of the Bible. However, given the particulars of his own scholarly background, it was natural for Erasmus to seek the familiar avenue of classical languages and cultures in his approach to the authors of the New Testament scriptures and the figures described therein. In the case of Jesus and the original Apostles, however, Erasmus' formidable knowledge of classical languages and cultures was often a hindrance to his efforts to understand the main figures of the Gospels. Jesus and his early disciples were not neo-Platonic philosophers, which dramatically limits Erasmus' aim "to know the philosophy of the gospel, which was given us by the Son of God himself."[10] Erasmus himself, despite his warning to others, confused the discernment of things through inaccurate syntax: he conflated the linguistic medium of the scriptures, Greek, with the culture and language of the people depicted in the narratives of the New Testament.[11]

9   See, e.g., Erasmus, *The Godly Feast*, in *Ten Colloquies*, trans. and ed. Craig R. Thompson (New York: Macmillan, 1987) [hereafter: Erasmus, *Colloquies*], pp. 130–74ff. In fact, as early as 1501 Erasmus was proclaiming the necessity of studying Hebrew to truly understand the scriptures.

10 Desiderius Erasmus, *Paraphrase on Mark*, trans. Erika Rummel, ed. Robert D. Sider, The Collected Works of Erasmus 49 (Toronto: University of Toronto Press, 1988) [hereafter: Erasmus, *Paraphrase on Mark*], p. 75. Throughout this Paraphrase, Erasmus contrasts the "darkness," "fear," and "despair" given to men through the "carnal" Law with the "light," "sweetness," and "love" given to them by the Gospel. See pp. 14–16, 21, 24, 26, 30–31, 59, 86–87, 103, and 132–33.

11 On this subject, a cursory review of Erasmus' scholarly apparatus is most telling: references to Hebrew terms number about a score in most of the

As with his rhetorical anthropology, Erasmus' tendency to fall back on familiar and beloved concepts resulted in some curious interpolations and assertions in his biblical writings. In his *Paraphrase on Hebrews*, the staff of Moses is described in terms lifted from Homer's *Iliad*, while his account of the furnishings and layout of the temple is halting and confused.[12] In his *Annotations on Romans*, as noted above, Erasmus asserted that the change of Saul's name to Paul was mainly the result of a program of Hellenization in the Mediterranean in the wake of Alexander's military conquests, despite ample Jewish scriptural parallels to individuals being renamed when their true vocation was made known to them by the Lord.[13] Similarly, in his *Paraphrase on John*, Erasmus assumed that the Roman custom of burying the dead along major roadways must have also been a feature of life in ancient Bethany.[14] These anachronisms result as much from Erasmus' intentional effort to link Jesus and his disciples as closely as possible with Antique culture, as from his eschewal of Old Testament culture and rites.

> modern editions of his *Annotations*, and many of these notes are merely imported from patristic sources, while individual Greek and Latin terms run to well over six double-columned pages of references. The same proportion of references is to be observed even in his *Paraphrase on Hebrews*, where such expertise would seem to be invaluable for establishing the authentic sense of the text.

12 Thus he speaks of "lights" in the Holy of Holies, rather than lamp stands, and asserts that there were seven loaves of the Presence, or Shewbread, upon the altar, although the text of Hebrews simply mentions loaves, and the related Old Testament scriptures speak of twelve loaves of Presence. See Erasmus, *Paraphrase on Hebrews*, p. 235, and editor's notes 4, 5, and 7. It is tempting to view Erasmus' interpolations as veiled allusions to the "lights" or candles maintained in Christian sanctuaries and the seven traditional sacraments of the Church.

13 See Erasmus, *Annotations on Romans*, p. 3. Erasmus nowhere mentions that, in the absence of any Greek political processes, Abram becomes Abraham in Genesis 17, Jacob becomes Israel in Genesis 32, and Simon becomes Peter in Matthew 16. The appeal of a Hellenistic etiology for Paul's name change was so powerful for Erasmus that he even challenged the commentary of his beloved Chrysostom on this point.

14 Erasmus, *Paraphrase on John*, p. 143 and accompanying editor's note 29.

Erasmus and Cambridge

Writing from prison in the 1550s, Ridley touchingly recalled his fondness for Cambridge, describing the University as "my lovyng mother and tender nurse."[15] Indeed, understanding just how steadily Cambridge nourished Ridley on the intellectual ideals of Erasmus is crucial to understanding his own thought. Nicholas Ridley's advent to Cambridge forms part of the larger story of University patronage from the northern counties starting in the 1480s. This initiative brought talented and serious men, like John Fisher and Nicholas' uncle, Robert Ridley, to Cambridge from in and around Northumberland, Durham, and Westmoreland. The pattern held, not just for the University in general, but for Nicholas' own College, Pembroke, in particular.[16] Fisher, having taken all of his degrees at Cambridge and subsequently been raised to a number of important administrative posts, was serving as University Chancellor by 1504. Constant in the promotion of Humanist studies at Cambridge, he was instrumental in having Erasmus appointed in 1511 to lecture in Greek and Theology.[17]

Erasmus was not the first to teach Greek at Cambridge, but he appears to have been the first to do so in an official capacity with the support of a regular stipend. His early lectures in the language were rudimentary lessons in grammar, while his Theology lectures focused on the works of St. Jerome.[18] Erasmus' time at Cambridge was also a remarkably productive period for his own scholarship: while continuing with other projects, he translated two of Plutarch's shorter works, edited Jerome's letters, and translated St. Basil's commentary on

---

15 Ridley's *Last farewell* letter in Miles Coverdale, *Certain most godly, fruitful, and comfortable letters of such true saintes and holy martyrs of God, as in the late bloodye persecution here within this realme, gaue their lyues for the defence of Christes holy gospel written in the tyme of their affliction and cruell imprysonment* ([STC 5886] London: John Day, 1564) [hereafter: Coverdale, *Comfortable Letters*], fol. 91ff.

16 See Damien Leader, *A History of the University of Cambridge, Volume 1, The University to 1546* (Cambridge: Cambridge University Press, 1988) [hereafter: Leader, *History of Cambridge*], p. 283.

17 Leader, *History of Cambridge*, pp. 264, 292–93.

18 Leader, *History of Cambridge*, pp. 293–95.

Isaiah.[19] Erasmus also finished the Latin translation for his *Novum Instrumentum* while at Cambridge, although it would not be published until 1516. This was his most ambitious project up to that time for amending the text of the Vulgate.

The seeds of Erasmus' legacy at Cambridge would be planted not just in texts, however, but in the personal relationships he established among his pupils on the one hand, and with his fellow lecturers on the other. Erasmus' work with Thomas Lupset suggests that there was a neat dovetailing of his university friendships and his Cambridge scholarship. Lupset, a student of Pembroke College who assisted Erasmus with revisions for the *Novum Instrumentum* in 1513, conducted this work not for pay, but in exchange for private lessons in Greek.[20] Several of Erasmus' pupils who assisted him with specific projects were later to serve Cambridge as lecturers themselves, or hold high office within the University. Robert Aldrich studied Seneca and St. Jerome with Erasmus as an undergraduate, and eventually became Vice Chancellor of the University.[21] John Bryan served Erasmus as his scribe, and went on to deliver Humanist lectures on Aristotle for the University in 1518.[22]

---

19 Leader, *History of Cambridge*, pp. 293–95.

20 See Leader, *History of Cambridge*, p. 296. Lupset would go on to have an impressive career in his own right as a Humanist scholar, and was an inveterate supporter of Erasmus during the controversy with Edward Lee that erupted when the second edition of Erasmus' *Novum Instrumentum*, now styled the *Novum Testamentum*, was published in March of 1519. See T. F. Mayer, "Lupset, Thomas (c. 1495–1530)," *Oxford Dictionary of National Biography*, Oxford University Press, 2004 [http://www.oxforddnb.com/view/article/17201, accessed 16 June 2006].

21 See Leader, *History of Cambridge*, p. 296. Aldrich would later assist Erasmus in his preparations for a new edition of Seneca by collating Cambridge manuscripts. In July of 1537, Aldrich was nominated by Henry VIII to serve as Bishop of Carlisle, and although very conservative in his views, he retained his episcopate until his death in Mary's reign. See Angelo J. Louisa, "Aldrich, Robert (1488/9–1556)," *Oxford Dictionary of National Biography*, Oxford University Press, 2004 [http://www.oxforddnb.com/view/article/315, accessed 16 June 2006].

22 See Leader, *History of Cambridge*, pp. 296–97. Bryan was last accounted

Erasmus also inspired a number of older men who were already lecturers and leaders within the University when he arrived. John Watson, junior proctor and Lady Margaret preacher at Cambridge by 1505, became one of Erasmus' closest English friends. Taking a Doctor of Theology in 1517, Watson wrote to Erasmus declaring that he had solemnly resolved to "devote the rest of my life exclusively to biblical and sacred studies."[23] Like Robert Aldrich, Watson was also later Vice Chancellor of Cambridge.[24] Henry Bullock's case was similar: he held the University lectureship in Mathematics between 1510 and 1513, but also took up the study of Greek under Erasmus. By 1517, he was teaching Matthew's Gospel to undergraduates, with the use of Erasmus' own lecture notes on the text.[25] While Erasmus' sojourn at Cambridge was quite brief, ending just twenty-six months after he took up his duties in the University,[26] the friendships he cultivated with Aldrich, Bryan, Bullock, and Watson were lasting. His influence upon them and other Cambridge men in the second decade of the sixteenth century would thereby prove decisive for the generation of scholars who came up to the University in the 1520s.

During this period, Erasmus himself repeatedly wrote in glowing terms about the University, especially about her students' assiduous and "tranquil" study of Greek.[27] By the time Nicholas Ridley arrived at Cambridge, about 1518, he entered a university already bustling with

as a member of Cambridge in 1521. See S. F. Ryle, "Bryan, John (b. 1492/3, d. after 1521)," *Oxford Dictionary of National Biography*, Oxford University Press, 2004 [http://www.oxforddnb.com/view/article/3789, accessed 16 June 2006].

23 See Judith Ford, "Watson, John (d. 1537)," *Oxford Dictionary of National Biography*, Oxford University Press, 2004 [http://www.oxforddnb.com/view/article/28843, accessed 30 May 2006].

24 See Leader, *History of Cambridge*, p. 323.

25 See S. F. Ryle, "Bullock, Henry (d. 1526)," *Oxford Dictionary of National Biography*, Oxford University Press, 2004 [http://www.oxforddnb.com/view/article/3921, accessed 30 May 2006].

26 Erasmus was to have taught at Cambridge through 1514, but left amid the Plague of Michaelmas term in 1513. See Leader, *History of Cambridge*, pp. 292, 297.

27 In notable contrast to his descriptions of the study of Greek at Oxford. See Leader, *History of Cambridge*, pp. 298, 300.

Erasmian texts, concepts, and disciples. Two individuals in particular were to shape Nicholas' intellect and interests at Cambridge, and both had long personal associations with Erasmus: Robert Ridley, Nicholas' uncle, and Richard Croke, most likely Nicholas' instructor in Greek. Robert Ridley was Terrence professor in the faculty of arts at Cambridge during the opening decade of the sixteenth century, and defrayed Nicholas' expenses at university. Robert Ridley was a personal friend and long-time correspondent of the distinguished scholar of Rotterdam, and was also a key influence on young Thomas Cranmer.[28] He was instrumental in bringing the first printing press to Cambridge, and one of the volumes it produced was Erasmus' *De conscribendis epistolis*.[29] Early in his nephew's studies at Cambridge, Robert Ridley likely introduced Nicholas to the writings of Erasmus. Richard Croke, Erasmus' erstwhile pupil from the University of Paris, eventually inherited his mentor's role, becoming professor of Greek at Cambridge the same year that Nicholas Ridley entered. Croke retained this title and function within the University until 1526.[30] Nicholas was likely all the more attached to Erasmian principles for having had such close, constant, and

28 See Susan Wabuda, "Ridley, Nicholas (c. 1502–1555)," *Oxford Dictionary of National Biography*, Oxford University Press, 2004 [http://www.ox-forddnb.com/view/article/23631, accessed 23 February 2006]. See also Richard Rex, "Ridley, Robert (d. 1536?)," *Oxford Dictionary of National Biography*, Oxford University Press, 2004 [http://www.oxforddnb.com/view/article/68881, accessed 23 February 2006].

29 Leader, *History of Cambridge*, pp. 318.

30 See Leader, *History of Cambridge*, p. 298. If Ridley held much fondness for Croke in his early years at Cambridge, relations between them were drastically changed by the mid-1550s. Ridley clearly distrusted Croke by then, refusing to believe his report of John Hooper's execution. See *Comfortable Letters*, fols. 70–71, and Ridley, *The Works of Bishop Ridley*, ed. Henry Christmas, for the Parker Society (Cambridge: Cambridge University Press, 1841) [hereafter: Ridley, *Works*], p. 373. Croke also attended Ridley's 1554 disputation and examination by Mary's commissioners at Oxford, and was the first to testify against Cranmer at the Archbishop's trial in September 1555. See Jonathan Woolfson, "Croke, Richard (1489–1558)," *Oxford Dictionary of National Biography*, Oxford University Press, 2004 [http://www.oxforddnb.com/view/article/6734, accessed 30 May 2006].

living contact with the Humanist's colleagues and friends in youth, in the very earliest stages of Nicholas' own intellectual and professional formation. With the rest of his peers, Nicholas Ridley's private volumes and many of his classroom texts were probably works of Erasmus, whose writings "are ubiquitous in the surviving library catalogues and personal library lists of sixteenth-century Cambridge men."[31]

Ridley's early education in 1520's Cambridge was likely decisive in his development, often for what that experience did *not* contain, as room was being made in the University curriculum for the leading pursuit of Erasmian studies and skills. Many of the men who shaped Nicholas Ridley's thought were a generation older, and often esteemed Erasmus' close study of the Greek New Testament, although they disagreed with some of his interpretations of the text. Robert Ridley and John Fisher did not embrace all of Erasmus' theological opinions, even as they admired his scholarship.[32] For this generation of scholars, Erasmus' was but one voice in an international movement, and they had direct contact with both Erasmian and Italian Humanism. They were also steeped in Aristotelian logic, metaphysics, and natural philosophy, which were substantially displaced in Cambridge by the 1520s.[33] Nicholas Ridley and many of his peers would therefore have not had the same grounding in the philosophical underpinnings of Aristotelian concepts that related to the doctrine of transubstantiation, for example. For men coming up to Cambridge around the third decade of the sixteenth century, the pursuit of humane and divine letters was directed chiefly by the voice of Erasmus, especially for men like Nicholas Ridley, who had had

---

31 See Leader, *History of Cambridge*, p. 306. Cf. p. 317.
32 For Fisher's theological and exegetical differences with Erasmus, see Maria Dowling, *Fisher of Men: A Life of John Fisher, 1469–1535* (London: Palgrave, 1999), pp. 44–46. For Robert Ridley's preaching in defense of relics, a topic frequently the object of Erasmus' ridicule, see Richard Rex, "Ridley, Robert (d. 1536?)," *Oxford Dictionary of National Biography*, Oxford University Press, 2004 [http://www.oxforddnb.com/view/article/68881, accessed 23 February 2006].
33 For the dominance of a Humanist emphasis on ethics at the expense of logic and metaphysics, see Leader, *History of Cambridge*, pp. 308–10. Cf. pp. 301, 136–38.

little or no direct exposure to academic trends beyond their own university or on the Continent.[34]

What is certain is that Ridley's Cambridge education led him to embody, in very personal and real ways, a number of Erasmian ideals. In the 1520s, he was engaged in committing the New Testament to memory, precisely as Erasmus had urged all godly preachers to do in his 1521 double biography of John Colet and the Franciscan, Jean Vitrier.[35] Ridley vividly recalled from prison some thirty years after the fact that at Pembroke College, "thy Orcharde (the wals, buttes, and trees, if they could

34 In his extant writings, Nicholas Ridley refers only once to his academic studies in Paris, reflecting on his treatment during the 1554 disputation at Oxford: "The Sorbonical clamours (which at Paris I have seene in time past when Popery most raigned) might be worthely thought (in comparison of this thrasonical ostentation) to have had muche modestie." See John Foxe, *Actes and Monuments of matters most speciall and memorable, happenyng in the Church, with an Universal history of the same, wherein is set forth at large the whole race and course of the Church, from the primitive age to these latter tymes of ours, with the bloudy times, horrible troubles, and great persecutions agaynst the true Martyrs of Christ, sought and wrought as well by Heathen Emperours, and now lately practised by Romish Prelates, especially in this Realme of England and Scotland* ([STC 11225] London: John Daye, 1583) [hereafter: Foxe, *Actes and Monuments*], p. 1463 and Ridley, *Works*, p. 303. Even this comment probably reflects his Cambridge Humanist education, as "thrasonical" is an allusion to a boastful character in Terrence's comedy, *Eunuchus*. Ridley is also thought to have studied at the University of Louvain during the sole period of his life that he is believed to have been abroad, sometime between 1527 and 1530. See *Works*, p. iii.

35 Coverdale, *Comfortable Letters,* fols. 92–93. See also Susan Wabuda, *Preaching During the English Reformation* (Cambridge: Cambridge University Press, 2002) [hereafter: Wabuda, *Preaching*], p. 71. For Erasmus' biographies of Colet and Vitrier, see *Opus epistularum Des. Erasmi Roterodami,* eds. P. S. Allen, H. M. Allen and H. W. Garrod (Oxford, 1922), vol. V, no. 1489. For an English translation of this lengthy letter to Jodocus Jonas, see *The Correspondence of Erasmus,* trans. and eds. R. A. B. Mynors and D. F. S. Thomson, The Complete Works of Erasmus 8 (Toronto: University of Toronto Press, 1974), pp. 225–44. For Erasmus' endorsement of memory work for preachers, see his descriptions of Vitrier's exertions, in *Correspondence*, pp. 227–28.

speak, would beare me witnesse) I learned without book almost all Paules Epistles; yea and I weene all the Canonicall Epistles save only the Apocalypse."[36] This scheme accords closely with the structure of Erasmus' *Novum Testamentum* of 1519, and it is quite likely that Ridley employed that volume for his solemn purpose. Ridley's Erasmian education instilled in him such familiar acquaintance with the *Colloquies* that he could borrow lines from them to ridicule opponents in debate decades later.[37]

In Ridley's surviving writings, Erasmus and Erasmus' exegetical hero, Laurentius Valla, are positively mentioned several times.[38] These commendations of Erasmus and Valla are even more illuminating when one considers that not one continental Protestant theologian is similarly celebrated in these texts. In fact, in the whole of Ridley's extant writings, he reserves unqualified praise for the scholarship of only two men: Thomas Cranmer[39] and Erasmus. In Ridley's attacks on Stephen Gardiner's objections to the *Opus Imperfectum in Mattheum*, the former asserts: "Erasmus which was a man that coulde understande the wordes and the sense of the wrytor . . . declareth playnely that this

36 Coverdale, *Comfortable Letters,* fol. 92. Valla's writings were also quite prominent at Cambridge in the 1520s. See Leader, *History of Cambridge,* pp. 302, 307.
37 See Ridley to Hooper on the Edwardine vestment controversy, John Bradford, *The Writings of John Bradford,* vol. 2, ed. Aubrey Townsend, for the Parker Society (Cambridge: Cambridge University Press, 1840) [hereafter: *Bradford,* vol. 2], p. 393: "What is this else than to play the part of him that is mentioned in Erasmus his *Colloquies,* that did steal the priest's purse, and yet cried as he ran, 'Stay the thief, stay the thief!' and thus crying escaped; and yet he was the thief himself."
38 See, e.g., *Works,* pp. 33, 374; *Bradford,* vol. 2, p. 393.
39 See Ridley's description of the *Book of the Sacrament,* produced by Cranmer in Edward's reign, and falsely attributed to Ridley by the Queen's examiners in 1553, Ridley *Works,* p. 159: "Mayster Secretary . . . that booke was made of a great learned man, and him which is able to do the like again: as for me I ensure you (be not deceived in me) I was never able to do or write any such like thing, he passeth me no lesse, then the learned mayster his yong scholer." Foxe, *Actes and Monuments,* p. 1427 and Ridley, *Works,* p. 159.

saying of this wrytour is non otherwise to be understanden."[40] In time, Ridley came to follow in the footsteps of both Erasmus and Richard Croke, becoming professor of Greek at Cambridge in 1535, a post he occupied until 1537–38.[41]

Protestants and Purgatory

At Cambridge during the 1520s and 1530s, Ridley would have absorbed much of the ethical dimensions of Erasmus' *philosophia Christi*, with its concern for the welfare of fellow Christians, especially the poor.[42] In the 1530s, Hugh Latimer and Edward Crome launched a series of pulpit attacks on the doctrine of Purgatory, preaching that the practices associated with requiem Masses were merely financial exploitation of the laity by venal clerics.[43] Perhaps it was a preoccupation with these themes that gradually drew Ridley more directly into the orbit of Cranmer, Latimer, and the other Henrician reformers. Ridley's precise views on Purgatory in the 1530s are not known, since unfortunately, none of his sermons has survived to us. Perhaps it was Ridley's willingness to sign the decree against papal supremacy at Cambridge in 1534 that brought him eventually into Cranmer's service. Whatever the nature of Ridley's theological principles in the 1530s, it is rather

40   Nicholas Ridley, *A Brief Declaracion of the Lordes Supper* ([STC 21046] (Emden: Egidius van der Erve, 1555) [hereafter: Ridley, *Brief Declaration*], sig. D.6, *verso* and *Works*, p. 33. Ridley's additional reflection on this passage also seems to indicate that he is aware that Erasmus raised doubts about the authenticity of this work, attributed from his own time to a fifth-century Arian author: "Whether the autor was John Chrisostome him self, the Archebishop of Constantinople, or no: that is not the mater. For of all it is graunted, that he was a writour of that age, and a man of great learnyng." See Ridley, *Brief Declaracion*, sig. D.5, *recto*, and Ridley, *Works*, p. 33.

41   Ridley's stipend was, as ordered by the royal injunctions, provided by the colleges of the University. As such, this was the first post Ridley assumed that was directly shaped by the Henrician reforms. See Leader, *History of Cambridge*, pp. 337.

42   See Leader, *History of Cambridge*, p. 265. Cf., e.g., Erasmus, *Enchiridion*, and *Colloquies*, pp. 92–112.

43   See Wabuda, *Preaching*, pp. 56, 61.

unlikely that he would have been tapped for the honor of serving as one of Cranmer's chaplains in 1537 if he did not show some continued enthusiasm for Henrician reforms. Although it is impossible to know for certain, it is a distinct possibility that Ridley read Luther's writings as a student, given the influx of the Wittenberg Reformer's works into Cambridge in the 1520s and 1530s.[44]

The controversy surrounding the idea of "soul sleep," as with the Eucharist, illustrates another of the difficulties that continental Protestants discovered in attempting to establish a consensus on scripture and ecclesiology in the early sixteenth century. While Luther, Zwingli, and Calvin all sought to ground church polity on the clear word of God in scripture alone, they often drew very different conclusions from the same text. Luther and Calvin were united in the belief that they could not discover in scripture the formal doctrine of Purgatory traditionally taught in the Church, but they were sharply divided beyond this common point. Luther, who abandoned his belief in Purgatory around 1530, thereafter promoted the idea that the souls of the dead sleep until the final judgment. Calvin's first theological tract, probably written in 1534, was an assault on this idea, and was entitled *Psychopannychia*. Ironically, the term *Psychopannychia* came to mean "soul sleep" in later Protestant discourse, even though Calvin asserted the exact opposite idea: his title is Greek for "the all night vigil of the soul."[45]

Calvin himself, not known to yield much ground to his adversaries, did concede when pressed by Cardinal Sadoleto that "as to Purgatory, we know that ancient churches make some mention of the dead in their prayers."[46] Indeed, prayers for the deliverance of departed souls are not

---

44   The works of Luther feature prominently in the controversies and persecutions at Cambridge from the late 1520s. See, e.g., See Leader, *History of Cambridge*, pp. 320–25.

45   See Diarmaid MacCulloch, *The Reformation* (New York: Viking, 2004) [hereafter: MacCulloch, *The Reformation*], pp. 561–62. Cf. John Calvin, *The Institutes of Christian Religion, 1559*, trans. Ford Lewis Battles, ed. John T. McNeil (Philadelphia: Westminster John Knox Press, 1960) [hereafter: Calvin, *Institutes*], III.xxv.6, pp. 996–98.

46   See *John Calvin and Jacopo Sadoleto: A Reformation Debate*, ed. John Olin (Grand Rapids: Baker Book House, 1976) [hereafter: Calvin,

only found in countless inscriptions in the Christian catacombs of Rome, but were also clearly advocated by several major patristic authors. In the early third century, Origen was already writing of the "cleansing fire" that would purify souls after death.[47] Tertullian, also writing in the early third century, advised a widow "to pray for the soul of her husband, begging repose for him," urging her to "make oblations for him on the anniversary of his demise."[48] Cyril of Jerusalem noted in the fourth century that many of the ancient liturgies of the Church are concerned with prayers for the dead.[49] Augustine, reflecting on Matthew 12:32, asserted that there must be some possibility of forgiveness in the hereafter, since Christ refers to the sin against the Holy Ghost not being forgiven in this world or the world to come.[50] Despite the wealth of patristic evidence promoting prayers for the dead, Calvin alleged that the practice must be wholly discarded, because of the "impostures that avarice has here fabricated, in order to milk men of every class."[51]

In England, similar attitudes were reshaping church polity by the mid 1530s, largely as a result of Erasmus' Humanist biblical scholarship.[52] Portions of Erasmus' retranslation of the Vulgate in his 1516 *Novum Instrumentum* and 1519 *Novum Testamentum* were understood to undermine traditional views of Purgatory, especially in his

---

Reformation Debate], p. 73. Cardinal Sadoleto, also a Humanist scholar and friend of Erasmus, addressed a letter to the city council of Geneva in March 1539 asking them to reconsider their schism and return to the Catholic Church. Although Calvin had already left Geneva for Strasbourg, the city fathers asked him to reply to Sadoleto, which he did in September of the same year. The full text of both letters can be found in Olin's volume.

47 Origen, *Homilies on Jeremias*, in *P.G.*, ed. Jacques-Paul Migne, vol. XIII, cols. 445, 448.

48 Tertullian, *De monogamia*, *P.L.*, ed. Jacques-Paul Migne, vol. II, col. 912.

49 St. Cyril of Jerusalem, *Catechetical Lectures*, *P.G.*, ed. Jacques-Paul Migne, vol. XXXIII, col. 1116.

50 Augustine, *City of God*, trans. Henry Bettenson (New York: Penguin Books, 1984), XXI.24, p. 1003.

51 Calvin, *Reformation Debate*, p. 73.

52 See Wabuda, *Preaching*, pp. 56–58, 64–80.

rendering of 1 Corinthians 15:51 as "we shall not all sleep."[53] The changing perspective on Purgatory was also a reaction against the highly elaborate and often exorbitant funeral rituals associated with popular lay piety in late medieval England. As Diarmaid MacCulloch notes, many of these rites involved the multiplication of masses for the repose of souls, and reveal an obsession with neatness and numbers.[54] The most intricate of the rituals associated with purgatorial piety was probably the Pope Trental, so named because popular legends connected it with Pope Gregory the Great. This line of pious fiction claimed to recount the efforts of St. Gregory to succor the soul of his mother in Purgatory, and how he managed to release her from her pains with a set formula of Masses that she indicated to him in a vision. The Pope Trental prescribed thirty Masses as most fitting for the deceased, and involved saying three of them on each of the ten major feasts of Christ and Mary within the liturgical year: Christmas, Epiphany, Candelmas, Annunciation, Easter, Ascension, Pentecost, Trinity, Assumption, and the Nativity of the Virgin. The rite also enjoined a number of ascetical acts upon the priest who would perform it, including periodic bread and water fasts.[55]

For a man like Ridley, who had taken up Erasmus' own profession as a scholar of Greek, these rituals must have seemed heavy-laden with the superstitions so regularly derided by the Humanist scholar of Rotterdam. In his *Colloquies*, Erasmus regularly lampooned multiple burial Masses and monastic funerary rites.[56] Ridley probably found it a short

---

53 As opposed to the Douay-Rheims' "we shall all indeed rise again." See Wabuda, *Preaching*, pp. 74–75.

54 MacCulloch, *The Reformation*, p. 12–13. Cf. Eamon Duffy, *The Stripping of the Altars* (New Haven: Yale, 1992) [hereafter: Duffy, *Stripping of the Altars*], pp. 373–74. For more on the origins of and practices associated with trental Masses, see Duffy, *Stripping of Altars*, pp. 43, 74, 76, 293–94. Cf. Francis Clark, S. J. *Eucharistic Sacrifice and the Reformation* (Oxford: Basil Blackwell, 1967) pp. 56–72.

55 Duffy, *Stripping of the Altars*, pp. 370–71. MacCulloch urges that we must understand these preoccupations with the multiplication of Masses against the background of the Black Death that swept Europe in the late fourteenth century, when people were buried hurriedly and often with little or no ceremony at all. See MacCulloch, *Reformation*, p. 13.

56 See, e.g., Erasmus, "The Funeral," in *Colloquies*, pp. 92–112 where he

step from Erasmus' treatment of such devotions to the idea that they were best eliminated altogether. This is not to say that Ridley and Erasmus held identical views on what constituted "superstition." Yet, often what Erasmus was content to label and ridicule under that title, was closely related to practices that Ridley wished to have eradicated completely from the church, particularly after the 1540s. Ridley's 1550 *Visitation Injunctions* for the diocese of London, for example, commence with an attack on multiplying eucharistic services: "Fyrst, that there bee no readynge of such injunctions as extolleth and setteth for the the popishe masse, candels, ymages, chauntries; neyther that there be used any superalteries, or trentalles of Communions."[57] Ridley takes aim here at the very same target as Erasmus, in naming "trentalles," of Communion services. His is, however, a more direct assault: rather than mere ridicule of such practices, Ridley declares that they must be abolished from the English church. This line of reasoning is also clear in Ridley's arguments for the removal of altars from London churches, where the opening line read: "First, the forme of a table shall more move the simple from the superstitious opinions of the Popish Masse, unto the right use of the Lordes supper. For the use of an altare is to make sacrifice upon it: the use of a table is to serve for men to eate upon."[58] While Erasmus does not appear to have advocated the removal of church altars, he did urge that superstition be eliminated from lay piety.[59] Ridley may have viewed his efforts then to have certain church

---

offers a riposte on multiple burial Masses, funerary processions, and papal dispensations from the pains of Purgatory in this 1526 production.

57 Ridley, Visitation injunctions as Bishop of London, ([STC 10247] London: Reynolde Wolfe, *Cum privilegio ad imprimendum solum*, 1550) [hereafter: Ridley, *Visitation Injunctions*]. Item I and also Item V urge the use of a table in the place of an altar: "the forme of a table may more move and tourne the simple frome the olde supersticious opinions of the Popish masse and to the right use of the lordes supper." Cf. Ridley's insistence to the Marian Bishop of Lincoln that removal of altars restored "the rites and usage of the primative Church," in the elimination of superstition, Foxe, *Actes and Monuments*, p. 1765.

58 Foxe, *Actes and Monuments*, p. 1331 and Ridley, *Works*, p. 322.

59 See Erasmus, "The Funeral," in *Colloquies*, pp. 92–112.

furnishings removed as the swiftest and most direct route to reach an Erasmian ideal.

Although no other single figure is likely to have had the impact on Ridley's thinking, both directly through his writings and indirectly through his disciples, as Erasmus, there were certainly other influences on his thought, particularly in the years of his close association with Cranmer in the effort to reform the English Church. Doubtless Ridley was reading and meditating on the writings of continental Protestants from the 1520s and 1530s onward, given the influx of these materials to Cambridge during the period.[60] He reveals his awareness of various Protestant schools of thought, if only obliquely, in the opening section of his *Brief Declaration of the Lord's Supper*: "Thou knowest, (O heavenly father), that the controversie about the Sacrament of the blessed bodye and blood of thy deare sonne, our saveour Jesu Christ, hathe troubled, not of late only, thy church of Englande, Fraunce, Germanye, and Italie, but also many yeares agoo."[61] He also seems to have been familiar with the salient points of Melancthon's eucharistic thought: "As for Melancton . . . , I marvell that ye will alledge him, for we are more nye an agrement here in England, then the opinion of Melancton to you: for in this poynt we all agree here, that there is in the sacrament but one materiall substance: and Melancton as I weene, sayth there are two."[62] Identifying precisely which contemporary continental Protestants most shaped Ridley's own thinking at this time, however, is not easily established, since very few of his writings survive from the period that preceded his imprisonment in the summer of 1553. Equally vexing for the modern ecclesiastical historian is Ridley's habit, in true Humanist form, of borrowing concepts and marshalling arguments often without citing his source for an idea.[63]

Ridley's eucharistic opinions bear some family resemblances to

---

60 Especially the works of Luther in 1520s and 1530s Cambridge. See, e.g., See Leader, *History of Cambridge*, pp. 320–25.
61 Ridley, *Brief Declaracion*, sigs. A.2, *recto*-A.3, *verso*. Cf. *Works*, p. 5.
62 Foxe, *Actes and Monuments*, p. 1427.
63 In contrast to the Scholastic tradition of plainly citing an authority at the outset of an assertion. For the free use of sources as a distinctively Humanist trait, see O'Malley, *Praise and Blame*.

Calvin's conception of a true spiritual presence of Christ in the Eucharist, but the Englishman ascribes the active agency of that presence to Christ's divine nature, as opposed to Calvin's characteristic preoccupation with the Holy Spirit.[64] Ridley's focus on the power and promise of Christ in the Eucharist is a more characteristically Lutheran theme, as is his endorsement of private, auricular confession to a priest.[65] Even Ridley's conception of a true spiritual presence may not bear evidence of direct influence from Calvin, since many of the theologians of his time, in the wake of the well-known clashes between Luther and Zwingli in the 1520s, were attempting to discover a mediating eucharistic theory that might reconcile the quarrelling Protestant factions. Indeed, Zwingli's successor in Zurich, Heinrich Bullinger, was himself attempting to move away from the stark memorialism of his mentor in the 1540s.[66] Ridley's persistent emphasis on the natural properties of a

64 See Chapter I above for Ridley's eucharistic thought and the traces of continental thinkers that can be found in his writings on the subject. See Chapter II for the striking resemblances between the work of Peter Martyr and that of Ridley.

65 Ridley preached approvingly of auricular confession in the 1540s, even though he declared that "he could not find" this practice endorsed in scripture. See Susan Wabuda, "Ridley, Nicholas (c. 1502–1555)," *Oxford Dictionary of National Biography*, Oxford University Press, 2004 [http://www.oxforddnb.com/view/article/23631, accessed 23 February 2006]. Ridley still embraced this practice as late as his imprisonment in the 1550s. Writing to West, one of his former chaplains, he declared: "Confession unto the minister which is able to instruct, correcte, comforte, and enforme the weake, wounded, and ignoraunt conscience, in dede I ever thought myght do much good in Christs congregation, and so I assure you that I think even at this day." Coverdale, *Comfortable Letters*, fols. 40–41, and Ridley, *Works*, p. 338.

66 See, e.g., *Two Epystles, one of Henry Bullynger with the consent of all the learned men of Tigury* [Zurich]: *an other of Johan Calvyne, chefe preacher of the church of Geneve: whether it be lawful for a christen man to communicate or be partaker of the masse of the papists, without offending God and hys neyghbour or not.* ([STC 4080] London: Robert Stoughton, 1548) sigs. A.vi–A.ix, *verso*. Stoughton probably collated and printed Bullinger and Calvin's tracts together to suggest that there was some consensus emerging on Communion in the Swiss churches, at least. Cf. Andrew Pettegree,

human body and the seeming impossibility of Christ's body to be at once in Heaven and on the altar, is also characteristic of the theological thought not only of Calvin, but also Zwingli and Bullinger.

Before ascribing too much importance to Calvin himself in Ridley's own thinking in the 1540s and early 1550s, it is important to remember that although Calvin would play a dominant role in the theological underpinnings of the Elizabethan church, his period of greatest influence and fame only occurred after his wife's death in 1553.[67] It is certainly true that Ridley produced a tract, now lost, on Predestination when he was a prisoner of the Marian régime, but this was not a topic solely of interest to Calvin. Not only is this concept found in Augustine's writings, but it was the subject of lively debate in the ninth century. Ratramnus, whom Ridley credited with "opening his eyes" on the Eucharist, also wrote *De praedestione Dei libri duo*, which embraced a theory of double Predestination.[68] Perhaps Ridley's interest stemmed from his conversations with Peter Martyr Vermigli,[69] who was also a promoter of Predestination, taking his cues from Gregory of Rimini.[70]

Marian Protestantism: Six Studies (Brookfield, Vermont: Ashgate, 1996) [hereafter: Pettegree, *Marian Protestantism*], pp. 135–36. Pettegree emphasizes the developing concord between Zurich and Geneva, and Calvin and Bullinger's protracted dialogues to bring it about.

67 See Andrew Pettegree, *Foreign Protestant Communities in Sixteenth-Century London* (Oxford: Clarendon Press, 1986) [hereafter: Pettegree, *Foreign Protestant Communities*], pp. 72–73. Pettegree notes that Calvin had few direct links to the Edwardine Church, and that he was not well informed of events at the time.

68 For Ridley's lost work on Predestination, see *Works*, p. xv. Ratramnus' treatises on the subject, *De predestinatione in libri duo*, can be found in *P.L.*, ed. Jacques-Paul Migne, vol. CXXI, cols. 11–80.

69 See Chapter II above. See also Pietro Martire Vermigli, *A discourse or traictise of Petur Martyr Vermilla Flore[n]tine, the publyque reader of diuinitee in the Universitee of Oxford wherein he openly declared his whole and determinate judgemente concernynge the sacrament of the Lordes supper in the sayde Universitee* ([STC 24665] London: Robert Stoughton [i.e. Whitchurch], 1550) [hereafter: Martyr, *Judgemente concernynge the sacrament of the Lordes supper*].

70 Martyr studied the work of Gregory of Rimini at Padua. See Mark Taplin, "Vermigli, Pietro Martire [Peter Martyr] (1499–1562)," *Oxford Dictionary*

Whatever Ridley owed to contemporary continental Protestants, it does not appear that his exposure to or enthusiasm for them wholly displaced his appreciation for Erasmus and his scholarship. The extent to which Erasmus inspired Ridley's own theological vision is apparent from Ridley's views on the church and her ministry, especially as they appear in his writings and in the Edwardine religious reforms that he helped to draft, promulgate, and defend, not only in his own diocese of London, but throughout the entire realm. When the key aspects of his outlook on ecclesiology are compared with the work of Erasmus, especially on the proper role of ministers and charitable lay piety, a remarkable congruence between their minds is revealed. The result of these Erasmian influences on Ridley's thought was that the Edwardine Bishop of London would come to see the role of ordained clergy as restricted to a merely pedagogical role in the life of the laity, who, in turn, were to celebrate almsdeeds as the highest form of altar worship in the English church.

Purgatory and the Poor Men's Chest in Edwardine England

For lay Christians in early-modern England, traditional purgatorial piety was gradually re-directed from intercessory prayer to sermons, through the establishment of preaching chantries.[71] Susan Wabuda's research, for example, reveals that leading clergy attempted not simply to eradicate the devotions dedicated to departed souls, but to train these impulses in a new direction through the endowment of preaching benefices. This harnessing of energies associated with purgatorial piety was also accompanied by a certain liturgical pedagogy that was especially directed towards almsdeeds. The Protestant establishment under Edward VI was firmly committed to such a program of devotional re-formation which, both in its didactic character and in its emphasis on social concerns, was likely shaped by Erasmus' call for a renewed Christian society led by ministers whose primary task was to teach true piety to the laity through

of National Biography, Oxford University Press, 2004 [http://www.oxforddnb.com/view/article/28225, accessed 23 July 2007].

71   Wabuda, *Preaching*, pp. 20–63.

godly sermons. As Wabuda notes, early English Protestants readily "greeted the ideal of the Erasmian teacher as a worthy and attainable goal for the clergy to reach."[72] That Ridley took pains to embody this Erasmian ideal of a preaching and teaching bishop is readily apparent in several aspects of his administration of London Diocese in the 1550s.

The Edwardine Reformers' implementation of the "poor men's chest" is a portion of their reform program that has received very little scholarly attention. It was, in fact, a central part of their efforts to redirect funds and lay attention away from several traditional devotions associated with purgatorial piety. They intended the "poor men's chest" literally to supplant parish rituals associated with Purgatory and Masses for the dead. Their aims at liturgical displacement are made plain in item twenty-nine of Edward VI's 1547 religious injunctions, where pastors are informed that "they shall provide and have within three months after this visitation, a strong chest with a hole in the upper part thereof, to be provided at the cost and charge of the parish. . . . Which chest you shall set and fashion near to the high altar, to the intent the parishioners should put into it their oblation and alms, for their poor neighbours."[73] The goal was to establish a public ritual for the collecting and distributing of alms: "the parson, vicar and curate shall diligently from time to time, and specially when men make their testaments, call upon, exhort and move their neighbours to confer and give (as they may well spare) to the said chest."[74]

Charity of this kind was to be extolled as a virtue, in an orchestrated contrast with memorials for the dead. When the call for alms was delivered, the presiding cleric was charged to admonish the laity, "declaring unto them, whereas heretofore they have been diligent to bestow much substance otherwise than God commanded upon pardons, pilgrimages, trentals, decking of images, offering of candles, giving to friars and upon other like blind devotions, they ought at this time to be much more ready

---

72 Wabuda, *Preaching*, p.65.
73 See *The Edwardian Injunctions, 1547*, No. 29, in *Documents of the English Reformation*, ed. Gerald Bray (Minneapolis: Fortress Press, 1994) [hereafter: *The Edwardian Injunctions, 1547*], p. 255.
74 *The Edwardian Injunctions, 1547*, No. 29, p. 255.

to help the poor and needy, knowing that to relieve the poor is a true worshipping of God, required earnestly upon pain of everlasting damnation."[75] The congregants were also to be reminded that in providing for the poor, "whatsoever is given for their comfort is given to Christ himself and is so accepted of him, that he will mercifully reward the same with everlasting life. The which alms and devotion of the people, the keepers of the keys shall . . . take out of the chest and distribute the same in the presence of the whole parish, one sixth of them to be truly and faithfully delivered to their most needy neighbours."[76] Clergy were also to see to it that "the money which riseth of fraternities, guilds and other flocks of the Church . . . shall be put into the said chest and converted to the said use, . . . and money given or bequeathed to the finding of torches, lights, tapers and lamps, shall be converted to the said use."[77] This last provision makes clear that any residual trappings of Purgatory devotions would be assimilated into the rite of the "poor men's chest." The hope of Ridley and the other Edwardine Reformers was that the poor box would occupy a central place, not only in the sanctuary, but also in the conscience of the people.

The promotion and use of the "poor men's chest" was consciously pitted against the former centrality of burial memorials and ritual practices associated with Purgatory. Edward's religious injunctions advanced these efforts at liturgical displacement on several fronts at once. The chest itself was to hold a place of honour, "near the high altar," where it might vie for the attention once lavished upon the reserved host.[78] The

---

75 *The Edwardian Injunctions, 1547*, No. 29, p. 255.
76 *The Edwardian Injunctions, 1547*, No. 29, pp. 255–56.
77 *The Edwardian Injunctions, 1547*, No. 29, p. 256.
78 Naturally these provisions had to be modified in practice at least when, in 1550, there were widespread efforts to remove altars altogether from Edwardine churches. Ridley's visitation injunctions call for the removal of altars, but do not specify the precise location for "the poor men's chest." We may safely assume that it was still centrally located within the worship space of the church, since he suggests that people contribute to it in the middle of the communion service. See Ridley, *Visitation Injunctions*, Item VI, and *Works*, p. 320. Despite the Reformers' general concern that worship conform to those rites expressly instituted or endorsed by Christ in

giving of alms is contrasted with both trental masses, and memorials for departed fellow guild members, while the people are urged to rely upon the eternal good to be had by the use of providing for the poor upon their deaths, as opposed to "pardons, pilgrimages, trentals, decking of images, offering of candles, giving to friars and . . . other like blind devotions."[79]

Upon being installed as bishop of London in April of 1550, Ridley issued a series of detailed *Visitation Injunctions*, and then proceeded to visit each parish personally and to examine all of the clerics under his jurisdiction. Since Ridley himself drafted and saw to the implementation of these articles, they remain an invaluable source for investigating his understanding of the nature and purpose of the church and her ministers. The bulk of Ridley's injunctions are concerned with establishing the normative use of the communion service of the 1549 *Book of Common Prayer*. He forbade all traditional eucharistic devotions at the altar, commanding "that no minister do counterfait the popish masse, in kissing the Lords borde, washyng his handes or fingers after the gospell, or the receyte of the holye Communion; . . . saiyng the Agnus before the Communion, shewynge the sacramente openly before the distribution, or makynge any elevation therof, ryngyng of the sacrying belle, or settyng any light upon the Lordes boord."[80] Lest this catalogue of proscribed acts prove inexhaustive, Ridley further enjoined "that the minister, in the time of the holy communion, doo use onely the ceremonies and gestures appointed by the boke of common prayer, and none other."[81] Ridley hereby made it clearly known that he desired strict conformity of worship in the Diocese of London. To obtain such uniformity, he knew that he would have to exclude the rituals and customs associated with the traditional Mass service and purgatorial piety. In fact, his visitation articles begin abruptly with the assertion that there will "bee no readynge of such injunctions as extolleth and setteth for the the popishe masse, candels, ymages, chauntries; neyther that there be used any superalteries,

---

scripture, the "poor men's chest" ritual does not seem to have been established upon these criteria.

79 *The Edwardian Injunctions, 1547*, No. 29, p. 255.
80 Ridley, *Visitation Injunctions*, Item II, and *Works*, p. 319.
81 Ridley, *Visitation Injunctions*, Item II, and *Works*, p. 319.

or trentalles of Communions."[82] Ridley proved vigilant in imposing the uniform adoption of the newly authorized ecclesiastical reforms throughout his jurisdiction.

In addition to the Protestant Reformers' desire to bring the Church's ritual practice in line with only the doctrines explicitly articulated in scripture, where no self-evident mention is made of Purgatory, they objected to Masses for the dead based upon two other interrelated concerns. First, they suspected that the institution of masses for the dead invited people to contemplate a final escape from the consequences of an immoral existence as a substitute to godly living. Calvin expressed this idea succinctly in Book IV of the *Institutes*: "and what is the purpose today of yearly memorials and the greater part of masses, except that those who throughout life were the cruelest tyrants, or the most rapacious robbers, or men who stooped to every infamy, should, as if redeemed by this price, escape the fire of Purgatory?"[83] Secondly, although the Reformers rarely expressed this concern directly or systematically, they believed that the institutions of chantries and their associated benefices seemed to link salvation with money, raising alarm that some might attempt literally to purchase salvation. Here again, the observations of Calvin may be taken as representative of the concerns of continental Protestants. Berating venal clerics, he declared, "It was their choice to apply it [the merits of the mass] . . . to everyone who was willing to buy such merchandise with coin. Now, although they could not reach Judas' price, still to resemble their author in some respect, they have kept a similarity in number. Judas sold him for thirty pieces of silver [Matt. 26:15]; these persons, according to the French reckoning, sell him for thirty pieces of copper; Judas once; these, as often as they find a buyer."[84]

For these reasons, Protestant Reformers throughout continental Europe asserted that chantries were an abomination, and that their elimination was best accomplished through a total repudiation of the doctrine of Purgatory. In England, Ridley and his fellow Reformers sought to suppress many of the pious articles and practices associated with the doctrine of

82 Ridley, *Visitation Injunctions*, Item I and *Works*, p. 319.
83 Calvin, *Institutes*, IV.xviii.15, p. 1443.
84 Calvin, *Institutes*, IV.xviii.14, pp. 1442–43.

Purgatory: "Item, that none mainteine purgatory, invocacion of saintes, the sixe articles, bederoules, ymages, reliques, rubrict primars with invocation of saintes, justificacion of man by his owne workes, holy breade, palmes, ashes, candels, sepulcher, paschall, creepyng to the crosse, halowyng of the fyer or altar, or any other such lyke abuses and superstitions, nowe taken awaye by the kinges graces moste godlye procedynges."[85] The motivation that propelled the English Reformers to such action was closely related to the second type of general objection to chantries and benefices, but their campaign against the doctrine of Purgatory and its ritual trappings was pursued under the banner of poor relief.

Ridley decries the idea that salvation can be purchased with money in his fourth visitation article: "Item, that none make a marte of the holye communion, by bying and sellyng receite therof for money, as the Popish masse in tymes past was wonte to be."[86] Here as elsewhere among the English Reformers was an effort to displace practices associated with traditional teachings, to more readily move the laity to embrace novel doctrinal concepts. For Ridley and his fellow reformers in England, the chantry structure represented a misdirection of funds that could be best spent on poor relief. Expressly associating this reinvigoration of almsgiving with the new communion liturgy, Ridley urged "[t]hat the minister in the tyme of the communion, immediately after the offertory, shal monishe the communicantes, saying these wordes, or such like, Now is the tyme, yf it please you, to remember the poore mens cheste with your charitable almes."[87] Here Ridley's injunction articles touched directly

---

85 Ridley, *Visitation Injunctions*, Item X, and *Works*, p. 320.
86 Ridley, *Visitation Injunctions*, Item IV, and *Works*, p. 319. Ridley's statement here is somewhat disingenuous, in that he was undoubtedly aware that no Church authority ever promoted the selling of Masses *per se*, but that donations and benefices were meant to meet the financial needs of ministers who served the faithful in that capacity. He himself was the beneficiary of this system, and sought similar earnings for several of his protégés in the reigns of Henry VIII and Edward VI. Certainly Ridley would have abjured the claim that offertory contributions to support his ecclesial work were nothing more than the mere purchasing of Communion services, sermons, and baptisms.
87 Ridley, *Visitation Injunctions*, Item VI, and *Works*, p. 320.

upon the religious act of 1547, urging observance of the "poor men's chest" to take place "in the time of communion" in the place reserved "near the high altar," as specified in the Edwardine articles.

Ridley's *Visitation Injunctions* for London also echoed the Edwardine religious articles in prescribing that the *Paraphrases* of Erasmus on the New Testament were to be set up in every church for the laity to consult at will.[88] Ridley's visitation articles assiduously promoted the Erasmian dimensions of the 1547 legislation, insisting in the very first question to be addressed under the heading "Of Bookes" whether "every minister, under the degree of bachelor of divinitie, hath of his owne, the new Testament both in English and latin, with Paraphrasis of Erasmus upon the same, and doo diligently studie the same in conferring the one with the other."[89] Ridley's vision for the Diocese of London was not merely that the laity should be able to consult Erasmus' *Paraphrase*, but that the minister should have his own copies, to be regularly consulted in the study of the scriptures. It was not the doctrinal work of continental Protestants that featured large in Ridley's recasting of religion in London, but the reforming ideas of Desiderius Erasmus in biblical interpretation. Significantly, Ridley requires ministers to own and consult copies of the New Testament, with no such provision made for the Old. In privileging the New Testament in this way, Ridley was again promoting an Erasmian concept, in the view that the rites and themes of the Old Testament were not required study for the preacher and teacher of Christ's religion. Ridley clearly intended for lay access to the Bible and Erasmus' work to be left unhindered by the ministers, so long as these texts were read in a quiet and respectful manner; he asked parishioners "[w]hether there be provided and set up in some convenient place of the churche, one boke of the whole Byble in the largest volume, in englysh, and the Paraphrasis of Erasmus upon the gospelles likewise in englyshe, and whether your minister doothe discourage any to loke and rede theruppon, so that it bee done quietlely withoute contencion."[90]

---

88 For the Edwardine prescription for Erasmus' *Paraphrase* to be available in every parish, see *The Edwardian Injunctions, 1547*, no. 7, p. 250.

89 Ridley, *Visitation Injunctions*, Interrogatory 28.

90 Ridley, *Visitation Injunctions*, Interrogatory 29.

One key piece of contemporary evidence suggests that the early reception of Ridley's Erasmian model of ministry and scriptural dissemination was somewhat cool. Richard Phinch, inspired by Ridley's initial visitation of London Diocese, completed a tract entitled *The Epiphanie of the Church*, on 11 July 1550.[91] In the opening lines of the dedicatory epistle, Phinch identifies himself as "the unworthie minister to the small congregation of Eastham."[92] Overall, Phinch's dedication is a consolatory piece, aimed to bolster Ridley's courage: "After I perceived (very reverend father) that your good travell amongest us had not so good successe, as the unfaithfull and superfluous doinges of other sometimes doe obtaine, I . . . mused with myself what should be the cause."[93] According to Phinch, Ridley's insistence that the faith of the people be "tried by the Gospel" was the chief reason that the new bishop was not immediately embraced: "this unwont maner and strangenesse made your godly indevors, of some not to be so thankfully received."[94] From this inauspicious beginning in London, Ridley would have just three years and ten days to implement the Reformation in his new diocese.[95] Phinch's tract suggests that there were few people in London well disposed to Ridley's alterations in religion in the months following Bonner's trial and removal from the see of London.

Phinch's *Epiphanie of the Church* is remarkable not only as an unusually frank account of popular reaction to the early work of Cranmer and his leading ministers, but also because it intentionally connects Ridley with the wider work of the Edwardine religious settlement, and the exegetical writings of Erasmus. Recounting for Ridley the dissent that had met the reform-minded ministers of Henry VIII in the latter 1530s, Phinch urges Ridley to press on with his work: "How thankefully those

---

91 This date is indicated in full on the final page of the work. See Richard Phinch, *The Epiphanie of the Church* ([STC 10877.5] London: Roger Ward, 1590) [hereafter: Phinch, *Epiphanie*], sig. G.2, *verso*.

92 Phinch, *Epiphanie*, sig. A.2, *recto*.

93 Phinch, *Epiphanie*, sig. A.2, *recto*.

94 Phinch, *Epiphanie*, sig. A.2, *recto*.

95 Ridley was seized by Queen Mary's men at Ipswich on 21 July 1553. See Jasper Ridley, *Nicholas Ridley* (London: Longmans, Green & Co. LTD, 1957), pp. 306–07.

things were then of some received, their setting forth and teaching of the same plainly shewed. I do well remember that many were as loth then to forgoe theyr purgatory, as they be now unwilling to take downe their altars, the monuments of the the same."[96] Throughout Phinch's rehearsal of the progress of the Reformation in England during the 1530s and 40s, he refers repeatedly to the necessity of the laity being properly taught. At last he is brought to the Articles of Religion proclaimed by Edward VI, referring to them by number, and extols the plan to make available to all the faithful "the paraphrase of that learned father Erasmus, to the great comfort of the simple who are willing to learne."[97] Phinch was clearly delighted to see in Ridley a man working to advance an Erasmian-inspired, didactic view of faith formation.

Pupils, Pulpits, and the Poor

In promoting this pedagogical and socially oriented vision of ecclesiology, Ridley showed himself most indebted to the man whose biblical scholarship he so admired, Desiderius Erasmus. Throughout Ridley's treatises, and especially in his *Injunctions for the Diocese of London*, he expressed the need to have the charges in his care properly taught. He had a didactic aim in view, even when his topic was the proper furnishings for church sanctuaries: "for that the forme of a table may more move and tourne the simple frome the olde supersticious opinions of the Popish masse and to the right use of the lordes supper, we exhorte the curates, church wardens, and questmen here present, to erect and set up the Lordes bourd, after the forme of an honest table decently covered."[98] The challenge of moving and turning "the simple" from the "olde" superstitions meant that no opportunity was to be missed in

96 Phinch, *Epiphanie*, sig. A.3, *verso*.
97 Phinch, *Epiphanie*, sig. A4, *verso*. For the Edwardine prescription for Erasmus' *Paraphrase* to be available in every parish, see the *Edwardine Injunctions*, no. 7, p. 250. This legislation itself was perhaps yet another instance of the Protestant effort to forge a link, although somewhat disingenuous, between their views and those of Erasmus. See the observations of Wabuda, *Preaching*, pp. 91–94.
98 Ridley, *Visitation Injunctions*, Item V, and *Works*, p. 320.

instructing them in the "new learning" of the Protestant gospel. In fact, a didactic program of ministry would follow naturally from a disciple of Erasmus, since according to John O'Malley, the dominant role Jesus plays in the *philosophia Christi* is that of a pedagogue: "Although Christ is described [by Erasmus] in a number of different terms like 'leader,' 'prince,' or 'head,' nonetheless the 'image' of him that predominates is that of teacher. Christ's redemptive mission is consequently, sapiential, even educational."[99] That Ridley's teaching ministry was focused on social concerns suggests that he fully embraced Erasmus' concept of true piety being anchored not in specific liturgical rites, but in care for the poor.[100] Ridley and his allies managed to resolve this dilemma by placing a ritual aimed at poor relief at the very heart of the Communion rite itself.

Ridley's efforts to teach and lead the faithful were consistently in tune with Erasmus' lead concept of the church as the school of Christ. Viewed from the angle of pedagogy, Ridley's role in preparing the Catechism of 1543, his promotion of Protestant preachers, his public articulation of Protestant views of the Eucharist in the 1549 disputation at Cambridge, his visitation of the whole diocese of London at his accession in 1550, and his prison tracts all served the fundamental purpose of exhorting and instructing, and together they are but various subparts of a single educational labor.

By the 1550s, Ridley's removal of altars from London churches made plain, if any were still in doubt, that he little esteemed the oblational dimensions of traditional priestcraft: "Nowe when we come unto the Lordes boorde, what do we come for? To sacrifice Christe agayne, and to crucifie hym againe? or to feede uppon hym that was once onely crucified, and offered up for us?"[101] Ridley was quite candid in linking these ideas to a

99 O'Malley, "Grammar and Rhetoric," p. 94.
100 For the Humanist's concern for social piety, see, e.g., Erasmus, *Enchiridion*.
101 Cf. the fourth argument on this same topic: "The forme of an aultar was ordained for the Sacrifices of the Lawe, and therfore the aultar in Greeke is called θυσιαστήριον. *Quasi Sacrificii locus*. But nowe bothe the lawe and the Sacrifices thereof doe cease: Wherefore the fourme of the aultare used in the Lawe, ought to cease wythall." Foxe, *Actes and Monuments*, p. 1331.

pedagogical effort to lead or guide the laity from "superstition." As he noted in his visitation articles, his aim was to "tourne the simple from the olde supersticious opinions of the Popish masse. . . . that none mainteine purgatory, invocacion of saintes . . . bederoules, ymages, reliques . . . halowyng of the fyer or altar, or any other such lyke abuses and supersticions, nowe taken awaye by the kynges graces moste godlye procedynges."[102] Likewise, Ridley took aim at the "superstition" of an oblational priesthood in enquiring "[w]hether the minister receiveth the sacrament excepte there be one at the least to communicate with hym," and "whether there be any that privately in the private house have theyr masses, contrary to the forme and order of the boke of Communion."[103] His administration of London Diocese was an effort to promote a counter expression to earlier forms of ministry, in an Erasmian model of the bishop as a teacher, a cherished ideal to be personally embodied by Ridley himself. Under his visitation articles and those of the Edwardine religious settlement, a direct and public act of charity stood at the center of a new order of worship, such that not just biblical texts, but the Eucharistic rite itself would now become a didactic allegory, teaching true, simple piety. It is hard to see where the Erasmus of the *Paraphrase on John* could find much fault with such worship: "By my flesh and my blood I mean my teaching, if you take it eagerly through belief and pass it into the bowels of your mind."[104] These features of the Edwardine religious settlement

102 Ridley, *Visitation Injunctions*, Item I and X. Cf. Ridley's advice to those who chose not to flee England in the reign of Mary: "Thou must be a contributor to the charges of al the disgised apparel, that the popish sacrificing priest, like unto Aaron, must play his part in. Yea when the pardoner commeth about, or the flatteringe frier, to begge for the mayntenaunce of supersticion, except thou doe as thy neighboures doe, loke not longe for to live in rest." Nicholas Ridley, *A Pituous Lamentation of the miserable estate of the church. . . .* ([STC 21052] London: Willyam Powell, dwelling in Fletestrete, at the signe of the George, nere to Sainct Dunstons Church, 1566) [hereafter: Ridley, *Pituous Lamentation*], sig. c.7, *verso*, and *Works*, p. 67.

103 Ridley, *Visitation Injunctions*, Interrogatories 37 and 45, under the heading, "Of the sacramentes and other rites and ceremonyes."

104 Erasmus, *Paraphrase on John*, p. 88 and accompanying editorial notes. See also Brian Gogan, "The Ecclesiology of Erasmus of Rotterdam: A

suggest that it was perhaps much more consciously Erasmian in form and purpose than has been commonly thought, especially when one considers that curates were asked to provide, at half their own expense, Erasmus' *Paraphrases* in every church. Next to the Bible itself, these were considered the most important texts for parishioners to read and study for their spiritual edification.[105]

Through Ridley and his allies, a didactic vision of ecclesiology and soteriology was made incarnate in the reign of Edward VI: Believers would be instructed in Erasmus' own *Paraphrases* in their preparations to hear godly ministers, who were to be preachers and teachers of the Word. While the *philosophia Christi* was not the "new learning" of Protestantism, the former could be brought to serve the purposes of the latter.[106] The hope of the English Reformers, in a manner largely consistent with the publicly stated aims of Erasmus before them, was that the laity would literally learn, even in the sanctuary, to supplant traditional aspects of eucharistic devotion with charitable deeds.

King Edward VI himself subscribed to the idea that true devotion to God should be centered on care for the poor. Tellingly, it was through

Genetic Account," *The Heythrop Journal* 21 (1981): pp. 393–411, which gives a useful overview of scholarship on Erasmus' thinking and re-thinking the role of the Church and the legitimate role of ecclesial authority. There is some evidence that he may have been recanting some of his more radical critiques of the Church in his closing years. For a brief but insightful analysis of Erasmus exegetical principles and their impact on his ecclesiology, see Thomas F. Torrance, "The Hermeneutics of Erasmus," in *Probing the Reformed Tradition, Historical Studies in Honor of Edward A. Dowey Jr.*, eds. E. A. McKee and B. G. Armstrong (Louisville: John Knox Press, 1989), pp. 48–76.

105 "They shall provide within three months next after this visitation, one book of the whole Bible, of the largest volume, in English. And within one twelve-months next after the said visitation, the Paraphrasis of Erasmus also in English upon the Gospels, and the same set up in some convenient place, within the said church that they have cure of, whereas their parishioners may most commodiously resort unto the same and read the same," *The Edwardian Injunctions, 1547*, no. 7, p. 250.

106 For the use and misuse of the term "new learning" in Reformation scholarship, see Richard Rex, "The New Learning," *Journal of Ecclesisatical History* 44 (1993): pp. 26–44.

the prodding of Ridley that Edward directly acted to provide for them. Responding to one of Ridley's court sermons on the needs of the poor in London, Edward VI wrote to him to discover what specific steps might be taken to remedy their needs: "I took myself to be especially touched by your speech, as well in regard of the abilities God hath given me, . . . for as our miseries stand most in need of aid from him, so are we the greatest debtors . . . and therefore, my lord, as you have given me, I thank you, this general exhortation, so direct me (I pray you) by what particular actions I may this way best discharge my duty."[107] In response to Edward's enquiry, Ridley met with the mayor and aldermen of London to consider what was to be done to provide for the poor of the city. Ridley, the mayor, and the aldermen resolved to address poverty in London by considering the various root causes of penury among the city's inhabitants.

The commission discerned three basic types of impoverished persons. First were those who were unable to work as a result of their physical circumstances or a permanent infirmity of the body or the mind. This group included orphans, the elderly, the insane, and the physically or mentally disabled. Poor people whose lives were beset by such circumstances were to be housed, educated, and maintained through charitable endowments. Edward accordingly donated the recently confiscated property and buildings of Grey Friars' Church near Newgate Market for this purpose. The second group consisted of those who were unable to work due to illness, disease, injuries, or war wounds. For these people, Ridley and the aldermen of London recommended that they be housed and their injuries and sicknesses treated, so as to cure as many as possible. Because their treatment required the establishment of a medical facility, Edward donated the property of St. Bartholomew's near Smithfield. The third type of poverty discerned by Ridley and the London aldermen involved people who were poor due to sheer idleness, whom they considered vagabonds and loiterers. For these people, Ridley seems to have envisioned something of a reform school, where the shiftless were to be chastened and "brought to good order."[108] Edward

107 "A Letter of Edward VI to Nicholas Ridley," in Ridley, *Works*, p. xiii.
108 For the details of Ridley's work with the mayor and aldermen of London

relinquished the old royal palace at Bridewell for the establishment of such an institution.

Ridley and the other Edwardine Reformers did not view the plight of the poor merely as a matter of private piety, but as a scourge to be addressed by the realm at large, through its governmental administration. They were particularly desirous of having the property and revenues of recently repressed religious houses and churches used for poor relief. While they labored to make such high ideals a reality, they were hindered in these efforts by the greed of courtiers and nobles.[109] While Ridley, Knox, Latimer, and others, with the aid of young Edward VI, successfully labored to have some buildings and goods donated to alleviate the plight of the poor in London, royal ministers helped themselves to the majority of the spoils of the chantries and religious houses.

Ridley thought that this greed in the spoliation of the religious foundations brought God's wrath on the realm of England, sweeping away the Protestant government and permitting Mary's accession to the throne: "I have hearde that Cranmer, and an other whom I wyll not name, were both in high displeasure, the one for shewinge his conscience secretly, but plainly and fully, . . . for repugning as they might against the late spoile of the church goodes, taken away only by commaundement of the hygher powers, wythoute any lawe or order of justice, and withoute any requeste of consente of them to whome they dyd belonge."[110] Noting that he and several other leading Edwardine ministers did in vain strive to "cure" the "disease" of greedy courtiers, he laments: "for all that could be done of al handes, their disease dydde not minishe, but dayly didde encrease, whyche, no doubt, is no smal occasion in that

and King Edward VI, see the synopsis provided by the editors of the Parker Society's volume of his writings, Ridley, *Works*, p. xiii. With respect to St. Bartholomew's, Edward was probably enlarging upon the foundation established by his father in the previous reign.

109 For the broader context of these initiatives and concerns for Ridley and his closest associates, Cranmer and Latimer, see Wabuda, *Preaching*, pp. 130–38.

110 Ridley, *Pituous Lamentation*, sigs. B.5, *recto*-B.6, *verso*, and Works, pp. 58–59. The "other" that Ridley did not name in the matter of reproving, and incurring the wrath of, the Edwardine magistrates, was himself.

state, of the heavy plague of god, that is poured upon England at this day."[111] Despite the earnest diligence of the Edwardine Reformers, their high ideals for the nation were not to be achieved.

Notwithstanding these reversals, Ridley was confident that the attempt to re-shape devotional and pious practice in the realm was a godly enterprise. Drawing attention to what he had been able to accomplish for the poor, he continued to maintain a sharp contrast between the ritual practices associated with an oblational priesthood and Protestant efforts to supplant chantry foundations with almsgiving: "as for almes dedes, which ar taught in gods word . . . as to provyde for the fatherlesse, infants and orphanes, for the lame, aged, and impotent poore nedy folke, . . . in these works, I say, how wayward were many, in comparison . . . of that greate prodigalitie, whereby in times paste they spared not to spende upon flatteryng fryers, false pardoners, painting and gilding of stockes and stones, to be set up and honored in churches, plainly against gods worde."[112] Such charitable provisions, according to Ridley, were advanced in the Epistle of James as "parte of true religion," calling for the rejection of other kinds of devotional sacrifice: "S. James sayth . . . he setteth more by [alms deeds] then by sacrifice."[113] That Ridley views God as justly chastising England for a lack of charity shown to the poor is a regular theme of his prison writings: "All these thynges doe mynyster matter of more mournynge and bewailing the miserable state that now is, for by this it maye be perceayved, howe well Englande hath deserved this just plague of God. And also it is greatly to be feared that those good thynges, whatsoever they were that had their beginnynge in the time when Goddes word was frely preached, nowe with the exyle and banishment of the same, they wil departe agayne."[114] Ridley was understandably bitter at seeing his pedagogical labors undone by the Marian régime, and such concerns were well founded: Sir Richard Dobbes, whom Ridley praised by name for helping to establish the poor houses in London, was buried according to the old Catholic rites during

---

111 Ridley, *Pituous Lamentation*, sig. B.6, *verso*, and *Works*, pp. 58–59.
112 Ridley, *Pituous Lamentation*, sig. B.7, *recto*, and *Works*, p. 60.
113 Ridley, *Pituous Lamentation*, sig. B.7, *recto*, and *Works*, p. 60.
114 Ridley, *Pituous Lamentation*, sig. B.8, *recto*, and *Works*, p. 61.

Mary's reign, complete with dirige, requiem, and month's mind Masses.[115]

Polity and Polemics

Another dimension of Ridley's effort to teach the laity and provide for the poor in London was his involvement with John Hooper and the so-called "Stranger Church." As with Ridley's aim to establish an Erasmian model of ministry for his diocese, he would also revisit his interactions with Hooper while in prison. In the summer and autumn of 1550, Ridley and Cranmer were involved in the establishment and regulation of the "Stranger Church" in London, which was to be an ecclesial home to hundreds of exiled continental Protestants in Edwardine England. The leaders of the Stranger Church were generally more advanced in their reformation agenda than many of the leading English Reformers were yet prepared to go.[116] Despite misgivings regarding the beliefs and practices of these continental exiles, Cranmer pressed for them to have a regular place of worship in London primarily because this type of centralization would more readily permit the scrutiny and regulation of the radicals' activities. Cranmer's efforts met with some opposition from Ridley, who continued to harass the members and leaders of the Stranger Church—especially for nonconformity in their refusal to worship according to the norms of the *Book of Common Prayer*.[117]

To understand the friction between Cranmer and Ridley on the issue of the Stranger Church, it must be noted that Ridley's visitation articles for London at his translation speak of the need for "a godly unitie to be observed in all our diocesse." In fact, the colophon of the

115 See Susan Brigden, *London and the Reformation* (Oxford: Clarendon Press, 1989) [hereafter: Brigden, *London and the Reformation*], p. 583.
116 See Pettegree, *Foreign Protestant Communities*, pp. 26–31.
117 For more on the Ridley's view of the Stranger Church as a "nuisance" in his diocese, see Diarmaid MacCulloch, *Thomas Cranmer: A Life* (New Haven: Yale University Press, 1996) [hereafter: MacCulloch, *Cranmer*], pp. 477–79. Ridley's opposition to these non-conforming congregations in London was still being felt by Laski as late as October 1552. See Pettegree, *Foreign Protestant Communities*, pp. 42–43.

printed visitation articles declares that they are being issued "for an uniformitie in the Diocesse of London."[118] Ridley understood that it would be very difficult for him to compel traditionalist priests and laity to conform to the new forms of worship if these same rubrics were being flouted by a large and active community of foreign Protestants in the very heart of his episcopal see. Given his decidedly Protestant bent by 1550, Ridley's opposition to the foundation and ritual practices of the Stranger Church may seem odd on first appearances, but we must remember that the campaign for conformity required reigning in both conservative and radical forces, lest one cite the example of the other as an argument for noncompliance. In fact, the nonconformity of Protestants to the new ecclesiastical reforms was probably more repugnant to Ridley than nonconformity among traditionalists, because divisions among the former gave occasion to Catholics to question whether or not the efforts of the Reformers were really led by the Holy Spirit, since they were often divided rather than united in their "recovery" of the ancient faith.[119]

While the membership of the Stranger Church consisted mainly of Italian, French, and Dutch Protestants, its drastically reformed structure and practices were also embraced and promulgated by John Hooper. Hooper was an exile from Henrician England who took up residence in Zurich in the 1540s.[120] Returning home after the death of Henry VIII, he became a well-known evangelical preacher in Edwardine England

118 Ridley, *Visitation Injunctions*, Item V and *Works*, p. 320. Cf. Ridley, *Works*, p. 319.

119 Ridley's concern for the scandal of Protestantism's fractious nature is apparent in the opening section of his *Brief Declaration of the Lord's Supper*, where he admonished those who "pretende therto to be controversies, wher as non suche are in dede; and so to multiplye the debate, the which, the more it dothe encreace, the further it dothe departe from the unitie, that the true christian should desyre." See *Brief Declaracion*, sig. A.7, *verso*, and *Works*, p. 10.

120 For more on Hooper's life and his discipleship to Zwingli and Heinrich Bullinger, see D. G. Newcombe, "Hooper, John (1495x1500–1555)," *Oxford Dictionary of National Biography*, Oxford University Press, 2004 [http://www.oxforddnb.com/view/article/13706, accessed 23 February 2006].

with connections at Court. His experiences in Zurich furnished him with a combined enthusiasm for continental Protestantism, and a personal sympathy for religious exiles. Hooper, like his friend, Jan Laski, certainly saw in the Stranger Church a luminous model for English reform, and was an energetic and articulate supporter of its religious practices and principles. Indeed, so long as the cause of the Stranger Church found favor in Edward VI's Council, so did Hooper.[121] Hooper and Laski hoped that the Stranger Church's radical, Zurich-inspired ecclesial polity would rapidly push England beyond the temporizing formularies found in the 1549 *Book of Common Prayer*.[122] Cranmer and Ridley, despite their quarrel over endowing the Stranger Church with a prerogative for nonconforming worship, were certainly agreed that it was not to be a model for English church reform in 1550. As Hooper attempted to vociferously promote the forms and usages of the continental exiles, Ridley and Cranmer became more resolute in resisting these same efforts. The matter came to a head in a full-blown, public controversy concerning clerical vestments in the fall and winter of 1550. Although Hooper had been designated as the bishop-elect of Gloucester in July, he had been barred from assuming the episcopal see because of his refusal to wear the traditional vestments of a bishop for the ordination service. Ridley simply refused to ordain Hooper without them, despite the latter's having been authorized by the Privy Council to be ordained in attire of his own choosing.[123] Hooper publicly and repeatedly claimed that traditional clerical garments were visible trappings of the "priesthood of Aaron," a phrase in constant use among all the reformers to allude to the Roman priestly hierarchy.

Ridley, already disgruntled by the very presence of the Stranger Church in his diocese, had little patience or sympathy for Hooper's celebration of the exiles' view of clerical vestments. Ridley challenged the bishop-elect's assertions, first exchanging ecclesiological broadsides with him in writings that both men submitted to the Privy Council in

---

121 For more on Hooper and his ardor for the Stranger Church, see MacCulloch, *Cranmer*, pp. 477–84.
122 See Pettegree, *Foreign Protestant Communities*, pp. 32–37.
123 See Pettegree, *Foreign Protestant Communities*, pp. 38–39.

August of 1550.[124] Ridley's written response to Hooper is one of only a handful of extant pieces preserved prior to Ridley's imprisonment by the Marian régime. Unlike his prison writings, this treatise to Hooper was completed a full two years before it became clear to English Protestants that Ridley was to be a martyr to their cause, and it is therefore remarkable that this treatise was preserved at all.[125] Ridley's earnest expression of his views of church order and administration in this short work are all the more valuable, since they were crafted under less adverse circumstances than he was to know from the summer of 1553 onward. Ridley's manuscript is also of immense historical value because in it he cites specific passages of Hooper's petition to the Council, setting them off in quotes. This feature of the work gives us some insights into Hooper's own views, as does the fragment of Hooper's treatise that was printed by Gloucester Ridley in his eighteenth-century biography of his kinsman, Nicholas.[126]

Nicholas' answer to Hooper on the question of clerical vestments outlines Ridley's principles of responsible Church reform. In this treatise, Ridley is primarily concerned to underscore the proper distinction between essential and "indifferent" or *adiaphora* matters in church structure and administration. The first line of Hooper's rejection of traditional episcopal vestments rested on the assertion that they were not an "indifferent matter," because in a reformed church, their use represented a scandalous retention of forms associated with the abominable Roman priestly hierarchy. The second line of Hooper's defense was to declare that if the use of traditional vestments was indeed an *adiaphora* matter, then his failure to employ them could not be held against him. Ridley readily exploited the essential contradiction in Hooper's premises.[127]

---

124 See "Martin Micron to Heinreich Bullinger," in *Original Letters Relative to the English Reformation*, vol. 2, ed. H. Robinson, for the Parker Society (Cambridge: Cambridge University Press, 1847), pp. 567–69.

125 See *Bradford*, vol. 2, p. 373. See *ibid.* pp. 375–95 for the text of Ridley's treatise. At the time that it was printed by the Parker Society in the mid-nineteenth century, the manuscript of Ridley's tract was in the collection of Sir Thomas Phillips "of Middlehill, near Worcester."

126 See *Bradford*, vol. 2, p. 373.

127 For example, Hooper's reference to Paul's retention of *adiaphora* Hebrew

Consistent in form with Hooper's objections, Ridley's response presents a two-fold division of the matter, although he takes up the topics in reverse order by explicating the doctrine of adiaphorism in general before addressing the issue of vestments in particular. Hooper's basic charge against Cranmer, Ridley, and the other leading English Reformers is that their insistence on the use of traditional episcopal vestments for ordination added something more to ecclesiastical polity than what is required by scripture.[128] This was the very claim that the Reformers had laid against Rome, and so naturally provoked a mordant response from Ridley. To Hooper, an *adiaphora* matter of ritual practice was one in which neither commission nor omission held significant consequences for the church. Ridley sought to disabuse Hooper of this view, which to the Bishop seemed a clear misapprehension of the concept of adiaphorism: "many things of themselves be indifferent, whereof the use is profitable, and the non use harmful; . . . as the times appointed for common prayer, preaching of God's word and receiving of the sacraments. The due use of these and such like do profit, for they do edify."[129]

As ever, Ridley's concern with a "godly order in the church" is central both to his vision of church reform and proper ecclesiastical polity. In these remarks, there is more than a hint that the real rub for him is Hooper's attempt to force the practices of Zurich onto the English Church. Given Ridley's consistent focus on ecclesiastical order and his original misgivings with regard to the Stranger Church, it is hard to imagine that Hooper's stated opposition to vestments did not elicit a reproach from Ridley to Cranmer.[130]

rituals (see, e.g., Acts 15 and Galatians 2 on the circumcision controversy surrounding the admission of Gentiles among the original Hebrew Christian communities) receives Ridley's sardonic remark: "Here methinketh that the writer hath forgotten what he said before, that the vestments were Aaronical, which if they be granted to be, then his answer maketh all against himself. And therefore I say once again, *Conveniet nulli, qui secum dissidet ipse*: [He will agree with no man, who himself differs with himself]," *Bradford*, vol. 2, p. 392. Cf. the fragment of Hooper's text, *ibid.* p. 373.

128 Hooper, *Bradford*, vol. 2, p. 373.
129 Ridley, *Bradford*, vol. 2, p. 376. See Pettegree, *Foreign Protestant Communities*, pp. 38–39.
130 See MacCulloch, *Cranmer*, pp. 477–84.

By bringing forth examples to highlight the erroneousness of Hooper's view that disregard of an "indifferent" thing in church order was of no real consequence, Ridley had won only half the battle. To fully reprove Hooper on the true meaning of adiaphorism, Ridley had also to show that there were necessary matters of church polity wherein scripture provided very little guidance. One passage of Hooper's tract in particular, in which he asserts that absolutely nothing in the Church should be done without the express command of scripture, is sharply rebuked by Ridley: "For how is it possible [to] receive the holy communion, but thou must either sit, stand, kneel, or lay? Thou must either take it at one time or another, fasting or after meat, clothed or naked, in this place or in another. Without the sum of these circumstances it is impossible to do that that the Lord biddeth thee." However: "none of all these circumstances are commanded in scripture."[131] The gist of Ridley's argument is that while the times, places, and postures for worship are "indifferent" matters to be determined by church leaders, they require devout submission on behalf of the ministers and laity once established by the proper authorities. For Hooper, any "indifferent" matter could be observed or omitted on the discretion of each minister.[132] Ridley rejects this individualist view of adiaphorism, reserving such discretion solely to the highest levels of ecclesial leadership. Once the national ecclesial body made a determination as to what was best in administrative matters, the clergy associated with that church were expected to observe the established rules of polity.

Ridley obviously suspects that Hooper's ideas concerning church polity and the rule of scripture are akin to the negative hermeneutic of the Anabaptists, who also insisted that positively nothing is to be considered necessary for the right order of the church that is not expressly affirmed in scripture.[133] The Bishop of London pointedly draws out the similarities between Hooper's position on ecclesiology and that of the Anabaptists: "If this reason should take place, 'The apostles used it not,

---

131 Ridley, *Bradford*, vol. 2, pp. 390–91.
132 See Pettegree, *Foreign Protestant Communities*, p. 38. Cf. Pettegree, *Marian Protestantism*, p. 142.
133 See Pettegree, *Foreign Protestant Communities*, p. 38.

ergo it is not lawful for us to use it'—or this either, 'They did it, ergo we must needs do it'—then . . . we may have no ministration of Christ's sacraments in churches, for they had no churches, but were fain to do all in their own houses; we must baptize abroad in the fields as the apostles did." Ridley extends his *reductio ad absurdum*: "We may not receive the holy communion but at supper, and with the table furnished with other meats, as the Anabaptists do now stiffly and obstinately affirm that it should be; our naming of the child in baptism, our prayer upon him, our crossing, and our threefold abrenunciation, and our white chrisom, all must be left, for these we cannot prove by God's word, that the apostles did use them."[134] In effect, Ridley turns Hooper's argument back upon him: since priestly vestments are not expressly condemned by scripture, any assertion that they are forbidden or evil is an "ungodly adding to God's word."[135] Taken to their logical conclusion, Ridley's arguments also raise sharp questions against the concept of scripture's ruling authority itself, in matters of ecclesiology, given the number of necessary things he enumerates that he cannot locate within the books of the Bible.

Hooper built his scriptural case on a passage from St. Paul concerning the Gospel's supersession of the Law: "If I build up again those things which I tore down, then I prove myself a transgressor."[136] To understand how and why Hooper linked the use of episcopal vestments, the priesthood of Aaron, and Roman Catholic eucharistic rituals together requires some insight into the early Protestants' application of the Letter to the Hebrews to their contemporary historical context. In the seventh chapter of that book, the author compares and contrasts the Levitical priesthood with that of Melchizedek. The behavioral code and obligations of the sons of Levi are described in the Old Testament Books of Exodus and Leviticus with a great deal of ritualistic formalism.[137]

134 Ridley, *Bradford*, vol. 2, pp. 382–83.
135 Hooper, *Bradford* vol. 2, p. 373. Cf. Ridley, *Bradford* vol. 2, p. 382.
136 For Hooper's use of Galatians 2:8 (which speaks to the issue of circumcision and Gentile admission into the original Christian Hebrew communities), see *Bradford* vol. 2, p. 373.
137 See especially Exodus 28 in regard to the foundation of the Priesthood of Aaron and the garments and sacrifices associated with the office.

Against this "priesthood of the law," the author of Hebrews compares the figure of Melchizedek, a mysterious priest king of Salem who, according to the Book of Genesis,[138] proceeds to bless Abraham following a successful military campaign. As a figure, Melchizedek merely materializes within the Old Testament canon, without any hint of a blood kinship to any member of the Levitical priesthood, an hereditary office passed from father to son. Because Melchizedek is both priest and king, neither of which power appears to be derived from any genealogical descent, the author of Hebrews likens him to Christ. The comparison to Jesus is made even more apparent in that the blessing that Melchizedek extends to Abraham is an offering of bread and wine. The author of Hebrews declares that Jesus was a priest after the Order of Melchizedek, rather than after the Order of Aaron, a descendant of Levi. The comparison is made in order to establish that the intercessory work of Christ, as both priest and victim, supersedes the priesthood of the Law, with blood rites that involve the sacrificing of animals as atonement for sin.

Ridley and other early English Protestants were eager to declare that theirs was a priesthood of the Gospel according to the Order of Melchizedek, superseding that of the Law, which they represented as the Catholic priestly hierarchy with its accent on the sacrificial character of the Eucharist. In the same way that the author of Hebrews suggests that the Levitical priesthood has its end in the salvific work of Christ, so Protestants believed their new clerical order spelled the abolition of the traditional Roman priestly hierarchy. In this multivalent comparison, Hooper viewed the use of traditional clerical vestments as forms associated with the practices of the "Aaronical priesthood" of Rome.[139]

Ridley attacked Hooper's historical and theological construct on several fronts simultaneously. The Bishop first asserts that the priesthood of Aaraon was, according to scripture, founded on divine revelation: "where it is said [of clerical vestments] that 'they show the pharisaical superstition

138 For the first mention of Melchizedek in scripture, see Genesis 14. Cf. Psalm 110 and Hebrews.
139 See Hooper, *Bradford* vol. 2, p. 373, where the author links the Catholic priesthood to that of Aaron. Cf. Ridley, *Bradford* vol. 2, p. 380; Cf. Ridley, *Pituous Lamentation*, sig. c.7, *verso*, and *Works*, p. 67.

and priesthood of Aaron,' first, if it be meant that Aaron's priesthood was pharisaical superstition, it is blasphemously spoken against God's Holy ordinance."[140] Early on in his treatise against Hooper, Ridley urges that things that might be readily reformed ought to be retained in the Church: "if the right use be profitable, and may be restored, and the abuse more easily taken away than the thing itself, then such are not, because they have been abused, to be taken away, but to be reformed and amended, and so kept still."[141] On these grounds, Ridley challenges Hooper to show that the historical origins of vestments resulted from the work of impious individuals or corrupt circumstances: "He saith, [clerical vestments] were brought into the church by them that abused both God and man: and yet he doth not deny but they were before the usurpation of the pope. Then let him show the first author of them, and then men shall judge the better, whether they were such that did abuse both God and man."[142]

For Hooper's part, even these devastating critiques by Ridley did not immediately reduce him to comply with the English statutes then in force. He remained obstinate, and published a further defense of his views in December of 1550. This move exasperated even Cranmer, who had the bishop-elect of Gloucester confined to Lambeth that same month. Probably urged on by his friend, Jan Laski, Hooper was still obdurate, and the Privy Council had him committed to prison proper in late January 1551. Only after two weeks' stay in the Fleet did Hooper yield, being consecrated in full Episcopal regalia by Cranmer and Ridley on 8 March 1551.[143]

It is tempting to view Ridley's spirited defense in 1550 of the utility of clerical vestments as a solemn nod to Church tradition. In reality, his treatise discloses that the English Reformers had more drastic changes for ecclesial polity in mind well before the 1552 *Book of Common Prayer* was issued: "The church hath received these vestments by lawful

---

140 Ridley, *Bradford* vol. 2, p. 380. For the establishment of the priesthood of Aaron and the garments prescribed by the authority of God, see Exodus 28.
141 Ridley, *Bradford* vol. 2, p. 378.
142 Ridley, *Bradford* vol. 2, p. 393.
143 See Pettegree, *Foreign Protestant Communities*, pp. 38–42.

authority, and with an agreeable consent, for causes to them seen good and godly: and, until it shall be otherwise dispossessed by order and good authority, we will plead a possession."[144] We should note that Ridley does not question *if* the use of traditional clerical vestments will be "dispossessed by order and good authority," but rather states that an imminent dispossession is no hindrance to defending vestments "until" their use be repressed by statute.[145]

In fact, in 1550 Ridley was no less willing than Hooper to force Aaron and Melchizedek to bear arms in contemporary theological battles. In this same treatise to Hooper, Ridley declared that clerical vestments were not necessary for proper ministry: "For so to say were indeed to defend the papistical and Aaronical priesthood both, against Christ's gospel."[146] Thus, Ridley intentionally coupled Catholic conceptions of ministry in his own day to the traditional Jewish priesthood as outlined in Exodus and the other books of the Old Covenant.

Ridley's premeditated plan to further alter the practices of the English church in 1553 accounts for his reflexive condemnation of traditional clerical vestments just two years later. In 1555, using words that could have been penned by Hooper himself, Ridley warned Protestants who did not flee Marian England that they would otherwise be forced to support Catholic usages: "Thou must be a contributor to the charges of al the disgised apparel, that the popish sacrificing priest, like unto Aaron, must play his part in. Yea when the pardoner commeth about, or the flatteringe frier, to begge for the mayntenaunce of supersticion, except thou doe as thy neighboures doe, loke not longe for to live in rest."[147] There is little in

144 Ridley, *Bradford* vol. 2, p. 386
145 Nor was Ridley's later opposition to traditional priestly vestments merely theoretical. His final act of direct resistance of the Marian régime was refusal to wear such garments at his official degradation, on 15 October 1555, the day before he was burned. See Foxe, *Actes and Monuments*, p. 1768 and Ridley, *Works*, pp. 286 ff. For this insight, I am indebted to Patrick Collinson, *The Elizabethan Puritan Movement* (Oxford: Oxford University Press, 1989), p. 96.
146 See Ridley to Hooper on the Edwardine vestments controversy, *Bradford* vol. 2, p.375. Cf., e.g., Ridley, *Works*, p. 195.
147 Ridley, *Pituous Lamentation*, sig. c.7, *verso*, and *Works*, p. 67.

this statement that would have failed to satisfy the bishop-elect of Gloucester in 1550. Indeed, at that period of his life, Ridley actively sought reconciliation with Hooper, then a fellow prisoner in Marian England, suggesting that relations between the two had remained tense up to that point.[148]

Ridley's desire to pit the priesthood of Aaron against that of Melchizedek is not only reminiscent of Hooper, however, but also of Erasmus. Recalling that Ridley's Aaron and Melchizedek typology is a kind of Protestant shorthand for the ministries of the Law and of the Gospel respectively, Ridley is contrasting the two here in a manner wholly consistent with Erasmus' "New Testament of Light and Old Testament of Darkness" dualism.[149] As the Edwardine program of religious reform advanced, Ridley seems to have increasingly followed Erasmus' lead in his view of the relationship between the Old and New Covenants. In Ridley's 1555 disputation at Oxford, for example, he reprised his rival Law and Gospel forms of ministry theme, declaring: "It is likewise doubted, after what order the sacrificing Priest shall be, whether after the order of Aaron, or els after the order of Melchisedech. For as farre as I know, the holy scripture doth allow no moe."[150]

Altered Worship

The deliberate contrast Ridley drew between the Old and New Covenants in his writings, intentionally attempting to distance Christianity from the religion of Israel, fit well with his having altars destroyed and removed from London churches, including St. Paul's Cathedral. Ridley was explicit about this aim, arguing that the retention of altars in churches gave too strong a similitude to Levitical rites: "The form of an altar was ordained for the sacrifices of the Law, and therefore the altar in Greek is

---

148 See Ridley's reference to their past clashes and the fact that he now looks upon Hooper as a brother in *Works*, p. 355.

149 See, e.g., Erasmus, *Paraphrase on Mark*, p. 75, and throughout the entire work where the "darkness," "fear," and "despair" given to men through the "carnal" Old Covenant is repeatedly contrasted with the "light," "sweetness," and "love" given to them by the New Covenant. See esp. pp. 14–16, 21, 24, 26, 30–31, 59, 86–87, 103, and 132–33.

150 Foxe, *Actes and Monuments*, p. 1442, and Ridley, *Works*, p. 195.

called θυσιαστήριον, *quasi sacrificii locus*. But now both the law and the sacrifices thereof do cease: wherefore the form of the altar ought to cease withal."[151] Like Ridley's hero, Erasmus, the Bishop of London's knowledge of the Old Testament Levitical prescriptions is secondhand, not rooted in a firm knowledge of biblical Hebrew, but refracted through his understanding of Greek and Latin linguistic concepts. These features of his ecclesiology owe much to Erasmus, whose learning Ridley so admired and attempted to emulate as a professor of Greek. As Richard Phinch clearly recognized in 1550, Ridley's promotion of the Edwardine religious settlement was part and parcel of his effort to personally embody the Erasmian ideal of a teacher in the administration of the diocese of London. That these guidelines for the instruction of the laity called for the use of Erasmus' own *Paraphrases* of the Gospels to be set up in every church in England, and consulted regularly by all ministers, was certainly no coincidence.

151 Ridley, *Works*, p. 323.

The Main Façade of Rochester Cathedral

Rochester Cathedral, episcopal see of St. John Fisher, from 1504 to his death in 1535, and of Nicholas Ridley, from 1548 to 1550.

Chapter Door, Rochester Cathedral

Erected by Bishop Haymo in the fourteenth century, the Chapter Door at Rochester was then part of a new passageway by which the monks entered the Cathedral to pray the hours of devotion. The door features the figures of Ecclesia and Synagoga, to left and right, respectively.

Chapter Door, Rochester Cathedral, Figure of Ecclesia

Detail of Ecclesia from the Chapter Door at Rochester Cathedral. The figure was decapitated by Protestant iconoclasts during the Reformation and restored in the nineteenth century.

Chapter Door, Rochester Cathedral, Figure of Synagoga

Detail of Synagoga from the Chapter Door at Rochester Cathedral. By the hands and posture of the figure, it is evident that the original face was of an aged woman, similarly attired to Ecclesia, on the opposite side of the entrance. The figure was decapitated by Protestant iconoclasts during the Reformation and restored in the nineteenth century.

The Door of the Prison Cell that held Ridley, Latimer, and Cranmer at Bocardo Prison, Oxford

Although the Bocardo Prison at Oxford was destroyed by fire in the early 1770s, the Bishop's Door, so called because it secured the cell that held Nicholas Ridley, Hugh Latimer, and Thomas Cranmer, was preserved. It can be seen today in the tower of St. Michael's at the North Gate, Oxford.

Execution Site of Ridley, Latimer, and Cranmer at Oxford

On October 16, 1555 Nicholas Ridley and Hugh Latimer were burnt at this site, now in the middle of Broad Street, Oxford. Five months later, Thomas Cranmer was put to death here by the same means, on March 21, 1556.

Churchyard of St. George's, Southwark and Remains of Marshalsea Prison

This plot of ground formed part of the churchyard of St. George's South-wark in the sixteenth century, where the body of Edmund Bonner was originally laid to rest. The low brick wall in the background is all that remains of the Marshalsea Prison, where Bonner was held from 1549 to 1553 under Edward VI, and again under under Elizabeth I from 1560 until his death on September 5, 1569.

Altar and Central Apse, Copford Church, Colchester

In 1809, a workman reported the discovery of Edmund Bonner's coffin here, under the floor at the north side of the altar. John Morren or Morwen, chaplain and secretary to Bonner, was rector of Copford from 1558-1559. Because of his close association with Bonner and intimate knowledge of Copford Church, Morren likely orchestrated or assisted with the effort to have Bonner's remains relocated from their original resting place in the churchyard of St. George's, Southwark.

The Poor Men's Chest of Copford Church, Colchester

The poor men's chest at Copford Church, Colchester, not only features the original, working keys, but the tool that was used to fasten the bolts on the heavy iron bands that still make it nearly impregnable today. Complete with slots cut through the thick wood of the lid, it was likely used as a part of the revised liturgy promulgated under Edward VI in 1547.

Poor Men's Chest, St. Michael's at the North Gate, Oxford

This chest was purchased in 1652 for the use of the Church of St. Michael's at the North Gate, Oxford. In keeping with the Edwardine tradition of the poor men's chest, it features three locks. The usual practice for distributing monies from the alms chest called for three members of the congregation—usually the Church Wardens—to all be present together to open the coffer.

Poor Men's Chest, St. George's, Southwark

This chest has been in use at St. George's, Southwark since 1738. Despite the fact that the lid has been replaced, it still serves as a poor chest. In the tradition of the Edwardine religious injunctions, the inscription suggests that its contents were managed by three wardens: William Hill, Thomas Lambe, and William Oldham.

Modern Poor Men's Chest, Canterbury Cathedral

This modern alms box stands in Canterbury Cathedral, and forms part of the long tradition of the poor men's chest stretching back to mid-Tudor times and the reign of Edward VI.

Chapter 4
Bonner on Biblical Interpretation

In contrast to Erasmus and Ridley, Edmund Bonner's principles for interpreting scripture are clearly in line with the epideictic tradition of Humanist exegesis. Although Erasmus preferred deliberative oratory, coupled with a Platonist view of Christ in the notion of a *philosophia Christi* that often induced him to present the relationship between the Old and New Testaments in a dualistic fashion,[1] early modern advocates of demonstrative or epideictic forms of classical rhetoric tended to read scripture inter-textually, as a single, comprehensive narrative of the salvific and monumental acts of God recounted in two Testaments.[2] This method of bringing classical rhetorical themes to bear on questions of exegesis was characteristic of Italian Humanism, and resulted in a more integrated and harmonious depiction of the relationship between the Old Covenant and the New.

The exegetical writings of John Colet, early English Humanist, Dean

---

1   See Chapter II above on Ridley's Exegetical Method and John W. O'Malley, "Grammar and Rhetoric in the Pietas of Erasmus," *The Journal of Medieval and Renaissance Studies* 18.1 (1988) [hereafter: O'Malley, "Grammar and Rhetoric"]: pp. 89, 94, and 99.

2   John W. O'Malley, *Praise and Blame in Renaissance Rome: Rhetoric, Doctrine and Reform in the Sacred Orators of the Papal Court, c. 1450–1521*, vol. 3 of *Duke Monographs in Medieval and Renaissance Studies* (Durham: Duke University Press, 1979) [hereafter: O'Malley, *Praise and Blame*], p. 49. Over against Erasmus' deliberative emphasis in exegesis, the author states that the epideictic rhetoric typical of the Papal Court sermons of the late fifteenth and early sixteenth centuries: "evince a tendency to look upon scripture more as a history of God's actions and less as a manual for doctrinal proof-texts or a book of artfully disguised philosophical principles." Cf. *ibid.* pp. 38–49 and O'Malley, "Grammar and Rhetoric."

of St. Paul's Cathedral School, and friend of Erasmus, offer a representative pattern of demonstrative rhetorical exegesis. Colet studied in Paris and Italy between 1493 and 1496, becoming an ardent advocate of Italian Humanism in biblical scholarship. Colet's later exegetical clashes with Erasmus reveal the signal differences between Italian and Erasmian Humanism in the sphere of scriptural interpretation.

The writings of William Peryn and Henry Pendelton, who worked closely with Bonner in his efforts to challenge and intellectually discredit Protestant ideas in the Diocese of London during the 1540s and 1550s, reveal that Bonner's ideas and circle of friends were deeply indebted to Italian Humanism. Peryn and Pendleton are of particular interest because they assisted Bonner in the administration of the Diocese of London under Mary I by writing portions of the *Homelies* and aiding Bonner in the composition of the *Necessary and Profitable Doctrine*. A study of their work, as well as the earliest editions of John Foxe's *Actes and Monuments* (commonly known as the *Book of Martyrs*), sets the stage for a reappraisal of Bonner's writings and labors within the context of the Italian Humanist tradition.

Classical Rhetoric and the
Renaissance Renewal of Biblical Studies

John O'Malley, S.J., leading scholar of the Renaissance revival of classical rhetoric, sketches Italian Humanism's key divergences from Erasmian Humanism by examining sermons preached at the Papal Court between 1450 and 1521.[3] He notes that the Italian Humanist tradition was more concerned with the deeds of God in Salvation History than is often seen in an Erasmian landscape.[4] O'Malley believes the differences in Erasmian and Italian Humanism result in different models of soteriology, the branch of theology concerned with Christ's salvation of man.

A consideration of the classical rhetorical triad or triangle is helpful in distinguishing the divergent Erasmian and Italian Humanist approaches

---

3   See O'Malley, *Praise and Blame.*
4   O'Malley, *Praise and Blame*, p. 49. Cf. *ibid.* pp. 38–49 and O'Malley, "Grammar and Rhetoric," pp. 89, 94, and 99.

to biblical exegesis and soteriology. In classical rhetoric, students were often urged to think about the relationships between the speaker, the speech or text, and the audience. For Erasmus and his disciples, this triad is composed of God as the speaker, Christ as the speech, and man as the audience. The identification of Christ as the "speech of God" in this triad results in an oracular concentration on the words of Christ recounted in the Gospels as the chief way of knowing what God wants to say to all mankind. By contrast, devotees of Italian Humanism consider the whole of scripture, the Old Covenant and the New, to be the "speech" of God. In this conception, the broad narrative, or the whole of salvation history, is God's message or speech to man. This model does not require that God's "speech" to man prior to the advent of Christ be disvalued or discounted. For this reason, followers of the Italian Humanist tradition tended to place less opposition between Old and New Testament rites and themes, since Christ is seen as the culmination or fullest expression of God's communications with man, rather than a wholly new message. This approach to biblical exegesis, because it is focused on God's relationship with man from Creation onward, also does not devote exclusive attention to God's words alone, but also considers His acts in human history, as recounted in both Testaments.

An awareness of these different conceptions of God's message to all humanity helps to account for the fact that not every Humanist became an ardent reformer, let alone a Protestant, in early modern Europe. The Erasmian and Italian Humanist traditions diverge at key points from each other, yet both are authentically humanistic in their concern for the reception, promulgation, and living out God's message or plan for the salvation of mankind. John Colet, Edmund Bonner, William Peryn, and Henry Pendleton were indeed Humanists, despite their lack of enthusiasm for Erasmian or Protestant re-appraisals of the role of Christ or the Church in Salvation History. Colet and Bonner share with Ridley and Erasmus a deep concern to explicate the historical dimensions of the biblical text, as well as a focus on particular linguistic terms in the source languages of biblical passages. Colet and Bonner, however, are less concerned than Erasmus and Ridley with interpolation or drawing the words of scripture into a different historical and religious context from what is presented in the Old Testament. In contrast to Erasmus and Ridley, neither Colet nor Bonner focuses on Christ's words as a completely new or different message from God's self-revelation to the Hebrew people in the Old Covenant.

With respect to Colet, the resemblance of his exegetical method to the contemporary work of late fifteenth-century papal preachers is substantial, owing probably to his residing and studying in Rome during the 1490s. Colet had living contact with this strand of Humanist Biblicism near the middle of the very period that O'Malley highlights. Bonner is likewise more concerned with the deeds of Christ in his explications of scripture than Erasmus' more exclusive concentration on the words of Jesus. It is possible that Bonner was partially influenced in this regard through Colet's lasting legacy in the diocese of London, most notably in the foundation of the Cathedral School at St. Paul's, where there was a strong emphasis on the boy Christ as a teacher.[5] It is more likely, however, that it was Bonner's own contact with Italian Humanism that accounts for his focus on the acts of Christ in a way that recalls Colet. In April 1530, Bonner wrote to Thomas Cromwell to borrow copies of the *Triumphs* of Petrarch and Castiglione's *The Courtier* in Italian. These readings would have acquainted Bonner with two major champions of the Italian Renaissance. Bonner was also resident at the Papal Court from 1532–1533, where he served as Henry VIII's ambassador to the Pope.[6]

The Hermeneutic Feast

Colet's understanding of the relationship between the Old and New Testaments is plainly revealed in the contrast between his and

---

5   See Susan Wabuda, *Preaching During the English Reformation* (Cambridge: Cambridge University Press, 2002) [hereafter: Wabuda, *Preaching*], pp. 147–48.

6   Gina Mary Vere Alexander, "The Life and Career of Edmund Bonner, Bishop of London, Until His Deprivation in 1549," unpublished doctoral dissertation (University of London: 1960) [hereafter: Alexander, "Bonner Until His Deprivation"], p. 53. We should also note that Cardinal Pole, though English by birth, was an exile in Rome for two decades and a member of a circle of impressive Italian Humanists before returning to England as papal legate under Mary. See Eamon Duffy, *Saints and Sinners: A History of the Popes* (New Haven: Yale University Press, 2001), pp. 210–11.

Erasmus' treatments of 1 Corinthians 10. The Epistle opens with Paul's famous double analogy of the Red Sea and Christian baptism, the manna provided to Israel in the wilderness with the Eucharist. Constrained by the circumstances of the text, Erasmus made a rare acknowledgment of the similitude between the signs given to Israel and their full revelation in Christ. Yet he could not leave the topic without placing a sharp interpolative rebuke of the Hebrews on the lips of Paul: "Because they fell again to lust, to idolatry . . . they fell from the grace of God. . . . So that in this day, no nation is more rejected of God than the Hebrews."[7]

The exegetical difference between Erasmus and Colet with respect to these verses is striking. Colet likens the Old and New Testaments to a lavish table setting. In the Old Testament, "the dishes are concealed and covered, and all is sealed. The setting aside of the covers is in the New Testament, with the revealing of the rich banquet of truth and an invitation to eat. The Master of the Feast has opened all." The preparations for the feast begun in the Old Testament are neither tainted nor merely incidental: "He [Christ] first in magnificent fashion piled the table high—through the ministry of Moses—with the covered dishes, and he was present there as Ruler of the Banquet, but unseen. And afterwards he himself struck off the covers, offering himself, Truth itself,

---

7   Erasmus, *Paraphrasis in Epist. Pauli ad Cor. 1*, Cap. VII, in vol. VII of *Desiderii Erasmi Roterdami Opera Omnia*, ed. Jean Leclerc (Leiden: Lugduni Batavorum, 1706), p. 892, col. C: "*Illi quonium ad luxem, ad idolatrum . . . redibant, exciderunt à gratia Dei; . . . Quin hodie nullum hominum genus longius rejectum est à Deo, quam Judæorum.*" Cf. Colet's reflections on the same theme, the relationship of the Hebrews to the New Covenant: "This more abundant law is the excellence of that City of Christ, *set on a hill*, which is the church of the faithful, and is formed of Jews and Gentiles. *For there is no difference.* Without any distinction, as God wills, does His grace take hold upon both Jews and Gentiles. Out of sinners, as materials, he has built up His holy church." John Colet, *Exposition of St. Paul's Epistle to the Romans*, in *Letters to Radulphus on the Mosaic Account of the Creation, Together with Other Treatises*, trans. and ed. J. H. Lupton (Cambridge: Cambridge University Press, 1876) [hereafter: Colet, *Exposition of Romans*], emphasis original as the passage includes citations of Matthew 5:17 and Romans 3:21, p. 105.

for the plentiful banqueting of his chosen guests."[8] Colet asserts the superiority of the New Covenant without totally denigrating the people and religion of the Old, a move that stands at some distance from Erasmus' explication of this same text. Not proceeding from a neo-Platonic dualism with respect to the religion of Israel and Christianity, Colet did not attempt to draw the sharpest contrast possible between the Books of Moses and the Gospel of Christ, as did Erasmus.

Colet's banquet analogy also served him well in illustrating the crucial matter at stake in Paul's prohibition of meat offered to idols: "Only with Christ, then, should we be banqueters, at the splendid table of the Scriptures; and in the New Testament we should feast the more abundantly, since there the water of Moses has been changed by Christ himself into wine" [John 11: 1–11].[9] Colet extended this motif to treat the matter of pagan philosophy's relationship to the Gospel: "At other tables, in other books—those of the pagans—where there is nothing with the savor of Christ and nothing without the savor of the Demon—in those places, surely, no Christian man ought to seat himself, unless he should wish to appear a guest of the Demon rather than of the Lord."[10] It goes without saying that such intellectual exclusivity was hardly in keeping with Colet's own precepts, most notably in the pagan sources he approved for teaching boys good Latin in the curriculum of the St. Paul's school.[11] Such a statement does, however, highlight how far Colet was from joining with Erasmus in the curious devotion, "*sancte Socrate, ora pro nobis.*"[12] Colet did not share the

8   John Colet, *Commentary on First Corinthians*, trans. and eds. Bernard O'Kelly and Catharine Jarrott, Medieval and Renaissance Texts & Studies 21 (Binghamton, New York: Medieval & Renaissance Texts & Studies, 1985) [hereafter: Colet, *Commentary on First Corinthians*], p. 217.

9   Colet, *Commentary on First Corinthians*, p. 217.

10   Colet, *Commentary on First Corinthians*, p. 217.

11   See editor's note 13 to Colet, *Commentary on First Corinthians*, p. 217.

12   Erasmus, *The Godly Feast*, in *Ten Colloquies*, trans. and ed. Craig R. Thompson (New York: Macmillan, 1987), p. 134. The divergence between Colet's sacred banquet analogy here and Erasmus' *Godly Feast* could not be more complete. In the Erasmian analogue, the focus of the meal is nothing so material as food, but rather the delicious conversation of the guests and the texts they sample, many of which are wise pagan aphorisms, that

bold confidence displayed in Erasmus' *Enchiridion Militis Christiani* that "not only [the Platonists'] ideas but their very mode of expression approaches that of the Gospels."[13]

The rich interplay of Old and New Testament themes in the exegetical writings of Colet can also be seen in his reflections on Paul's *Epistle to the Romans*. In this commentary, Colet was at pains to show the continuities between the Old Covenant and the New, noting that Christ, as the very archetype of virtue, better establishes and perfects the Law of Moses: "For he was all righteousness; that He might Himself appear a full and complete law to men, and that, by believing in Him, they might need no other law besides. And thus the faith of Jesus does not *make void the law*, but *establishes* and builds it up, advances and perfects it."[14] Far from abrogating the Old Testament, Colet urged that "He who gives a better development to anything, is not doing away with it, but rather settling and confirming it. By His new and more perfect Covenant, Jesus threw light upon the Old Covenant of God. He did not destroy, but established, that Covenant. He completed God's will, and joined in attesting, as a present witness, the half-completed testament."[15] Thus while Colet could allow a qualitative difference between the Old Testament and the New, his remarks on the subject never devolve into the stark darkness-and-light dualism of

they in turn liken to the Gospels and the *philosophia Christi*. Throughout this colloquy, Platonist themes are positively compared to Christian fasts and rituals, which are decried as "Jewish." See, e.g., pp. 148–50. Erasmus is mistaken here, however, in the identity of Socrates' interlocutor; it was not to Crito that his remarks were made concerning God's acceptance of his labors, but Simmias and Cebes. See editor's note 47.

13   Desiderius Erasmus, *The Handbook of the Militant Christian* (*Enchiridion Militis Christiani*), in *The Essential Erasmus*, trans. and ed. John P. Dolan (New York: Meridian, 1993) [hereafter: Erasmus, *Enchiridion*], p. 36.

14   Colet, *Exposition of Romans*, p. 109. Emphasis original, as the citation includes terms drawn directly from Romans 3:31.

15   Colet, *Exposition of Romans*, p. 109. In several key respects, Moses assumes a similar role in the exegetical thought of Colet as Christ does for Erasmus. In Colet's *Letters to Radulphus*, it is Moses who is a pedagogue, setting forth Platonic wisdom in a series of metaphors accommodated to the uneducated. See Colet, *Exposition of Romans*, pp. 3–28.

Erasmus.[16] In fact, Colet argued that faithfulness to the Old Covenant enabled Abraham to have a foreknowledge of the future ministry of Christ.[17] These emphases in his thought indicate a clear divergence from an Erasmian approach to the relationship between the Old and New Testaments.

Nevertheless, Colet's clashes with Erasmus[18] resulted as much from what he held in common with the Rhetor of Rotterdam as from their differences. Since both men subscribed to the view that there was a single, unitive meaning of the biblical text to be discovered, any substantial conflict of interpretation must necessarily result from an error on the part of one scholar or the other. The most volatile element in their new program of exegesis was this interpretive exclusivity, wedded to historical and linguistic analyses. Whereas medieval conflicts of interpretation could be and often were resolved by appealing to different layers or strands of meaning in scripture, no such accommodation is possible in a system that promotes a single meaning for the text. When that single meaning is in turn established on the basis of philological and historical analysis, variant interpretations can be viewed only as resting on more or less error and ignorance than their rivals.

The innate divisiveness of Humanist exegesis was so strong that it

16 See, e.g., Erasmus, *Paraphrase on Mark*, p. 75, and throughout the entire work where the "darkness," "fear," and "despair" given to men through the "carnal" Old Covenant is repeatedly contrasted with the "light," "sweetness," and "love" given to them by the New Covenant. See esp. pp. 14–16, 21, 24, 26, 30–31, 59, 86–87, 103, and 132–33. See also Manfred Hoffman, *Rhetoric and Theology: The Hermeneutic of Erasmus* (Toronto: University of Toronto Press, 1994), p. 160.

17 Colet, *Exposition of Romans*, p. 122. Colet has in mind here John 8:56–58 [Douay-Rheims]: "Abraham your father rejoiced that he might see my day: he saw it and was glad. . . . Amen, amen, I say to you, before Abraham was made, I am."

18 See Chapter II above, and Charles Béné, *Érasme et Saint Augustin*, Travaux d'Humanisme et Renaissance 103 (Geneva: Droz, 1969), pp. 109–12, 189–194. For Colet's criticism of Erasmus' *Commentary on Romans*, see J. B. Trapp, "Colet, John (1467–1519)," *Oxford Dictionary of National Biography*, Oxford University Press, 2004 [http://www.oxforddnb.com/view/article/5898, accessed 1 Feb 2007].

threatened to rend the new enterprise itself, even as it was being formed. In the last years of his life, Colet urged reverence on Erasmus with increasing earnestness.[19] Intriguingly, a work of Johann Reuchlin (1455–1522), the German Humanist and Hebrew Scholar, on Cabbalistic theology spurred Colet to chide Erasmus in 1517: "For (as the author instructs us), words in Hebrew have in their characters and combinations something transcending mere human knowledge. Erasmus, there is no end to books or to knowledge. But our lives are brief, and there is nothing we can do with them better than to live them in innocence and holiness, and daily spend our efforts to the end that we may be purified, and enlightened, and made perfect." Colet concluded curtly: "Leaving the roundabout and enigmatic ways, then, let us go the short way to the truth. Insofar as my own strength permits, that is what I wish to do. Farewell."[20] Colet's letter was prompted by Erasmus' choosing to send Reuchlin's work first to John Fisher.[21]

These early tensions between Erasmus and Colet were rooted in rival Humanist approaches to exegesis. Their disputes both presaged and were wholly overshadowed by larger controversies soon to follow. Erasmus had hoped the promotion of scripture would lead to a pious transformation of all Christendom into a culture of authentic charity.[22] Despite such noble aims, the equating of theology with exegesis, in fact, led swiftly to permanent schism in the West, as interpreters brought forth rival and unyielding interpretations of *the* Word.[23] Just some four months after Colet wrote to Erasmus, Luther drafted and distributed his *Theses* in and

19 See editor's remarks in Colet, *Commentary on First Corinthians*, p. 15.
20 Colet, "Letter to Erasmus," in the editors' introduction to his *Commentary on First Corinthians*, p. 15. This translation varies in only minor points from the version found in Desiderius Erasmus, "Letter 593, from John Colet," in *The Correspondence of Erasmus, Letters 446–593, 1516–17,* trans. and eds. R. A. B. Mynors and D. F. S. Thomson, The Complete Works of Erasmus 4 (Toronto: University of Toronto Press, 1977) [hereafter: Colet, "To Erasmus"], p. 398.
21 Colet, "Letter to Erasmus," in *Commentary on First Corinthians*, p. 15. Cf. Colet, "To Erasmus," p. 398.
22 See, e.g., Erasmus, *Enchridion.*
23 See Euan Cameron, *The European Reformation* (Oxford: Clarendon Press, 1991), pp. 139–44.

around Wittenberg.[24] While Colet and Erasmus explicated scripture to define the principles of proper Christian moral conduct, this endeavor was not far removed from looking to scripture as propositional for the establishment of Church polity in general. Although Colet did not live to see it, this was precisely the route that Luther took in his *Babylonian Captivity* and *Freedom of a Christian Man*, both printed in 1520.[25]

By the early 1520s, a whole new cohort of biblical scholars was being formed at Cambridge. Unlike Colet and Fisher in the previous generation, the primary and dominant exposure these younger men would have to Humanism would be almost exclusively Erasmian.[26] One such man was John Frith, who left Eton for Cambridge, taking his B.A. at King's College in 1525. Frith became a very able scholar in both Latin and Greek and excelled in his studies with Stephen Gardiner as his tutor.[27] Frith's talents were such that he came to the attention of Wolsey and was made a junior canon of Cardinal College at Oxford. However, Frith was soon imprisoned with several other young scholars for espousing reformist views. He was released on condition that he stay within ten miles of Oxford, but fled to Antwerp, where he assisted William Tyndale with a number of printing projects, including preparation of his famous Bible. Throughout the late 1520s, Frith studied the works of

24 Heiko A. Oberman, *Luther: Man Between God and the Devil*, trans., Eileen Walliser-Schwarzbart (New York: Double Day, 1992) [hereafter: Oberman, *Luther*], p. 16.

25 Colet died in 1519, just six months after the printing of Erasmus' *Novum Instrumentum*. On Luther's circumscription of ecclesiology to the limits of *sola scriptura*, see, e.g., *The Freedom of a Christian Man*, in *The Protestant Reformation*, ed. Hans J. Hillerbrand (New York: Harper & Row, 1968), pp. xxvi–28. See also Anthony N. S. Lane, "*Sola Scriptura?* Making Sense of a Post-Reformation Slogan," in *A Pathway into the Holy Scriptures*, eds., Philip E. Satterwhite and David F. Wright (Grand Rapids: Eerdmans, 1994) [hereafter: Lane, "Sola Scriptura?"], pp. 297–327.

26 On the work of Erasmus and his disciples at Cambridge in the first and second decades of the sixteenth century, see Chapter III above.

27 See David Daniell, "Frith, John (1503–33)" *Oxford Dictionary of National Biography*, Oxford University Press, 2004 [http://www.oxforddnb.com/view/article/10188, accessed 1 Febuary 2007] [hereafter: Daniell, "Frith"].

several continental Protestants, and even attended the Marburg Colloquy where Luther and Zwingli worked in vain to harmonize their disparate views on the Eucharist in 1529. While he absorbed some Lutheran concepts on the Continent, Frith became primarily an admirer of Oecolampadius, an early disciple of Zwingli.[28]

In 1531, Frith made two trips back to England. The first, in Lent, was quite brief, while the second, in July, proved fateful: he was arrested as a vagabond, but then released when he impressed Leonard Cox, a former schoolmaster, with his knowledge of Latin and Greek.[29] Frith's controversial publications on the Continent, however, in which he had attacked both Thomas More and John Fisher, had made him a wanted man in England. More learned that Frith was again in England, and issued a warrant for his arrest under a charge of heresy. Frith was seized at Milton Shore in Essex while trying to leave once more for Antwerp.[30] For a time, More and Gardiner dealt gently with Frith, attempting by these means to persuade him to recant his heretical opinions. This effort may have been partially motivated by a desire to please Henry VIII, whose councilors, especially Thomas Cromwell, hoped that Frith's learning and acumen might be applied to building up the case for the King's divorce.[31] In the end, the energies Gardiner and More

---

28 Daniell, "Frith."
29 Cox was also a committed disciple of Erasmus. See S. F. Ryle, "Cox, Leonard (*b. c.*1495, *d.* in or after 1549)," *Oxford Dictionary of National Biography*, Oxford University Press, 2004 [http://www.oxforddnb.com/view/article/6525, accessed 13 August 2007].
30 Daniell, "Frith."
31 See Foxe's account of Frith's imprisonment, controversies with More, and execution, in John Foxe, *Actes and Monuments of matters most speciall and memorable, happenyng in the Church, with an Universal history of the same, wherein is set forth at large the whole race and course of the Church, from the primitive age to these latter tymes of ours, with the bloudy times, horrible troubles, and great persecutions agaynst the true Martyrs of Christ, sought and wrought as well by Heathen Emperours, and now lately practised by Romish Prelates, especially in this Realme of England and Scotland* ([STC 11225] London: John Daye, 1583) [hereafter: Foxe, *Actes and Monuments*], pp. 1031–36, and p. 1215. See also Richard Marius, *Thomas More: A Biography* (New York: Vintage Books, 1985), pp. 428–30.

devoted to persuading Frith to abandon his extreme opinions on the Eucharist and other controversial views were in vain. In the summer of 1533, Henry finally ordered Frith to recant or be condemned. Frith refused, and was subsequently examined at St. Paul's on 20 June by Gardiner and Edmund Bonner, among others. He signed a statement reiterating his rejection of Purgatory and the real presence of Christ in the Eucharist, and was handed over by Bonner to the secular powers and burned on 4 July.[32]

Martyrdom was not inevitable for early Protestants in Henrician England, and it is certainly a marvel to compare the careers of John Frith and Edward Crome (d. 1562) during this same period. As an early advocate of radical ecclesiastical reform, Crome preached regularly in the 1530s against purgatory and the intercession of the saints. Despite his delivery of an equivocating recantation of these views in 1531, he was offered, through the entreaties of Anne Boleyn, the wealthy living of St. Mary Aldermary in London. He was also granted the prebendary stipend of South Grantham in Lincolnshire in 1537.[33] Crome was one of the few Henrician divines who openly opposed the passage of the Act of Six Articles in 1539. His supporters included Thomas Cranmer himself, who unsuccessfully attempted to have Crome named Dean of the new foundation of Canterbury in 1541.[34] Early that year, Crome again offered a prevaricating recantation of his opinion that Masses for the dead were superstition. On this occasion, his deliberate equivocation met with less success and he was not permitted to preach again for several years.[35]

32 Daniell, "Frith."
33 See Susan Wabuda, "Equivocation and Recantation During the English Reformation: The 'Subtle Shadows' of Dr. Edward Crome," *The Journal of Ecclesiastical History* 44.2 (1993) [hereafter: Wabuda, "Subtle Shadows," pp. 224–42.
34 Susan Wabuda, "Crome, Edward (d. 1562)," *Oxford Dictionary of National Biography*, Oxford University Press, 2004 [http://www.oxforddnb.com/view/article/6749, accessed 23 February 2006] [hereafter: Wabuda, "Crome"].
35 Wabuda, "Crome." Despite this high favor with the leaders of English reform, Crome was not favorably portrayed in the latter editions of the *Actes and Monuments*, revealing Foxe's growing distaste for dissemblers. See Wabuda, "Subtle Shadows."

In Lent 1546, however, Crome returned to the pulpit and sparked a controversy from London with far-reaching implications through a series of sermons against transubstantiation. With Henry's health waning, tensions ran high between Conservatives and Reformers as to who would hold the reins of power in the next régime. The substance of Crome's preaching in Henry VIII's last spring was that the Mass was a memorial rite of Christ, and that he was not present in the consecrated elements of the sacrament. Once more Crome was charged to recant, and several of the Reformers, including Nicholas Ridley, then chaplain to the king, urged Crome to submit to Henry's will. When Crome offered another ambiguous recantation on 27 June, several members of the nascent Protestant party who sympathized with Crome lost their resolve: sixty fled, while several others were tortured, leading to more investigations for heresy. The episode ended with the burning of three individuals charged as heretics on 16 July.[36] The victims included Anne Askew, who had both attended Crome's sermons and was reading John Frith's writings in her final months.[37] Unlike Frith and Askew, Crome survived the Henrician heresy investigations and lived into the first years of Elizabeth's reign.

36 Wabuda, "Crome." On Ridley's role in Crome's examination in summer 1546, see Diarmaid MacCulloch, *Thomas Cranmer: A Life* (New Haven: Yale University Press, 1996) [hereafter: MacCulloch, *Cranmer*], p. 355.
37 While Askew did present a book to one of her examiners that was not written by Frith, the uniform witness of her contemporaries that she was his disciple is not to be discounted by this one exchange. See Anne Askew, *The first examinacion of the worthy seruaunt of God, Mastres Anne Askew the yonger doughter of Syr William Askew Knyght of Lyncolne shyre: lately martyred i[n] Smythefelde, by the Romyshe Popes vpholders. Anne Askewe stode faste by this veritee of God, to the ende.*, ([STC 852] London: W. Hill, 1548?) [hereafter: Askew, *Examinacion*]. Cf. Diane Watt, "Askew, Anne (c.1521–1546)," *Oxford Dictionary of National Biography*, Oxford University Press, 2004 [http://www.oxforddnb.com. /view/article/798, accessed 13 August 2007]. See also Sarah E. Wall, "Editing Anne Askew's *Examinations*: John Bale, John Foxe, and Early Modern Textual Practices," in *John Foxe and his World*, eds. Christopher Highley and John N. King (Burlington, Vermont: Ashgate, 2002), pp. 249–62.

Peryn and Pendleton:
The New Learning and Veteran Polemics

Edmund Bonner had already begun to recruit and license a band of excellent homilists for faith formation in London diocese by the early 1540s. These efforts were almost certainly motivated in part to meet the claims of Cranmer that there was not enough solid preaching in the realm.[38] Bonner provided for highly skilled, but thoroughly traditional preachers to address many points of doctrine, especially on ecclesiology and the sacraments, during this more conservative moment of the Henrician reformation. Bonner's preachers focused regularly on the historicity of the events related in the Old and New Covenants, and their interconnectedness in the larger narrative of salvation history. One of the preachers Bonner deployed for the dissemination of orthodox teaching in the 1540s was William Peryn, a former Dominican friar.[39] In 1546, Peryn launched a series of conservative sermons as a counter to Crome's attacks on the sacrament. Peryn preached and then printed *Thre godly and notable Sermons of the moost honorable and blessed sacrament of the Aulter*, which he dedicated: "Unto the ryght reverend father in god, and his special good lorde and mayster, Edmund (by the grace of God) byshoppe of London."[40] This set of homilies is replete with references to the Old Testament prefigurations of the Eucharist.

Peryn's *Thre godly sermons* is a fascinating study in Catholic theological polemic on the eve of a more radical shift in liturgical and

38 See Susan Wabuda, "Bishops and the Provision of Homilies, 1520 to 1547," *Sixteenth Century Journal* 25.3 (1994): pp. 551–66, esp. pp. 563–64.

39 Peryn went into exile shortly after the proclamation of the Royal Supremacy in 1534, but returned to England in 1543, taking his Bachelor of Theology from Oxford that same year. See L. E. C. Wooding, "Peryn, William (d. 1558)," *Oxford Dictionary of National Biography*, Oxford University Press, 2004 [http://www.oxforddnb.com/view/article/22007, accessed 1 Feb 2007] [hereafter: Wooding, "Peryn"].

40 See original colophon of William Peryn, *Thre godly and notable Sermons of the moost honorable and blessed sacrament of the Aulter* ([STC 19785.5] London: John Hereforde for Robert Toye, 1546) [hereafter: Peryn, *Thre godly sermons*].

sacramental reform in sixteenth-century England. In this series, delivered during Lent,[41] Peryn adopted an expressly Trinitarian structure for his explication of the scriptural and patristic underpinnings of traditional teaching on the Eucharist. In his first sermon, Peryn catalogued and explicated the miracles wrought by God the Father in the Old Testament that were "shadows" of the "verity" of the Eucharist. Peryn's Dominican training is fully, if only implicitly, displayed in this approach to the subject, given Thomas Aquinas' constant allusions to the "types and shadows" of the Eucharist to be found in the Old Testament. In sermon two, Peryn turned to consider the relationship of God the Son to these Old Testament prefigurations of his total self-sacrifice. In sermon three, Peryn surveyed the work of the Holy Ghost in guiding the Church in development of orthodox eucharistic doctrine over the centuries, with copious citations from the Church Fathers. In the closing section of this final sermon, he lined up several sacramentarian arguments against the real presence, and worked to contravene them on the basis of scripture, rational argument, and patristic insights.

Peryn's chief point throughout his *Thre godly sermons* was that if the Eucharist is understood as a mere figure or mnemonic for Christ's passion, then the Church possesses rather less than did the Temple of the Old Covenant, where true ritual sacrifices were presented to God on behalf of the people.[42] He argued further that if the sacrifice of the Eucharist is only the congregation's offering of praise and thanksgiving to God, such prayer was already a feature of synagogue worship. He also noted that the concept of a sacrifice of praise does not escape the alleged dangers of works righteousness, in that doxology is a human act: "But

41 Susan Brigden has suggested that they may have been delivered in Lent of that year. See Susan Brigden, *London and the Reformation* (Oxford: Clarendon Press, 1989) [hereafter: Brigden, *London and the Reformation*], p. 398. Emphatic references to Maundy Thursday and Easter in the text support Brigden's surmise, and the three-part Trinitarian structure and multiple references to the Resurrection being an act of God that transcends our reason in a manner not unlike Christ's corporal presence in the Eucharist, would certainly make for a solid Triduum series.

42 See, e.g., Peryn, *Thre godly sermons*, sigs. D.7, *recto*-D.8, *verso*. Cf. sigs. I.7, *recto*.

yet a craftye heretike will understande, (or rather wreaste) this prophe-cye, unto the oblacyon or sacrifice of faith, of prayer, and of al other godli dedes. That can not be so, after Luther's opinion, for al our good dedes (with him) are synfull."[43] These statements were probably veiled references to the ideas of Anne Askew and her companions.[44]

Peryn's subject matter naturally led him to ponder the interrelation-ships between Old Testament and New Testament concepts and events: "Ther are more fygures, lefte unto us wrytten, under the lawe naturall, and the lawe Moysaical (that which prefigured thys blessyd sacrament) then ther are of ani other sacraments. . . . The which figures (by the syn-guler wyssedom of god) were preordeyned and set in use, longe before the institution of this holy sacrament, as a preamble, and an introduction, towardes the commyng of the more holy and more perfect sacrament."[45] In this context, Peryn took up the subject of the priesthoods of Aaron and Melchizedek, the same theme that would occupy Ridley so intensely in his broadsides with Hooper during the Edwardine vestment contro-versy four years later.[46] Peryn reminds his readers that while Christ is rightly referred to as "a priest forever according to the order of Melchizedek" in the Letter to the Hebrews,[47] that for his bloody self-sacrifice at Calvary, Christ can just as appropriately be described as a priest "after the order of Aaron."[48] Peryn concluded this portion of his argument with a dazzling passage that linked the priesthoods of Aaron and Melchizidek to Christ's institution of the Eucharist in the context of a Passover meal: "In the sacryfice of breade and wyne of Melchisidek, was fygured, the kyndes or outward apparens of thys blessed sacrament, whiche beareth the shape of bread and wyne. In the paschal lambe, was

43   Peryn, *Thre godly sermons*, sigs. D.7, *recto*-D.8, *verso*.
44   See Askew, *Examinacion*.
45   Peryn, *Thre godly sermons*, sig. C.4, *recto*.
46   On Peryn's treatment of Aaron and Melchizedek, see *Thre godly sermons*, sig. C.7, *verso*-D.5, *recto*. On Ridley's treatment of this topic in response to Hooper, see John Bradford, *The Writings of John Bradford*, vol. 2, ed. Aubrey Townsend, for the Parker Society (Cambridge: Cambridge Univer-sity Press, 1840) [hereafter: *Bradford*, vol. 2], pp. 375–95.
47   See Hebrews 7:17 and cf. Psalm 110:4.
48   Peryn, *Thre godly sermons*, sig. C.8, *verso-recto*.

figured, the very substance, that is contayned in the sacrament, whych is the substance of Jesus Christe, the very lambe of God, that taketh away the sinnes of the worlde."[49] Peryn's closing phrase tied Jesus' sacrifice to the Mass in a clear allusion to the *Agnus Dei*. By highlighting the fact that the ritual setting of the Last Supper was a Passover meal, Peryn focused the reader's attention on the deeds and Old Testament religious identity of Jesus in a way that diverges sharply from contemporary Protestant analyses that concentrated almost exclusively on Jesus' speech in the institution narratives of the synoptic gospels.[50]

Bonner's chaplains and preachers consistently focus on the larger sweep of salvation history in their exegetical writings. In contrast to what is often seen with Erasmus and Ridley, Bonner's chaplains concentrate their attention not on a single phrase or verse of scripture, but on an entire biblical episode or story. Among such homilists promoted by Bonner, after he was restored to his jurisdiction under Mary, was Henry Pendelton.[51] In 1555, Pendelton would write: "The holye catholyke churche . . . hath bene lately assaulted by sundrye sectes and heresies, and so sore shaken, that many (more is the pitie) hathe separate themselves from the same, and wylfully have runne astraye beyenge ledde and caried with every wave and winde of newe learning. . . ."[52]

---

49 Peryn, *Thre godly sermons*, sig. D.5, *verso*. Cf. sigs. F.4, *verso*-F.5, *verso*.

50 See, e.g., Ridley's *A Brief Declaracion of the Lordes Supper* ([STC 21046] Emden: Egidius van der Erve, 1555) [hereafter: Ridley, *Brief Declaracion*]. Cf. Nicholas Ridley, *The Works of Bishop Ridley,* ed. Henry Christmas, for the Parker Society (Cambridge: Cambridge University Press, 1841) [hereafter: Ridley, *Works*], pp. 5–45.

51 Henry Pendleton, styled "H. Pendilton," was chaplain to Bonner and Professor of Sacred Theology. He wrote two of the sermons included in Bonner's *Homelies*. See L. E. C. Wooding, "Pendleton, Henry (d. 1557)," *Oxford Dictionary of National Biography,* Oxford University Press, 2004 [http://www.oxforddnb.com/view/article/21863, accessed 1 Feb 2007] [hereafter: Wooding, "Pendleton"].

52 *Homelies sette forth by the righte reuerende father in God, Edmunde Byshop of London, not onely promised before in his booke, intituled, A necessary doctrine, but also now of late adioyned, and added therevnto, to be read within his diocese of London, of all persons, vycars, and curates, vnto theyr parishioners, vpon sondayes, [and] holydayes,* ([STC 3285.4])

Thus he opened his homily "Of the Churche, what it is, and of the commodity thereof,"[53] in the volume of related sermons "sette forth by the reverende father in God, Edmunde Byshop of London. . . ." Pendelton knew whereof he wrote: despite being an early and vocal critic of Luther, he held strong Protestant views in the reign of Edward before reconverting to Catholicism under Mary.[54]

Knowledge of the careers of those who assisted Bonner in the effort to preach and teach in the diocese of London in the 1540s and 1550s illustrates how much more compatible Italian Humanism was with traditional theology than was the work of Erasmus. Peryn's training as a Dominican preacher made him invaluable in Bonner's administration of the Diocese of London in the 1540s. The fact that Pendleton was both a strong preacher[55] and had returned to Catholicism under Mary made him an important ally for Bonner in the 1550s. As someone who had once subscribed to Protestant exegesis, ecclesiology, and apologetics, Pendleton was intimately familiar with reformist concepts. Pendleton's chief service in Bonner's cause was to consistently point to the fact that scripture speaks of a visible and united Church.[56] Enlisting men with such first-hand experience of Protestantism enabled Bonner to set forth strong and incisive arguments for the restoration of Catholicism under Mary. Peryn and Pendleton's work have deep biblical roots and reveal a concern for the larger narrative of salvation history. Peryn and Pendleton's combined learning and experiences lent considerable gravitas to Bonner's polemical productions. Bonner's choice of them reveals in turn that he was quite astute in marshaling the talent and resources available to him in the administration of his diocese.

London: In Poules churcheyarde, at the sygne of the holy Ghost, by Ihon Cawodde, 1555) [hereafter: Bonner, *Homelies*], fol.32.

53 Bonner, *Homelies*, fols. 32–36.
54 Wooding, "Pendleton."
55 Pendleton is said to have drawn a crowd of 20,000 to a sermon he preached at the Spital on Easter Monday, 1557, with the mayor, aldermen, and judges of London in attendance. See Wooding, "Pendleton."
56 Wooding, "Pendleton."

Restoration, Episcopal Visitation, and Lay Formation

Although the Edwardine commission to deprive Bonner did not pronounce against him until 1 October 1549, he had already been imprisoned by late September of that year.[57] Bonner was officially pardoned by Queen Mary and released from the Marshalsea on 5 August 1553.[58] When Bonner launched a sweeping visitation of his cure on 3 September 1554,[59] he was therefore resuming active oversight as Bishop of London nearly five years to the day that he was first committed to prison by Cranmer, Ridley, and the other royal commissioners appointed by Edward VI. Bonner's episcopal visitation, begun with the proclamation of 133 articles for examination, concluded in October 1554.[60] By that point he had, no doubt, discovered a great deal about the nature of belief in London Diocese.

As a result of his episcopal visitation, Bonner came to understand that a coherent program of lay formation was needed in his diocese to

---

57   See Alexander, "Bonner Until His Deprivation," p. 451.
58   See Kenneth Carleton, "Bonner, Edmund (d. 1569)," *Oxford Dictionary of National Biography*, Oxford University Press, 2004 [http://www.ox-forddnb.com/view/article/2850, accessed 23 Feb 2006] [hereafter: Carleton, "Bonner, Edmund"]. Cf. Alexander, *Marian Persecutions*, p. 158. Alexander appears to have confused the starting year of the visitation, dating it to 3 September 1553, which is unlikely given that Bonner was not released from prison until 5 August 1553, and his Visitation Articles were published first in 1554. See *Articles to be enquired of in the generall visitation of Edmonde Bisshoppe of London exercised by him the yeare of oure Lorde. 1.5.5.4. in the citie and diocese of London. . .* ([STC 10248] London: John Cawood, September 1554). Cf. *Iniunctions geuen in the visitatio[n] of the Reuerend father in god Edmunde, bishop of London begunne and continued in his cathederal churche and dioces of London, from the thyrd day of September the yere of oure Lorde god, a thousand fiue hundreth fifty and foure, vntill the. viii. daye of October, the yeare of our Lord a thousand fiue hundreth fifty and fiue then nexte ensuing* ([STC 10249] London : In Paules churcheyard, at the signe of the holy ghost, by Iohn Cawood, 1555).
59   Gina Alexander, "Bonner and the Marian Persecutions," in *The English Reformation Revised*, ed. Christopher Haigh (Cambridge: Cambridge University Press, 1987) [hereafter: Alexander, "Marian Persecutions"], p. 168.
60   See Alexander, *Marian Persecutions*, p. 168.

reach those who were not convinced Protestants, but merely confused by all of the official changes in religion that had come to pass since Henry VIII had first proclaimed himself head of the English Church. Having served Henry and Cromwell faithfully in the 1530s, few men were better placed than Bonner to understand what was ultimately at stake. After four years of imprisonment under Edward, Bonner needed little persuading that there were no fixed limits to doctrine once a key component of ecclesiology, such as the papal primacy, was cast aside. The various examinations he conducted for heresy can only have served to more firmly fix those convictions in his mind. Ralph Allerton, brought up for heresy charges and questioned by Bonner, opined on the religious climate of the realm: "My lorde, there are in England three religions." When Bonner asked him to elaborate, Allerton exclaimed: "The first is that whiche you holde: the seconde is cleane contrary to the same: and the thirde is an Neuter, being indifferent, that is to say, observing all things that are commaunded, outwardly, as though he were of your part, his heart being set wholy against the same."[61] While Bonner was quite willing to see those who were committed members of Allerton's second group be tried and burnt, he also labored diligently to reach those belonging to Ralph's "neuter" religion. Bonner was determined to address the questions and concerns of waverers, those who had flirted with Protestantism but who were not certain enough to risk death in the defense of novel doctrines.

To meet the objections of this group, Bonner developed an ambitious campaign of lay formation, which began in earnest in the summer and autumn of 1555.[62] Bonner's *Necessary and Profitable Doctrine*

---

61 See Alexander, *Marian Persecutions*, p. 167 and Foxe, *Actes and Monuments*, p. 2014.

62 Gina Alexander asserts that Bonner had the *Homelies* published in July 1555, and that they were followed two months later by his *Profitable and Necessary Doctrine*. See Alexander, *Marian Persecutions*, p. 170. While Bonner's preface to the *Homelies* indicates that he wrote it on 1 July 1550, it would seem that Alexander has reversed the chronology of these two productions, since the full title and preface of the *Doctrine* assert that there will be a collection of homilies appended to it, but none are found in the text. See *A profitable and necessarye doctryne with certayne homelies*

was published in the capital in July, and was structurally modeled on the *King's Book* of 1543. Building on this most conservative formulary of doctrine set forth under Henry VIII, Bonner retained some materials unchanged, such as the section on faith, but added much new material, particularly on the Eucharist, Confirmation, and Extreme Unction.[63] This work was characterized by long quotations from the Gospels, the Epistles of Paul, and early patristic sources. It was an effort at intelligent enquiry based on primary source materials, designed to meet Protestant arguments on their own ground.[64] By choosing to leave aside medieval commentators or scriptural glosses in the writings they produced under Mary, Bonner and his preachers sought to prove the

---

adioyned thervnto set forth by the reuerende father in God, Edmonde byshop of London, for the instruction and enformation of the people beynge within his diocese of London, [and] of his cure and charge ([STC 3281.5] London: John Cawood, 1555) [hereafter: Bonner, *Necessary and Profitable Doctrine*], sig. A.3, *recto*. Cf. Bonner, *Homelies*, colophon. The full title includes the statement that the *Homelies* were: "*not onely promised before in his boke intituled, A necessary doctrine, but also now of late adjoyned, and added thereunto, to be reade in his diocese of London, of all persons, vycars, and curates, unto theyr parishioners, upon sondayes, & holydayes.*" On the force of this primary evidence, the analysis that follows presumes that Bonner's *Doctrine* was printed before the *Homelies*.

63 See Alexander, *Marian Persecutions*, p. 170 and C. D. C. Armstrong, "English Catholicism Rethought?" *The Journal of Ecclesiastical History* 53.1 (2002): p. 721.

64 See Alexander, *Marian Persecutions*, p. 170. Determining how much of Bonner's productions were his own and how much of the work was undertaken by his chaplains was a problem even for his contemporaries. During his deprivation trial, Bonner himself remarked: "My Chapleins . . . be much suspected for my doings in many things, and sometimes I for theirs, when there is no cause why." See Foxe, *Actes and Monuments*, p. 1317. Cf. p. 1319 where Bonner describes the process of drafting notes for his set-piece sermon, and p. 1325 when Bonner charged his chaplains to be "as mery as I am" for his tribulations at the hands of Edward VI's Council. Given his close, personal supervision of affairs in London for the second portion of his episcopate, we can say with certainty that neither the *Doctrine* nor the *Homelies* promote any theological concept that Bonner did not also endorse.

coherence between contemporary Catholic doctrine and the primary textual sources of Christianity.[65] This tack skillfully raised hard challenges against Protestant claims that sixteenth-century Catholicism was a "Romish" invention inimical to the precepts of the Gospel and the apostolic Church.

Gina Alexander, the only modern biographer of Edmund Bonner, maintains that the Bishop of London did not likely write much of the *Necessary Doctrine*, due to his heavy involvement with heresy proceedings during the spring and summer of 1555. Such a conclusion is something of a *non sequitur*, however, in that the *Doctrine* would have been composed well before it was printed, which was actually two months earlier than Alexander believed.[66] These heresy inquests honed Bonner's arguments against Protestant doctrinal positions, but also revealed to him the broad variance of opinion among individual Protestants themselves. Questioning suspected heretics on a daily basis, Bonner confronted many of them with the same textual and doctrinal points that would later appear in the *Necessary and Profitable Doctrine*. In addition, there are several personal digressions throughout the *Doctrine* where Bonner refers to books in his library, his involvement with Parliamentary proceedings, etc., which strongly suggest that he was either directly involved with much of the composition, or that he edited the whole near the point of publication.

The Old Law and the New

When stylistically compared with the *Paraphrases* of Erasmus or Ridley's prison tracts, Bonner's *Necessary and Profitable Doctrine* stands out as a quite different kind of production, in that it did not rely so much on interpolative arguments as on extended excerpts from key texts. Whereas Erasmus and Ridley tended to build a theme by grafting their ideas directly onto a term or concept found in the recorded sayings of

---

65   See William Wizeman, S.J., *The Theology and Spirituality of Mary Tudor's Church* (Burlington, Vermont: Ashgate, 2006) [hereafter: Wizeman, *Mary Tudor's Church*], pp. 57–62.

66   See note 62 above.

Jesus, or the words of Paul,[67] the *Doctrine* rendered biblical passages at length, with the text itself set off in a different typeface.[68] The use of alternating typefaces is also scrupulously applied to shorter citations of the Bible within the declarative portions of the text. By these means, Bonner and his chaplains showed themselves as responsible editors and expositors, delineating for the reader precisely where a biblical or patristic theme concluded, and where their own arguments commenced. This textual form invited the reader to consider how true or foreign the theological argument might be from the ground of the source text. This was a mode of explication targeted to challenge, persuade, and correct those members of the laity whom Ralph Allerton had described to Bonner as belonging to a "neuter" religion, conforming to Catholicism outwardly, but inwardly feeling the attractions of Protestantism.

The substance of the *Doctrine* is also strikingly different from the work of Erasmus and Ridley in several key respects, but nowhere more so than in the handling of the relationship between the Old and New Covenants. While Ridley and Erasmus would draw out as sharp a contrast as possible between Old and New Testament religious themes, Bonner and his chaplains portrayed the content of the two Testaments as mutually reinforcing. In this aspect of his thought, Bonner was certainly much nearer the mind of John Colet than to either Ridley or Erasmus.

We have already noted that Colet, unlike Erasmus, treated Old and New Testament concepts as naturally allied rather than mutually opposed. Colet's banquet analogy in his *Commentary on First Corinthians* plainly reveals this aspect of his thinking. He likened the Old and New Testaments to a lavish table setting: "He (Christ) first in magnificent fashion piled the table high—through the ministry of Moses . . . afterwards he himself struck off the covers, offering himself, Truth itself, for the plentiful banqueting of his chosen guests."[69] Throughout the

67 See Chapters II and III above.
68 See, e.g., the long quotations from Luke in *The Exposition of the Sacrament of Confirmation*, in Bonner, *Necessary and Profitable Doctrine*, sig. O.2, verso-recto.
69 Colet, *Commentary on First Corinthians*, p. 217.

Doctrine and the *Homelies*, we see the same focus on the compatibility of Old and New Testament themes that we find in the exegetical work of Colet.

Bonner's *Exposition of the Ten Commandments* is typical of his efforts throughout the *Homelies* and *Necessary and Profitable Doctrine*: while seeking scriptural sanction for his assertions, he draws upon Church history, patristic insights, and historical linguistics to defend and promote Catholic doctrine. Bonner's explication of the commandments comprises the fourth section of his *Necessary and Profitable Doctrine*, and is the first section of that work concerned directly and systematically with portions of scripture. It is preceded by declarations of what faith is, the Apostles' Creed, and the seven sacraments.[70] Bonner opened his commentary on the commandments with a preface that outlined their significance for the faithful. He wished to impress four principal points on his readers: first, what the will or law of God is; second, how the commandments are to be observed; third, what punishments will come to those who fail to observe God's law; and finally, the rewards in store for those who keep the law of God. Bonner asserted that the commandments were given as a compass or guide for believers, and likens them to the rule or square of a stone mason.[71]

From the outset, Bonner's commentary is firmly legalistic, an aspect of these writings that likely results both from his formal training in Canon Law and the actual nature of the subject matter itself. The juridical character of his reflections on the commandments are made explicit when, paraphrasing Paul, Bonner declares that the law was given not only on stone tablets to Moses, but also to each of us upon the tablets of our hearts: "The commaundementes are geven to us of God . . . [who] hath, both (throughe the lawe of nature) in our hartes prynted them, and also in the lawe of Moyses with his owne fynger, (that is to saye, by the vertue of the holy spyryte) in two tables of stone wrytten them." Bonner goes on to say: "Laste of all our saviourer Chryste, beyinge both God and man, hath ratified and expounded them in the new lawe of the

---

70 See Bonner, *Necessary and Profitable Doctrine*, sigs. A.1-EE.2. The section on faith in the *Doctrine* is identical to the *King's Book* of 1543.

71 Bonner, *Necessary and Profitable Doctrine*, sig. FF.1, *verso-recto*.

Gospell . . . that with all diligence we shoulde studye to observe and kepe the . . . commaundments . . . especially because that thei are geven to us of God, who thereby doth declare to us his godlye wyll and pleasure, unto whom both we, and all creatures els, are bounde to be obedient."[72] Bonner did not hesitate to refer to the Gospel itself as the "new *law*." Here and elsewhere in his *Doctrine*, as we shall see, he consistently expounded the New and Old Testaments as mutually reinforcing, rather than mutually displacing.

Following several scriptural citations concerning those who distinguished themselves in faithfulness to God's law, Bonner made several sharp remarks about the prisoners of the Marian régime and their efforts at doctrinal reform under Edward VI. He introduces the topic by alluding to 2 Maccabees: "We wyl not stay upon the seven brethern and theyr mother, spoken of in the second boke and seventh chapiter of Machabees, of whiche one of the chyldren sayde: 'We are redy rather to die, then to breake or transgresse the lawes of God which our fathers kepte.'" Bonner continues to draw out his contrast between the Macabees and Edward's leading divines: "But of late dayes, in the tyme of oure pestiferous scisme, the new broched brethern, rather would tumble to hel headlonge, then they would doo as the catholyke Churche from Chrystes tyme hetherto hath done, concernynge the lawes of God, and the rytes of the sayde catholyke churche. And yet forsoth they wyll chaleng martyrdome, but those seven innocents do condempnest them in this case."[73] Bonner's point is that normatively, martyrdom is understood as remaining steadfast in the faith handed on from earlier generations, even to the point of death. For him, obeying God's law will therefore inevitably carry ecclesial dimensions. Bonner completed his preface by underscoring Christ's endorsement of the law: "We will here conclude repeatinge agayne one shorte sentence of our saviour Chryst in the nineteenth of Matthew, 'Yf thou wylt entre into lyfe, kepe the commaundements.'"[74]

---

72 Bonner, *Necessary and Profitable Doctrine*, sig. FF.1, *recto*. Cf. 2 Cor. 3:3.
73 Bonner, *Necessary and Profitable Doctrine*, sig. FF.3, *recto*. I have omitted the citation of the Latin text that precedes Bonner's excerpt from 2 Maccabees 7:2.
74 Bonner, *Necessary and Profitable Doctrine*, sig. GG.1, *recto*. Cf. Matthew 19:17.

Bonner opened his exposition of the first commandment by again linking the Old and New Covenants, comparing and contrasting the manner in which the commandments were given on Mt. Sinai with the descent of the Holy Spirit on the Apostles in the upper room at Pentecost: "In the olde testamente, as also in the gyvinge of the evangelicall lawe, in the newe testamente, there was a high place in which the lawe was gyven, and also there was fyre." Bonner goes on to extend his analogy: "In the olde testamente the lawe was gyven upon a grosse and earthly mountayne whych was called Syna or Synai, takyng the name of a precepte or commaundemente, in as much as the preceptes or commaundements were geven in it, to brydle and kepe under the headye rebellious and stiffenecked people, not suffred to come up to it, but commaunded to be under it. . . ." He concluded by noting: "In the new testamente, the law is gyven in dede in a mountaine but yet not called Syna or Sinai, but called Sion, which by interpretation dothe sounde or signifye a beholdynge place, from whense all earthly thynges may be considered or loked upon, and from whense being high and nighe unto heaven, heavenlye and celestiall thynges may be beholden."[75] These remarks by Bonner are a rare example of his use of an anagogical approach to scripture. Nevertheless, even here he was closely focused on issues of linguistics in the etymology of place names, and the historicity of events related by the Bible.

Bonner continues to relate Pentecost to the Sinai Covenant by noting the similarities and differences in the dispensations of the Old Covenant and the New: "In the giving of the lawe in Mount Syna, there was fyre, lyghtnyng, and thunder, and dyverse other thynges very terrible, to signifye the cheife strengthe of the lawe to consyste in terror, and fearfulnes, accordynge whereunto St. Paule in the fourth chapter to the Romaynes, dothe saye: 'The lawe dothe worke or brynge furthe wrathe.'" He continues: "In the gyvynge of the lawe in Mounte Syon, there was a vehement spyryte or blaste, but yet bryngyng with it alacrity and Joye, and a fyre there was, but yet not brening the body, but lightening the blynde harte or mynde of man, . . . soo that not by terror or feare compelled as in the old law, but incited and moved by harty love, he runneth in the

75 Bonner, *Necessary and Profitable Doctrine*, sig. GG.2, *verso-recto*.

waye of the commaundementes."[76] Bonner's references to a "vehement spyryte or blast" at Pentecost in the descent of the Holy Ghost is an allusion to the Greek word πνεῦμα, which can mean both "wind" and "spirit." Bonner does not dwell on such linguistic issues at length, since he is writing primarily for a lay readership. Yet he does not omit such philological material altogether, despite the fact that his English translations of biblical passages are chiefly based upon the Latin Vulgate.[77]

It might at first appear that Bonner's mention of fear at Sinai and joy at Pentecost is in keeping with an Erasmian contrast between the darkness of the Old Testament and the light of the Gospel, but instead Bonner moves directly from this idea to a discussion of the proper fear of the Lord that all Christians should have. Touching upon the first article of the Decalogue, Bonner stated: "In this commaundement God requireth of us four thinges, in which consisteth his chief and principall honour, it is to wytte, feare, fayth, hope and charitie." He goes on to cite a pair of biblical verses, one from the Old Testament and one from the New on fear of God: "Saloman in the ix chapiter if his proverbs playnely and briefly declareth . . . 'The beginninge of wisedome, is the feare of God.' And of this feare, our saviour Christ hymselfe, speaketh in the xii of Luke: '. . . feare him who, after that he hath slaine or killed the body, hath power to put or cast into hel: thus I saye unto you, feare him.'"[78]

Bonner's arrangement of these passages is typical of his use of scripture throughout the *Necessary and Profitable Doctrine*: he links portions of the Old and New Testaments so that parallels between both Covenants are readily apparent to, and better appreciated by, his readers. Bonner

---

76 Bonner, *Necessary and Profitable Doctrine*, sigs. GG.2, recto-GG.3, *verso*.
77 See, e.g., his explication of the Sacrament of Penance, in Bonner, *Necessary and Profitable Doctrine*, sigs. P.3, *recto*-S.4, recto, esp. sig. R.2, *recto* and ff, where Bonner repeatedly renders ***poenitentiam*** as "do penaunce," rather than "repent." Cf. sig. HH.4, *verso*, where it is declared that the first commandment has been variously translated lately from Hebrew, but the authors "have (as becometh us to do) folowed the latin translation, commonlye receyved throughout the hole catholyke Churche." This statement may have been intended as a passing shot at Erasmus' *Novum Instrumentum*.
78 Bonner, *Necessary and Profitable Doctrine*, sigs. GG.4, *verso-recto*.

applied this parallel explication of Old and New Testament scriptures throughout his treatment of faith and hope or trust due towards God.[79] Concerning the love that we should have for God, Bonner coupled Ecclesisaticus 2:8 with Jesus' summary of the Decalogue: "'You that feare our Lorde, love ye him, and your hartes shalbe illumynated.' But howe or in what sorte we maye or oughte to performe thys true love and charitie towards God, that doth our Savyour Chryste himself in the tenth chapter of Saynte Luke teach us, saying, 'Thou shalt love thy Lord God, with all thy harte, with all thy soule, with all thy strengthe, and with all thy minde.'" Bonner asserted that this declaration of Jesus' is "as yf he hadde . . . sayde, let all thy thoughtes al thy wittes, and al thy understandyng, al the partes or powers of thy soule, al thy strength, travayle and laboure, be directed to the service . . . of God, of whom thou hast receyved bodye, soule, and all the gyftes wherewith thy saide body and soule are endued, yea and not onelye thou hast receyved them, but also besides, thou hast receyved all thy temporall goodes, fruytes, and commodities whatsoever."[80] Bonner's intent here is to remind Christians that we are to worship and proclaim a God from whom we have not only all possessions, but also all that we are.

Bonner also weighed the issue of the order and form of the commandments. In keeping with several patristic commentators, he noted that the Decalogue is arranged in a descending order of primacy, with the first commandment being the greatest of the ten.[81] Furthermore, there is an internal division within the Decalogue, as the first portion or "table" speaks to our obligations to God, while the latter portion or "second table" addresses our obligations to other people.[82] Despite this division, Bonner urged that the issues raised in both parts of the Decalogue are profoundly inter-related: "Yet heare must you marke that thys seconde table dothe issue or come from the fyrst table, so that the workes of the second table cannot truely be done withoute the workes and dedes of

---

79 See Bonner, *Necessary and Profitable Doctrine*, sigs. GG.4, *recto*-HH.1, *verso*.

80 Bonner, *Necessary and Profitable Doctrine*, sig. HH.1, *recto*.

81 Bonner, *Necessary and Profitable Doctrine*, sig. GG.4, *verso*.

82 Bonner, *Necessary and Profitable Doctrine*, sig. GG.3, *verso*.

the fyrst table." Bonner goes on to explicate this idea: "For then in dede we maye be sene ryghtly and well to love our neighbour, when . . . withoute anye worldely or carnall respectes, we do onelye love him for Goddes sake, and do embrace and cheryshe hym as our own selves, bycause that God, in whome is all our hope and trust, and to whome in harte and mynde, we have joyned our selves, doth soo wyll us and commaunde us to do."[83] Bonner's description of the interconnections between the two portions of the Decalogue is analogous to his view of the relationship between the Old Covenant and the New. He characteristically views the Gospel as based upon and "issuing forth" from the cultic context of Old Testament rites.

Despite his confessional bias, Bonner was often quite candid in recounting the historical differences of opinion among the Fathers. He explored this issue at some length in a consideration of the proper numbering or ordering of the Ten Commandments. He noted that Augustine arranges them such that three commandments refer to our relationship with God, while the final seven outline our relationships with other people. This order enabled Augustine to emphasize Trinitarian themes in his commentary on the Decalogue, although he allows that the commandments may be validly ordered in a four and six arrangement, separating the first two clauses and combining the last two. Both Origen and Jerome followed this alternative order, which, by separating the clauses of the first item of the Decalogue, enables one to emphasize human susceptibility to both internal and external idolatry. For his own commentary on the commandments, Bonner has resolved to follow the ordering of Origen and Jerome.[84]

Bonner asserted that those who fail to fear, believe in, trust, and love God, transgress the first commandment. Among others, he berated pagans, Jews, Turks, those who place material goods ahead of God, those who presume that God will be merciful to them while failing to

---

83   Bonner, *Necessary and Profitable Doctrine*, sig. GG.3, *verso-recto*.
84   Bonner, *Necessary and Profitable Doctrine*, sigs. GG.3, *verso*-GG.4, *verso*.
     On divergent approaches to ordering the Decalogue by Catholics and Lutherans on the one hand, and other Protestants on the other, see MacCulloch, *Cranmer*, pp. 192–93, and 388.

repent, and those who practice magic or consult "Conjurers."[85] In all such cases, the individuals and groups he cites have placed their trust or faith in something other than Christ, which underscores Bonner's Christocentric focus throughout the *Necessary Doctrine*. These passages are also a thrust at the implicit rationalism of Protestantism, which by the measure of Bonner and his allies was a betrayal of faith to the limits of what seemed possible to the human mind.[86] Bonner's exhaustive list of those who fail to keep this portion of the Decalogue reveals the legalistic cast of his mind: he is attempting to address every conceivable failure of loyalty towards the Triune God. His remarks on the language of the commandments were lawyerly indeed: "Ye shall note, both touching thys, and the rest of the commaundements, that they are, for the moste parte, uttered in the negatyve, and not in the affirmative speche, not onely for that the negatyve doth bynde ever and for ever, and is more vehement then is the affirmative, But also for that the negatyve doth accustomably requyre, on the contrary syde the affyrmative, and denying or forbydding doth imploye in it a contrary commaundement." According to Bonner: "In these preceptes it is not alonely to be considered what is forbydden and denyed unto us, but also what God (thoughe therein he do not use formall or expresse wordes) doth requyre in the contrary of us. . . . Therefore thys precepte in the negatyve speach it is sayd, 'Thou shalt not have straunge Godes before me,' there must by this negatyve, be understande the affyrmatyve, that is to saye, 'thou shalt onely have me for thy true God.'"[87] The negative form of language employed in this commandment denies cover to those, like the Samaritans, who worship the one God, but do so syncretistically, mixing pagan and heathen rites with praise of the Lord God of Israel.[88]

As Bonner turns his attention to the second commandment, he makes several philological observations about traditional and recent translations of it. His rendering of this portion of the Decalogue is "Thou

---

85 Bonner, *Necessary and Profitable Doctrine*, sig. HH.2, *verso-recto*.
86 Wizeman, *Mary Tudor's Church*, pp. 55–56.
87 Bonner, *Necessary and Profitable Doctrine*, sig. HH.3, *recto*.
88 Bonner, *Necessary and Profitable Doctrine*, sig. HH.4, *verso*.

Shalt not make to the any graven thinge, nor any likenesse of anye thing that is in heaven above, and that is in earth beneth, nor of them that be in the waters under the earth, thou shalt not adore them, nor honor them, with gods honor."[89] Bonner was especially incensed by late Protestant translations of this commandment that offer "image" for *sculptile* and *idolum*, rather than "graven thing" or "idol." To prove his claim that these recent translations of the second commandment are disingenuous, Bonner cited the text of a singularly intriguing source: "Almost eight score yeare agone our owne countrey men even in time of heresye dyd oute of Latyne translate thys place into Englyshe, and ye maye the better beleve me herein for that I have thys booke in parchement fayre and truly written to be shewed at all tymes to any well dysposed person that shall desyre it. . . ." Bonner's intent in offering this heretical text to all takers is that, "Thereby shall indifferent men perceyve that the procedynge preachers, or rather praters, takynge scuptile and idolum for an Image, and confoundyng the one with the other have greatly abused and deceyved the people."[90]

Bonner goes on to quote the relevant passages of Exodus, Leviticus, and Deuteronomy as rendered by what is apparently an early Wycliffite translation of these scriptures.[91] Citing this early heretical translation of Deuteronomy 5, Bonner made several pointed remarks about Protestant understandings of the second commandment: "In the fifth chapiter of Deuteronomye it is written thus: 'Yee schalte not have alyen Goddys in my syght, yee schalte not make to yee graven thinge ne lyckenesse of alle thinges that in heven ben above. Ande in erth bynethe, and that dwellin in waters under erth, yee schalt not honour hem ne herthe.'" Bonner railed, "By these places so translated even in the noughtye tyme, it is evident that men were not then so impudent and false as they in oure time have bene, for they neyther coulde nor durst as some in our tyme falsely have done, translate an Idoll or a graven thinge in to anye Image, for you must understand, that betwene an Image (which is a name of reverence) and an Idol (which alwayes with the good is abhominable)

---

89 Bonner, *Necessary and Profitable Doctrine*, sig. HH.4, *recto.*
90 Bonner, *Necessary and Profitable Doctrine*, sig.HH.4, *recto.*
91 Bonner, *Necessary and Profitable Doctrine*, sigs.HH.4, *recto*-KK.1, *verso.*

there is a very notable difference."[92] Bonner claimed that the crucial distinction lies in the original referent of images and idols. The original of the image is God or one of the saints, who did actually dwell among us, providing us with godly models for our own lives. Idols, however, are based on "deities" which are "very untrue and clerely false."[93] Whereas the idol has no true original, the image has its original in Christ, upon which it is based, since Christ really was both true man and true God. Given the propensity of early Protestant apologists to argue that the tradition of their church was a uniform rejection of Catholicism through the centuries, citing precedents in the followers of Hus and Wycliffe, Bonner may also be attempting to sweep the ground from under such dubious assertions.[94]

The remainder of Bonner's commentary on the second commandment suggests that his grasp of Church history and his training in Canon Law are mutually reinforcing aspects of his thought. He turns to consider what the Church proclaimed about sacred images at the Seventh Ecumenical Council. He urged his readers: "Consider what the churche dyd in thys matter about eyght hundred yeares agoo, at which time there was a greate controversie in this matter, whereupon the cheif and most lerned men of all christendome did assemble oute of all partes of the worlde to the citie of Nyce, in the Cuntrye of Bithinia, being in Asia the lesse." Bonner goes on to consider what the Council Fathers accomplished: "They, after longe deliberation, diligent searchyng, and most advysed perusinge of the bokes written by the Auncient fathers, whyche were before those dayes, dyd conclude that the use of images in the catholyke churche is in no wise repugnante, with this second commandment."[95]

---

92 Bonner, *Necessary and Profitable Doctrine*, sig. II.1 (erroneously marked as KK on the leading signature, but corrected on following ones in the original), *verso-recto*.
93 Bonner, *Necessary and Profitable Doctrine*, sig. II.1, *recto*.
94 For Protestant efforts to establish a tradition to support doctrinal innovation, see Chapter III above and Alec Ryrie, "The Problems of Legitimacy and Precedent in English Protestantism, 1539–1547," in *Protestant History and Identity in Sixteenth-Century Europe*, vol. 1, *The Medieval Inheritance*, ed. Bruce Gordon (Brookfield, Vermont: Scolar Press, 1996), pp. 78–92.
95 Bonner, *Necessary and Profitable Doctrine*, sig. II.2, *verso*.

As he reviewed the canons and decrees of the Council, Bonner simulta-neously rehearsed the definitive arguments set forth at the time of the Iconoclast Controversy. His specific references to the time and place of the Council establish it as a real historical event. To determine the proper English sense of *sculptile* and *idolum*, he turned to patristic and conciliar sources. His efforts here, as in the writings of Ridley, illustrate how read-ily textual interpretation turned to issues of philology and ecclesiastical history in sixteenth-century England.[96]

Of special significance to Bonner was the Council Fathers' view of the Old Covenant scriptures and worship in ancient Israel. They "then dyd playnelye declare that in the olde testament were many images, and lykenesses or similitudes, not onely without the tabernacle and the tem-ple, but also within the same, made, had, and used by Goddys expresse commaundemente."[97] The utility of images lies in their ability to stir up our love and devotion to Christ and the saints. Such images are honored not for the wood or metal in them, nor for their workmanship, but for what they depict: "We beholding the pictures or Images, might be brought thereby in remembraunce of them, there lyves, doinges, and deathes, whose Images they are, or whome they represent, and thereupon imitate, and diligently followe, to our power, al the same, as when we ernestly, and intentyvely doo behold, the Image of the Crucifix, we then have good occasion to remember, the incarnation, lyfe, passion and death of our Saviour Chryste."[98] Similarly, liturgical reverence is paid to the Gospels with no thought of idolatry: "The same Connsayle also hath this other example, that lykewise as when we do kysse the boke of the Gospells, we have not such affection, and love, to the parchment, paper, or letters made with ynke, as for theyr sakes to kysse the boke, but hav-ing onelye respecte to those holsome comfortable, and holy sayings which are in the boke conteyned, do, for that respect, kysse and embrace the boke most joyfully."[99]

---

96 On the pattern of swift movement from biblical to patristic sources in six-teenth-century theological debates, see, MacCulloch, *Cranmer*, p. 489.
97 Bonner, *Necessary and Profitable Doctrine*, sig. II.2, *verso*.
98 Bonner, *Necessary and Profitable Doctrine*, sig. II.2, *recto*.
99 Bonner, *Necessary and Profitable Doctrine*, sig. II.3, *recto*. For late me-

Bonner was aware however, that the Protestant attack on the veneration of images extended beyond the objects themselves, to the very concept of a cult of the saints. He therefore spoke to the issue of why the saints are venerated in the first place: "We do not worshyppe those outwarde shapes or fygures, but we do worshyppe the giftes, graces, and vertues whych god hath wrought in those sainctes, whose Images they are: for we do prayse the godlynes of theyr lyves, and styre up our selves thereby, to imytate and followe theyr fote steppes, and there withall we do make prayer unto almighty God that he wylbe mercifull and bountifull unto us, through the intercession and merytes of them."[100] Bonner listed a number of the patristic sources cited by the Seventh Ecumenical Council, and then proceeded to quote many of these authorities at first hand.[101] He made clear that he was citing these passages "out of the very actes and recordes of the same Counsayle."[102] Among others, Bonner quotes passages from the writings of Athanasius and Basil the Great.[103]

Bonner selected his sources to emphasize that the veneration of the saints and their images was an ancient practice in the Church. His citation of Germanus, Patriarch of Constantinople from A.D. 715–730, was representative of his endeavors here: "There was in the sayde seventh generall counsayle alledged, the aucthorytie of Germanus, patriarche of

dieval and Reformation rituals of the kissing of the pax in England, and use of the Mass book as a pax, see Eamon Duffy, *The Stripping of the Altars* (New Haven: Yale University Press, 1992), pp. 11–12, 29, 116–29, and 497.

100 Bonner, *Necessary and Profitable Doctrine*, sig. II.3, *recto*.

101 Bonner, *Necessary and Profitable Doctrine*, sigs. II.3, *verso*-KK.1, *recto*.

102 Bonner, *Necessary and Profitable Doctrine*, sig. II.4, *verso*.

103 Bonner, *Necessary and Profitable Doctrine*, sig. II.4, *verso-recto*. The decrees and canons of the Seventh Ecumenical Council, held at Nicea in A.D. 787, can be found in *Enchiridion Symbolorum Definitionum et Declarationem de Rebus Fidei et Morum*, eds. Henry Denziger and Adolph Schönmetzer (Rome: Herder and Herder, 1976), p. 200ff. The opening section on the approbation of sacred images includes a citation from paragraph 45 of St. Basil's *De Spiritu Sancto*. For a modern English translation of the passage of Basil's text cited here by Bonner, see St. Basil the Great, *On the Holy Spirit* (Crestwood, New York: St. Vladimir's Seminary Press, 1980) [hereafter: St. Basil, *The Holy Spirit*], p. 72.

Constantinople, who sayd thus: 'Let it offende no man, that before the ymages of saynctes, Candels, and swete savourynge encens are brente. For we must thinke that these thinges are done mysticallye, not unto the very wood or stones, but in, and for the honoure of them, whose rest is with Christ, the honour of whiche saynctes repayreth or commeth agayne unto Christ.'" To drive home the point of Church authority more firmly, Bonner goes on to quote Germanus' use of Basil the Great: "Basyll [testifies to] the same . . . saying, that the honour done to oure fellowe servauntes being good, doth geve or exhibit a commen token, or signe of benevolence to oure Lord, or master him selfe. For the sensible lyghtes, or candelles, are a signe of that pure and immateriall lyght geven of God. And the burning of fraken encense, doth signify the pure, and the ful or hole inspiration, and replenishing of the holye ghost."[104] By quoting such early and noteworthy figures among the Greek Fathers, Bonner was able to show that the veneration of the saints through sacred art is a common custom of the Church, both in the East and in the West, with a tradition stretching back long before the Great Schism.

Bonner brought his commentary on the second commandment to a close by noting that the Council's final and unanimous determination

---

104 Bonner, *Necessary and Profitable Doctrine*, sig. KK.1, *verso*. The extant writings of St. Germanus I, Patriarch of Constantinople A.D. 715–730, can be found in Migne, P.G., vol. XCVIII, cols. 35–454. These include three letters on the veneration of images. Germanus' letters cite in turn a letter attributed to Basil the Great, "Of the Holy Trinity, the Incarnation, the Invocation of Saints, and their Images." See Phillip Schaff, gen. ed. *Nicene and Post-Nicene Fathers*, ser. II vol. viii (Grand Rapids: William B. Eerdmans, 1894), pp. 614–15. The translator, Blomfield Jackson, raises doubts about the authenticity of this letter. Nevertheless, the idea that reverence of the image passes from it to its "original" is certainly authentic to Basil's thought: "The honor given the image passes to the prototype." See St. Basil, *The Holy Spirit*, p. 72. This is the very passage cited by the Council Fathers in the opening section of the decrees and canons of the Seventh Ecumenical Council. Bonner himself cites this same letter of Basil the Great. See Bonner, *Necessary and Profitable Doctrine*, sig. II.4, *verso-recto*. The original text of the letter [306] "Of the Holy Trinity, the Incarnation, the Invocation of Saints, and their Images" can be found in Migne, P.G., vol. XXXII, cols. 1099–1100.

was that there was a real distinction to be made between *latria* (from the Greek verb, λατρεύειν, "to worship"), which is worship proper, due unto God alone, and the sort of reverence that is paid to images and to the saints.[105] Quoting Paul from Colossians 3:17, Bonner asserted that the veneration of the saints is done in the name of Christ: "'Every thinge whatsoever ye doo in worde or in dede, do ye al thinges in the name of our Lord Jesus Chryste, gyvinge thanks to GOD and the father by or through Chryste.' Whiche rule who that foloweth in the use of these Images (as the hole Catholyke Churhe, heretofore hath, and nowe doth) can not justlye, nor ought not be reprehended or misliked, nor rekened to have done a mysse, or to breake thys seconde commaundement." Bonner clarified his point by adding, "For by the very wordes therein conteyned, we be not forbydden to make or to have similitudes or Images, but onely we be forbydden to make or to have them to the intent to gyve Gods honoure unto them, or to take them as Gods, as it appeareth in the 26th chapiter of Leviticus."[106]

Bonner's final points about the use of images in churches were pastoral in focus. He described images as "books" for uneducated laity: "The sayd ymages may well be sette up in churches, to be as bokes for unlearned people, to put them in remembraunce of those saynctes, of whom they maye learne examples of fayth, humilitie, charitie, pacience, temperance, and all other theyr vertues and gyftes of God, which were in them."[107] Despite his august endorsement of images, however, Bonner believed that their proper use should be taught to the people by educated and diligent clergy: "Ymages maye be set in the churche, and oughte not to be despysed, but to be used reverently, although we be forbydden

---

105 Bonner, *Necessary and Profitable Doctrine*, sig. KK.2, *verso*.

106 Bonner, *Necessary and Profitable Doctrine*, sig. KK.2, *recto*.

107 Bonner, *Necessary and Profitable Doctrine*, sig. KK.3, *verso*. Bonner's assertion that images may serve as books for the unlearned recalls Fisher's account of the crucifix as a book depicting the passion and death of Christ for the illiterate. See Susan Wabuda, "The Woman with the Rock: the Controversies on Women and Bible Reading," in *Belief and Practice in Reformation England: A Tribute to Patrick Collinson from His Students*, eds. Susan Wabuda and Caroline Litzenberger (Aldershot: Ashgate, 1998), p. 51.

to geve goddes honoure unto them. These lessons should be taught by every curate to theyr parysheners."[108]

Bonner's remarks about the curate's role in teaching and forming the laity betray his concerns about the education and dedication of clergy in sixteenth-century England. Similar contemporary reflections are sprinkled throughout his commentary on the Decalogue. For example, in his exposition of the eighth commandment, which prohibits stealing, Bonner took a passing shot at lackluster and absentee clergy: "all they who doo receyve rent or stipend, for any offyce, spirituall or temporall, and yet do not thyer offyce belonging thereunto, they, (I say) are transgressors of thys commandment."[109] Occasionally, Bonner expressed his concern for clerical depravity alongside sharp rebukes of the Henrician and Edwardine reforms. As he continued his discussion of the eighth commandment and what constitutes stealing, Bonner lamented, "There is an other grevous kynde of theft, and that (the more is the pitie) commonly used, which is called Symony, taking name of Simon Magus, who fyrst attempted with mony to purchase spiritual offyce or function (which eyther to sel or bye is damnable)."[110]

This passage directly precedes a lengthy rant on the late spoliation of churches: "Now emongst other special kindes of theft, none was ever more dredfullye punyshed in scripture, than sacrilege (whiche is thefte, spoyle, and robbery commited in suche thynges, as are dedicated or gyven to the honor of God specially, as are all churches, and al the ornamentes, plate, treasure, landes, and goodes to the same belongynge)." Bonner proceeded to buttress this claim with a characteristic appeal to scripture: "as appeareth in the fifth of Danyell, by the example of kynge Balthasar, and in the seconde booke of the Machabies, and the thyrde chapiter, of Heliodorus, who goinge aboute the spoyle of the temple of Hierusalem, for the threasors sake of the same, sodenly was throwen doune to the grounde, and beyng sore strycken with blyndnes, was caryed spechles also out of the temple halfe deade."[111] Likening

108 Bonner, *Necessary and Profitable Doctrine*, sig. KK.3, *verso*.
109 Bonner, *Necessary and Profitable Doctrine*, sig. RR.3, *verso*.
110 Bonner, *Necessary and Profitable Doctrine*, sig. SS.1, *verso*.
111 Bonner, *Necessary and Profitable Doctrine*, sig. SS.1, *verso-recto*.

Heliodorus to those nobles who seized or were lately awarded Church lands and goods under Edward, Bonner declared, "Whiche kynde of punyshment, if it had bene used in Englande, so ofte as sacrilege hath bene commyted, what a number shoulde there have bene of them that shulde have bene punyshed? But the thynge beynge of that sorte that it hath bene, and we not able to amende it, we wyll yet here admonysh all men from hensforth, to make, and kepe theyr handes pure from al sacrilege."[112] In these remarks, Bonner made it clear that his dissatisfactions with ignorance and abuse among Catholic clergy did not outweigh his antipathy for Protestant ideals or initiatives.

In addition to such explicit repudiations of Protestant endeavors in sixteenth-century England, Bonner also rebuked their labors implicitly. Writing on the sixth commandment, Bonner describes one aspect of what it means not to kill another: "The soule, beynge the cheyfe parte of man, doth incomparablye passe the bodye, . . . ye shall here note, that, by this commaundement we are muche more forbydden to kyll or murder our neyghbours soule, whiche kynde of murder and slaughter of the soule, they do commyt, who by pernitious, hereticall, and ungodlye doctryne, or by evyll counsayle, seduce the soule of theyr neyghbour, causinge it thereby to dye everlastynglye in hell." With alacrity, Bonner immediately pointed out those he believed to be guilty of this sin: "And specially they herein doo offend, who not onelye . . . with thyr teachinge by mouthe, do infecte theyr hearers, but with theyr moost venemous bookes lefte behynd them, doo stynge to death the soules of as manye, as by the readyng therof, doo consente to theyr develyshe doctryne. . . . As such theyr bookes or wrytynges doo remayne, infectynge other, so longe doth the damnation of the aucthors of suche bookes, and heresies, continuallye . . . increase."[113]

Although he goes on to cite the example of Arius and the perennial influence of his erroneous teachings, it is all too likely that Bonner also has in mind here the writings of the Protestant prisoners of the Marian régime. While there were a spate of heretical books being circulated in Marian England, the work of Ridley in Bonner's own diocese cannot

---

112 Bonner, *Necessary and Profitable Doctrine*, sig. SS.1, *recto*.
113 Bonner, *Necessary and Profitable Doctrine*, sigs. QQ.1, *recto*-QQ.2, *verso*.

have been far from his mind in this regard. In his preface to the *Neces-sary and Profitable Doctrine*, Bonner thanks King Phillip and Queen Mary for their efforts at restoring sound doctrine within the realm. He declares that he has earnestly travailed with his chaplains and friends "[t]hat errours, heresies and noughtye opinions may be cleane weeded, purged, and expelled out of my diocese (a great help whereunto is geven by dyverse provisions made by the Kynges and Queenes mooste excel-lent Majesties, and especyallye by that godlye proclamation, whiche of late was sente forth by theyr graces, concerninge the bringinge in of cer-tayne hereticall and noughtye bokes)."[114]

As lively and intriguing as his remarks are about contemporary events, these comments were peripheral to Bonner's main purpose in the *Necessary and Profitable Doctrine*. His essential aim was to expli-cate scripture, treating it primarily as a source of biblical history. Even in the portions of his work that are strictly concerned with prayer, Bonner remained sharply focused on the historical dimensions of biblical texts. In all of these elements, he is employing an essentially Humanist method of exegesis, yet not in the Erasmian mold of a sharp separation of Old and New Testament themes. His remarks also reveal the potency of texts in sixteenth-century England, expressed in the need to have the right books, especially the *Necessary Doctrine*, disseminated to a wide lay

114 Bonner, *Necessary and Profitable Doctrine*, sig. A.2, *verso*. In December 1554 and January 1555, the covert activities of Ridley himself came to the attention of Marian authorities when one of his former chaplains provided the Queen's men with several manuscript tracts that he had written even as he was held in prison. For his part in smuggling these writings out of jail and transcribing them, Ridley's brother-in-law was incarcerated. As a reward for his work, Ridley's Chaplain, Master Grimbold (Grimald), was set free from prison. Grimbold embraced Catholicism, recanting the Pro-testant ideas that he had helped Ridley promote under Edward. See *Brad-ford* vol. 2, pp. 207–08. See also Michael G. Brennan, "Grimald, Nicholas (*b.* 1519/20, *d.* in or before 1562)," *Oxford Dictionary of National Biogra-phy*, Oxford University Press, 2004 [http://www.oxforddnb.com/view/ar-ticle/11629, accessed 13 August 2007]. For more on the sale and distribution of Protestant writings in Marian England, see Philippa Tudor, "Protestant Books in London in Mary Tudor's Reign," *London Journal* 15 (1990): pp. 15–28.

readership, alongside the discovery and destruction of the wrong books from his diocese and the realm at large.

The History of Salvation

In his explication of the *Ave Maria*, Bonner reviewed several key passages of the New Testament. Throughout his reflections on this prayer, he was concerned with the historicity of the events related about Mary and the Incarnation in scripture. His heading for this section of the *Necessary and Profitable Doctrine* emphasized that this prayer is largely taken from scripture: "Here foloweth The Salutation of the Archaungell Gabriell made to the blessed Vyrgin Mary, taken oute of the first chapiter of S. Luke commonly called the *Ave Maria*, with the exposition or declaration thereof."[115] Bonner opened his exposition of this prayer by noting that we humans have greater cause than Gabriel to sing Mary's praise: "The high messenger of almyghty God, and heavvenly spirite Gabriell, dyd most joyfully with thys salutation greet the Vyrgyn Mary, [she] beynge than a mortall woman, lyvinge on the earth, and not havyng than conceyved in her undefiled, and chaste wombe, our saviour Christ. . . ." By way of comparision with the Archangel, Bonner exclaimed, "Howe much more ought we mortall, earthly, and synfull creatures, with all promptnesse and alacritie to salute with the selfe same wordes, that blessed Vyrgyn nowe, when as not onelye she hath brought forth our saviour and redemer Christ, but also she her selfe is exalted in heven above all angels, and Archaungels."[116] Foremost in Bonner's mind was to impress upon the reader that the historical fact and circumstances of the Annunciation bear ongoing implications for human devotion and reflection.

Turning to consider the meaning and appropriateness of the term "hail" in Gabriel's greeting: "Truelye thys worde 'Hayle,' or 'be joyful'

115 Bonner, *Necessary and Profitable Doctrine*, sig. AAA.2 *recto*. By underscoring the scriptural nature of the *Ave Maria*, Bonner fulfills his oft-repeated promise "not to omit our accustomed maner in alledginge scripture for the confirmation of assertions made in this booke," sig. RR.3, *recto*.

116 Bonner, *Necessary and Profitable Doctrine*, sigs. AAA.3, *recto*-AAA.4, *verso*.

is a word most mete and convenient for the Angell (comminge on a message) to begynne his salvation with all. For never was, there Creature, that hadde soo greate and Juste cause, to rejoyse for anye Benefytte receyved at gods handes, as had the blessed virgin Mary. . . ." Bonner made plain the "Juste cause" of Mary's joy: "For that it pleased allmightie god to chuse specially and appoynte her, to that most excellente, and incomparable dignitie, that of her shuld be conceyved and borne, Chryst, beinge both God and man, the saviour, and redemer of all mankynde."[117] Bonner stated that the Incarnation could not have occurred in the way it did without Mary's consent.[118] These events should bring all believers to recognize and acknowledge the immensity of God's miraculous grace, that he should send his Son to redeem us after the Fall, and that a virgin should conceive and bear a child without sin.[119]

Bonner next turns his attention to the words of St. Elizabeth, "blyssed is the fruyte of thy wombe."[120] In this portion of his reflections, Bonner characteristically coupled the Old and New Covenants. He relates the two by focusing on the term "fruit," and its inter-textual meaning: "He may well be called the blessed fruyte, for that he hath saved us, and gyven us lyfe, contrarye to the cursed fruyte, which Eve gave to Adam, by which we were distroyed, and broughte to deathe. But blessed is the fruyte of thys wombe, whiche is the fruyte of lyfe everlasting."[121]

Bonner ends his explication of the *Ave Maria* with another jab at the late form of religion under Edward. He noted that the Church's liturgical use of the Hail Mary has come at the conclusion of the *Pater Noster*, partially in praise of Christ, and partially to put us in mind of the virtuous Mary.[122] Such use has not prevailed in recent times, however: "Who is there now that hath a good Christen hart, and considereth the meanyng, . . . the aucthor, and other the cyrcumstances of the Ave Maria that wyll not counte, and judge them unworthy of the name of Chrysten men, who

117 Bonner, *Necessary and Profitable Doctrine*, sig. AAA.4, *verso-recto*.
118 Bonner, *Necessary and Profitable Doctrine*, sig. BBB.1, *verso*.
119 Bonner, *Necessary and Profitable Doctrine*, sig. BBB.1, *verso*.
120 Bonner, *Necessary and Profitable Doctrine*, sig. BBB.1, *verso*.
121 Bonner, *Necessary and Profitable Doctrine*, sig. BBB.1, *recto*.
122 Bonner, *Necessary and Profitable Doctrine*, sigs. BBB.1, *recto*-BBB.2, *verso*.

of late yeares, not onely have, in all theyr bokes, and other prynted papers, of purpose lefte oute this Godlye salutation, disdaynyng at the honour of the blessed virgin Mary." Bonner lamented those who, "[t]o the uttermost of theyr power, by theyr envying agaynste the commen, commendable, and devoute use thereof, [have] gone about to plucke it cleane out of mennes hartes, and myndes, and so for ever to abolyshe the memorye of her blessednes, moost contrary to . . . the holye gooste, by the mouth of the same vyrgin declared when she said: 'Behold verely from hence forth all generations shall call me blyssed.'"[123]

Although he draws strikingly different historical conclusions from the scriptures than Ridley, Bonner's fundamental exegetical method is quite similar to the Protestants whose work he so firmly denounces. Like Ridley, Bonner attaches ultimate significance to the historical facts related by the text, even when he is discussing the devotional dimensions of scriptural verses. He also paid careful attention to the hidden significance and proper interpretation of specific terms found in the text, as his reflections on "hail" and "fruit" make plain in his explication of the *Ave Maria*.

Apart from his ecclesiological allegiances, what distinguishes Bonner's scriptural reflections from Ridley's is not the basic historical and philological methods employed, but a persistent concern to show that the Old and New Covenants are mutually interdependent. Above all else, Bonner emphasized the similitude between God's original Covenant with Israel and his Covenant with the new Israel, the Church. Even as he reflected on the *Pater Noster*, Bonner asserted that part of its utility for Christians lies in the fact that its petitions recapitulate the devotional content of both testaments: "This prayer of our Lorde is so profounde, so aboundaunt and so plenteous, that there is no prayer, whether it be wrytten in the olde testament, or in the newe, but that the summe and effect thereof is conteined in some of these seven petitions. Wherefore we exhorte all people to saye this prayer ofte, distinctly, and devoutlye."[124] What Bonner hoped to demonstrate by drawing out the

---

123 Bonner, *Necessary and Profitable Doctrine*, sig. BBB.2, *verso-recto.*
124 Bonner, *Necessary and Profitable Doctrine*, sigs. UU.3, *recto*-1UU.4, *verso.*

continuities between the Old Testament and the Gospel is to show that Jesus, the archetype for all believers, was faithful to the Covenant of Israel.

Commenting on the fifth commandment, Bonner indicated that Jesus not only told us to honor our parents, in keeping with the Law, but did so himself. Bonner noted that in the seventh chapter of Mark, Christ states: "'Honor thy father and thy mother. He that doeth curse father or mother, shall dye the death.' And Christ himselfe gave herein unto us example, both of oure subjection, and also of obedience, to be geven and done unto our natural parentes, as appeareth in the seconde of Luke, where it is wrytten thus: 'And he (that is to saye, Christe) dyd goo downe wyth them, and came to Nazareth, and was subject, or obedient unto them.'"[125] By the use of such examples, Bonner wanted his readers to draw the conclusion that Jesus' faithfulness to the Old Covenant is analogous to Christian faithfulness to the Church. For Bonner, Christians may only claim the name when they embrace the traditions of the Church, modeling their actions on Jesus' faithfulness to the rites of the Old Covenant. Bonner's fundamental claim then, is that true obedience to Christ inevitably carries sacramental and ecclesiological dimensions for believers.

Administration and Defamation

Ironically, Bonner had been removed from his office as Bishop of London when he provoked the wrath of the King and his counselors in 1549, but his visitation articles in 1554 were deliberately promulgated without the consent of the Queen and her Council. When questioned about his actions, Bonner responded that the visitation was "a matter pertaining to his own post" and that he had "acted out of zeal for God's service." Nevertheless, he tellingly conceded that he "knew that if he had told the Council about it there would have been opposition."[126]

---

125 Bonner, *Necessary and Profitable Doctrine*, sig. OO.4, *recto*.
126 *Calendar of State Papers, Spanish*, eds., P. de Gayangos, G. Mattingly, A. S. Hume, and R. Tyler, vol. XIII (H.M.S.O. 1862–1964), pp. 66, 68. See Alexander, *Marian Persecutions*, p. 168.

Bonner's instincts about the Marian Council proved sound: for the duration of her reign, even the internal administration of his diocese was directed by leading Council members, acting in various capacities. On 2 April 1557, commissioners appointed by Mary for London ordered all parsons, curates, and churchwardens in the diocese to locate and identify people who avoided confession, attendance at Mass, and reception of the Eucharist. The following year, they issued a manual of *Interrogatories*, to enquire of all churchwardens their knowledge of married clergy, their doctrinal views, and urging them to help in the discovery and suppression of "heretical, naughty, or seditious erroneous" books and Bibles.[127] On 24 May 1555, the King and Queen personally reminded Bonner by letter that his jurisdiction had been restored to him to ensure the swift execution of government policy in matters of religion.[128] On three separate occasions between 1554 and 1556, Bonner was directed by the Council to send his preachers and commissaries into Essex.[129] The royal policy that they wished to carry out by these means was the discovery and execution of unrepentant Protestants.[130]

Although Bonner did not protest the Marian policy of persecution, he appears less sanguine and more patient, even in the chronicles of John Foxe, than some of Mary's other ministers. We catch such glimpses of a more empathetic Bonner, for example, in John Philpot's account of his several examinations before the Queen's commissioners: it was Bonner who repeatedly offered hearty food, good wine, and kind words to Philpot.[131] By contrast, Dr. Story jeered: "I dispatched them [Latimer, Cranmer, and Ridley] and I tell thee that there hath bene yet never a one burnte, but I have spoken with him, & have bene a cause of his dispatch. . . . I tell thee I will never be confessed therof."[132] At his sixth examination, Philpot himself declared of his treatment by Bonner, "for my part I might say that I have found more gentlenesse at his Lordships handes

127 Alexander, *Marian Persecutions*, pp. 162–63.
128 Alexander, *Marian Persecutions*, pp. 160–61. For the text of this letter, see Foxe, *Actes and Monuments*, p. 1582.
129 Alexander, *Marian Persecutions*, p. 161ff.
130 Alexander, *Marian Persecutions*, pp. 161–70.
131 See Foxe, *Actes and Monuments*, pp. 1798ff.
132 Foxe, *Actes and Monuments*, p. 1805.

then I dyd at myne owne Ordinaries for the time I have bene wythin his prison."[133]

It is somewhat puzzling, then, that Foxe went to such lengths to single out Bonner as the Archfiend of the Marian persecution, bestowing upon him the enduring epithet "Bloody Bonner" in the *Actes and Monuments* (commonly called *Foxe's Book of Martyrs*). Foxe consistently excoriated Bonner as a man determined to destroy as many Protestants as possible, even when those examined by the Bishop paint a very different portrait of Bonner's words and deeds. In fact, many of the materials that Foxe incorporated into his ponderous tome reveal Bonner as long-suffering, personally concerned for, and generally attempting to persuade and teach heretics rather than peremptorily despatching them to the magistrates and the stake. As with other aspects of his duties, Bonner's proceedings with respect to many accused heretics during the reign of Mary reflect not his personal convictions, but the will of leading governmental officials. Philpot's case is a prime example: while Bonner sought more time to work with the accused, Dr. Story insisted to Bonner's chaplains: "One of you tell my lord, that my commyng was to signifi to his Lordshyp, the he must out of hand rid this heretik away."[134] That the Council and royal commissioners were directing the actions of the Bishop in heresy proceedings, against his will at many points, is quite clear from even Philpot's perspective.[135]

To fully understand Foxe's creation of the figure "Bloody Bonner," we must read the sometimes conflicting accounts of Bishop Edmund Bonner in the *Actes and Monuments* with an eye to modern scholarship on the martyrologist and his sources. As Patrick Collinson has pointed out, Foxe was steeped in a classical tradition stretching back to Plutarch that portrayed virtuous men and women as calm, stable, and rarely driven to anger or vindictiveness.[136] Foxe's aim in his great work was to

133 Foxe, *Actes and Monuments*, p. 1806. Cf. Patrick Collinson, *The Elizabethan Puritan Movement* (Oxford: University Press, 1989), pp. 265, 378.
134 See, e.g., Foxe, *Actes and Monuments*, pp. 1798–99.
135 Bonner actually confessed to Philpot that he had displeased the Council in tarrying so long in working to persuade him. See Foxe, *Actes and Monuments*, p. 1805.
136 This ideal of personified virtue was characteristic of Aristotle. See Patrick

provide a total contrast between his martyrs and their persecutors. While the "godly" were typically described by him as placid and prayerful even in the fire, Bonner is portrayed as possessing a vitriolic temper when confronted with mere words, whether delivered orally, or written scripture verses on the walls of churches.[137]

Another aspect of Bonner's inconstancy, from Foxe's perspective, was the preface he had written to Stephen Gardiner's *De vera obedientia* in 1535. In an effort to remain in favor with Henry, Gardiner and Bonner had joined forces to craft a strong rebuke of papal primacy. Foxe reprinted the whole of Bonner's preface, where it was declared: "And this is no new example, to be against the tyrany of the Byshop of Rome, seeing that not only this man, but many men often times, yea and right great learned men afore now, have done the same even in writing, whereby they both painted him out in his right colours, and made his sleightes, falshoode, fraudes, and deceiptfull wyles, openly knowne to the world."[138] Given Bonner and Gardiner's volte-face under Mary on the role of the Petrine ministry for ensuring unity in Church doctrine, Foxe's citation of Bonner's own words was devastating. Michael Riordan and Alec Ryrie have noted that Gardiner's turn to embrace the pope in the 1550s made him an object of derision.[139] In their review of Gardiner's depiction in the *Actes and Monuments*, they have perfectly

Collinson, "'A Magazine of Religious Patterns': An Erasmian Topic Transposed in English Protestantism," in *Godly People: Essays in English Protestantism and Puritanism* (London: Hambledon Press, 1983) [hereafter: Collinson, *An Erasmian Topic*], pp. 499–526.

137 Relating the events of Bonner's Deprivation trial in 1549, for example, Foxe repeatedly refers to the Bishop's anger, declaring he was "in a raging heate, as one cleane voyd of all humanity." *Actes and Monuments*, p. 1318. Cf. Foxe's description of Bonner being "in a great and stoute rage" when the actual charges were brought against him in the same trial, *Actes and Monuments*, p. 1325. Similarly, Bonner and his ministers are rebuked for "theyr malicious rage agaynst the Lord and his word" in the painting over of scripture verses in Marian churches. *Actes and Monuments*, p. 1475.

138 Foxe, *Actes and Monuments*, p. 1060.

139 See Michael Riordan and Alec Ryrie, "Stephen Gardiner and the Making of a Protestant Villain," *Sixteenth Century Journal* 34 (2003) [hereafter: Riordan and Ryrie, "Making of a Protestant Villain"]: pp. 1039–65.

captured a central point in Foxe's own thinking: the marginal note following Bonner's preface decries "[t]he inconstant mutabilitye of Wint. and Boner."[140] Bonner's rage and shifting doctrinal opinions marked him out, for Foxe, as untrustworthy and irregular.

Were Bonner and Gardiner really more "inconstant" than their opponents? Did they really exhibit a greater degree of "mutabilitye" than Cranmer and Ridley? They were, after all, advocating much the same doctrine in the early 1550s as they did before Henry's break from Rome. By concentrating on the change in Bonner and Gardiner's views between 1535 and 1553, Foxe perhaps succeeded in distracting his readers from another key question that might naturally suggest itself: why had the doctrinal opinions of early English Protestants shifted so dramatically during this same period? With respect to the Eucharist alone, once the unity of tradition was broken by Luther and Zwingli, a great variety of Protestant opinions immediately sprang up. Cranmer had, in turn, embraced nearly all of them, from belief in transubstantiation to holding to a Lutheran notion of real presence in the 1530s, then promoting a Bucerian view of the sacrament in the later 1530s, and finally, under Ridley's direction, adopting a doctrine of a hypostatic presence of Christ in the sacrament by the later 1540s. Ridley's own eucharistic opinions were also in flux during these same years, not to mention his and Cranmer's shifting views on the papacy, images, relics, and vernacular liturgy.[141] The fact that constancy was a cardinal virtue for sixteenth-century English Protestantism explains both Foxe's focus on Bonner and Gardiner's turn-about on papal primacy, and the Martyrologist's decision to purge Crome from his book of Protestant martyrs in the 1530s and '40s. To maintain the contrast he wished to present between the "true" Church and the "false" one, Foxe's characters had to exhibit steadfastness in the former case, and exhibit "rage" and "mutabilitye" in the latter.

From the many details supplied by his sources, Foxe was certainly aware that Bonner occupied an unenviable position between the gears of governmental and ecclesiastical heresy investigations in London. Foxe even quotes Bonner as saying that "they report me to seeke bloud,

140 Foxe, *Actes and Monuments*, p. 1060.
141 See, e.g., MacCulloch, *Cranmer*.

and call me bloudy Boner, where as God knoweth, I never sought any mans bloud in all my life."[142] However, it was never Foxe's intention to present a disinterested account of the Marian persecutions. As Patrick Collinson notes, Foxe himself demanded of his critics: "Why should I be restrained from the free walke of a story wryter . . . ?"[143] Collinson states that it is the drama of Foxe's story that gave it the verve essential to forming an English Protestant national consciousness.[144] Foxe certainly denounced Queen Mary and her policies, but had much too good

142 Foxe, *Actes and Monuments*, p. 1692.
143 Foxe, *Actes and Monuments*, p. 702. See Patrick Collinson, "Truth and Legend: The Veracity of John Foxe's Book of Martyrs," in *Elizabethan Essays* (London: Hambledon Press, 1994) [hereafter: Collinson, "Truth and Legend"], pp. 151–77. Collinson is persuaded that the question of Foxe's historical accuracy is essentially settled in the affirmative, once allowance is made for mistakes of names, places, and dates, and for the fact that some themes were part of "a tradition which was in a literal and strict sense fabulous." Although he has discovered that Foxe removed and willfully repressed evidence from original sources that would have disclosed some of his alleged Protestant martyrs as having denied the Resurrection and the Trinity, Collinson does not think this a grave matter, but rather a "pardonable handicap." For Foxe's removal of nine folio pages from the trial register of a special Marian commission on heresy for the diocese of Canterbury, see "Truth and Legend," pp. 166ff.
144 Protestant monopoly of the printing press from the reign of Elizabeth onward was also decisive in this regard. See Elizabeth Evenden and Thomas Freeman, "Print, Profit, and Propaganda: The Elizabethan Privy Council and the 1570 Edition of Foxe's 'Book of Martyrs,'" *The English Historical Review* 119 (2004), pp. 1288–1307. This article reminds modern scholars that, in the absence of anything resembling public libraries in sixteenth-century England, having copies secured in local parish churches was the best and most convenient way to ensure the dissemination of the "useful messages," from the Government's perspective, contained in the *Actes and Monuments*. For the Elizabethan régime's appreciation of "the propaganda value of history," see pp. 1296–1303. On the similar initiative to have Bibles placed in Henrician churches, see Margaret Aston, "Lap Books and Lectern Books: The Revelatory Book in the Reformation," in *The Church and the Book: Papers Read at the 2000 Summer Meeting and the 2001 Winter Meeting of the Ecclesiastical History Society*, ed. R. N. Swanson (Rochester, New York: Boydell Press, 2004) pp. 163–88, esp. p. 180ff.

an eye for drama to cast something as impersonal as a council or royal commission as the central villain of his story. Foxe's dualistic narrative of the pure Church and the utterly corrupt one called for a central human figure to better raise and focus the ire of his audience.[145]

Under such circumstances, we might imagine that the sadistic Dr. Story, gleefully naming for Philpot those whom he had personally examined and "dispatched,"[146] would become the Archfiend of Foxe's tale. Foxe's was an ecclesial drama, however, an epic of the battle between the forces of Christ and Antichrist. For this purpose, Bonner made a much more suitable *bête noire* in the narrative, because he was a Bishop, by Foxe's reckoning, in the Church of Antichrist.[147] In terms of office, Cardinal Pole might stand nearer Antichrist himself, the Pope, as Foxe cast his characters, but Pole's comparatively lenient treatment of heretics meant that Bonner was the best candidate for the role of master villain in the "*Actes and Monuments of these . . . perillous dayes . . . wherein have been . . . described the great persecutions & horrible troubles that have been wrought and practised by the Romishe Prelates. . . .*"[148]

Inverted parallelisms were a staple of early Protestant polemics, and they are found as readily in Foxe as in Richard Phinch's "*Epiphanie of the Church . . . plainly shewwing, both the Church that cannot but erre, and also the Church that cannot erre.*"[149] Foxe actively heightened the juxtapositions of the protagonists and villains in his book of martyrs by intentionally excluding stories of Protestant equivocators from his

---

145 Riordan and Ryrie, "Making of a Protestant Villain."

146 See Foxe, *Actes and Monuments*, p. 1805.

147 That Foxe's singular scorn for Bonner results in part from the martyrologist's dramatic flair seems apparent from his own manuscript notes, where he sums up Story's career with rare concision: "Story worsse then Boner." See Julian Lock, "Story, John (1503/4?–1571)," *Oxford Dictionary of National Biography*, Oxford University Press, 2004 [http://www.oxforddnb.com/view/article/26598, accessed 1 Feb 2007]. Lock is citing from Landsdowne MS 109, fol. 52, *recto*, in the British Library Collection. Cf. Foxe's similar vilification of Gardiner in Riordan and Ryrie, "Making of a Protestant Villain."

148 See Foxe, *Actes and Monuments*, colophon.

149 See Richard Phinch, *The Epiphanie of the Church* ([STC 10877.5] London: Roger Ward, 1590) [hereafter: Phinch, *Epiphanie*], colophon.

narrative.[150] He also recast key details of some stories that were passed to him. The examination of Thomas Tomkins, a weaver from Shoreditch, is a case in point: the Spanish Ambassador recounted the bravado of Tomkins who, being questioned by Bonner, voluntarily asked for a lighted candle to be brought to him so that he might demonstrate the pain he could endure to his hand.[151] Foxe told of the same events, but asserted that Bonner, again in a rage, snatched Tomkins' hand and held it to the flame until the skin swelled with blisters that then burst asunder.[152] With this animus, Foxe's forced contrasts between the "true" Bishop, Ridley, and the "false" Bishop, Bonner, would have been plain to his audience. The stratagem clearly worked: in the mid-nineteenth century, the editors of the Parker Society simply reprinted Foxe's account of the contrasting characters of Bonner and Ridley to serve as the greater part of their introduction to Ridley's collected works.[153]

As Thomas Betteridge has noted, the "true" image of the "false" bishop is an explicit theme in a famous woodcut of Bonner included in the *Actes and Monuments*.[154] The illustration is entitled: "The right picture and true Counterfet of Boner, and his crueltie, in scourging of Gods Sainctes, in his Orcharde at Fulham."[155] It depicts Bonner flailing the bare backside of a Protestant prisoner, a bundle of switches clutched in each hand. A third figure, presumably a fellow prisoner to the victim, peeks between his fingers at Bonner's fury, being forced himself to hold with his legs the head of his *confrère*. Betteridge asserts that this image is constructed such that the reader of the *Actes and Monuments* is called to identify more with the figure being forced to hold down the victim than with the victim himself.[156] In this way, the woodcut paradoxically

150 Wabuda, "Subtle Shadows," pp. 224–42.
151 See Alexander, *Marian Persecutions*, p. 157.
152 Foxe, *Actes and Monuments*, p. 1534ff.
153 See the editor's preface to Ridley, *Works,* pp. iv–xi.
154 Thomas Betteridge, "Truth and History in Foxe's *Acts and Monuments*," in Christopher Highly and John King, eds., *John Foxe and His World* (Aldershot: Ashgate, 2002) [hereafter: Betteridge, "Truth and History"], pp. 145–59, esp. p. 153.
155 Foxe, *Actes and Monuments*, p. 2043.
156 Betteridge, "Truth and History," p. 153. That this interpretation requires

becomes an "implicit demand that in reading Foxe's work one moves from passivity to activity and from watching to doing."[157] Betteridge believes that the woodcuts in *Actes and Monuments* impel the reader to action because they capture the violence and fury of "papistry," thereby stabilizing the meaning of Foxe's text.[158]

Betteridge's point about the active brutality depicted in the woodcuts that accompany the *Actes and Monuments* is certainly well taken, but we should also note that part of their power will always lie in a contrary direction, in the way they actually arrest action: Bonner in this depiction is forever frozen as an icon of aggressive sadism. Wholly excluded from such an image is any kindliness that he may have ever shown another person, or any crime or act of hostility that his victim may himself have ever committed. Both men are stationary caricatures of their respective personalities and deeds, both physically and doctrinally. Immortalized in the gritty lines of Foxe's woodcuts, each of them has been stripped of the fullness of their humanity, in that this image encapsulates all that we see of them.

Yet there is another, more subtle, and ultimately for Foxe, more consequential action or movement associated with Bonner than those depicted in the woodcut images of the *Actes and Monuments*: Bonner's characterization as one who turned away from Protestantism after having at first promoted it. In a passage that does not appear in the 1563 edition of the *Actes and Monuments*, Foxe urges his readers in 1570 to "understand (good reader) that this Doct. Boner all this while remayned yet (as he seemed) a good man, and was . . . a favourer of Luthers doctrine." Further along in this section Foxe declares, "The world and all posteritye maye see, how the comming up of Doct. Boner was onely by the Gospell (how so ever he is now unkynd unto the Gospell)."[159] It is important to

Betteridge to abandon, without explanation or apology, the highly-structured typology for interpreting the woodcuts that he has been using up to this point in his article, seems to have escaped his notice. Prior to his discussion of the Bonner woodcut, Betteridge maintains that the reader is to identify with the central-most figure or object in these images.

157 See Thomas Betteridge, "Truth and History," p. 153.
158 See Thomas Betteridge, "Truth and History," pp. 153–57.
159 Foxe, *Actes and Monuments*, 1570 edition (STC 11223), pp. 1239–40.

recall here both that Bonner died in September 1569, and that Foxe came by stages in later editions of his work, to place great significance in the quasi-Stoic, unmoving constancy of his martyrs, often portrayed as unflinching, even in the flames of the stake.[160] What we might be tempted to construe as an effort on Foxe's part at a more evenhanded or realistic portrayal of Bonner, in the charge that he once was "a favourer of Luthers doctrine," was really meant to highlight the changeable, shifting, unfixed character of the arch-villain of the *Actes and Monuments*. In Foxe's narrative, constancy in religious conviction in the face of terror and torture serves as a validation of the individuals whose stories he champions. In this same regard, we also know that Foxe purged from his *magnum opus* even the stories of committed Protestants, if they were also known by him to be equivocators.[161] Neither the fact that dissembling was crucial to the survival of English Protestantism at points, nor that it was respected among the early Reformers, could lead Foxe to look at it favorably.[162] With increasing scrupulosity, Foxe came to scorn mutability in the religious attitudes of the people he profiled in the *Actes and Monuments*.

Bonner's activities inevitably provided a wealth of source material for Foxe's martyrology, since he served as the spiritual head of the most determinedly Protestant diocese in the whole of Marian England. With the Council, royal commissioners, and local magistrates all referring suspects to him to be tried for heresy, Bonner's prominent role in the persecution was as certain as it was inescapable. The zeal of Mary's ministers in London Diocese resulted in some 113 men and women being burnt for heresy, accounting for about two-thirds of all of the known victims for the whole realm. Nevertheless, throughout the *Actes and Monuments*, Foxe mentions at least another seventy suspects who were either

Throughout the rest of this study, we have cited exclusively from the 1583 edition, following STC 11225. Cf. p. 1088 of this edition with pp. 1239–40 of the 1570 edition.

160 Collinson, "Truth and Legend," pp. 174–75.

161 Wabuda, "Subtle Shadows."

162 See Andrew Pettegree, "Nicodemism and the English Reformation," in *Marian Protestantism: Six Studies* (Brookfield, Vermont: Ashgate, 1996), pp. 86–117.

reconciled by Bonner and his officers, released at trial, or died in prison before they could be examined.[163] Bonner's efforts to labor long and closely with educated suspects, to gain their conversion, had the unintended effect of furnishing Foxe with great stores of polemical ammunition against the Bishop since the prisoners' accounts were often written out and were eventually delivered to the martyrologist. Bonner's attention to legal detail, a natural quality in a career lawyer and diplomat, meant that he saw closely to the execution of the law once sentence had been pronounced against an individual heretic. Ninety-eight of the surviving ninety-nine London significations, or writs from Chancery for excommunications, bear Bonner's own signature.[164]

Reappraisal of Bonner's Life and Work

We cannot today assess and understand Bonner's character in a way that is not partially colored by Foxe's treatment of him as "the Bloody Bishop." It is certainly clear, however, that Bonner was not very enthusiastic about carrying out orders to condemn suspects for heresy, even when urged onward by members of the Privy Council or the King or Queen. Foxe's portrayal of Bonner as eager to conduct such proceedings is a contrived image, with contours re-shaped to fit neatly into the Protestant martyrologist's black and white tableau of plain villains and pure victims.

A close study of Bonner's work, however, especially the *Necessary and Profitable Doctrine*, reveals a mind that is far-ranging though scripturally focused in theological argument, concerned for historical and dogmatic precedent, and well acquainted with the Greek and Latin Church Fathers and Humanist philological principles in exegesis. While Bonner's chaplain might decry "every wave and winde" of Protestant opinion, it would be a mistake to assume that no similarities of exegetical method are to be found between the theological works of leading Catholic clergy in the reign of Mary Tudor, and their contemporary archrivals. Although swearing off Protestant "new learning," Bonner and

---

163 See Alexander, *Marian Persecutions*, p. 167.
164 See Alexander, *Marian Persecutions*, p. 174.

his associates regularly employed some of the exact same Humanist interpretive tools in their exegetical works that we find in the writings of leading ministers of reform under Edward VI.[165]

Bonner relies on the Humanist tools of historical consciousness and philology no less than Ridley does for the explication of scripture, yet for very different ends. The great divide between Bonner and Ridley is not exegetical method *per se*, but their divergent views of the relationship between the Old and New Covenants, and of the person and work of Christ. These concepts coalesce around Bonner's understanding of the role of the Church in salvation history, and he treats them in a fashion that is reminiscent of the work of John Colet.

The similarity of Bonner's thought to that of Colet is most fully revealed in the Bishop's ecclesiology. For both men, a profound appreciation of Old Testament typology is fundamental to their understanding of the work of the Church. Bonner and Colet view the Church as a sacramental extension throughout the ages of the presence and salvific labors of Christ, Paschal Victim and High Priest. Their focus on themes that connected the Old Covenant with the New, even while highlighting the historical and philological aspects of biblical texts, discloses their indebtedness to Italian Humanism. Under the influence of this strand of Humanist exegesis, both Colet and Bonner direct the reader's attention to the great deeds of Christ in the Redemption of man.

---

165 Indeed, Pendleton's own homilies are very much concerned with historical consciousness in biblical exegesis. See, e.g., Bonner, *Homilies*, fols. 37–42. Here Pendleton questions the Apostolicity of any form of *sola scriptura*, noting that the New Testament scriptures were not written down until many years following Pentecost.

Chapter 5
Bonner on the Nature and Role of the Church

Bonner's philological digressions on terms such as *idolum, sculptile,* and Sinai, coupled with the historical consciousness evident in his work, suggest that he is employing key Humanist tools for exegesis in a fashion that recalls the work of Ridley. Despite applying the same basic interpretive methods of close historical and linguistic enquiry to explicate scripture, the two men nevertheless arrive at widely divergent interpretations of the texts themselves and of what the text enjoins upon believers.

Ridley and Bonner arrive at different exegetical destinations because they are travelling along different paths of Humanist biblical interpretation. Ridley's Erasmian Humanism leads him down the path of ignoring or dismissing the Old Testament context of Jesus' words in the New Testament, while focusing narrowly on the words of Jesus as a series of propositions that Ridley believes are aimed at establishing the proper form of the Church. Ridley relies repeatedly on interpolation to make these arguments stand firm. In this model of exegesis, Christ and the establishment of the Church are presented as a *de novo* re-founding of God's relationship with man, rather than a new stage of building that rests upon the foundation of God's covenant with Israel. By contrast, Bonner is following the Italian Humanist tradition, which leads him to major exegetical departures from the path taken by Erasmus and Ridley. Among those departures are two key aspects of Bonner's work that conform fully to the aims of Italian Humanist exegesis: focusing the reader's historical consciousness on the events and religious culture of the Old Testament when explicating the New Testament, and giving ample scope to the deeds of God throughout salvation history, rather than focusing exclusively on the words of God as recounted in the Old and New

Testaments. These emphases give rise to Bonner's ecclesiology, which of necessity, then, is both sacramental and encyclopedic in linking Church rites to the covenant history of ancient Israel.

These ecclesiological themes are clearly evident in Bonner's *Homely on Christian Love*. In it, he declares: "The perverse nature of man, corrupt with synne . . . thinketh it against all reason, that a man should love hys enemye, and hath many perswasions, whyche enduceth hym to the contrary. Agaynste all whyche reasons, wee ought as well to set the teachynge, as the lyvynge of our savioure Chryste."[1] This focus on "the lyvynge" as well as "the teachynge" of Christ is characteristic of several selections penned by Bonner and his chaplains in Reformation London. A consideration of the living of Christ leads to a different view of ministry and sacramental practice than that advocated by Erasmus and Ridley.

For Bonner, it is only within the sacramental framework of the Church that believers have any reliable encounter with the New Covenant established by Christ. This position is the natural result of Bonner's parallel constructs of Christ's faithfulness to the Old Covenant and Christians' faithfulness to Jesus. Bonner's concern for the "lyyvnge" of Christ recalls John Colet's emphasis on Jesus as a moral exemplar primarily by virtue of His actions. By consistently noting the direct example of Christ's actions as recounted by the New Testament authors, Bonner reveals himself as exegetically and ecclesiologically nearer to Colet than to Erasmus or Ridley. This characteristic emphasis of Italian Humanism guides Bonner's exegetical method, and thereby gives shape to his ecclesiology. The same patterns of emphasis are evident in the writings of Bonner's chaplains, John and Nicholas Harpsfield. To better understand how exegesis gives shape to ecclesiology, and to see how rival Humanist traditions led to different models of

---

1   *Homelies sette forth by the righte reuerende father in God, Edmunde Byshop of London, not onely promised before in his booke, intituled, A necessary doctrine, but also now of late adioyned, and added therevnto, to be read within his diocese of London, of all persons, vycars, and curates, vnto theyr parishioners, vpon sondayes, [and] holydayes,* ([STC 3285.4]) London: In Poules churcheyarde, at the sygne of the holy Ghost, by Ihon Cawodde, 1555) [hereafter: Bonner, *Homelies*], fol. 25, *verso*.

ministry and church practice in early modern Europe, it will be helpful to consider Erasmus' and Colet's respective commentaries on First Corinthians and Romans.

Fellow-working with Christ

According to John O'Malley, a leading author on the Renaissance and the Reformation, the most common portrayal of Jesus arising from Erasmus' *philosophia Christi* is that of a pedagogue or teacher: "Although Christ is described [by Erasmus] in a number of different terms like 'leader,' 'prince,' or 'head,' nonetheless the 'image' of him that predominates is that of teacher. Christ's redemptive mission is consequently, sapiential, even educational."[2] For O'Malley, this "image" of Christ is the direct result of Erasmus' subscription to the *genus deliberativum* of classic oratory, the branch of that discipline concerned with persuading or leading a hearer to a particular conviction or course of action. It tends to concern itself more with the speech and words of the subject than the *genus demonstrativum*, which weighs the actions of an individual with an aim to assigning "praise and blame."[3] O'Malley is firmly persuaded

---

2 John W. O'Malley, "Grammar and Rhetoric in the Pietas of Erasmus," *The Journal of Medieval and Renaissance Studies* 18.1 (1988) [hereafter: O'Malley, "Grammar and Rhetoric"]: p. 94.

3 O'Malley, "Grammar and Rhetoric," pp. 94–95. Cf. John W. O'Malley, *Praise and Blame in Renaissance Rome: Rhetoric, Doctrine and Reform in the Sacred Orators of the Papal Court, c. 1450–1521*, vol. 3 of *Duke Monographs in Medieval and Renaissance Studies*, (Durham: Duke University Press, 1979) [hereafter: O'Malley, *Praise and Blame*], p. 39–49. See also O'Malley, "Erasmus and the History of Sacred Rhetoric: The Ecclesiastes of 1535," in *Religious Culture in the Sixteenth Century* (Brookfield, Vermont: Variorum, 1993), p. 14, where the author indicates that Erasmus' placement of preaching in the *genus deliberativum* not only brings a more moralizing but also "a more decidedly didactic" emphasis to preaching. The third division of classical rhetoric, the *genus iudiciale* or judicial oratory, was principally a courtroom form, and was little applied to the explication of biblical texts or preaching in the Renaissance. See *ibid.* p. 46. On O'Malley's view that Jesus remains primarily a sacred pedagogue for Erasmus, see his "Erasmus and Luther, Continuity and

that it is his adherence to deliberative oratory that accounts for "Erasmus' relatively scarce interest in the deeds and actions of the Jesus of Nazareth depicted especially in the Gospels of Mark and Luke."[4] In Erasmus' soteriology, then, Christ's redemptive work is primarily rhetorical: Jesus is, quite literally, the Speech of God.[5] Christ's words as recounted in the New Testament, not his actions, are therefore the primary *scopus* of Erasmus' exegetical labors.[6]

The contours of Erasmus' rhetorical soteriology become more defined when his exegetical writings are contrasted with those of John Colet on identical passages of scripture. In their rival commentaries on First Corinthians, for example, Colet and Erasmus display very different emphases and arrive at opposite interpretations of the verses in Paul's

Discontinuity as Key to Their Conflict," *The Sixteenth Century Journal* 4.2 (1974) [hereafter: O'Malley, "Erasmus and Luther"], p. 55, where Jesus' "redemptive and reforming mission" is described as "inseparable from his office as teacher" in the work of Erasmus. Cf. the observation of Charles Trinkhaus that Erasmus is the expositor of a "rhetorical theology," *In Our Image and Likeness: Humanity and Divinity in Italian humanist Thought,* (London: Constable, 1970) I, pp. 126–28, 141–42. O'Malley also notes that in Erasmus' soteriology, "Christ becomes the teacher rather than the prophet; . . . he is more a purveyor of philosophy than a proclaimer of judgment; he saves through the illumination of the soul rather than through action." O'Malley, "Grammar and Rhetoric," p. 98.

4   O'Malley, "Grammar and Rhetoric," p. 94.

5   On Erasmus' recasting of the Prologue to John's Gospel, proclaiming Christ as the *Sermo Dei,* see Margery O'Rourke Boyle, *Erasmus on Language and Method in Theology* (Toronto: University of Toronto Press, 1977) [hereafter: Boyle, *Erasmus on Language and Method*] and Chapter III above. Cf. the observation of Susan Wabuda that Erasmus' chief argument for broad dissemination of the scriptures was that Jesus barred no one from the sound of his voice. See Susan Wabuda, *Preaching During the English Reformation* (Cambridge: Cambridge University Press, 2002) [hereafter: Wabuda, *Preaching*], p. 76. Wabuda is here paraphrasing a portion of Erasmus' *Paraclesis,* later revised and reissued as the *Exhortation ad studium Euangelicae lectionis.* Erasmus refers other key points of Church doctrine to aspects of Jesus' speech throughout his explication of First Corinthians. See Chapter II above.

6   On Erasmus' description of Christ as the *scopus* of exegesis and devotion, see Chapter II above.

epistle that relate to the subjects of chastity and celibacy.[7] Erasmus places a line on Paul's lips that refers the matter to Jesus' speech: "Truly, that thing that Christ demanded not of his, I dare not demand of you."[8] This interpolation, which reflects Erasmus' approbation of clerical marriage,[9] is aimed to deflect attention from Paul's encomia on celibacy: "It is good for a man not to touch a woman. . . . For I would wish that all were even as myself. . . . I say to the unmarried, and to the widows: It is good for them if they so continue, even as I."[10] Colet, however, stresses that Christ's chaste example in this regard is the true model that all should strive to emulate: "[Christ] was the first to set forth the features and countenance of the good. And this he did not so much in words as in the reality, in himself rather than extrinsically, in his own life, in which the good and true manner of living was portrayed. Christ is, therefore, the first in this kind of being, and the measure, and the standard."[11] For Colet, close attention to Jesus' actions is crucial for any authentic life of faith, since Christ is "That exemplar of the truth toward which all his followers ought to strive; and the closer you come to him, the more you will become perfect. For Christ, who came to teach perfection and draw men to it, was the perfection itself of human life."[12]

The idea that exegesis and devotion should take their cues from the New Testament record of Jesus' deeds as well as his words also finds expression in Colet's *Commentary on Romans*. Here Colet refers repeatedly to Christ's words and deeds as complementary and integral parts of the one work of redemption: "For it is in Jesus . . . in the hearing [of] His

---

7 See Chapter II above and 1 Corinthians 7:1–10.

8 Erasmus, *Paraphrasis in Epist. Pauli ad Cor. 1*, Cap. VII, in vol. VII of *Desiderii Erasmi Roterdami Opera Omnia*, ed. Jean Leclerc (Leiden: Lugduni Batavorum, 1706), p.880, col. C: "*Verum, quod Christus non exigit à suis, non ausim à vobis exigere.*"

9 See Ashley Null, *Thomas Cranmer's Doctrine of Repentance* (Oxford: Oxford University Press, 2000), p. 107, n. 113.

10 Douay-Rheims, 1 Corinthians 7: 1, 8, and 9.

11 John Colet, *Commentary on First Corinthians*, trans. and eds. Bernard O'Kelly and Catharine Jarrott, Medieval and Renaissance Texts & Studies 21 (Binghamton, New York: Medieval & Renaissance Texts & Studies, 1985) [hereafter: Colet, *Commentary on First Corinthians*], p. 141.

12 Colet, *Commentary on First Corinthians*, p. 141.

teaching, in the imitation of His life—that our one and only and surest hope consists of eternal life in Him."[13] Similarly, believers are admonished: "The teaching of Jesus must be listened to; His life must be ever kept before our eyes."[14] Colet's emphasis on the active nature of faith in his *Commentary on Romans* is as constant as it is conspicuous. He insists that "True Christianity" involves "the performance of every good," and is rooted in "the conduct of him who . . . acts well to the utmost of his power . . . satisfied with his own good action."[15] Faith for Colet must always be "coupled with an imitation and setting forth of [Christ]."[16]

So committed is Colet to promoting Christian faith as active, that he adds: "and the imitation of Jesus" to charity, as the greatest of the theological virtues.[17] Colet insists that the righteous man, "[b]y doing the will of God, confesses God in his works."[18] Such themes read almost as if they were conceived as a corrective to Erasmus' *philosophia Christi* and his consequent preoccupation with Christ as a sacred rhetor. Indeed, in one remarkable passage of Colet's *Commentary on Romans*, he explicitly raises the subject of a philosophy of Christ, in a fashion that is clearly not consonant with Erasmus' oracular soteriology. Colet asserts: "This sect and school of philosophy of Christ is one not so much in words, as in deed, in works, in life itself; and a justifying faith implies in its very nature an imitation of Christ and fellow-working with Him; being elsewhere called by St. Paul, *faith which worketh by love.*"[19] Even

13 John Colet, *Exposition of St. Paul's Epistle to the Romans, in Letters to Radulphus on the Mosaic Account of the Creation, Together with Other Treatises*, trans. and ed. J. H. Lupton (Cambridge: Cambridge University Press, 1876) [hereafter: Colet, *Exposition of Romans*], pp. 106–07. "Of" here is merely a typographical correction of the printed text.

14 Colet, *Exposition of Romans*, p. 107.

15 Colet, *Exposition of Romans*, pp. 107–08.

16 Colet, *Exposition of Romans*, p. 107.

17 Colet, *Exposition of Romans*, p. 118. Paul discusses faith, hope, and charity in 1 Corinthians 13:13.

18 Colet, *Exposition of Romans*, p. 118.

19 Colet, *Exposition of Romans*, p. 118. Lupton's transcription of the Latin text of Colet's original manuscript can be found in the same volume: "*Haec secta Christi et philosophatio non tamen est verbis quae re, operibus, et vita ipse. Et fides iustificans importat in suo significantu imitationem*

here, Colet is propelled to further emphasize the idea that true faith is an active imitation of the deeds of Christ: "He who works in the Holy Spirit, is reckoned to hope in God, and believe in Christ. *Faith without works, says James, is dead.* And St. John adds his testimony: *He that saith he abideth in him, ought himself also to walk, even as he walked.*"[20] Colet's concentration on the believer as a "fellow-worker" with the deeds of Christ results in a soteriology that is far removed from Erasmus' consistent appeal to the oral teachings of Jesus alone.

Text, Context, and Controversy

The controversy over exegesis and ecclesiology that characterized the early decades of sixteenth-century England was sparked in large part by Erasmus' New Testament scholarship, and went far beyond the arguments between Erasmus and Colet on the interpretation of specific passages of the Bible. Erasmus introduced a revolution in textual interpretation in late February of 1516 with his *Novum Instrumentum*. In it, he translated the

> *Christi, et cooperationem cum illo, quam alibi vocat Paulus 'fidem quae per dilectionem operantur,'"* p. 298. The translator's rendering of Galatians 5:6b is nearly identical to the Douay-Rheims: "Faith that worketh by charity."

20 Colet, *Exposition of Romans*, p. 118. Lupton's transcription of the Latin text of Colet's original manuscript can be found in the same volume: "*Is censetur sperare in Deo et credere in Christo, qui operantur in Spiritu sancto. Fides, inquit Jacobus apostolus, sine operibus mortua est. Et Joannes subscribit: 'Qui dicit se in Christo manere, debet, sicut ille ambulavit, et ipse ambulare,'"* p. 298. Colet's original text suggests a rather more firm relationship between the citations from James 2:20 and 1 John 2:6 than merely "adding testimony," but rather declares that John "underwrites" or "endorses" James' assertion that faith without works is dead. For an excellent summary of the perennial debates over faith, works, and human merit, see Richard H. Bulzacchelli, *Judged by the Law of Freedom: A History of the Faith-Works Controversy and a Resolution in the Thought of St. Thomas Aquinas* (New York: University Press of America, 2006). Through an appeal to the Aristotelian-Thomistic conception of co-proximate causality, Bulzacchelli suggests that human cooperation with God gradually restores a pre-fall human *posse* in humanity which makes possible a form of relative merit in man, through divine grace.

Greek term λόγος as *Sermo* in Latin, in opposition to the Vulgate's *Verbum*. With this substitution, the passage in question became: "In the beginning was the Speech, and the Speech was with God, and the Speech was God." A floodgate of controversy opened with the printing of Erasmus' diaglott New Testament in Latin and Greek, and this particular passage was singled out for strident criticism and heated debate.[21] Nevertheless, the pericope thus rendered succinctly captures the chief note of Erasmus' Christology: Jesus is the divine Speech incarnate.[22] By the time Erasmus completed his revisions to the *Novum Instrumentum* in 1519, Luther was already appealing to scripture as an independent and higher authority for establishing ecclesial polity than the teaching office of the Church. Thus, due both to its fateful timing and audacious emendation of the Vulgate, Erasmus' *Novum Testamentum* embroiled him in lengthy attacks on his character even from its inception.[23]

The long struggles of the English clergy against Lollardy, which was characterized by the clandestine production and dissemination of vernacular translations of scripture, predisposed traditionalists to be wary of any effort to make biblical texts the sole measure and arbiter of

21 For a brief introduction to the early controversy surrounding Erasmus' *Novum Instrumentum*, see Boyle, *Erasmus on Language and Method*, pp. 1–31. Erasmus felt the static and singular concept of *Verbum* or Word was too restrictive to indicate the full range of oral teachings handed down by Christ. He actually preferred the term *Oratorio* or Oration as even more precise, but thought better of this course because the gender of *Oratorio* in Latin is feminine. See *ibid.* pp. 33–57. Cf. Wabuda, *Preaching*, Chapter II.

22 Cf. Boyle, *Erasmus on Language and Method*. It is likely that this concept represents another Platonic strand in his thinking on the *philosophia Christi*, since speech, as indicated in Plato's *Dialogues*, enjoys a privileged place for instructing the individual in piety, virtue, and knowledge.

23 See Wabuda, *Preaching*, pp. 72–73. Cf. Brian Cummings, *The Literary Culture of the Reformation: Grammar and Grace*, (Oxford: Oxford University Press, 2002) [hereafter: Cummings, *Literary Culture of the Reformation*], p. 104, where the author asserts that Erasmus' 1516 *Novum Instrumentum* "[m]arks [his] ultimate failure," in that it led "not to a new consensus in religion," but rather made Humanist studies "party to a new schism."

theology and ecclesiology. Against the backdrop of Luther's denial of four of the Church's seven sacraments according to his own interpretation of the New Testament, Erasmus' assertion that scripture was "self-authorizing, virtually self-interpreting," while "all other forms of knowledge [were] *abditum et retrusum*, [hidden and obscure]," led many to be suspicious of his own motives.[24] Among English divines of the period, alarm at both Lutheran doctrine and Erasmus' presumption in editing and publishing on his own authority a "correction" of the received text of the New Testament scriptures erupted into philippics.[25] These circumstances "created the condition for the demise of [Erasmus'] personal reputation and associated his name with unorthodoxy, sometimes heresy."[26] It did not help matters that Erasmus insisted that the biblical text made Christ more "fully present" than his human body, a claim that was implicitly subversive of the Church's eucharistic theology.[27]

While the principle of *sola scriptura* first emerged from the mind of Luther, even there it was not a settled matter, since the Wittenberg reformer himself admitted that "a person cannot be persuaded by another's inner conviction" of the meaning of scripture.[28] Nevertheless, as Erasmian biblicism and Luther's principle of an ecclesiology restricted to self-evident scriptural references gradually took hold in England, debate on those practices that derived from the oral traditions of the apostolic deposit of faith were derided as "unwritten verities."[29] In the 1530s and 1540s, Tyndale and Cranmer, among others, printed tracts that attempted to prove that scripture pointed only to itself as an

---

24 Cummings, *Literary Culture of the Reformation*, p. 105. Cf. Marshall, *Henry VIII's England*, pp.82–83.
25 This was the substance of Edward Lee's original attack on Erasmus. See Wabuda, *Preaching*, pp. 72–74. For the career and labors of Lee, see Claire Cross, "Lee, Edward (1481/2–1544)," *Oxford Dictionary of National Biography*, Oxford University Press, 2004 [http://www.oxforddnb.com/view/article/16278, accessed 1 Feb 2007].
26 Cummings, *Literary Culture of the Reformation*, p. 104.
27 Cummings, *Literary Culture of the Reformation*, p. 106.
28 Cummings, *Literary Culture of the Reformation*, p. 174.
29 See Wabuda, *Preaching*, pp. 76–89. See also Marshall, *Henry VIII's England*.

authority.[30] The very fact that they felt compelled to argue this case raises questions about whether any form of *sola scriptura* is a self-evident tenet of scripture itself.[31] In the long run, these efforts were greatly complicated by several political and ecclesiological circumstances, not least of which was Henry's own religious conservatism, resulting in the preservation of many ecclesial practices such as "creeping to the cross" on Good Friday, that could not be explicitly located in scripture.[32] In

30 See Peter Marshall, *Religious Identities in Henry VIII's England*, (Aldershot: Ashgate, 2006) [hereafter: Marshall, *Henry VIII's England*], p. 85. While the author appears to accept Tyndale and Cranmer's proposition, labeling the contemporary Catholic effort to promote the idea of an unwritten deposit of faith as "*post hoc* rationalism," we should note that the entire chapter Marshall devotes to this debate in Henrician England does not include a direct citation of any patristic source. Although he describes Thomas More's notion of "a Christianity without scripture" as "counter-factual," Marshall later concedes the historical fact that the Church "preceded [the New Testament scriptures] in time." Cf. pp. 84, 85 and p. 89. Since Christ is recorded as telling his disciples that they are bound to heed the sayings of even the Pharisees, because they occupy the seat of Moses, it would seem that the question of scripture's promotion of itself as an independent authority is still an open matter. See *The Byble in Englyshe of the largest and greatest volume* . . . . ([STC 2073] London: Edwarde Whitchurch [or Rycharde Grafton] *cum priuilegio ad imprimendum solum*, 1541) [hereafter: *The Great Bible*], Matthew 23:1–3: "Then spake Jesus to the people, and to his disciples, saying: 'The Scribes and Pharises syt in Moses seate. All therefore whatsoever they bid you observe, that observe you and do: But do not ye after their workes: for they saye, and do not.'" Given that more than three centuries elapsed before the Church had a definitive canon of New Testament writings, it is rather unlikely that *sola scriptura* was an apostolic teaching, the Reformers' claim to be recapturing the ethos of the "primitive church" notwithstanding.

31 See Cummings, *Literary Culture of the Reformation*, p. 235, where the author wryly notes: "Cranmer's definition of the Bible as self-explicating . . . . is a claim not borne out by the need for a thousand folio pages of Erasmian paraphrase alongside it." It is also not borne out by Cranmer's reliance on an allegory drawn from Ezekiel 44:1–3 to assert that the perpetual virginity of Mary was plainly established in scripture. See Marshall, *Henry VIII's England*, p. 86.

32 See Marshall, *Henry VIII's England*, pp. 90–94, esp. 93.

addition, even the leading Edwardine divines held to the doctrine of the perpetual virginity of Mary because this concept served to undermine Anabaptist notions of Christology.[33] The plain, self-interpreting text of scripture led to ever-greater divisions among Protestants in England up to and beyond the Marian restoration of Catholicism. This fact was disconcerting to those who promoted the idea of scripture as the highest authority in Church polity, including Ridley himself.[34]

Heresy and Homilies: Nicholas and John Harpsfield

In the mid-1550s, *scriptura* was the alleged authority that governed both the official Edwardine settlement in religion, and the affairs of the "Freewillers," a radical sect whose members rejected predestination. It was in this setting, characterized by very wide divergences in Protestant practice, that Bonner assembled the ablest talent available to him for restoring Catholicism in the Diocese of London.[35] Among those who joined in his efforts to re-establish orthodoxy in the capital was Nicholas Harpsfield, Oxford canon lawyer, and a man with long-standing and very close ties to the friends and relatives of Thomas More—most notably More's son-in-law, William Roper.[36] With the accession of Edward VI,

33 See Marshall, *Henry VIII's England*, pp. 86–89.
34 Cummings, *Literary Culture of the Reformation*, pp. 241–43, which touch briefly on Ridley's 1552 investigation of "Freewillers" in Kent, and a resurgence of this debate when he, Bradford, and Henry Hart were in prison, shortly before Bradford was burnt.
35 The controversies between Ridley, Hooper, and the Stranger Church also owe much to the volatile principle of *sola scriptura*, as Ridley, Hooper, and Laski all claimed to be building up the church according only to the Word of God, yet the particulars of their ecclesiological visions were in fateful conflict. This problem is likely rooted in the effort to establish proper and firm limits to ecclesiology from documents that do not have this purpose as their primary aim: none of the New Testament writings is concerned explicitly and exclusively with the proper form of the Church. On Ridley's clashes with Hooper and the leaders of the Stranger Church, see Chapter III above. Cf. Marshall, *Henry VIII's England*, pp. 96–99.
36 See Thomas S. Freeman "Harpsfield, Nicholas (1519–1575)," *Oxford Dictionary of National Biography,* Oxford University Press, 2004

Harpsfield found Oxford considerably less congenial, and in 1550, he took up residence in Louvain with Antonio Bonvisi, formerly one of Thomas More and Erasmus' greatest friends. Members of More's family also resided with Bonvisi during Harpsfield's sojourn in Louvain. During this period, Harpsfield wrote most of his biography of Thomas More, a work which even today is still credited for its accuracy and completeness.[37]

Returning to England when Mary came to the throne, Harpsfield rapidly ascended the ladder of ecclesiastical preferment, being first named archdeacon of Canterbury, then becoming principal agent to Cardinal Pole, and eventually vicar-general of London. In this capacity, Harpsfield worked closely with Bonner in the execution of the Marian anti-heresy laws. The visitation of London Diocese conducted by Harpsfield between November 1554 and March 1558 resulted in investigations of nearly four hundred suspected heretics within Bonner's diocese. For these efforts and Harpsfield's similarly thorough proceedings in the diocese of Canterbury, he received rough treatment from Foxe in the *Actes and Monuments*.[38]

[http://www.oxforddnb.com/view/article/12369, accessed 1 Feb 2007] [hereafter: Freeman, "Harpsfield, Nicholas"].

37 Freeman, "Harpsfield, Nicholas."

38 Freeman, "Harpsfield, Nicholas." See also Collinson, *Truth and Legend*, p. 166. Nicholas Harpsfield was also credited with writing *Cranmer's Recantacyons* during the reign of Mary, while his *Dialogi sex contra summi pontificatus, monasticae vitae, sanctorum, sacrarum imaginum oppugnatores, et pseudomartyres* (Christopher Plantin: Antwerp, 1566), written while he was imprisoned by the Elizabethan régime, led Foxe himself to correct a number of errors and mischaracterizations that appeared in the 1563 edition of his *Actes and Monuments of matters most speciall and memorable, happenyng in the Church, with an Universal history of the same, wherein is set forth at large the whole race and course of the Church, from the primitive age to these latter tymes of ours, with the bloudy times, horrible troubles, and great persecutions agaynst the true Martyrs of Christ, sought and wrought as well by Heathen Emperours, and now lately practised by Romish Prelates, especially in this Realme of England and Scotland* ([STC 11225] London: John Daye, 1583) [hereafter: Foxe, *Actes and Monuments*]. Cf. *Bishop Cranmer's Recantacyons*, ed. Lord Houghton (London: Philobiblon Society Miscellanies, 1877).

Nicholas' older brother, John, also made common cause with Bonner under Mary, although his career was rather more ambiguous than that of Nicholas up to that time. John was Oxford's first Regius Professor of Greek in 1541 and engaged in a number of Humanist translation projects, one of which was dedicated to Henry VIII himself.[39] John contributed one selection to Cranmer's *Book of Homilies*, "Of the misery of all mankynde." In it, he stressed the role of divine grace in human salvation. Unlike Nicholas, John did not flee to the Continent under Edward VI, but retained his post as a fellow of New College, Oxford until 1551. That same year, John became, through the auspices of the traditionalist Bishop, George Day, prebend of Chichester cathedral.[40]

After the death of Edward VI, John Harpsfield preached in support of Catholic restoration before Convocation in October of 1553. In the same year that his brother Nicholas became archdeacon for the diocese of Canterbury, John was made archdeacon of London. In this capacity, John assisted in the examination of Ridley and was very active in the final proceedings against Cranmer. John Harpsfield was an accomplished preacher, being called upon to deliver sermons for a number of official government functions in the reign of Mary, including the funerals of several high officials.[41]

A Polemical Presence

John Harpsfield also bore the brunt of the labor for Bonner's *Homelies*, writing nine of the thirteen selections that comprise the work.[42] For

---

39 See William Wizeman "Harpsfield, John (1516–1578)," *Oxford Dictionary of National Biography,* Oxford University Press, 2004 [http://www.ox-forddnb.com/view/article/12368, accessed 1 Feb 2007] [hereafter: Wizeman, "Harpsfield, John"].
40 Wizeman, "Harpsfield, John."
41 Wizeman, "Harpsfield, John." Both Nicholas and John Harpsfield were jailed in 1559 with the accession of Elizabeth, and would not be set at liberty again until 1574, when they were released from prison for health reasons. Nicholas died the following year, while John lived until 1578. See Freeman, "Harpsfield, Nicholas."
42 See the closures that follow each selection, in Bonner, *Homelies*. One of

Harpsfield, a focus on the deeds of Christ led naturally to a consideration of Old and New Testament intertextuality. In the eleventh homily, *Of the true presence of Chrystes bodye and bloud in the sacrament of the Aultar*, Harpsfield weighs both the actions of Christ and his Old Testament religious heritage in explicating the institution of the Eucharist. In this vein, Harpsfield connects Christ simultaneously to the paschal and priestly dimensions of the old covenant: "In that our savyour dyd eate of the paschal lambe with his apostles, immediately before he did institute this sacrament, it most playnely declareth unto us, that this sacrament is a marveylous worthye misterye and that very thing, which the eating of the paschal lambe, in the olde lawe did prefygurate, for whyche cause, when this was instituted that was abrogated."[43] We should note that Harpsfield considers the Passover Feast to be abrogated not because it is an empty ritual, or its annual celebration is a vain human tradition, but because Jesus, presiding at this Passover rite, put something substantive and correlative in its place. To Harpsfield's mind, the Last Supper carried priestly dimensions from the very beginning, by virtue of the company assembled: "Nether is it without a merveylouse consideration that Chryst at that heavenly banket, would of purpose, nother have the blessed Vyrgyn Mary his mother, presente with him, nor anye other of his dyscíples, save onely the twelve Apostles, whome he appointed to be the heade ministers of all his misteries here on the earth, and specially to be the ministers of this most blessed sacrament, and the instructours of al other, touchynge the same."[44]

Following these observations, Harpsfield applies his historical and analytical skills to gain insight into the institution narratives of the Gospels. He notes that, according to Chrysostom and Theophylact, the synoptic evangelists wrote their chronicles of Jesus' ministry at different times, separated by a span of several years.[45] Despite this remove from

these, "Of the misery of all mankynde," was a revision of the piece he had written for Cranmer's *Book of Homilies* in the 1540s. See Wizeman, "Harpsfield, John."

43 Harpsfield, in Bonner, *Homelies*, fol. 56, *verso*.
44 Harpsfield, in Bonner, *Homelies*, fol. 56, *verso*.
45 Harpsfield, in Bonner, *Homelies*,, fol. 56, *recto*. The original supplies only a marginal note indicating Chrysostom and Theophylact, but not a proper

each other in time, "it is to be well noted that the three Evangelystes, Matthewe, Marke, and Luke did all three agree in the maner of the institution of thys sacrament."[46] Even more remarkable, in Harpsfield's estimation, is that none of the Evangelists undertook to explicate or clarify Jesus' words at the Last Supper: "In doubtefull speaches of our saviour Chryst, some one or other of the Evangelists evermore openeth playnely the very meaning of the speches, yet touching these wordes, this is my body, no one of them, maketh anye declaration upon the same, but they all leve them to be taken of us, as they sounde, and (as of most playne words) they make no exposityon or interpretation of them at all. Whyche point muste be well consydered."[47]

The force of Harpsfield's argument about a lack of clarifying remarks from the Evangelists concerning Jesus' words "This is my body," only becomes apparent in light of the counter examples he cites. He notes that when Jesus declared, "Loose you this temple, and in thre daies shal I builde it up againe,"[48] John clarifies that Jesus, "By the temple ment his body."[49] Again, when Jesus says in John 7:38, "He that beleveth in me, as the scrypture sayeth, 'there shal ryvers of quycke water flow out of him," Harpsfield notes that, "because thys saying is obscure S. Jhon to make it open sayethe, that he spake these wordes, of the spirit, which they that beleved in him shoulde receyve."[50] Harpsfield's point is that the Gospel writers consistently explicate any saying of Jesus that is not to be taken literally. Since none of them makes any effort to indicate a metaphorical meaning for Jesus' declaration that the blessed bread was

citation. In his 23rd Homily on John's Gospel, St. John Chrysostom does comment on the fact that the Evangelists and Paul wrote at different times, and both after Jesus spoke about his body and the temple (John 2:18–19). See P. G., ed. Jacques-Paul Migne, vol. XLIX, cols. 137–43 and "Homily XXIII," in *Nicene and Post-Nicene Fathers*, ser. I, vol. xiv, ed. Phillip Schaff (Grand Rapids: William B. Eerdmans, 1894), p. 82.

46 Harpsfield, in Bonner, *Homelies*, fol. 56, *recto*.
47 Harpsfield, in Bonner, *Homelies,* fol. 56, *recto*.
48 John 2:19.
49 John 2:20, cited by Harpsfield, in Bonner, *Homelies*, fols. 56, *recto*-57, *verso*.
50 See Harpsfield, in Bonner, *Homelies*, fol. 57, *verso*.

his body, we may safely assume that the direct sense was the one they intended to convey.

Harpsfield concludes these observations with a three-fold assertion: that Jesus' presence in the sacrament is neither beyond his love for us, nor beyond his power, and is also prefigured in nature. In the first instance, Jesus has expressed his intention to be in the sacrament, and his love for humanity extends to the full agony of the Crucifixion as a reparation for our sins.[51] Secondly, in language strikingly similar to St. Ambrose's writings on the Eucharist, Harpsfield appeals to Jesus' divinity: "in the Sacrament of the aultare, there is the verye body and bloud, of our saviour Christe, worthye of al honour and glorye, the selfe same in substaunce, that is in heaven; whych thyng for Christ to bryng to passe, is a thyng most easye, he being God almightye, maker of heaven and earth."[52] Thirdly, he says: "nother is it finally unfytte for hys wysedome, seeynge he hathe ordeyned, that everye naturall mother, nouryshe her chyldren, wyth the substaunce of her owne body."[53]

Bonner's own reflections on the real presence occupy the final place in the *Homelies* and read as if they were designed to be a point-by-point attack on the eucharistic thought of Ridley. Despite repeated assaults on the teachings of Edwardine Protestant leaders, Bonner does not refer to any of them by name. Yet, by any number of ways, it is quite likely that Bonner had a firm knowledge of Ridley's eucharistic views. Ridley held the episcopal see of London just prior to Bonner's reinstatement, and so his books and notes were probably perused by Bonner and his chaplains when they took possession of the bishop's estates. In fact, early in his imprisonment, one of Bonner's chaplains, Secretary Bourn, made an informal examination of Ridley's sacramental views while he was in the

---

51 Harpsfield, in Bonner, *Homelies*, fol. 57, *recto*.
52 Harpsfield, in Bonner, *Homelies*, fol. 57, *recto*. Touching on the theme that it is fully within God's power to perform acts that transcend human reason, Harpsfield's homily also bears resemblance to Peryn's *Thre godly sermons*. Cf. St. Ambrose "On the Mysteries," in *Nicene and Post-Nicene Fathers*, ser. II, vol. x, ed. Phillip Schaff (Grand Rapids: William B. Eerdmans, 1894), p. 325. St. Ambrose's original text can be found in P. L., ed. Jacques-Paul Migne, vol. XVI, cols. 405b–410.
53 Harpsfield, in Bonner, *Homelies*, fol. 57, *recto*.

Tower of London. At the end of their conversation, Bourn admitted that at one time, he had been given all of Ridley's books.[54] In addition, a number of Ridley's treatises came into the hands of Marian authorities in December 1554 or January 1555, when Grimald (or Grimbold), one of Ridley's former chaplains, betrayed both him and Ridley's brother-in-law, George Shipside or Sheepside.[55] When Ridley was brought from the Bocardo jail to debate with the Queen's commissioners, Dr. Weston, the interlocutor, informed Bonner in great detail of the proceedings. Finally, a Master Harpsfield, either John, who assisted Bonner by writing the bulk of the *Homelies*, or Nicholas, his brother, Vicar-General to Bonner, engaged Ridley in that debate.[56] Through all of these means, Bonner would have had considerable knowledge of Ridley's theological ideas.

Bonner's *An homely wherein is aunswer made to certayne common objections, agaynst the presence of Christes bodye, and blounde in the sacrament of the Aultar*, is the single largest selection in the whole volume of the *Homelies*. Throughout the piece, Bonner's central point is that rejection of the real presence is based mainly on the protests of human reason. He repeatedly refutes the notion that bare rationalism is compatible with Christian faith. He opens this homily with a series of excerpts from Paul on the subject of faith and reason: "Saynt Paule in the tenth chapyter of his second epistle to the Corinthians, geveth us an example . . . howe we should always brynge reason in subjection to fayth, sayeng, 'The wepons of oure warfare are not carnall, but myghtye in God, to overthrowe stronge holds, to destroie counselles, and every hyghe thinge that exalteth itselfe agaynst the knowledge of God, and to brynge in captivity unto the servyce of Chryst, all underdtandynge.'"[57]

---

54   Foxe, *Actes and Monuments*, p. 1427 and Nicholas Ridley, *The Works of Bishop Ridley*, ed. Henry Christmas, for the Parker Society (Cambridge: Cambridge University Press, 1841) [hereafter: Ridley, *Works*], p. 165.

55   See Michael G. Brennan, "Grimald, Nicholas (*b.* 1519/20, *d.* in or before 1562)," *Oxford Dictionary of National Biography*, Oxford University Press, 2004 [http://www.oxforddnb.com/view/article/11629, accessed 13 August 2007].

56   For Weston's reports to Bonner, and John Harpsfield among the Catholic disputants, see Ridley, *Works*, pp. 189, 191.

57   Bonner, *Homelies*, fol. 63, *verso*. The verses cited are from 2 Cor. 10:4–5.

Bonner suggests that if the limits of human reason were the true foundation of Christian faith, then Jesus' message would originally have met no resistance. He points out, however, that even from the beginning Jesus' teachings were received only by a small minority of his own people: "What, (thinke you) is the cause whye the Jewes beleve not on Chryst? Verelye fyrste, because he was borne of a Vyrgyn, which is contrary to the course of nature." Bonner continues: "Secondly likewyse, he was in unitie of person, God and man, whych how it may be no mans wyt is able, by natural power, to conceave, thirdly because he beynge God and man, suffered the deth of the crosse, which for God to be content to do, semeth to natural reason a thing moste absurde, but good chrysten folke, gevyng place to faith, do most undoubtedly beleve on Chryst, God and man crucified."[58] By referring to Jesus' virgin nativity, divinity, and crucifixion, Bonner is building his argument on the articles of the Nicene-Constantinopolitan Creed. He is suggesting that if Christian faith is circumscribed to the limits of the human mind, then no portion of this ancient profession of faith may long stand.

After reinforcing these points by citing Paul's admonition to the Corinthians, that "[their] faith might not stand on the wisdom of men, but on the power of God,"[59] Bonner urges that such counsel "ought so to staye us in the fayth of the catholyke churche that nether carnall reasons, grounded upon the feble intellygence of mans natural wyt, nether the deceatefull judgement of our selves, shoulde make us once to doubte, of any one truth in Chrystes religion were it never so contrarye to the course of nature, never so farre above our capacities, and never so absurde to the appearaunce of our outward senses."[60]

It is clear from Bonner's remarks that he intends his response to objections against the doctrine of the real presence as an answer to the sacramental thought of the Edwardine Reformers: "Through the iniquitie

---

58 Bonner, *Homelies*, fol. 63, *verso*.

59 Citations from both 1 Corinthians 1:23–24, and 2:3–4, are to be found in Bonner, *Homelies*, fol. 63, *verso-recto*. The verse quoted here, 1 Corinthians 2:5, is the Douay-Rheims rendering.

60 Bonner, *Homelies*, fol. 63, *recto*. Cf. William Wizeman, S.J., *The Theology and Spirituality of Mary Tudor's Church* (Burlington, Vermont: Ashgate, 2006) [hereafter: Wizeman, *Mary Tudor's Church*], pp. 54–56.

of these latter evyll yeares, dyvers have hadde sondrye fonde dowtes and scruples, put into theyr heades . . . agaynst the presence of Chrystes body and bloud, in the Sacrament of the aultar, and through suche dowtes have swarmed from the true belefe therein, therefore here shall folowe aunsweres, and solutyons, to such dowtes as have ben most common, that from henceforth no man shall nede to be seduced by them or lyke."[61] While many of the arguments against the real presence that Bonner meets in this homily could have been taken either directly from Ridley's prison writings, or from the transcript of his statements made during his examination at Oxford, we will consider only the most salient resemblances to Ridley's thought addressed by Bonner in this piece.

The first objection that Bonner takes up is the idea that, since Christ declared that the Eucharist was to be celebrated in memory of him,[62] such a remembrance necessitates the absence of Jesus himself.[63] Bonner responds to this challenge by applying a common Humanist principle for scriptural analysis: close inter-textual comparison of related biblical pericopes.[64] He refers the issue to what Paul says he "received from the Lord" concerning the Eucharist in 1 Corinthians 11. There, Paul rehearses Jesus'

61   Bonner, *Homelies*, fol. 63, *recto*.
62   See, e.g., Luke 22:19, Douay-Rheims: "Do this for a commemoration of me."
63   Bonner, *Homelies*, fols. 63, *recto*-64, *verso*. This was a favorite argument of Ridley: "If, therefore, he be now really present in the body of his flesh, then must the supper cease: for a remembrance is not of a thing present, but of a thing past and absent," Ridley, *Works*, p. 199, as he declared in his examination at Oxford before the Queen's commissioners.
64   Bonner also employs this method when discussing a similar argument based upon Matthew 26:11, where, after being anointed with nard by a woman with an alabaster flask, Jesus says to Judas (according to the Douay-Rheims), "For the poor you have always with you: but me you have not always." Bonner says that Jesus makes plain, when Matthew and Mark are compared together, that this act was to prepare his body for burial. His flesh had no need of anointing after the resurrection, nor was it to be among the disciples in the form of an incarnate man after the Ascension. He concludes by asserting that Christ's presence in the sacrament is to provide nourishment for believers, and is not for the purpose of presenting himself as a human body for anointing. See Bonner, *Homelies*, fols. 64, *verso*-65, *recto*.

institution of the Eucharist, presenting Jesus' words almost identically as they are recorded in the Synoptic Gospels. However, in the verse immediately following "Do this in remembraunce of me," Paul says, "As oft as you eat of that bread, and drink of that cuppe, you shal shew forth the Lordes death until he come."[65] Therefore, Bonner concludes, "the remembraunce whyche oure savyoure there requyreth of us, is in the remembraunce of hys death, whych is past, and not present, and therefore after most proper maner of speache, may well be remembered."[66] Among other points he raises in response to this objection, Bonner notes that the sacrament might well be a remembrance of Calvary, where Jesus' flesh, there in the form of a man, hung upon the cross when his blood was shed as a sacrifice for the sins of the world. Similarly, since the Word has become flesh, the sacrament may be a commemoration of his whole ministry, especially the Incarnation.[67]

The next objection that Bonner singles out for refutation is built upon John 6:63: "It is the spirite whiche geveth lyfe, and that the flesh profiteth nothyng."[68] Partially from this passage and partially from Paul's description of the Eucharist as a spiritual food and spiritual drink,[69] many were convinced that they had discovered clear biblical proof that Jesus was not substantially present in the sacrament. Bonner opens his response by pointing out the various meanings that "spirit" and "spiritual" may carry in the Bible. He notes that often, a physical substance is also called spiritual in the scriptures: "for example, the bodye of man after the resurrection, shall (as S. Paule wytnesseth in the fifteenth chapter of hys fyrst Epystle to the Corinthians) be spiritual, and yet it shalbe then the same in substance, that it is nowe."[70] As he so often does, Bonner follows Paul's lead in linking the New Testament with the Old: "Agayne, Manna a meate which God sent to the children of Israel in the

---

65 1 Corinthians 11:25–26, as cited in Bonner, *Homelies*, fol. 64, *verso*.
66 Bonner, *Homelies*, fol. 64, *verso-recto*.
67 Bonner, *Homelies*, fol. 64, *verso*.
68 Bonner, *Homelies*, fol. 65, *recto*.
69 The passage in question is 1 Corinthians 10:4–5. These verses, along with John 6:63, were often quoted by Zwingli and his Strassbourgian and English disciples, including Ridley. See, e.g., Ridley, *Works*, pp. 15–16.
70 Bonner, *Homelies*, fols. 65, *recto*-66, *verso*, citing 1 Cor. 15:35–55.

wylderness, is both in Scripture, and of the catholyke churche also, called a spiritual meat, and, the water lykewyse which God gave them out of a rocke, is called a spiritual drynke, and yet as well Manna, as the water, were of a bodily substance."[71] Likewise, Bonner notes that "in the sixth [chapter] to the Galatians, sainct Paule calleth mortall men, living then on the earth, spiritual. Wherefore spirituall, is not so to be taken alwayes, as to exclude corporall, but that thynge whatsoever it be, may be called spirituall, wherein is a worke wrought by God, above nature."[72] Bonner's philological analysis of "spiritual," as it is encountered in scripture, leads him to other possible meanings of the term than "something that is not physical."

Bonner next turns his attention to arguments alleged from the Nicene-Constantinopolitan Creed against the real presence. Among other points, he rebukes: "objectyons upon three partyculer artycles of our crede whyche are, that Christ is ascended, and sytteth at the ryght hand of God the father, and from thense shall come to judge the quicke and the deade."[73] Once more, Bonner asserts that this argument is an attempt to set up human reason as a judge over the content of faith. These very same articles make several assertions about Christ's body that are just as far beyond human understanding as the notion that he is simultaneously in heaven and on earth in the sacrament, Bonner argues. He states that this portion of the creed, "ryghtly understanded shoulde rather confyrme us in the true catholyke belefe, of the presence of Christes body in the sacrament of the aultare" because, he says, "It is above nature for a manes bodye to ascende, and above the worthynes of manes nature, to syt at the ryghte hande of God the father, that is, to be of equal power,

71 Bonner, *Homelies*, fol. 66, *verso*.
72 Bonner, *Homelies*, fol. 66, *verso*. See Galatians 6:1a [Douay-Rheims], "Brethren, if a man be overtaken in any fault, you, who are spiritual, instruct such a one in the spirit of meekness."
73 Bonner, *Homelies*, fol. 68, *verso*. Again, this idea is frequently encountered in Ridley's writings. He rehearsed this very argument at his examination at Oxford, proclaiming that the doctrine of the real presence "varieth from the articles of the faith: 'He ascended into heaven, and sitteth on the right hand of God the Father, from whence,' (and not from any other place . . .), 'he shall come to judge the quick and the dead,'" Ridley, *Works*, p. 199.

and glorie with God the father, and fynallye, as it is above the authoritie of mans nature, to gyve sentence of eternall deathe, and lyfe, upon all mankynde."[74] Bonner is once more indicating that the overwhelming bulk of Christian doctrine transcends the narrow boundaries of our rational understanding. Of the Ascension and final judgment, in contrast to those who would restrict Christ's power to limits of human comprehension, Bonner says the faithful man, "stedfastlye beleveth al these supernatural powers in Christ, touching his manhed, bycause he is both God and man, and to God nothyng is impossible."[75] Likewise, he declares, "should we with like belefe, knowinge that Christ is omnipotent, credite all other thinges done, or spoken by Chryst, and be moost certen, that how that so ever they seme in appearaunce to our reason, yet in very dede they agree, and stand ryghte well with those foresayd three articles of the crede."[76]

Bonner also takes aim at various efforts to construe Jesus' statements "this is my body," and "this is my blood" as merely metaphorical speech. Against those who pointed out that Christ likened himself to a vine, a door, and other things, Bonner maintains that a demonstration that Jesus occasionally employed symbolic language is no proof that he relied exclusively upon metaphors throughout all his discourses.[77] The issue of Jesus' language in the institution narratives goes to the heart of the New Testament's relationship to the Old, for Bonner. He asserts, "yf in the sacrament of the aulter were not the true body of Christ, but a figure, and a signification onely of it, than the sacramants of the new testament should have nothing more, but rather lesse, then the sacraments of the old testament had, which is against the catholyke doctrine of the churche, and against al good reason."[78]

---

74 Bonner, *Homelies*, fol. 68, *verso*.
75 Bonner, *Homelies*, fol. 68, *verso*.
76 Bonner, *Homelies*, fol. 68, *verso-recto*.
77 Bonner, *Homelies*, fols. 72, *verso*-73, *recto*. Bonner's strategy here was essentially to turn a common Protestant theme on its head: where Ridley points out that Christ's speech was not always literal, Bonner asserts that this fact does not establish that every statement of Christ is therefore to be taken as necessarily figurative. Cf., e.g., Ridley, *Works*, p. 20–21.
78 Bonner, *Homelies*, fol. 72, *recto*.

Bonner also addresses a very specific variation on the "symbolic speech" argument concerning the institution narratives: "An other objection is . . . Christ . . . takyng the chalice . . . dyd . . . saye: 'This cup is the new testament, in my bloud.' And seyng these wordes must nedes, as they say, be taken fyguratively, inasmuch as the very material cup it selfe, was neyther the new testament, ne yet the bloud of Christ, therefore lykwyse, these wordes also whiche Christ, takyng bread into his handes, blessing it, saying, 'thys is my bodye,' must nedes be taken figurativelye."[79] For Bonner, this argument is no stronger than the objection that Christ also said, "I am the vine." In response, he reiterates that the observation that Jesus did indeed use metaphors does not prove that he used only metaphors, whensoever he spoke.[80]

Among Bonner's parting shots in the *Homelies* is a firm rejection of the idea that Christ's divinity and his humanity can be separated from one another. Bonner's argument is in complete harmony with the *Definition of Chalcedon* of A.D. 451, the Church's definitive dogmatic statement on the divine and human natures in the one person of Christ, and the relationship between them. The *Definition of Chalcedon* states that Christ's divine and human natures are joined in an essential (or hypostatic) union, and for that reason, Jesus' two natures cannot be contrasted with respect to location.[81] On the unity of Christ's natures, Bonner asserts, "the dyvinitie is, in unitie of person, inseparably united, and joyned to the sayd bodye and bloude, therefore we must saye and beleve, that the godhed of Chryste is in the sacrament of the aultar, with his humanitie."[82]

---

79 Bonner, *Homelies*, fol. 72, *recto*. This particular objection is not frequently encountered in the writings of the leading Edwardine Reformers, but it is, however, explicated in detail in Ridley's *A Brief Declaracion of the Lordes Supper* ([STC 21046] Emden: Egidius van der Erve, 1555) [hereafter: Ridley, *Brief Declaration*]. See, Ridley, *Works*, pp. 20–21.

80 Bonner, *Homelies*, fol. 72, *recto*.

81 Bonner, *Homelies*, fol. 74, *recto*. Cf. *The Chalcedonian Definition* in *Creeds of the Churches*, ed. John Leith, third edition (Louisville: John Knox Press, 1982) [hereafter: Leith, *Creeds*], pp. 34–36.

82 Bonner, *Homelies*, fol. 74, *recto*. The counter proposition, that Christ's body remains in heaven, while his divinity is encountered in the sacrament, is expressly stated by Ridley in his *Brief Declaracion*. See Ridley, *Works*, p. 13.

In such remarks we can see that Bonner holds the historical deliberations and dogmatic definitions of Church councils in high esteem.

Nevertheless, Bonner's typical response to what he views as heresy is to focus his attention on the scriptures. As his progress in this homily makes plain, he employs the Humanist tools of linguistic and textual analysis, comparing the use of particular terms and themes throughout the books of the canon. He also treats scripture as an historical record, pouring over the written accounts of Jesus' ministry to determine the sacramental and ecclesiological implications of Christ's words and deeds for his faithful followers. In all of these things, he is employing fundamentally the same exegetical method as Ridley, despite his arrival at a very different view of the Church than his archrival in the Diocese of London.

Covenant and Sacrament

Among other documents that reveal Bonner's fundamental conformity with the principles of Italian Humanist biblical exegesis and ecclesiology is his "treatyse of the seven Sacramentes."[83] Here, issues of Old and New Testament intertextuality, covenant, sacrament, and ecclesiology naturally coalesce. Bonner opens this section of his *Necessary and Profitable Doctrine* with a consideration of the general concept of a sacrament. Bonner's point of departure is a philological investigation of the term "sacrament" itself, as he notes that among profane Latin authors, it is "pryncipally called, an obligation or promysse made and confyrmed by an othe."[84] In scripture, the term appears to have two basic senses, generally to describe a mystery of the faith, and secondly and more specifically, to indicate a sign or token of something both hidden and holy. Hence, Paul speaks both of the "sacrament" of God's will being opened

---

83 *A profitable and necessarye doctryne with certayne homelies adioyned thervnto set forth by the reuerende father in God, Edmonde byshop of London, for the instruction and enformation of the people beynge within his diocesse of London, [and] of his cure and charge* ([STC 3281.5] London: John Cawood, 1555) [hereafter: Bonner, *Necessary and Profitable Doctrine*], sig. L.3, *recto*.

84 Bonner, *Necessary and Profitable Doctrine*, sig. L.4, *verso*.

to us through Christ in Ephesians 1:9, and also of Jesus himself as a sacrament of godliness "shewed in the fleshe," in 1 Timothy 3:16.[85] Bonner asserts: "Thys worde sacramente . . . signifieth the sygne of a holye thynge, whiche beareth the similitude or likenes of the thing, whose sygne it is. After which sort the signes and figures of the olde testamente are called sacramentes, and so the auncient Fathers, speakyng of the signes of the olde testament, do use commonly and frequentlye to name them." Bonner goes on to cite Augustine to substantiate his claim that the rites of the Old Testament were viewed by the Fathers as preadumbrations of the Christian sacraments: "Accordyng whereunto S. Augustyne in the 12th chapiter of his nineteenth boke agaynst Faustus doth saye: 'The fyrste Sacramentes whiche were observed and celebrated by the lawe, were prenunciative of Chryste to come.'"[86] By quoting Augustine on the subject of the old testament "sacraments," Bonner advances two of his major objectives at once, showing both that it is reasonable to couple the signs of the Old Covenant with those of the New, and that such a comparison is in no way a recent innovation, but a traditional feature of patristic scriptural commentary.

Bonner declares that "in thys treatice," a sacrament is to be understood as: "a visible signe of an invisble grace of God, which grace, God effectually and certaynly doth worke in it, so that the same be dulye handled, and not unworthelye receaved. Accordyng to which definition, there are seven sacraments of the churche. . . to wytte: Baptisme, Confyrmation, Penaunce, Eucharistie (or the sacramente of the aulter), Order, Matrimonye, and extreme unction."[87] Bonner fleshes out his definition of a sacrament with an analogy of the ring a lord gives to a vassal. Such a ring is simultaneously a token both of the vassal's fidelity to the lord, and the lord's pledge of a titular inheritance to the vassal, such that the giving of

---

85 Bonner, *Necessary and Profitable Doctrine*, sig. L.4, *verso-recto*. The Vulgate's rendering of this verse indicates that the mystery of God's will involves the whole of Christ's redemptive work: "*Et manifeste magnum est pietas sacramentum quod manifestum est in carne iustificationem est in spiritu apparuit angelis praedicatum est gentibus creditum est in mundo adsumptum est in gloria.*"

86 Bonner, *Necessary and Profitable Doctrine*, sig. L.4, *recto*.

87 Bonner, *Necessary and Profitable Doctrine*, sigs. L.4, *recto*-M.1, *verso*.

the ring seals or ratifies "a certayne covenant" between Lord and vassal. The vassal who receives a ring of fidelity from his lord may rightly say that he has not a ring only, but a title of inheritance. Bonner's ring analogy, like Peryn's *Thre godly sermons*, recalls the Eucharistic controversy between Thomas More and John Frith in the 1530s.[88] More, defending the doctrine of the real presence, likened the Eucharist to a bridal ring, saying that only a mean-spirited soul would try to persuade the betrothed maid that the ring was nothing more than the base metal or stones in it, rather than a pledge of love and fidelity from her groom. Frith countered that, to his mind, the doctrine of the real presence was akin to someone informing the bride that the groom was the ring.[89] While we do not know if Bonner was consciously following More here, we do know that he believed that Jesus chose and ordained signs that invest us of his grace, to unite believers to him in "a spirituall bonde or covenaunt."[90]

For Bonner, Christ is the consummation of the word or law of God in the old covenant. He asserts that the Incarnation itself was something of a sacrament: "Whereas in olde tymes God by manye meanes and by sondry wayes did speake in his prophetes, and gave counsayle, as by worde, by the lawe, by signes and wonders, he hath nowe last of all spoken in or by his onely sonne our Lord, whom his wyll was to take our flesh on him and be crucified for us." Therefore, it is only fitting "that we casting our eyes and considerations upon hym, beynge made like unto us visible and palpable, and as a most myghty signe, sent and given of God, and hearynge him speake, myght begyn in him to knowe God, beleve and put our hole confydence in God, and fynally to love God above all thinges ells."[91]

88 On Peryn's references to Fryth, see Chapter I above, p. 9, note 26.
89 See John Frith, *A Treatise Agaynst the Boke M. More Made*, in William Tyndale, *The whole workes of W. Tyndall, Iohn Frith, and Doct. Barnes, three worthy martyrs, and principall teachers of this Churche of England: collected and compiled in one tome togither, beyng before scattered, [and] now in print here exhibited to the Church. To the prayse of God, and profite of all good Christian readers* ([STC 24436] London: John Daye, 1573), pp. 120–21.
90 Bonner, *Necessary and Profitable Doctrine*, sig. M.1, *verso-recto*.
91 Bonner, *Necessary and Profitable Doctrine*, sig. M.1, *recto*.

This rather Pauline recapitulation of salvation history, with its Old and New Covenant intertextuality, stands at the heart of Bonner's view of the Church and scripture. What connects the New Testament with the Old is Christ's submission to the Old Covenant, fulfilling it in an act of obedience, even to the point of death. In Bonner's view, the Crucifixion is not the categorical abrogation of the Law, but its consummation. Bonner suggests that the difference between the Old Covenant and the Gospel is qualitative, and that the New Covenant is not something of a wholly different order or species than the signs that came before in the Old: "The sacramentes . . . of the newe testamente, are . . . instituted, that they might be certayne and efectuall sygnes to oure outwarde sence, of the wyll and grace of God. . . . They are . . . remedies agaynst synne, and do fare passe those of the old law. For they were the shadows of thynges to come, and as signes and fygures were abolyshed, (Christ after hys commynge havinge fulfilled them): and they were therefore abolyshed, because they were fulfilled."[92] As Christ's crucifixion was the consummation of the law, so he also established certain sacramental signs to assure us that we are incorporated into and saved by his passion and resurrection.[93] Throughout this ecclesiological tract, Bonner makes explicit the connections between particular rituals of the Old Covenant, and the sacramental rites of the Gospel.

Thus, in his consideration of baptism, Bonner emphatically employs the patristic and scriptural convention of comparing it with circumcision. Here, as elsewhere, Bonner's ecclesiology is firmly covenantal because it rests upon an Italian Humanist method of exegesis. He raises the subject of circumcision in connection with recent controversies about infant baptism: "As the infancye of the chyldren of the Hebrews, in the olde testamente, dyd not let, but that they were made participante of the grace and benefytte geven in Circumcision, even so in the newe Testamente, the infancye of chyldren doth not let, but that they maye and ought to be baptysed and so receyve the graces and vertues of the same."[94] Bonner

---

92 Bonner, *Necessary and Profitable Doctrine*, sig. M.3, *verso*.
93 Bonner, *Necessary and Profitable Doctrine*, sig. M.2, *verso*.
94 Bonner, *Necessary and Profitable Doctrine*, sig. N.3, *recto*. This very theme occupies a great deal of attention in Colet's *Exposition of Romans*,

clearly states that circumcision was a ritual entry into the covenant that conferred grace upon the Hebrews.

Bonner marshals several passages from the writings of the Greek and Latin Fathers to make the case that the practice of baptizing infants, and also of the ritual exorcisms associated with the rite, were traditional features of the early church.[95] In addition to his use of Ambrose, Pseudo-Dionysius, Cyprian and Chrysostom, Bonner appeals to Augustine to make his case: "S. Augustine in his second boke, *De gratia Christi* and in his xl. chapiter doth saye thus: 'The very Sacramentes of the holye churche whiche she by so olde or auncient tradicion, together with other doth celebrate, sufficiently do declare, yonge chyldren even most newly or freshly cummen from byrthe, to be by the grace of Chryste, delivered from the servyce of the devyll.'" Bonner's citation from Augustine continues: "'For besydes that they be baptised, not with the deceateful, but with the true misterye, there is also fyrst in them exercysed, and exsufflate the contrarye power (meanynge thereby the Devyll) whiche contrary power, the childre (by the words of them that did heare them) make aunswere that they do renounce it.'"[96] Such passages from the writings of the Fathers totally discredit the claims of some who "of late, . . . have untruly preached, and reported, that the maner of baptysing or christening, nowe used in the Church, is not the same which was used in the primative Church."[97]

In response to the question of why children of baptized parents should likewise need to be cleansed of original sin, Bonner employs an agricultural analogy: just as grain can be completely purged of chaff, as soon as it is planted, it immediately brings forth chaff again.[98] Despite such digressions,

where he is even led to declare that Abraham had both the "token and reality" of justification in circumcision, since "he received the sacrament of faith, even fleshly circumcision." Colet, *Exposition of Romans*, p. 118.

95 Bonner, *Necessary and Profitable Doctrine*, sigs. N.1, *verso*-N.2, *verso*.
96 Bonner, *Necessary and Profitable Doctrine*, sigs. N.1, *recto*-N.2, *verso*. For the original text, see P. L., ed. Jacques-Paul Migne, vol. xliv, col. 408. Cf. *Nicene and Post-Nicene Fathers*, ser. I, vol. v, ed. Phillip Schaff (Grand Rapids: William B. Eerdmans, 1894), p. 232.
97 Bonner, *Necessary and Profitable Doctrine*, sig. N.1, *verso*.
98 Bonner, *Necessary and Profitable Doctrine*, sigs. N.2, *recto*-N.3, *verso*.

Bonner retains his emphasis on the covenantal nature of the rite: "Ye shall note concernyng thys sacrament of Baptisme, that it may well be called, a covenaunt between God and us, whereby God testifieth, that he for his sonne Christes sake, justifieth us, that is to say, forgyveth us our synnes. . . . And we agayne upon oure parte, oughte most diligently to remember and kepe the promysse, that we in baptysme have made to almyghtye God, that is, to beleve only in him, onely to serve hym, and obey him."[99]

Bonner's reflections on the sacrament of confirmation are likewise focused on parallels between the Old Covenant and the New. He begins this portion of the *Necessary and Profitable Doctrine* with a scriptural reflection that is a reminiscence of 1 Corinthians 10: "In the olde testamente, almyghtye God was beneficiall and good to the chyldren of Israel, whom he caused safely to passe the redde sea, drowning theyr enemies . . . as . . . in spreadyinge abroade over them the cloude in the daye, for theyr protection, as gevynge them fyre, to lyght them in the nyght . . . besydes the feadynge of them with celestiall fode, and refreshsshyng of them with water that yssued oute of the harde rocke." Similarly in the New Testament, "Our blessed Saviour Jesus Christ, havynge fulfylled the fygures and shadowes of the olde lawe, doth after baptysme, geve unto his Israelites, the Christian people, dyvers gyftes of the holy Ghost, and manyfolde graces, whereby he doth holde up, and confyrme or make stronge his sayd people."[100] Bonner says that the outward sign of this sacrament is the laying on of hands after baptism, an act described several times in the New Testament.[101]

Bonner notes that Jesus himself imparted the graces of the Holy Spirit to the disciples in stages, by breathing on them, and by telling

---

99 Bonner, *Necessary and Profitable Doctrine*, sig. N.4, recto.
100 Bonner, *Necessary and Profitable Doctrine*, sig. O.1, *recto*. Cf. 1 Corinthians 10:1–4 [RSV], "I want you to know brethren, that our Fathers were all under the cloud, and all passed through the sea, and all were baptized into Moses in the cloud and the sea, and all ate the same spiritual food and all drank the same supernatural drink. For they drank from the supernatural Rock which followed them, and the Rock was Christ."
101 Among other passages, Bonner points to the laying on of hands by Peter and John among the Samaritans, as recounted in Acts 8, and of Paul's doing likewise among the Ephesians in Acts 19. See *Necessary and Profitable Doctrine*, sig. O.2, *verso-recto*.

them to wait in Jerusalem for the Pentecost.[102] As proof that the completed gifts of the Holy Ghost bring a steadfast confirmation of faith, Bonner points to the example of Peter, who, although he must have been baptized already, yet denied Jesus before Pentecost, and yet was stout in the proclamation of the Gospel thereafter.[103] Characteristically, Bonner links the rite of confirmation to the Old Covenant. He compares chrysmation with the Passover blood ritual: "Inward shamefastness . . . is taken awaye by confyrmation, where in the forehead is made the sygne of the crosse. . . . As the distroyenge aungell, dyd forbeare and passe by those houses in Egypte, whose dore postes, and lyntell, he dydde see to be enoynted with the bloude of the lambe, so the wicked spryte beholdyng the person baptised, and confyrmed with the tryumphante sygne of the crosse is, discouraged to make anye hote assaulte agaynst hym."[104] As for the use of anointing oil, the testimony of Fabian, Tertullian, Cyprian, Jerome, and Augustine, among others, is sufficient to persuade Bonner that its use was both an ancient and universal practice in the early Church.[105]

Despite his love for and regular citations from the Fathers, Bonner is careful to ground his remarks in the New Testament scriptures. Noting that in ancient times, the rite was simply called the Imposition of Hands, Bonner asserts that Jesus himself instituted the sacrament of confirmation.[106] The most notable example of Jesus' imposition of hands in connection with this rite, according to Bonner, occurs in the tenth chapter of Mark, where Jesus tells the disciples to suffer the little children to come unto him.[107] In verse 16, we are told that Jesus: "Embrac[ed] them, and laying his hands upon them, he blessed them."[108]

---

102 Bonner, *Necessary and Profitable Doctrine*, sig. O.3, *verso-recto*. See Luke 24 and Acts 1. See also Wizeman, *Mary Tudor's Church*, pp. 118–23.

103 Bonner, *Necessary and Profitable Doctrine*, sigs. O.3, *recto*-O.4, *verso*. Cf. the opening chapters of Acts.

104 Bonner, *Necessary and Profitable Doctrine*, sig. P.2, *recto*.

105 Bonner, *Necessary and Profitable Doctrine*, sigs. O.4, *recto*-P.1, *verso*.

106 Bonner, *Necessary and Profitable Doctrine*, sig. P.2, *verso*.

107 Bonner, *Necessary and Profitable Doctrine*, sig. P.2, *verso*.

108 This is the Douay-Rheims rendering. Cf. the Vulgate: "*Et complexans eos et inponens manus super illios benedicebet eos.*"

In this context, Bonner might be expected to allege the "unwritten verities" delivered by Christ to the Apostles. However, Bonner makes no direct appeal to the closing verses of John 20 or 21, which state that Jesus said and did much more than the slender books of the New Testament could adequately record.[109] Bonner raises this point only indirectly, generally through one of his sources. Instead, he maintains that widespread witness from the Fathers, coupled with a lack of early controversy on the subject, is sufficient ground to postulate Christ's institution of any such rite. His observations on the textual evidence for the sacramental anointing of *confirmandi* are representative of this aspect of his thought. After rehearsing several patristic passages on the subject, he declares: "Agreynge with the auncient and holye Fathers of the churche, ye maye undoubtedly see and perceave, that this sacrament of confirmation, or imposition of the Byshoppes handes, is receaved, approved, and speciallye commended of all Catholique men, and at all tymes." Bonner continues: "Seinge then that this Sacrament of Confirmation . . . is so greatly to be estemed and regarded, not onely for the aucthorite of Christe, that did institute it, and the aucthoritie of the churche and of the Apostles that dydde receave and use it, but also for the commoditie and profyt whiche the sayd Sacrament doth brynge with it. Therefore they do verye wyckedlye, that in any wyse do contempne it."[110] Bonner moves freely from his patristic sources to the assertion that Jesus instituted this sacrament. He simply trusts that the early Fathers would not have practiced chrysmation and confirmation without a clear and substantial precedent from the Apostles, who in turn would not have so proceeded without sufficient instruction from Christ. Bonner's historical thinking appears to be the product of his probative legal training: positive biblical precedents are not essential where there is a lack of contravening evidence. To Bonner's mind, the absence of any biblical prohibition and a lack of controversy among the Fathers on the

---

109 John 20:30–31, Douay-Rheims: "Many other signs also did Jesus in the sight of his disciples, which are not written in this book. But these are written, that you may believe that Jesus is the Christ, the Son of God: and that believing, you may have life in his name."
110 Bonner, *Necessary and Profitable Doctrine*, sigs. P.1, *recto*-P.2, *verso*.

subject of anointing and confirmation indicate that the practice was universally received from Christ and the Apostles.

The Word Written and Verities Unwritten

Bonner's "lack of contravening evidence" principle enables him, by indirect means, to raise the question of an unwritten deposit of faith transmitted to the Apostles by Jesus. This principle is therefore part of Bonner's implicit challenge to the Protestant doctrine of *sola scriptura*, by pointing out that many key points of New Testament history or ecclesial doctrine are implied, but not directly stated, in the Gospels. Bonner employs this technique in his discussion of Peter's strident proclamation of the Gospel following Pentecost. In this section of the *Necessary and Profitable Doctrine*, immediately following Bonner's discussion of Peter's transformed character, Bonner proceeds with a definition of confirmation as a sacramental anointing and laying of hands on a baptized person.[111] Although Bonner says Peter was "washed and pronounced also to be pure and clene,"[112] Bonner is unable to cite biblical evidence for Peter's baptism. In fact, there is no direct scriptural proof that any of the Apostles was baptized. Furthermore, the New Testament canon does not contain a single narrative of Jesus himself baptizing anyone, and John 4:2 explicitly states: "Jesus himself did not baptize, but his disciples."[113]

While there is a lack of direct evidence concerning Peter's baptism, there is also no biblical indication that he was not baptized. In fact, there is ample warrant for Bonner to assume that Peter had received this ritual cleansing. Paul assumes the universality of baptism among the Christians to whom he writes, and Jesus not only permitted himself to be baptized by John, but also bade his Apostles: "Teach ye all nations; baptizing them in the name of the Father, and of the Son, and of the Holy Ghost. Teaching them to observe all that I have commanded you: and behold I am with you all days, even to the consummation of

---

111 Bonner, *Necessary and Profitable Doctrine*, sigs. O.3, *recto*-O.4, *recto*.
112 Bonner, *Necessary and Profitable Doctrine*, sig. O.4, *verso*.
113 This is the Douay-Rheims rendering of the verse.

the world."[114] Similarly, there is no account of the Apostles baptizing any person during Jesus' lifetime, but following Pentecost they baptize both individuals and groups, as recorded throughout Acts. It is unlikely then that Peter and the Apostles were required to administer a rite that had not been first ministered unto them, especially when such an act had confirmed Jesus' own mission.[115] Bonner rehearses the great commission and Peter's ritual immersion of Cornelius in the preceding section on the sacrament of Baptism,[116] so the reader has these portions of scripture in mind while considering Bonner's remarks on confirmation. The total effect of Bonner's selection and arrangement of biblical themes is to suggest that Jesus and the Apostles said and did more than the record of scripture expressly indicates. Bonner directs his readers' attention not just to the bare record of Jesus' words, but also towards a consideration Jesus' actual deeds, and those of the Apostles, that do not appear to have been recorded in scripture.

By touching on the subject of Peter's baptism in his presentation of Confirmation, Bonner is also advancing an *inter alia* assault on Protestant ecclesiology. English Protestants sought to retain baptism as a sacrament, alleging that both it and the Lord's Supper were personally instituted by Christ.[117] However, since all four Evangelists agree that John was baptizing the people of Judea prior to Jesus' ministry, and we have no record of Jesus baptizing anyone at all, the case for Jesus' having established the rite seems no stronger than claims that he established confirmation. Bonner thereby raises subtle questions here against all forms of *sola scriptura*; in other portions of the *Necessary and Profitable Doctrine*, such questions are made more explicit.

Bonner addresses the question of Jesus' training of the Apostles once more in his reflections on the sacrament of extreme unction. He notes: "We do rede in Mark 6 howe Chryst callynge unto hym his twelve Apostles, and sendyng them fourth bye two and two, dyd prescrybe unto them

---

114 Douay-Rheims, Matthew 28:19–20.
115 On Jesus' baptism, see, e.g., Matthew 3:13–17, and Mark, 1:9–11.
116 Bonner, *Necessary and Profitable Doctrine*, sig. M.4, *verso-recto*.
117 See, e.g. *The Forty-Two Articles* in *Documents of the English Reformation*, ed. Gerald Bray (Minneapolis: Fortress Press, 1994), esp. pp. 298–302.

a certaine forme of embassade, or message and dyd also gyve unto them a certayne power which they should occupye and use. And we do rede also there, that the Apostles so going forth . . . dyd cast fourth devyles, and also that they dyd anoynte with oyle many that were sicke, who therby were healed and cured."[118] Once more, Bonner is steadily directing the reader's attention to passages of scripture that implicitly suggest more information than they directly announce. As with baptism, we have no record of Jesus training the Apostles in the anointing of the sick, neither in the actions to be performed, nor the proper form of words to be used. Nevertheless, Jesus summons the Apostles with great purpose, enjoining a strict code of behavior upon them: "And he commanded them that they should take nothing for the way, but a staff only; no scrip, no bread, nor money in their purse, but to be shod with sandals, and that they should not put on two coats. . . . And going forth, they preached that men should do penance: And they cast out many devils, and anointed with oil many that were sick, and healed them."[119] Given such intentionality, it is highly unlikely then that Jesus sent the Apostles out, bereft of procedural details for anointing the sick, casting out demons, and the preaching of repentance, although the biblical text omits any mention of these instructions. In fact, while the closing verses declare that the Apostles healed many in body and soul, Jesus does not explicitly tell them in his charge to even carry oil, much less to actually anoint or exorcise anyone. Rather, the text records him saying only: "Wheresoever you shall enter into an house, there abide you till you depart from that place. And whosoever shall not receive you, nor hear you: going forth from thence, shake off the dust from your feet as a testimony to them."[120]

The Apostles then either transgressed the proper limits of their authority, which is unlikely since they were not subsequently rebuked by Jesus,[121] or they proceeded to execute several commands of Jesus not

118 Bonner, *Necessary and Profitable Doctrine*, sigs. DD.4, *recto*-EE.1, *verso*. See Mark 6:7–13.
119 Douay-Rheims, Mark 6:8–9, 12–13.
120 Douay-Rheims, Mark 6:10–11.
121 More than the other Synoptics and John, the Gospel of Mark is characterized by Jesus' relentless upbraiding of the disciples for not believing and heeding him. His failure to do so here, even though he is not even reported

revealed by the text itself. Through such citations, Bonner calls attention to the fact that certain portions of scripture only tangentially touch upon many of Jesus' words and deeds. He thereby indirectly challenges the plausibility of scripture as a full record of the words and deeds of Christ.

By linking the issue of sacramental anointing to the priestly ministry of the Apostles, Bonner strengthens his peripheral assaults on the idea that scripture is a complete historical record of Jesus' words and deeds. Bonner introduces this next topic by again appealing to patristic sources: "Takynge for a testimonye of the fundation and ground thereof, the sayd sixth chapter of Saynt Marke, so by the auncient Fathers of the churche most lernedly and godly expounded and interpretated, whereunto is adjoyned the testimonye of St. James in the last chapter of his canonical epistle."[122] After citing passages from key Church Fathers, including Chrysostom, Theophylact, Oecumenius, and Jerome, Bonner, as he so often does, allows Augustine the *coup de grâce*:

> "Saynt Augustyne . . . wryting to his Nephewe . . . giveth him this counsaile saieng, 'That commaundement of Saynt James the Apostle is not to be omytted or overpassed of the. "Is any man sicke emongest you? Let hym bring in the preystes of the churche that they may praye over hym, annointing him with the holy oyle in the name of our Lorde Jesus." Therefore desire thou, that of the, and for the, so it may be done, as Saynt James the Apostle, yea rather, our Lorde by his Apostle did say, for surely the anointing with the consecrate oyle is understand to be a typicall anointing of the holye Ghost.'"[123]

to have told them to carry oil, augurs even more strongly that they exorcised and anointed the people according to some prior instruction.

122 Bonner, *Necessary and Profitable Doctrine*, sig. EE.1, *verso*.

123 Bonner, *Necessary and Profitable Doctrine*, sig. EE.2, *recto*. This passage is from *De Visitationem Infirmorum*. See Migne, P.L vol. xl, col. 1154. Modern catalogues of Augustine's writings do not include this selection, and its listing in Migne suggests that the authorship of *De Visitationem Infirmorum* is uncertain. Nevertheless, unlike Ridley's use of Pseudo-Chrysostom's *Opus Imperfectum in Matthaeum*, there is no indication here or

The priestly aspects of James' description of anointing is enhanced in Bonner's well-chosen selection, since the oil used is here described as "consecrate," and its efficacy is ascribed to the work of Holy Ghost.

As with baptism, we have no direct evidence of Jesus laying hands on the Apostles expressly to ordain them as priests, and yet in the Epistle of James, in Acts, and in the writings of Paul, the Apostles clearly hold an authoritative ministry that is self-evidently clerical in its functions, ritual actions, and proclamation. Pentecost is not the sole origin of such an ordination because Mary and the other disciples assembled in the upper room appear to have no such authority following the advent of the Holy Spirit. Bonner himself, following patristic precedents, locates the ordination of the Apostles in Jesus' breathing on them, bidding them to receive the Holy Ghost, as recounted in John 20:19–23.[124] Jesus does indeed enjoin a special ministry on the Apostles in these verses, telling them "Whose sins you shall forgive, they are forgiven them; and whose sins you shall retain, they are retained," but he does not explicitly call them priests, neither here nor anywhere else in the New Testament. Again, the passage suggests, especially in the light of the preaching and rituals performed by the Apostles in Acts, that more transpired between them and Jesus on this subject than the text discloses.

Ordinarily then, Bonner merely hints that scripture is not a complete ecclesiological guide in the *Necessary and Profitable Doctrine*. In at least one instance, however, he addresses the question directly, while writing on the fourth commandment, "Remember that thou keep holy the Sabbath day."[125] Bonner's topic in this portion of the *Necessary and Profitable Doctrine* is the Church's ancient tradition of observing special holy feast days. As is his custom, Bonner permits Augustine to make the central point for him, that the Church retains apostolic customs that were not written down:

> S. Augustyne in his one hundred and eighteenth epystle, wrytten to Januarius sayth thus: "Concerninge those things

elsewhere that Bonner was aware that *De Visitationem Infirmorum* is not an authentic work of Augustine. See Chapter II above.

124 Bonner, *Necessary and Profitable Doctrine*, sig. AA.1, *verso*.

125 Bonner, *Necessary and Profitable Doctrine*, sigs. MM.4-OO.4.

whiche we doo kepe, not beynge wrytten, but by tradition lefte unto us, beynge suche whiche in dede are kepte throughoute the whole worlde, it is to be understanded, the same eyther of the apostles themselves, or of general counsails, (whose authority in the church is most holesome) commended and establyshed or decreed to be reteyned or kepte, as that the passion of oure Lorde and resurrection, and ascension into heaven, and the commyng of the holye goost from heaven, are with anniversarye, or yearlye solempnitie, celebrated."[126]

As usual, Bonner's selection from Augustine is expertly chosen to advance several concerns at once. With this patristic text, he is simultaneously able to show that the early Church observed special feast days while raising sharp doubts concerning the Fathers' subscription to the idea that *scriptura* should govern ecclesiology.

In the *Homelies*, the subject of "unwritten verities" is again addressed explicitly and at length, but not by Bonner himself, and not through an appeal to the celebrated closing verses of John 20 and 21. Rather, the matter is taken up by Henry Pendleton, one of Bonner's chaplains, in his work, *On the authority of the church*. Although the issue is analyzed more thoroughly than Bonner does himself, it may certainly be taken as congruent with his own thought.[127] Indeed, Pendleton's homily fleshes out Bonner's notion that the Fathers of the early Church did not hold with the view that scripture was a complete guide to ecclesiology.

At the start of his address, Pendleton indicates that scriptural inspiration and ecclesiology are mutually interdependent, since the Holy Ghost is the author of scripture and abides still in the Church.[128]

---

126 Bonner, *Necessary and Profitable Doctrine*, sig. OO.1, *verso*. This passage from Augustine's correspondence can be found in P. L., ed. Jacques-Paul Migne, vol. XXXIII, col. 200. See also "Letter LIV," in Phillip Schaff, gen. ed. *Nicene and Post-Nicene Fathers*, ser. I, vol. i (Grand Rapids: William B. Eerdmans, 1894), p. 301.
127 See both the colophon and preface of Bonner, *Homelies*.
128 Pendleton, in Bonner, *Homelies*, fols. 37, *recto*-38, *verso*.

Likewise, Jesus has pledged to remain with the Church, declaring: "Behold, I am with you, even to the ende of the worlde."[129] It is for these reasons, Pendleton argues, that the Fathers submitted their writings and opinions to the judgment of the Church.[130] He proceeds to show the mind of the Fathers on the question of authority and scripture. His first citations are from the second-century Church apologist, Irenaeus of Lyons (c. 130–200 A.D.): "The godly lerned . . . father Irenaeus, wrytyng agaynst schismaticall heresyes, sayeth thus: 'but what and yf there were contention concerning some smal question, were it not necessarye to returne to the mooste auncient churches? . . . What (sayeth thys holye father) yf the Apostles had lefte to us no scripture at all, had it not bene necessarye to folowe the order of tradytion, whyche they delyvered to those, to whome thye dyd bequethe the churche?'"[131] Pendleton's

---

129 Pendleton, citing Matthew 28:20, in Bonner, *Homelies*, fol. 38, *verso*. The marginal note erroneously assigns the passage to the eighteenth chapter of Matthew.

130 Pendleton, in Bonner, *Homelies*, fol. 38, *recto*.

131 Pendleton, citing Irenaeus in Bonner, *Homelies*, fol. 38, *recto*. This passage from Irenaeus' *Adversus Haeresis* can be found in P. G., ed. Jacques-Paul Migne, vol. VIIa, cols. 855 and 856. See also Susan Wabuda's illuminating treatment of the English flap over "unwritten verities" that opened in the wake of Erasmus' *Novum Instrumentum* and *Novum Testamentum*, in *Preaching*, pp. 72–80. As she indicates, William Hubberdine's assertion in 1533 that it was not necessary for the scriptures to have been written at all may have been "shocking" by sixteenth-century standards, especially among reform-minded authorities such as Thomas Cromwell, but as Pendleton's citation of Irenaeus' text makes plain, the same concept was being contemplated in the late second century. Cf. the assertion of Tertullian (circa A.D. 211) who defends Christians crossing themselves in prayer and observing special liturgical practices on the basis of unwritten tradition: "If you demand a scriptural injunction as the basis for these and other similar practices, you will not find any. The arguments for them will be tradition, usage, and faith." See Wiles and Santer, *Documents in Early Christian Thought* (Cambridge: Cambridge University Press, 1988) pp. 135–36. Tertullian's original text, *De corona militis*, can be found in P. L., ed. Jacques-Paul Migne, vol. II, cols. 73ff. The appeal to an unwritten Apostolic Tradition was certainly not an invention of sixteenth-century Catholic apologists, Marshall's description of their efforts in this regard

strongest challenge to the idea that the Fathers believed that scripture was to govern ecclesiology is an excerpt from Augustine: "Truly, I would not beleve the Gospel, onles that the aucthoritye of the catholyke churche did move me thereto."[132]

Pendleton's homily demonstrates that Bonner's historical focus in biblical exegesis and sacramental theology was not an idiosyncratic view among Marian Catholics. In fact, Pendleton's consideration of the Church's authority is specifically intended to point out the historical improbabilities associated with the Protestant concept of *sola scriptura*, in any of its forms.

as "*post hoc* rationalism" notwithstanding. See Marshall, *Henry VIII's England*, p. 85.

132 Pendleton, citing Augustine, in Bonner, *Homelies*, fol. 39, *recto*. The passage can be found in P. L., ed. Jaques-Paul Migne, vol. XLII, col. 176. See also "Against the Epistle of Manichæus called Fundamental," in *Writings Against the Manichaeans and Against the Donatists*, in *Nicene and Post-Nicene Fathers*, ser. I, vol. iv, ed. Phillip Schaff (Grand Rapids: William B. Eerdmans, 1894), p. 131. Augustine had good cause to be wary concerning the authority of spurious scriptures, since the Manichees, whose teaching he embraced in his youth, read and proclaimed the works of Manichæus. The chief extant work of this enigmatic religious leader is a most curious re-casting of some portions of the Gospel narratives, thoroughly mixed with Manichæus' own visions of shrieking vegetables and angels of light. See *The Cologne Mani Codex: Concerning the Origin of His Body*, trans. and eds. Ron Cameron and Arthur J. Dewey (Missoula, Montana: Scholar's Press, 1979). Despite Euan Cameron's assertion that the context undermines traditional appeals to this passage, it must be noted that Augustine does not refer to "unbelievers" and their abuse of scripture in this remark, but to his own convictions. See *The European Reformation*, p. 137. Arrayed with other citations from Irenaeus and Cyprian, as it is in Pendleton's sermon, the passage clearly indicates that the Church Fathers did not hold to a view of scripture alone as the only source of authority left to the Church by the Apostles. Augustine, who finally succeeded in his efforts to have a synod determine the definitive form of the New Testament canon at Carthage in 393 A.D., was certainly an unlikely candidate to advocate for the authority of scripture over the *magisterium* of the Church. A collection of excerpts from Origen, Tertullian, Dionysius of Alexandria, Theodore of Mopsuesta, and Augustine, that plainly reveal that the Fathers did not subscribe to *sola scriptura*, are assembled in Wiles and Santer, *Documents in Early Christian Thought*, pp. 127–58.

Pendleton indicates that Jesus entrusted the Apostles with an authoritative commission, which was in turn transmitted to their successors.[133]

Among other things that Pendleton posits to be within the purview of the Apostles and their successors, is the proper interpretation of scripture and the power to declare what is and what is not scripture.[134] Pendleton substantiates this point by indicating that several "gospels" ascribed to Jesus' disciples were rejected by the Church in the course of establishing the New Testament canon: "We ought here to consider, that after the ascension of our saviour Christe, for the space of certayne yeares, there was no gospell at all wrytten; but all thinges, concernyng the faythfull christians, were ruled, and governed by the disciples of Christ, being than the heades of the church." Furthermore: "We rede that dyvers of the dysciples of Chryste, dyd wryght Gospelles: as sainct Bartylmew, Nicodemus, and an other Gospel was called *Evangelium Nazareorum*, But the aucthoritie of the church, did onely admit those fower evangelistes, which now the whole churche dooth retayne."[135] By pointing out that the Gospels were not written page by page just as the historical action was unfolding, Pendleton all but declares *sola scriptura* to be an unmitigated anachronism.[136] Without an authoritative canon or any written Gospels whatsoever, the possibility that the early Church held to the principle that scripture should govern ecclesiology, seems rather remote. Pendleton's point here is also an ecclesiological

---

133 Pendleton, in Bonner, *Homelies*, fol. 37, *verso-recto*. Pendleton locates the Apostles' commission and authority in Matthew 10:40 [Douay-Rheims]: "He that receiveth you, receiveth me: and he that receiveth me, receiveth him that sent me." John 15:15, "I will not now call you servants: for the servant knoweth not what his lord doth. But I have called you friends: because all things whatsoever I have heard of the Father, I have made known to you," and John 20:21b, "As the Father hath sent me, I also send you."

134 Pendleton, in Bonner, *Homelies*, fol. 37, *recto*.

135 Pendleton, in Bonner, *Homelies*, sig. 39, *recto*.

136 Many of Pendleton's arguments here recall points made by John Standish in *A discourse wherin is debated whether it be expedient that the scripture should be in English for al men to reade that wyll* ([STC 23207] London: Robert Caly, 1554). In this treatise, Standish reminds his readers that: "Christ never bad goe write his gospell or holye worde, but badde preache it," sig. E.7, *recto*.

challenge to Protestant characterizations of the Catholic Church as the debauched "whore of Babylon," since this allegedly malevolent Church has, over time as he points out, brought forth the perfect and infallible canon of scripture.

Pendleton's attention to the anachronism inherent in the view that Jesus and the early Church subscribed to the principle that scripture alone was sufficient to establish the proper limits of ecclesiology, raises several key issues regarding the biblical text as a copious historical record of Jesus' earthly ministry. If it is acknowledged that a substantial portion of time elapsed between the Ascension and the writing of the Gospels, then not only is the Protestant principle of *sola scriptura* challenged, but so likewise is its Erasmian forerunner, the claim that the biblical text is a more true encounter with "the holy mind" of Jesus than a direct vision of him, such that "you would see less if you gazed upon Him with your very eyes."[137] As Pendleton suggests, the scriptures we do possess greatly limit the extent to which they can alone be considered a direct and full communion with Jesus, since they were written down a century or more after the original events transpired. Those events were chronicled by people two, three, or four generations removed from the historical facts, and preserved in a language other than Jesus' first tongue. Pendleton's sermon is certainly far removed from Erasmus or Ridley's near exclusive concern with Jesus' speech in the Gospels.

The Deeds of Christ

One of the characteristic interpretive emphases of Bonner that drives his work in a different direction than that of Erasmus and Ridley, despite his reliance on historical and philological techniques that recall their basic exegetical method, is his focus on Jesus' actions in the narratives of the New Testament.[138] This focus on the deeds of Christ surfaces

---

137 See Erasmus, "Paraclesis," in *Christian Humanism and the Reformation*, ed. John C. Olin (New York: Fordham University Press, 1975) [hereafter: Erasmus, *Paraclesis*], pp. 92–106. See also Chapter II above.

138 See, for example, his discussion of Jesus breathing on the Apostles in Luke 24 and Acts 1 as Bonner explicates the sacrament of Ordination, in

repeatedly in Bonner's writings, even when his main topic is not the institution of the Eucharist or any of the other sacraments. Bonner announces the need for us to consider not merely the words of Christ, but also his life and actions, "the lyvynge of oure savioure Chryste," as the Bishop says in the *homely of Christian love, or Charitie.*[139] Far from being an isolated or incidental point in the text, the concept of Jesus' living example is the organizing theme of Bonner's sermon on this subject. Bonner actually declares this aim explicitly in the opening section of his homily: "You shall heare now a true and playne descryption of charitie, not of men's imagination, but of the very woordes and example of oure savyoure Jesus Christe."[140]

Bonner asserts that true charity consists in the love of all men, both friend and foe: "for so Christ him selfe taught, and so also he performed in dede."[141] The living of example of Christ's charity was plainly evident throughout his ministry: "Thus . . . he dyd use hym selfe, exhortynge hys adversaryes, rebukynge the faultes of hys adversaryes, and when he coulde not amende them, yet he prayed for theym."[142] Christ maintained this high standard even in his Passion. Towards his final persecutors, Jesus "dyd good towarde theym. . . . When thy gave hym evyll woordes, he gave non evyll againe, when they dyd stryke hym, he did not smite againe."[143] Bonner urges every man to examine "hys lyfe and conversation," to see if he has acted "by the doctrine, as by the example of Christ him selfe."[144] Otherwise, "if we wyll have of God forgyvenes there is none other remedye, but to forgyve the offences done unto us, whyche be very small in comparison of our offences done againste God."[145]

Necessary and Profitable Doctrine, sig. O.3, *verso-recto*. Cf. his references to Christ's imposition of hands on the children in Mark 10:16 and the sacrament of Confirmation in *Necessary and Profitable Doctrine*, sig. P.2, *verso*.

139 See Bonner, *Homelies*, fol. 25, *verso*.
140 Bonner, *Homelies*, fol. 22, *recto*.
141 Bonner, *Homelies*, fol. 23, *verso*.
142 Bonner, *Homelies*, fol. 24, *verso*.
143 Bonner, *Homelies*, fol. 24, *recto*.
144 Bonner, *Homelies*, fol. 24, *recto*.
145 Bonner, *Homelies*, fol. 24, *recto*.

Edmund Bonner and the Legacy of Italian Humanism

The repeated references to the actions of Christ that we find in Bonner's homily are reminiscent of the scriptural commentaries of John Colet, who was a proponent of Italian Humanism. How is it that both Bonner and Colet place such similar emphasis on the deeds of Jesus that both men's exegetical writings are so sharply distinguished from an Erasmian preoccupation with the words of Christ to "his hearers"? It is comparatively simple to trace how the ideas of Erasmus would come to exert so much force on the thought of Ridley; but Bonner does not appear to have had any strong attraction to or connection with Colet and his work.

The scholarship of John O'Malley holds the key to understanding the family resemblance of Bonner's scriptural writings to those of Colet. O'Malley outlines two major but contrasting schools of thought in Renaissance Humanism with respect to biblical interpretation.[146] Erasmus' approach to scripture was firmly rooted in the *genus deliberativum* of classical oratory, the branch of that discipline concerned with persuading or leading a hearer to a particular conviction or course of action. This method tends to concern itself more with the speech and words of the subject than the *genus demonstrativum*, which weighs the actions of an individual with an aim to assigning "praise and blame."[147] O'Malley goes so far as to assert that it was a firm adherence to deliberative oratory that accounts for "Erasmus' relatively scarce interest in the deeds and actions of the Jesus of Nazareth depicted especially in the Gospels of Mark and Luke."[148] Demonstrative oratory, by contrast, was concerned with the "great deeds" of God in scripture, and was characteristic of the Italian school of Renaissance Humanism.[149]

---

146 O'Malley, *Praise and Blame*, pp. 39–49.
147 O'Malley, "Grammar and Rhetoric," pp. 94–95. Cf. O'Malley, *Praise and Blame*, p. 39–49, and Chapter II, above.
148 O'Malley, "Grammar and Rhetoric," p. 94.
149 Colet's focus on Jesus' actions is nearer the Italian Renaissance preachers at the papal court and their appropriation of the demonstrative or epideictic form of classical rhetoric. See O'Malley, *Praise and Blame* as well as his "Grammar and Rhetoric." The similitude of Colet's exegetical model to those of the papal preachers is probably not merely coincidental, since he

What little we know of Bonner's intellectual formation in the years after his legal education at Oxford, especially in connection with Italian Humanism, is pivotal. Already in April of 1530, he was writing to Thomas Cromwell to ask for the *Triumphs* of Petrarch and Castiglione's *The Courtier* in Italian. These readings would have acquainted Bonner with two major proponents of the Italian Renaissance.[150] From 1532–1533, Bonner served in Rome and elsewhere as Henry VIII's ambassador to the Pope, where, as a guest of the papal court, he regularly heard the kinds of sermons that O'Malley analyzes in *Praise and Blame*, homilies imbued with the Italian Renaissance emphasis on the great deeds of God in salvation history. In his later embassies, Bonner was always on good terms with the Italian ambassadors attached to the court he was serving.[151] Bonner continued to read and write Italian in his later years, and was still quoting Italian proverbs in a letter to his servant, Richard Lechmere, after his Deprivation (removal from episcopal office) in 1549.[152]

If both Colet and Bonner owe something to Italian Humanism in their exegetical work, that fact also explains why the two of them were much less likely than Erasmus to see the content and themes of the Old and New Testaments as mutually opposed. The orientation of a *genus demonstrativum* approach to the Bible and a consonant focus on God's great deeds would tend to result in a view of scripture as a single sweeping narrative of God's action in human history.[153] Rather than treating

studied in Italy, notably Rome, during the late 1490s, a portion of the very period that O'Malley highlights (1450–1521) in *Praise and Blame*.

150 Gina Mary Vere Alexander, "The Life and Career of Edmund Bonner, Bishop of London, Until His Deprivation in 1549," unpublished doctoral dissertation (University of London: 1960) [hereafter: Alexander, "Bonner Until His Deprivation"], pp. 53–54.

151 Alexander, "Bonner Until His Deprivation," p. 53.

152 Alexander, "Bonner Until His Deprivation," pp. 53–54. Bonner also came to be fluent in spoken Italian, and, as Ambassador to the Pope, was able to understand Clement's asides in Italian on the subject of Henry VIII's divorce suit.

153 O'Malley, *Praise and Blame*, p. 49. Over against Erasmus' deliberative emphasis in exegesis, the author states that the epideictic rhetoric typical of the Papal Court sermons of the late fifteenth and early sixteenth centuries

the Old Testament as a series of negative examples, as it is normatively in Erasmus' *Paraphrases*, Bonner and Colet both concentrate on the positive interrelationships between Old and New Covenant rites and concepts. It is also worth noting that beginning with Bonner's reconciliation with Stephen Gardiner in the early 1540s, and the selection of his chosen conservative preachers for the Diocese of London, he collected to himself a circle of friends who were mostly inimical to the work of Erasmus. The cloud of suspicion hovering over Erasmus' reputation in the wake of his *Novum Testamentum* and the use of his *Paraphrases* by the Protestant establishment under Edward VI meant that his work was not widely or enthusiastically embraced by Catholic divines under Mary. Rather, they continued to cite the Vulgate in their catechetical and polemical works and showered little praise indeed on the name of Erasmus of Rotterdam in their own writings. None of these figures would have needed much encouragement to adopt the principles of a rival school of opinion in the application of Humanist techniques to scriptural interpretation. As a result, not a single commendation of the work of Erasmus is to be found in the extant writings of Bonner or his chaplains composed under Mary Tudor.

"evince a tendency to look upon scripture more as a history of God's actions and less as a manual for doctrinal proof-texts or a book of artfully disguised philosophical principles." Cf. *ibid.* pp. 38–49 and O'Malley, "Grammar and Rhetoric," pp. 89, 94, and 99.

Conclusion

Synopsis

This study traces a set of themes through the writings of four authors of the early and middle sixteenth century with the aim of highlighting Renaissance Humanism's contributions to both Protestantism and Catholicism in England during this same period. The work of John Colet, Desiderius Erasmus, Nicholas Ridley, and Edmund Bonner has been sifted for expository clues on their use of philology and historical consciousness in exegesis, the relationship between the Old and New Covenants, and the person and role of Christ in ecclesiology. The congruencies and contrasts outline the inner logic of each author's ideas and serve to show how certain exegetical themes were carried forth in England from the Renaissance into the Reformation.

With respect to philology, all four authors are inclined to seize upon the significance of specific terms as integral to understanding a particular biblical text and to dwell on them at some length. This shared trait may be readily perceived in the work of each writer, despite Colet's frequent recourse to vignettes for explication, as with his banquet analogy for apprehending salvation history. With Erasmus, Ridley, and Bonner, the keen attention paid to particular words and their etymological origins is both consistent and pronounced in their work, even when they are writing for a broad readership.

Similarly, all four writers consider the scriptures to be chiefly historical source texts and seek to ground contemporary doctrinal or practical arguments in what they believe the historical narrative indicates. This tendency is at work in the writings of both Colet and Erasmus, despite the fact that both men arrive at opposite conclusions in their interpretations of First Corinthians and Paul's admonitions concerning marriage and chastity, for example. Likewise, Ridley and Bonner form rival arguments from the institution narratives of the Gospels, but both firmly hold that the texts themselves are primarily historical depictions of the events they relate.

The common philological and historical emphases exhibited in their writings reveal that each man stood within what we may describe as a Humanist tradition of biblical interpretation. This approach to scriptural exposition was relatively new when Colet and Erasmus began their close studies of the New Testament. It differed from dominant patristic and medieval exegetical emphases in the pursuit of a single sense for the text rather than weighing multiple meanings or multiple layers of meaning in scripture. The Humanist historical focus on individuals and events depicted in scripture also differed markedly from the mystical and devotional reflections on scripture that are characteristic, for example, of Athanasius' comments on the Psalms, Richard of St. Victor's meditations on the ark of the covenant, or Thomas à Kempis' *Imitatio Christi*, which went through several different editions in England on the eve of the Reformation. To a great extent, then, we may rightly speak of Colet, Erasmus, Ridley, and Bonner as all sharing the same rudimentary exegetical method.

Given this common basic interpretive method, what accounts for the rifts between this quartet of exegetes, among whom there is often anything but harmony? Their interpretive differences extend to outright conflict between Colet and Erasmus and to inimical confrontations between Ridley and Bonner. Certainly one might expect that any such divide would separate the earlier from the latter pair of scholars. Nevertheless, Ridley shares much more in common with Erasmus than with Bonner, who is much nearer to Colet in most of his exegetical observations.

One key feature of Humanist biblical exegesis ensured that it would lead ineluctably to strife and controversy: the insistence on a single, historically contextualized meaning for scriptural texts. Without this operative principle, there would have been much less exegetical controversy and friction between Colet and Erasmus on the one hand, and Bonner and Ridley on the other. The Humanist emphasis on a unitive meaning for biblical texts made reconciling rival views of a passage or book of the Bible much more difficult to accomplish. With the displacement of patristic and medieval exegetical methods, scholars of contrary opinion could not simply appeal to different strata in a controverted passage.

Instead, they were left to test who had a better or worse grasp of the historical context of a given pericope, a question which often could not be settled on internal grounds.

The other divisive aspect of Humanist biblical exegesis results from the fact that this tradition was not a seamless garment: from its inception, there were rival strands in it that emphasized different aspects of scripture and God's role in salvation history. This second-most divisive aspect of Humanism and its legacy for biblical interpretation has been masterfully explicated by John O'Malley. Any reader of the current study will realize how indebted it is throughout to his insights into Erasmus' inclination to deliberative oratory. For O'Malley, opting for one of the two major strains of classical rhetoric predisposed Renaissance scholars to a particular type of biblical explication. Erasmus' fondness for the *genus deliberativum* leads him to focus primarily on the oral and aural phenomena of Jesus' earthly mission, that is, his speech. It also inclines him to conceive of the person and work of Christ chiefly as a pedagogue. By contrast, Renaissance scholars influenced first or most deeply by Italian Humanism tended to embrace the demonstrative, or *epideictic*, form of classical rhetoric, focusing primarily on the deeds of Christ. I have argued here that Colet is quite likely to have been more indebted to Italian than Erasmian Humanism, and certainly his exegetical instincts are much nearer the Renaissance preachers at the papal court than to Erasmus on many points. The ground of this assertion is not mere speculation: Colet in fact studied in Rome during the late 1490s.

Their rival emphases on Jesus' speech and his deeds are as salient as they are persistent when Erasmus' and Colet's exegetical writings are compared. On the basis of internal structure and the content of their work, I have argued that Bonner and Ridley inherited something of this division from the generation of Renaissance biblical scholars that immediately preceded them. Ridley's connections to Erasmus were both personal, and academic, and it is therefore not difficult to work out how an early-sixteenth-century Cambridge professor of divinity might have come under the influence of the age's most celebrated Greek scholar. While we know little about Bonner's intellectual tastes and formation after his legal studies, we do know that he showed an early interest in key writings of the Italian Humanists, was fluent in Italian, and spent long periods of time at the papal court as ambassador for Henry VIII, so it is likely that he had some substantive and formative contact with Italian Humanism.

Pursuit of a single, historically contextualized meaning for sacred texts proved explosive even in the formative stages of Humanist biblical scholarship, and one only need review the strife between Colet and Erasmus to understand why. The Bible, perhaps uniquely so, is not the product of a single epoch or regional culture. Efforts to reconstruct its historical contexts, then, are necessarily selective or compromised, since one setting or another will be emphasized at the expense of others.

Erasmus often privileges the historical context of Roman Palestine, when Jesus and the Apostles lived and taught, while denigrating the Hebrew religious background of his subjects. Erasmus' reasons for proceeding in this fashion result first and foremost from his Platonic line of thought, which always reveals itself in a series of foils or dualities. As the logical counter to his Gospel of Light, he consistently and consciously contrasts the ritual content of the Old Testament, declaring it to be pure darkness and the "antitype of true religion," because it "consists in things visible." His glorification of Antique culture is entirely consistent with Erasmus' career and principal intellectual interests in the years leading up to his first efforts at biblical scholarship. In opposite fashion, Colet tends to privilege the Old Testament context of Jesus' life and work and does not attempt to explicitly connect Christ with any particular school of Ancient Philosophy. Thus, he and Erasmus cannot arrive at similar interpretations of key texts because they have sworn first allegiances to different layers of history and religious culture to be found in the scriptures they explicate. I have argued here that Colet's approach, to link the historical contexts of the Old and New Testaments, is more in keeping with the broad sweep of Christian exegesis and results in a more human and natural portrait of Christ and his early disciples than Erasmus' efforts to link Jesus and Paul directly to the philosophical systems and political phenomena of ancient Greece and the Roman Near East.[1]

---

1   In all of these observations on history, context, and biblical interpretation, I doubtless betray myself as a former pupil of David Steinmetz. See, e.g., David Steinmetz, "The Superiority of Pre-Critical Exegesis," *Theology Today* 37.1 (1980): pp. 27–38.

As noted in the opening sections of Chapters II–V, investigations into which strands of biblical history appeal most to a particular exegete will also throw light on their views of the relationship between the Old and New Testaments, and the closely connected subject of the import and role of Christ in their ecclesiology. To that extent, Erasmus' preoccupation with language, philosophy, and pedagogy lead almost ineluctably toward his portrayal of Christ as a teacher and founder of a *philosophia Christi*. Since he envisioned Church reform as a process of gradual re-education away from "superstition," this model of Christ was singularly apposite for his exegetical program. Similarly, Colet's more integral approach to Old and New Testament narrative and rites is certainly not unrelated to his portrayal of Christ as a living archetype of morality, not merely the giver of the New Law, but the keeper and exemplar of the same. For Colet, a strict moralist who longed for a return to the virtues of the primitive Church, Christ was necessarily depicted as faithful to the heart of the Law and Prophets.

Mutatis mutandis, the same connections between exegetical method, treatment of the two Testaments, and ecclesiology are to be observed among Ridley and Bonner. In those chapters that relate to Ridley's interpretive method and ecclesiology (II and III), I have argued that a great deal of his thought is probably consciously modeled on Erasmian precedents, and extends even to his vision of Jesus and the ministers who serve him as pedagogues. This is not to say that there are not key differences between Ridley, who views Christ as a teacher of true doctrine, and Erasmus, who typically promotes Christ as a teacher of true piety, but exegetically, they clearly hold more in common than either of them shares with Colet. While Ridley tends mostly to circumvent the issue of the Old Testament ritual context of Jesus' words and actions, when he does touch on the subject he is as severe as Erasmus. Perhaps most notably in this regard, he states plainly that his efforts to tear altars out of London churches are aimed to purge Christianity of semblances to the rites of the Law.[2]

2 Nicholas Ridley, *The Works of Bishop Ridley*, ed. Henry Christmas, for the Parker Society (Cambridge: Cambridge University Press, 1841), p. 323.

In the chapters that explore the exegetical work and ecclesiology of Bonner (IV and V), I have not argued that there is any direct connection between him and John Colet. There simply is no positive evidence upon which one could responsibly build such a case. Rather, I posit that a shared enthusiasm for and substantive contact with Italian Humanism helps to account for the many similarities that Bonner and Colet hold in common. As with Ridley and Erasmus, there are also important differences between Colet and Bonner. The former tends to view Christ as an exemplar of virtue, while Bonner is more consistent in emphasizing that Christ's faithfulness to the Law extends to his consummation of it as both priest and paschal victim. This same motif may certainly be found in Colet, but is clearly more emphatic in the work of Bonner, which is hardly surprising given the latter's context of eucharistic controversy and efforts to combat doctrinal schism.

Inferences and Questions

A smaller but fascinating area for more research suggested by this study focuses on the relationship between Edwardine and Marian church furnishings. It is curious that the tabernacle, a new feature for altars that emerged under Mary I, happened to have a shape, function, and placement not unlike that of the "poor men's chest," as authorized by Edward VI. It is just possible that the tabernacle actually evolved from the Edwardine poor chest, which would be a telling encapsulation on the shifting foci of devotion under the lesser Tudor monarchs in early modern England.

The second inference arising from this study is that it is not sufficient to speak simply of the effect of Humanism on the generation of divines living and writing in England in the middle of the sixteenth century without distinguishing between the competing Erasmian and Italian Humanist currents within the Renaissance tradition of biblical interpretation. One of the oldest and most critical questions for English Reformation scholarship is the role that Humanism may have played as a seedbed for Protestantism. Once accepted as axiomatic, the Whiggish notion that enthusiasm for Humanist ideas predisposed sixteenth-century Church leaders to Protestantism has come under hard scrutiny, especially in the last thirty years of research. One of the operating theses of the current study, reinforced by comparing the work of Erasmus and Ridley, is that Erasmian Humanism may have played such a role in the intellectual formation of its proponents, especially if it was the foundational contact a figure had with Humanist exegesis. However, substantial or primary contact with Italian Humanism may have actually had an opposite effect, given the similarly conservative concepts found in the work of Colet and Bonner.

A great deal more research, well beyond the scope of the current study, needs to be undertaken to thoroughly test this hypothesis. Still, it is important to note that Erasmus' closest contemporary friends in England all sooner or later found themselves at odds with him on one or more points of exegesis and doctrine. In their critiques of his ideas, Erasmus is not characteristically accused of being overly traditional. It may well be that earlier contact with Italian Humanism provided a perspective of distance and balance, enabling More, Fisher, Colet, and even Robert Ridley, to perceive and address particular issues in Erasmus' interpretations of biblical texts and the novel positions he assumed on certain Church teachings.

Conversely, it is clear that Catholic divines in the reign of Edward VI understood that the authority of Erasmus carried great weight among their rivals. Thus, the Bishop of Chichester dropped Erasmus' name in the Lords' debate on the first *Book of Common Prayer* in December 1548, even when the discussion was, perforce, focused on Patristic authors.[3] Similarly, Alban Langdale, one of the Catholic participants in the 1549 debate on the Eucharist at Cambridge, chided Dr. Madew, one of Ridley's *confrères*, thus: "I doe not a little marvell. Seeyng that, that most famous Clarke Erasmus whose authoritye and sentence you refuse at this present onely, yet neverthelesse he is very worthy in thys matter of farre better estimation amongst learned men. Wherefore I trust I

---

3   See Abbot Francis Aidan Gasquet and Edmund Bishop, *Edward the Sixth and the Book of Common Prayer-An Examination of its Origin and Early History: With an Appendix of Unpublished Documents*, third edition (London: Burns and Oates, 1891) [hereafter, Gasquet and Bishop, *Edward the Sixth*], p. 423.

shall not offend to alledge him before this learned and honourable auditorye."[4] It is interesting to note that Ridley himself interjected several comments directly at this stage of the debate when Langdale appeared to be getting the best of Maydew on the subject of Erasmus' understanding of the scriptures on the question of the real presence of Christ in the Eucharist.[5] Langdale's remarks at once suggest that contemporary Protestant divines had set great store by the name of Erasmus, but that not all of his opinions were considered "worthy" by traditionalists. The reader is also struck by the fact that there is not one commendation of Erasmus and his exegetical precepts to be found in any of the catechetical and homiletic projects Bonner coordinated during the reign of Mary I. A prosopographical study of Ridley's contemporaries on the episcopal bench, with an eye to which of them may have been well-disposed early on to either Erasmian or Italian Humanism, and their later alignment in the late 1540s when it became clear that there would be a fully Protestant religious establishment in England, would be most revealing.

The third major postulate suggested by the current study is that Erasmian Humanism may indeed have served to prepare the soil for the growth of Protestantism in some quarters, but likely accomplished this end passively rather than actively—not so much in what it did, but rather in breaking up what had come before. All of this is to say that what Heiko Oberman, the German Reformation scholar, calls Erasmus' "unremitting theological anti-Judaism" succeeded in tearing asunder the common exegetical convention of the patristic and medieval ages that Jesus' words and deeds be specifically interpreted in light of Old

---

4   John Foxe, *Actes and Monuments of matters most speciall and memorable, happenyng in the Church, with an Universal history of the same, wherein is set forth at large the whole race and course of the Church, from the primitive age to these latter tymes of ours, with the bloudy times, horrible troubles, and great persecutions agaynst the true Martyrs of Christ, sought and wrought as well by Heathen Emperours, and now lately practised by Romish Prelates, especially in this Realme of England and Scotland* ([STC 11225] London: John Daye, 1583) [hereafter, Foxe, *Actes and Monuments*], p. 1379.

5   See Foxe, *Actes and Monuments*, p. 1380.

Testament ritual precedents or "types." Erasmus' neo-Platonic propensity for mere juxtaposition of the two Covenants, and his privileging of Jesus' words often to the exclusion of his actions, served to dissolve the inter-textual bonds between Law and Gospel. The result was that exegetes like Ridley, just one generation removed from Erasmus, would weigh in on questions relating to the work and aims of Jesus at the Last Supper, often without a single reference to any of the Old Testament preadumbrations of the Eucharist.

Again, much more study needs to be devoted to this topic, but there is certainly strong evidence that English Protestants other than Ridley believed the work of the Gospel called for purging Christianity of Old Testament ritual references. One of the major features of Cranmer's liturgical work was that Old Testament allusions to Christian feasts and rites, so common to medieval orders of worship, were greatly abridged in both the 1549 and 1552 editions of the *Book of Common Prayer*.[6] Similarly, a thoroughgoing study of Erasmus and Luther on the subjects of Law and Gospel might throw light on why Erasmus resisted direct and public confrontation of Luther for so long. When contemporaries accused Erasmus of having laid the egg that Luther hatched, he did not deny the charge, but merely commented that he had expected quite a different bird. John O'Malley has done an excellent study of the contrasting views of Luther and Erasmus on the subject of pagan philosophy,[7] but the current study suggests that both men held very similar views on the relationship of the Old Testament to the Gospel and that this topic needs to be explored in its own right.

The fourth general surmise that can be made from the current study speaks to the still fashionable notion among Protestant historians that traditional Catholicism represented a filtering of lay experience of scripture, as compared with the direct access to the Old and New Testaments that were afforded to the laity during the Reformation. In the preceding chapters, it appears abundantly clear that whether one has in mind the

6   See Gasquet and Bishop, *Edward VI and the Book of Common Prayer*, pp. 277–307.
7   See John O'Malley, "Erasmus and Luther, Continuity and Discontinuity as Key to Their Conflict," *Sixteenth Century Journal* 5.2 (1974): 47–65.

Paraphrases of Erasmus, the Edwardine poor chest ritual, or Bonner's *Homelies*, lay access to scripture was still "filtered" by one or more conceptual, doxological, or homiletic constructs, no matter one's ecclesial allegiance. Even those relatively rare members of sixteenth-century society with sufficient education to read had to contend either with a Tyndale-based text that rendered "elder" for πρεσβύτερος, select portions of the Vulgate that offered "do penaunce" for *poenitentiam*, or *sermo* for λόγος in Erasmus' *Novum Instrumentum*. The enormous efforts at lay formation in Edwardine England were certainly not undertaken so that believers would be emboldened to interpret the scriptures in just any fashion they so pleased, as Ridley's polemical writings make plain. Similarly, Cranmer's *Homilies* and *Books of Common Prayer* were expressly designed to ensure that scripture was absorbed by the laity according to certain pre-determined exegetical categories and conditions.

The fifth cardinal conclusion that may be drawn from this study is that the early English Protestant effort to divine the proper form of the Church from the pages of scripture was highly problematic, both hermeneutically and practically. Historically, the Church preceded the New Testament, and not one document in the canon is dedicated explicitly or exclusively to the question of the shape and organization of the Church. Early English Protestants attempted then to invert the traditional relationship between ecclesiology and exegesis, urging that the text should determine the proper limits of dogma. However, despite Ridley's suggestion that all doctrinal problems could be resolved in the Church by consulting scripture, none of the major disputes arising in the sixteenth century was ever resolved by such means. In fact, during the four and a half centuries since he wrote, the world has come to know several thousand distinct Protestant denominations, all following God's Word, and none in full agreement on what that Word prescribes for authentic and pure Church polity.

An especially eloquent patristic allegory on the relationship of Mary to Christ, and of the New Covenant to the Old, can be found in the writings of St. Athanasius (297–373 A.D.), bishop of Alexandria and doctor of the Church. In one of his homilies on the Incarnation, he says of St. Mary: "O noble Virgin, truly you are greater than any other greatness. For who is your equal in greatness, O dwelling place of God the Word? To whom among all creatures shall I compare you, O Virgin? You are greater than them all. O Ark of the New Covenant, clothed with purity instead of gold! You are the Ark in which is found the golden vessel containing the true manna, that is, the flesh in which divinity resides."[8] Athanasius' description of Mary as "the Ark of the New Covenant" is more than a poetic likening of Mary to the Ark of Yahweh described in the Torah; it is also an implicitly ecclesiological claim. Amplifying earlier patristic statements on the role and person of Mary, it became increasingly common from the latter half of the fourth century for the Fathers to suggest that Mary was a "type" or figure of the Church.[9] While Athanasius was not primarily concerned with the relationship between the Church and the Christian scriptures, his description of Mary as the "dwelling place of God the Word," underscores the fact that the scriptures emerged from the Church, and not vice versa. This theme is reiterated in his comparison of the Theotokos to the Ark of the Covenant: just as Mary brought the infant Christ into the world, the Church is the Mother or womb that nurtured and brought forth the scriptures. Through such allusions, Athanasius and many other Church Fathers in both the East and the West gave witness, by indirect means, to the historical reality that the New Testament is the beloved child of holy mother Church, rather than the reverse. Because the New Testament canon was not fully formed until the middle of the fourth century, after the Nicene Creed was composed and adopted by the Church, the early Fathers had no thought that the scriptures preceded the Church in time or represented an independent source of authority that governed it. Early English Protestants insisted that they were reclaiming the au-

8 Luigi Gambero, *Mary and the Fathers of the Church* (San Francisco: Ignatius Press, 1999) [hereafter Gambero, *Mary and the Fathers*], p. 106.

9 Gambero, *Mary and the Fathers*, p. 19. See also the patristic authors cited in this work who make this very same comparison, both implicitly and explicitly, such as St. Ambrose of Milan on pp. 198–99, 367; St. Augustine of Hippo, pp. 222–25; St. Clement of Alexandria, p. 71; St. Ephrem, pp. 115–16; St. Epiphanius, pp. 124–25; St. Gregory the Great, p. 367; St. Gregory Nazianzen, pp. 163, 164; St. Isidore of Seville, pp. 376–77; and Sedulius, p. 290.

thentic ideas of the primitive Church, even as they attempted to invert the original relationship of ecclesiology to exegesis, urging instead that the Church become the progeny of Scripture.

Bibliography

Primary Sources

Scripture

The Holy Bible. Revised Standard Version, Catholic Edition. San Francisco: Ignatius Press, 1966.

The Byble in Englyshe of the largest and greatest volume, auctorysed and apoynted by the commaundemente of oure moost reboubted prynce and soueraygne Lorde Kynge Henrye the. viii. supreme heade of this his churche and realme of Englande: to be frequented and vsed in euery churche w'in this his sayd realme, accordynge to the tenoure of hys former iniunctions geuen in that behalfe. Ouersene and perused at the co[m]maundeme[n]t of the kynges hyghnes, by the ryght reuerende fathers in God Cuthbert bysshop of Duresme, and Nicolas bisshop of Rochester. (STC 2073) London: Printed by Edwarde Whitchurch [or Rycharde Grafton] *Cum priuilegio ad imprimendum solum,* 1541.

The Greek New Testament. 3ʳᵈ Edition, edited by Kurt Aland, Matthew Black, Carlo M. Martini, Bruce M. Metzger, and Allen Wikgren. Münster/Westphalia: United Bible Societies, 1983.

The Jerusalem Bible. Garden City, New York: Doubleday & Company, Inc., 1966.

The New King James Bible. Nashville: Thomas Nelson Publishers, 1982.

The New Testament of Our Lord and Savior Jesus Christ. A Revision of the Challoner-Rheims Version of the *Vulgate.* Patterson, New Jersey: St. Anthony Guild Press, 1941.

Bibliography

Manuscripts Consulted

Bonner, Edmund. Episcopal register as Bishop of London. MS 9531/12, pt. 1, Guildhall Library Collection, London.

Ridley, Nicholas. Episcopal Register as Bishop of London. MS 9531/12, pt. 2, Guildhall Library Collection, London.

Early Printed Materials

Askew, Anne. *The first examinacion of the worthy servaunt of God, Mastres Anne Askew the yonger doughter of Syr William Askew Knyght of Lyncolne shyre: lately martyred i[n] Smythefelde, by the Romyshe Popes vpholders. Anne Askewe stode faste by this veritee of God, to the ende.* (STC 852) London: W. Hill, 1548?

Bale, John. *The image of both churches.* (STC 1297) Antwerp, 1546?

Bonner, Edmund. *A profitable and necessarye doctryne with certayne homelies adioyned thervnto set forth by the reuerende father in God, Edmonde byshop of London, for the instruction and enformation of the people beynge within his diocesse of London, [and] of his cure and charge.* (STC 3281.5) London: John Cawood, 1555.

_____. *An Honest Godly Instruction, and information for the tra-dying, and bringinge up of Children, set furth by the Bishoppe of London. . . .* (STC 3281) London: 1556.

_____. *Homelies sette forth by the righte reuerende father in God, Edmunde Byshop of London, not onely promised before in his booke, intituled, A necessary doctrine, but also now of late adioyned, and added therevnto, to be read within his diocesse of London, of all persons, vycars, and curates, vnto theyr parishioners, vpon son-dayes, [and] holydayes.* (STC 3285.4) Imprinted at London: In Pou-les churcheyarde, at the sygne of the holy Ghost, by Ihon Cawodde, prynter to the Kynge and Queenes Maiesties, 1555.

_____. *Iniunctions geuen in the visitatio[n] of the Reuerend father in god Edmunde, bishop of London begunne and continued in his cathederal churche and dioces of London, from the thyrd day of Sep-tember the yere of oure Lorde god, a thousand fiue hundreth fifty and foure, vntill the. viii. daye of October, the yeare of our Lord a thousand fiue hundreth fifty and fiue then nexte ensuing.* (STC 10249) London: In Paules churcheyard, at the signe of the holy ghost, by Iohn Cawood, 1555.

_____. *Articles to be enquired of in the generall visitation of Edmonde Bisshoppe of London exercised by him the yeare of oure Lorde. 1.5.5.4. in the citie and diocese of London. . . .* (STC 10248) London: John Cawood, September 1554.

_____. *Admonicion.* In Aston, Margaret. "Lap Books and Lectern Books: The Revelatory Book in the Reformation." In *The Church and the Book: Papers Read at the 2000 Summer Meeting and the 2001 Winter Meeting of the Ecclesiastical History Society*, edited by R. N. Swanson, *The Ecclesiastical History Society*, volume 56, pp. 163–88. Rochester, New York: Boydell Press, 2004.

Bullinger, Heinrich. *Two Epystles, one of Henry Bullynger with the consent of all the learned men of Tigury [Zurich]: an other of Johan Calvyne, chefe preacher of the church of Geneve: whether it be lawful for a christen man to communicate or be partaker of the masse of the papists, without offending God and hys neyghbour or not.* (STC 4080) London: Robert Stoughton, 1548.

Calvin, John. *Two Epystles, one of Henry Bullynger with the consent of all the learned men of Tigury [Zurich]: an other of Johan Calvyne, chefe preacher of the church of Geneve: whether it be lawful for a christen man to communicate or be partaker of the masse of the papists, without offending God and hys neyghbour or not.* (STC 4080) London: Robert Stoughton, 1548.

Chertsey, Andrew. *Ihesus. The floure of the commaundementes of god with many examples and auctorytees extracte and drawen as well of holy scryptures as of other doctours and good auncient faders, the whiche is moche vtyle and prouffytable vnto all people. The. x. commaundementes of the lawe. Thou shalt worshyp one god onely. And loue hym with thy herte perfytely ... The fyue commaundementes of the chyrche. The sondayes here thou masse and the festes of co[m]maundement. ... The foure ymbres vigyles thou shalte faste, [and] the lente entyerly.* (STC 23876) London: In Flete strete at the sygne of the sonne by Wynkyn de Worde, 1510.

Coverdale, Miles. *Certain most godly, fruitful, and comfortable letters of such true saintes and holy martyrs of God, as in the late bloodye persecution here within this realme, gaue their lyues for the defence of Christes holy gospel written in the tyme of their affliction and cruell imprysonment.* (STC 5886) London: John Day, 1564.

Erasmus, Desiderius. *An Exhortation to the Diligent Studye of Scripture.* Edited by William Roye. (STC 10493) Antwerp, 1529.

Foxe, John. *Actes and Monuments of matters most speciall and memorable, happenyng in the Church, with an Universal history of the same, wherein is set forth at large the whole race and course of the Church, from the primitive age to these latter tymes of ours, with the bloudy times, horrible troubles, and great persecutions agaynst the true Martyrs of Christ, sought and wrought as well by Heathen Emperours, and now lately practised by Romish Prelates, especially in this Realme of England and Scotland.* (STC 11223) London: John Daye, 1563.

_____. *Actes and Monuments of matters most speciall and memorable, happenyng in the Church, with an Universal history of the same, wherein is set forth at large the whole race and course of the Church, from the primitive age to these latter tymes of ours, with the bloudy times, horrible troubles, and great persecutions agaynst the true Martyrs of Christ, sought and wrought as well by Heathen Emperours, and now lately practised by Romish Prelates, especially in this Realme of England and Scotland.* (STC 11225) London: John Daye, 1583.

Frith, John. *A Treatise Agaynst the Boke M. More Made*, in William Tyndale, *The whole workes of W. Tyndall, Iohn Frith, and Doct. Barnes, three worthy martyrs, and principall teachers of this Churche of England: collected and compiled in one tome togither, beyng before scattered, [and] now in print here exhibited to the Church. To the prayse of God, and profite of all good Christian readers.* (STC 24436) London: John Daye, 1573.

_____. *An Answere to the Treatise that M. More Made.* Edited by John Foxe. (STC 24436) London: John Daye, 1573.

Harpsfield, Nicholas. *Dialogi sex contra summi pontificatus, monasticae vitae, sanctorum, sacrarum imaginum oppugnatores, et pseudomartyres.* Christopher Plantin: Antwerp, 1566.

Mirk, John. *The festyuall.* (STC 17971) London: Wynkyn de Worde, 1508.

More, St. Thomas. *An Answere to the Treatise that M. More Made.* Edited by John Foxe. (STC 24436) London: John Daye, 1573.

Peryn, William. *Thre godly and notable Sermons of the moost honorable and blessed sacrament of the Aulter.* (STC 19785.5) London: John Hereforde for Robert Toye, 1546.

Phinch, Richard. *The Epiphanie of the Church.* (STC 10877.5) London: Roger Ward, 1590.

Ridley, Nicholas. *A Brief Declaracion of the Lordes Supper.* (STC 21046) Emden: Egidius van der Erve, 1555.

_____. *A pituous lamentation of the miserable estate of the churche of Christ in Englande in the time of the late revolt from the gospel, wherin is conteyned a learned comparison betwene the comfortable doctrine of the gospel, and the traditions of the popish religion: with an instruction how the true Christian ought to behaue himself in the tyme of tryall. Wrytten by that worthy martyr of god Nicolas Rydley, late Bysshoppe of London. Neuer before this tyme imprynted. Wherevnto are also annexed certayne letters of Iohn Careles, written in the tyme of his imprisonment. Perused and allowed according to the Quenes Maiesties iniunctions.* (STC 21052) London: Willyam Powell, dwelling in Fletestrete, at the signe of the George, nere to Sainct Dunstons Church, 1566.

_____. *Certen godly, learned, and comfortable conferences, betwene the two reuerende fathers, and holye martyrs of Christe, D. Nicolas Rydley late Bysshoppe of London, and M. Hughe Latymer sometyme Bysshoppe of Worcester, during the tyme of their emprysonmentes. Whereunto is added. A treatise agaynst the errour of transubstantiation, made by the sayd reuerende father D. Nicolas Rydley.* (STC 21048) Strasbourg: Heirs of W. Rihel, 1556.

_____. *Certein godly, learned, and comfortable conferences, betwene the two reuerende fathers, and holy martyrs of Christe, D. Nicolas Rydley late Bisshoppe of London, and M. Hughe Latimer, sometyme Bisshop of Worcester, during the tyme of their emprisonmentes.* (STC 21047.3) Emden: Egidius van der Erve, 1556.

_____. *Iniunctions geven in the visitation of the reverende father in God, Nycolas byshoppe of London for an vniformitie in the Diocesse of London, in the fourth yeare of our soueraygne Lorde Kynge Edwarde the syxt, by the grace of God Kyng of England, France, and Irelande, defender of the fayth, and in earthe, of the churche of England and also of Ireland, the supreme heade, nexte and immediatly vnder our sauioure Christ.* (STC 10247) London: Reynolde Wolfe, *Cum priuilegio ad imprimendum solum,* 1550.

Standish, John. *A discourse wherin is debated whether it be expedient that the scripture should be in English for al men to reade that wyll* (STC 23207) London: Robert Caly, 1554.

The Byble in Englyshe of the largest and greatest volume, auctorysed and apoynted by the commaundemente of oure moost reboubted prynce and soueraygne Lorde Kynge Henrye the. viii. supreme heade of this his churche and realme of Englande: to be frequented and vsed in euery churche w'in this his sayd realme, accordynge to the tenoure of hys former iniunctions geuen in that behalfe. Ouersene and perused at the co[m]maundeme[n]t of the kynges hyghnes, by the ryght reuerende fathers in God Cuthbert bysshop of Duresme, and Nicolas bisshop of Rochester. (STC 2073) London: Printed by Edwarde Whitchurch [or Rycharde Grafton] *Cum priuilegio ad imprimendum solum,* 1541.

Vermigli, Pietro Martire. *A discourse or traictise of Petur Martyr Vermilla Flore[n]tine, the publyque reader of diuinitee in the Universitee of Oxford wherein he openly declared his whole and determinate judgemente concernynge the sacrament of the Lordes supper in the sayde Universitee.,* (STC 24665) London: Robert Stoughton [i.e. Whitchurch], 1550.

Other Primary Materials

à Kempis, Thomas. *The Imitation of Christ in Four Books*. Edited by Clare L. Fitzpatrick. New York: Catholic Book Publishing Co., 1977.

St. Ambrose. "On the Mysteries." In *Nicene and Post-Nicene Fathers*, series II, volume X, edited by Philip Schaff. Grand Rapids: William B. Eerdmans, 1894.

_____. "On the Mysteries." In *Patrologia Latina*, volume XVI, edited by Jacques-Paul Migne.

Aquinas, St. Thomas. *Catena Aurea in Quatuor Evangelia*, vol. 1, *Expositio in Mattheum et Marcum*. Rome: Marietti Editori Ltd., 1953.

_____. *Summa Theologica*. Translated and edited by the Fathers of the English Dominican Province. New York: Benziger Brothers, Inc., 1947.

St. Augustine of Hippo. "Against the Epistle of Manichæus called Fundamental." In *Writings Against the Manichaeans and Against the Donatists*, series I, volume IV of *Nicene and Post-Nicene Fathers*, edited by Philip Schaff. Grand Rapids: William B. Eerdmans, 1894.

_____. "Against the Epistle of Manichæus called Fundamental." In *Patrologia Latina*, volume XLII, edited by Jacques-Paul Migne.

_____. *City of God*. Translated by Henry Bettenson. New York: Penguin Books, 1984.

_____. *De gratia Christi*. In *Patrologia Latina*, volume XLIV, edited by Jacques-Paul Migne.

_____. "On the Grace of Christ." In *Nicene and Post-Nicene Fathers*, series I, volume V, edited by Philip Schaff. Grand Rapids: William B. Eerdmans, 1894.

_____. "Letter LIV." In *Nicene and Post-Nicene Fathers*, series I, volume I, edited by Philip Schaff. Grand Rapids: William B. Eerdmans, 1894.

_____. *De Doctrina Christiana*. Translated and edited by Edmund Hill, O.P. New York: New City Press, 1996.

_____. *Expositions of the Psalms*. In *Nicene and Post-Nicene*

Fathers, series II, volume VIII, edited by Philip Schaff. Grand Rapids: William B. Eerdmans, 1888.

_____. "To the Enquiries of Januarius." In *Patrologia Latina*, vol. XXXIII, edited by Jacques-Paul Migne.

St. Basil the Great. "Of the Holy Trinity, the Incarnation, the Invocation of Saints, and their Images." In *Nicene and Post-Nicene Fathers*, series II, volume VIII, edited by Philip Schaff. Grand Rapids: William B. Eerdmans, 1894.

_____. "Letter 306, Of the Holy Trinity, the Incarnation, the Invocation of Saints, and their Images." In *Patrologia Graecae*, vol. XXXII, edited by Jacques-Paul Migne.

_____. *On the Holy Spirit*. Crestwood, New York: St. Vladimir's Seminary Press, 1980.

Bishop, Edmund and Gasquet, Abbot Francis Aidan. *Edward the Sixth and the Book of Common Prayer-An Examination of its Origin and Early History: With an Appendix of Unpublished Documents*. Third edition. London: Burns and Oates, 1891.

Bradford, John. *The Writings of John Bradford*, volume 2. Edited by Aubrey Townsend, for the Parker Society. Cambridge: Cambridge University Press, 1840.

Bucer, Martin. *Martin Bucer and the Book of Common Prayer*. Edited by E. C. Whitaker, for the Alcuin Club. Great Wakering: Mayhew-McCrimmon, 1974.

Calendar of State Papers, Spanish. Volume XIII, edited by P. de Gayangos, G. Mattingly, A. S. Hume, and R. Tyler. H.M.S.O. 1862–1964.

Calvin, John. *The Institutes of Christian Religion, 1559*. Translated by Ford Lewis Battles and edited by John T. McNeil. Philadelphia: Westminster John Knox Press, 1960.

_____. *John Calvin and Jacopo Sadoleto: A Reformation Debate*. Edited by John C. Olin. Grand Rapids: Baker Book House, 1976.

Chrysostom, St. John. "Homily XXIII on John's Gospel." In *Patrologia Graecae*, volume XLIX, edited by Jacques-Paul Migne.

_____. "Homily XXIII." In *Nicene and Post-Nicene Fathers*, series I, vol. XIV, edited by Philip Schaff. Grand Rapids: William B. Eerdmans, 1894.

Colet, John. "Introduction to Orders." In *Ecclesiastical Hierarchy*, vol. I, of *Super Opera Dionys*, translated and edited by J. H. Lupton. London: Bell and Daldy, 1869.

_____. *Commentary on First Corinthians*. Translated and edited by Bernard O'Kelly and Catharine Jarrott, Medieval and Renaissance Texts & Studies 21. Binghamton, New York: Medieval & Renaissance Texts & Studies, 1985.

_____. *Exposition of St. Paul's Epistle to the Romans*. In *Letters to Radulphus on the Mosaic Account of the Creation, Together with Other Treatises*, translated and edited by J. H. Lupton. Cambridge: Cambridge University Press, 1876.

_____. "Reply to Erasmus on the Agony in the Garden." In *Desiderii Erasmi Roterdami Opera Omnia*, volume V, edited by Jean Leclerc. Leiden: Lugduni Batavorum, 1703–1706.

Cranmer, Thomas. *Miscellaneous Writings and Letters of Thomas Cranmer, Archbishop of Canterbury*. Edited by John Edmund Cox, for the Parker Society. Cambridge: Cambridge University Press, 1846.

Creeds of the Churches. Edited by John Leith. Third edition. Louisville: John Knox Press, 1982.

St. Cyril of Jerusalem. *Catechetical Lectures*. In *Patrologia Graecae*, volume XXXIII, edited by Jacques-Paul Migne.

Edward VI. "To Nicholas Ridley." In *The Works of Bishop Ridley*, edited by Henry Christmas, for the Parker Society. Cambridge: Cambridge University Press, 1841.

Enchiridion Symbolorum Definitionum et Declarationem de Rebus Fidei et Morum, Edited by Henry Denziger and Adolph Schönmetzer. Rome: Herder and Herder, 1976.

Erasmus, Desiderius. "Letter 29, to Cornelius Gerard." In *The Correspondence of Erasmus*, translated and edited by R. A. B. Mynors and

D. F. S. Thomson. The Complete Works of Erasmus 1. Toronto: University of Toronto Press, 1974.

_____. "Letter 593, from John Colet." In *The Correspondence of Erasmus*, translated and edited by R. A. B. Mynors and D. F. S. Thomson. The Complete Works of Erasmus 4. Toronto: University of Toronto Press, 1977.

_____. "Letter to Jodocus Jonas." In *The Correspondence of Erasmus*, translated and edited by R. A. B. Mynors and D. F. S. Thomson. The Complete Works of Erasmus 8. Toronto: University of Toronto Press, 1974.

_____. "The Funeral." In *Ten Colloquies*, translated and edited by Craig R. Thompson. New York: Macmillan, 1987.

_____. "To Jodocus Jonas." In *Opus epistularum Des. Erasmi Roterodami*, volume V, no. 1489, edited by P. S. Allen, H. M. Allen, and H. W. Garrod. Oxford, 1922.

_____. *Annotations on Romans*. Translated and edited by John B. Payne, Albert Rabil Jr., and Warren Smith. The Collected Works of Erasmus 56. Toronto: University of Toronto Press, 1994.

_____. *Paraphrase on First Timothy*. Translated and edited by John Bateman. The Collected Works of Erasmus 44. Toronto: University of Toronto Press, 1993.

_____. *Paraphrase on Hebrews*. Translated and edited by John Bateman. The Collected Works of Erasmus 44. Toronto: University of Toronto Press, 1993.

_____. *Paraphrase on John*. Translated and edited by Jane E. Phillips. The Collected Works of Erasmus 46. Toronto: University of Toronto Press, 1991.

_____. *Paraphrase on Mark*. Translated by Erika Rummel and edited by Robert D. Sider. The Collected Works of Erasmus 49. Toronto: University of Toronto Press, 1988.

_____. *Paraphrases on Romans and Galatians*. Translated and edited by John B. Payne, Albert Rabil Jr., and Warren Smith Jr. The

Collected Works of Erasmus 42. Toronto: University of Toronto Press, 1984.

_____. *Paraphrasis in Epist. Pauli ad Cor. 1*. In *Desiderii Erasmi Roterdami Opera Omnia*, volume VII, edited by Jean Leclerc. Leiden: Lugduni Batavorum, 1706.

_____. *The Godly Feast*. In *Ten Colloquies*, translated and edited by Craig R. Thompson. New York: Macmillan, 1987.

_____. *Paraclesis*. In *Christian Humanism and the Reformation*, translated and edited by John C. Olin. New York: Fordham University Press, 1975.

_____. *The Handbook of the Militant Christian (Enchiridion Militis Christiani)*. In *The Essential Erasmus*, translated and edited John P. Dolan. New York: Meridian, 1993.

Fisher, St. John. *Exposition of the Seven Penitential Psalms*. Edited by Anne Barbeau Gardiner. San Francisco: Ignatius Press, 1998.

Gambero, Luigi. *Mary and the Fathers of the Church*. San Francisco: Ignatius Press, 1999.

St. Germanus I. Complete Extant Writings. In *Patrologia Graecae*, volume XCVIII, edited by Jacques-Paul Migne.

Harpsfield, Nicholas? *Bishop Cranmer's Recantacyons*. Edited by Lord Houghton. London: Philobiblon Society Miscellanies, 1877.

Hopf, Constantin. *Martin Bucer and the English Reformation*. Oxford: Basil Blackwell, 1946.

St. Irenaeus of Lyons. *Adversus Haeresis*. In *Patrologia Graecae*, volume VII B, edited by Jacques-Paul Migne.

Jones, Norman. "A Bill Confirming Bishop Bonner's Deprivation and Reinstating Bishop Ridley as the Legal Bishop of London, from the Parliament of 1559." *The Journal of Ecclesiastical History* 33.4 (1982): 580–85.

Luther, Martin. *The Freedom of a Christian Man*. In *The Protestant Reformation*, edited by Hans J. Hillerbrand. New York: Harper & Row, 1968.

_____. *The Pagan Servitude of the Church*. In *Martin Luther:*

Selections From His Writings, edited by John Dillenberger. New York: Anchor Books, 1962.

Manichæus. *The Cologne Mani Codex: Concerning the Origin of His Body*. Edited and translated by Ron Cameron and Arthur J. Dewey. Missoula, Montana: Scholar's Press, 1979.

Martin Micron. "To Heinreich Bullinger." In *Original Letters Relative to the English Reformation*, vol. 2, edited by H. Robinson, for the Parker Society. Cambridge: Cambridge University Press, 1847.

Origen. *Homilies on Jeremias*. In *Patrologia Graecae*, volume XIII, edited by Jacques-Paul Migne.

Plato. *Euthyphro, Apology, and Crito*. Translated and edited by J. F. Church. New York: Macmillan Library of Classics, 1985.

Pseudo-Augustine. *De Visitationem Infirmorum*. In *Patrologia Latina*, volume XL, edited by Jacques-Paul Migne.

Pseudo-Chrysostom. *Opus Imperfectum in Matthaeum*. In *Patrologia Graecae*, volume LVI, edited by Jacques-Paul Migne.

Ratramnus of Corbie. *De predestinatione in libri duo*. In Patrologia Latina, volume CXXI, edited by Jacques-Paul Migne.

Records of the English Bible: The Documents Relating to the Translation and Publication of the Bible in English: 1521–1611. Edited by A. F. Pollard. Oxford: Oxford University Press, 1911.

Ridley, Nicholas. *The Works of Bishop Ridley*. Edited by Henry Christmas, for the Parker Society. Cambridge: Cambridge University Press, 1841.

Sadoleto, Jacopo. *John Calvin and Jacopo Sadoleto: A Reformation Debate*. Edited by John C. Olin. Grand Rapids: Baker Book House, 1976.

Santer, Mark and Wiles, Maurice. *Documents in Early Christian Thought*. Cambridge: Cambridge University Press, 1998.

Tertullian. *De monogamia*. In *Patrologia Latina*, volume II, edited by Jacques-Paul Migne.

_____. *De corona militis*. In *Patrologia Latina*, volume II, edited by Jacques-Paul Migne.

The Dictionary of Early Christian Literature. Translated by Matthew O'Connell and edited by Siegmar Döpp and Wilhelm Geerlings. New York: Herder and Herder, 2000.

The Edwardian Injunctions, 1547. In *Documents of the English Reformation*, edited by Gerald Bray. Minneapolis: Fortress Press, 1994.

The First and Second Prayer Books of Edward VI. Edited by E. C. S. Gibson. London: J. M. Dent & Sons Ltd., 1910.

The Forty-Two Articles. In *Documents of the English Reformation*, edited by Gerald Bray. Minneapolis: Fortress Press, 1994.

Speculum Sacerdotale. Edited by Edward H. Weatherly. Reprint, Oxford: Early English Text Society, 1988.

Trapp, J. B. *Erasmus, Colet and More: The Early Tudor Humanists and Their Books*. London: The British Library, 1991.

Valla, Lorenzo. *The Treatise of Lorenzo Valla on the Donation of Constantine*. Translated and edited by Christopher B. Coleman. Buffalo: Renaissance Society of America Reprint Texts, 1993.

Zwingli, Huldrych. *Commentary on True and False Religion*. In *The Protestant Reformation*, edited by Hans J. Hillerbrand. New York: Harper & Row, 1968.

Secondary Sources

Aldridge, J. W. *The Hermeneutic of Erasmus*. Zurich-Richmond: John Knox Press, 1966.

Alexander, Gina Mary Vere. "Bishop Bonner and the Parliament of 1559." *The Bulletin of the Institute of Historical Research* 56 (1983): 164–79.

_____. "Bonner and the Marian Persecutions." In *The English Reformation Revised*, edited by Christopher Haigh. Cambridge: Cambridge University Press, 1987.

_____. "The Life and Career of Edmund Bonner, Bishop of London, Until His Deprivation in 1549." Unpublished doctoral dissertation, University of London: 1960.

Anderson, Marvin W. "Peter Martyr, Reformed Theologian (1542–1562): His Letters to Heinrich Bullinger and John Calvin." *Sixteenth Century Journal* 4 (1973): 41–64.

Armstrong, C. D. C. "English Catholicism Rethought?" *The Journal of Ecclesiastical History* 53.1 (2002): 714–28.

_____. "Gardiner, Stephen (c. 1498x8–1555)." *Oxford Dictionary of National Biography*. Oxford: Oxford University Press, 2004. http://www.oxforddnb.com/view/article/10364, accessed 1 March 2006.

Ashley Null. *Thomas Cranmer's Doctrine of Repentance*. Oxford: Oxford University Press, 2000.

Aston, Margaret. "Lap Books and Lectern Books: The Revelatory Book in the Reformation." In *The Church and the Book: Papers Read at the 2000 Summer Meeting and the 2001 Winter Meeting of the Ecclesiastical History Society*, ed., R. N. Swanson. Rochester, New York: Boydell Press, 2004.

Bakhuizen van den Brink, J. N. "Ratramn's Eucharistic Doctrine and its Influence in 16th Century England." *Studies in Church History* 2 (1965): 54–77.

Béné, Charles. *Érasme et St. Augustin*. Travaux d'Humanisme et Renaissance 103. Geneva: Droz, 1969.

Betteridge, Thomas. "Truth and History in Foxe's *Acts and Monuments*." In *John Foxe and His World*, edited by Christopher Highly and John King. Aldershot: Ashgate, 2002.

Bishop, Edmund and Abbot Gasquet. *Edward the Sixth and the Book of Common Prayer—An Examination of its Origin and Early History: With an Appendix of Unpublished Documents*. Third edition. London: Burns and Oates, 1891.

Boyle, Margery O'Rourke. *Erasmus on Language and Method in Theology*. Toronto: University of Toronto Press, 1977.

Bradshaw, C. "Old, John (d. 1557)." *Oxford Dictionary of National Biography*. Oxford: Oxford University Press, 2004. http://www.oxforddnb.com/view/article/20673, accessed 23 Feb 2006.

Brennan, Michael G. "Grimald, Nicholas (*b.* 1519/20, *d.* in or before 1562)." *Oxford Dictionary of National Biography*. Oxford: Oxford University Press, 2004. http://www.oxforddnb.com/view/article/11629, accessed 13 August 2007.

Brigden, Susan. *London and the Reformation*. Oxford: Clarendon Press, 1989.

Bulzacchelli, Richard H. *Judged by the Law of Freedom: A History of the Faith-Works Controversy and a Resolution in the Thought of St. Thomas Aquinas*. New York: University Press of America, 2006.

Cameron, Euan. *The European Reformation*. Oxford: Clarendon Press, 1991.

Caplan, H. "The Four Senses of Scriptural Interpretation and the Medieval Theory of Preaching." In *Of Eloquence: Studies in Ancient and Mediaeval Rhetoric*. Ithaca, New York: Cornell University Press, 1970.

Carleton, Kenneth. "Bonner, Edmund (d. 1569)," *Oxford Dictionary of National Biography*. Oxford: Oxford University Press, 2004. http://www.oxforddnb.com/view/article/2850, accessed 23 Feb 2006.

Cavendish, George. *The Life and Death of Cardinal Wolsey*. Edited by R. S. Sylvester. Early English Text Society 243. London: Published for the Early English Text Society by the Oxford University Press, 1959.

Chibi, Andrew A. *Henry VIII's Conservative Scholar: Bishop John Stokesley and the Divorce, Royal Supremacy and Doctrinal Reform*. Bern: Lang, 1997.

Clark, Francis, S.J. *Eucharistic Sacrifice and the Reformation*. Oxford: Basil Blackwell, 1967.

Collinson, Patrick. "'A Magazine of Religious Patterns': An Erasmian Topic Transposed in English Protestantism." In *Godly People: Essays in English Protestantism and Puritanism*. London: Hambledon Press, 1983.

_____. "Truth and Legend: The Veracity of John Foxe's Book of Martyrs." In *Elizabethan Essays*. London: Hambledon Press, 1994.

_____. *Archbishop Grindal 1519–1583: The Struggle for a Reformed Church*. London: Jonathan Cape, 1979.

_____. *The Elizabethan Puritan Movement*. Oxford: Oxford University Press, 1989.

Coulson, Ian. *The History of Health and Medicine in Kent*. Kent: West Kent Health Authority, 1998.

Cross, Claire. "Lee, Edward (1481/2–1544)," *Oxford Dictionary of National Biography*. Oxford: Oxford University Press, 2004. http://www.oxforddnb.com/view/article/16278, accessed 1 Feb 2007.

Cummings, Brian. *The Literary Culture of the Reformation: Grammar and Grace*. Oxford: Oxford University Press, 2002.

Dowling, Maria. *Fisher of Men: A Life of John Fisher, 1469–1535*. London: Palgrave, 1999.

Duffy, Eamon. *Saints and Sinners: A History of the Popes*. Yale: Yale University Press, 2001.

_____. *The Stripping of the Altars*. New Haven: Yale University Press, 1992.

Evans, G. R. *The Language and Logic of the Bible: The Earlier Middle Ages*. Cambridge: Cambridge University Press, 1984.

Evenden, Elizabeth and Freeman, Thomas. "Print, Profit, and Propaganda: The Elizabethan Privy Council and the 1570 Edition of Foxe's 'Book of Martyrs.'" *The English Historical Review* 119 (2004): 1288–307.

Ford, Judith. "Watson, John (d. 1537)," *Oxford Dictionary of National Biography*. Oxford: Oxford University Press, 2004. http://www.oxforddnb.com/view/article/28843, accessed 30 May 2006.

Freeman, Thomas S. "Harpsfield, Nicholas (1519–1575)," *Oxford Dictionary of National Biography*. Oxford: Oxford University Press, 2004. http://www.oxforddnb.com/view/article/12369, accessed 1 Feb 2007.

Gerrish, B. A. *Grace and Gratitude: The Eucharistic Theology of John Calvin*. Minneapolis: Fortress Press, 1993.

Gnuse, Robert K. *The Authority of the Bible: Theories of Inspiration, Revelation, and the Canon of Scripture*. New York: Paulist Press: 1985.

Gogan, Brian. "The Ecclesiology of Erasmus of Rotterdam: A Genetic Account." *The Heythrop Journal* 21 (1981): 393–411.

Hoffman, Manfred. *Rhetoric and Theology: The Hermeneutic of Erasmus*. Toronto: University of Toronto Press, 1994.

Anthony N. S. Lane. "*Sola Scriptura?* Making Sense of a Post-Reformation Slogan." In *A Pathway into the Holy Scriptures*, edited by Philip E. Satterwhite and David F. Wright. Grand Rapids: Eerdmans, 1994.

Leader, Damien Rihel. *A History of the University of Cambridge*, Volume 1, *The University to 1546*. Cambridge: Cambridge University Press, 1988.

Levering, Matthew. *Christ's Fulfillment of Torah and Temple: Salvation According to Thomas Aquinas*. Notre Dame: University of Notre Dame Press, 2002.

Loades, David. *The Oxford Martyrs*. London: Batsford, 1970.

Lock, Julian. "Story, John (1503/4?–1571)," *Oxford Dictionary of National Biography*. Oxford: Oxford University Press, 2004. http://www.oxforddnb.com/view/article/26598, accessed 1 Feb 2007.

Lockyer, Roger. *Tudor and Stuart Britain: 1471–1714*. Essex: Longman, 1985.

Louisa, Angelo J. "Aldrich, Robert (1488/9–1556)," *Oxford Dictionary of National Biography*. Oxford: Oxford University Press, 2004. http://www.oxforddnb.com/view/article/315, accessed 16 June 2006.

MacCulloch, Diarmaid. *The Reformation*. New York: Viking, 2004.

_____. *Thomas Cranmer: A Life*. New Haven: Yale University Press, 1996.

Maclure, Millar. *Register of Sermons Preached at Paul's Cross*. Toronto: University of Toronto Press, 1958.

Margolin, Jean-Claude. "The Epistle to the Romans (Chapter 11) According to the Versions and/or Commentaries of Valla, Colet, Lefevre, and Erasmus." In *The Bible in the Sixteenth Century*, translated by John L. Farthing, Duke Monographs in Medieval and Renaissance Studies 11, edited by David Steinmetz. Durham: Duke University Press, 1990.

Marius, Richard. *Thomas More: A Biography*. New York: Vintage Books, 1985.

Marshall, Peter. *Religious Identities in Henry VIII's England*. Aldershot: Ashgate, 2006.

Mayer, T. F. "Lupset, Thomas (c. 1495–1530)," *Oxford Dictionary of National Biography*. Oxford: Oxford University Press, 2004. http://www.oxforddnb.com/view/article/17201, accessed 16 June 2006.

McLelland, Joseph C. *The Visible Words of God: An Exposition of the Sacramental Theology of Peter Martyr Vermigli*. London: Oliver and Boyd, 1957.

Miles, Leland. *John Colet and the Platonic Tradition*. London: Allen and Unwin, 1962.

Newcomb, Mark A. "We Understand His Benefits to be Greatest in the Sacrament." *The Anglican* 26.2 (): 9–14.

Newcombe, D. G. "Hooper, John (1495x1500–1555)," *Oxford Dictionary of National Biography*. Oxford: Oxford University Press, 2004. http://www.oxforddnb.com/view/article/13706, accessed 23 February 2006.

Nichols, Aidan, O.P. *The Shape of Catholic Theology*. Collegeville, Minnesota: The Liturgical Press, 1991.

Oberman, Heiko A. *Luther: Man Between God and the Devil*. Translated by Eileen Walliser-Schwarzbart. New York: Doubleday, 1992.

O'Malley, John W. "Grammar and Rhetoric in the Pietas of Erasmus." *The Journal of Medieval and Renaissance Studies* 18.1 (1988): 81–98.

_____. *Praise and Blame in Renaissance Rome: Rhetoric, Doctrine and Reform in the Sacred Orators of the Papal Court, c. 1450–1521.* Duke Monographs in Medieval and Renaissance Studies 3. Durham: Duke University Press, 1979.

_____. "Erasmus and Luther, Continuity and Discontinuity as Key to Their Conflict." *The Sixteenth Century Journal* 5.2 (1974): 47–65.

_____. "Erasmus and the History of Sacred Rhetoric: The Ecclesiastes of 1535." In *Religious Culture in the Sixteenth Century.* Brookfield, Vermont: Variorum, 1993.

Payne, J. B. "Toward the Hermeneutics of Erasmus." In *Scrinum Erasmianum* II, pp. 13–49. Leiden: Brill, 1969.

Pettegree, Andrew. *Marian Protestantism: Six Studies.* Brookfield, Vermont: Ashgate, 1996.

_____. *Foreign Protestant Communities in Sixteenth-Century London.* Oxford: Clarendon Press, 1986.

Redworth, Glyn. *In Defence of the Church Catholic: The Life of Stephen Gardiner.* Oxford: Basil Blackwell, 1990.

Rex, Richard. "The New Learning." *The Journal of Ecclesisatical History* 44 (1993): 26–44.

_____. "Ridley, Robert (d. 1536?)," *Oxford Dictionary of National Biography.* Oxford: Oxford University Press, 2004. http://www.oxforddnb.com/view/article/68881, accessed 23 February 2006.

_____. *The Theology of John Fisher.* Cambridge: Cambridge University Press, 2003.

_____. "Vavasour, Thomas (d. 1585)," *Oxford Dictionary of National Biography.* Oxford: Oxford University Press, 2004. http://www.oxforddnb.com/view/article/53524, accessed 5 August 2007.

Ridley, Gloucester. *The life of Dr. Nicholas Ridley, sometime Bishop of London: shewing the plan and progress of the Reformation.* London: 1763.

Ridley, Jasper. *Nicholas Ridley.* London: Longmans, Green & Co. LTD, 1957.

Riordan, Michael and Alec Ryrie. "Stephen Gardiner and the Making of a Protestant Villain." *Sixteenth Century Journal* 34 (2003): 1039–65.

Ryle, S. F. "Bryan, John (b. 1492/3, d. after 1521)," *Oxford Dictionary of National Biography*. Oxford: Oxford University Press, 2004. http://www.oxforddnb.com/view/article/3789, accessed 16 June 2006.

_____. "Bullock, Henry (d. 1526)," *Oxford Dictionary of National Biography*. Oxford: Oxford University Press, 2004. http://www.oxforddnb.com/view/article/3921, accessed 30 May 2006.

_____. "Cox, Leonard (*b. c.*1495, *d.* in or after 1549)", *Oxford Dictionary of National Biography*. Oxford: Oxford University Press, 2004. http://www.oxforddnb.com/view/article/6525, accessed 13 August 2007.

Ryrie, Alec. "The Problems of Legitimacy and Precedent in English Protestantism, 1539–1547." In *Protestant History and Identity in Sixteenth-Century Europe*, volume 1, *The Medieval Inheritance*, edited by Bruce Gordon. Brookfield, Vermont: Scolar Press, 1996.

Sider, Robert D. "Historical Imagination and the Representation of Paul in Erasmus' Paraphrases on the Pauline Epistles." In *Holy Scripture Speaks: the Production and Reception of Erasmus' Paraphrases on the New Testament*, edited by Hilmar M. Pabel and Mark Vessey. Toronto: University of Toronto Press, 2006.

Steinmetz, David. Introduction to *The Bible in the Sixteenth Century*, Duke Monographs in Medieval and Renaissance Studies 11. Durham: Duke University Press, 1990.

_____. *The Superiority of Pre-Critical Exegesis. Theology Today* 37.1 (1980): 27–38.

Taplin, Mark. "Vermigli, Pietro Martire [Peter Martyr] (1499–1562)," *Oxford Dictionary of National Biography*. Oxford: Oxford University Press, 2004. http://www.oxforddnb.com/view/article/28225, accessed 23 July 2007.

Thompson, D. F. S. *The Latinity of Erasmus*. Edited by T. A. Dorey. Albuquerque: University of New Mexico, 1970.

Torrance, Thomas F. "The Hermeneutics of Erasmus." In *Probing the Reformed Tradition: Historical Studies in Honor of Edward A. Dowey Jr.*, edited by E. A. McKee and B.G. Armstrong. Louisville, Kentucky: John Knox Press, 1989.

Trapp, J. B. "Colet, John (1467–1519)," *Oxford Dictionary of National Biography*. Oxford: Oxford University Press, 2004. http://www.oxforddnb.com/view/article/5898, accessed 1 Feb 2007.

Trinkhaus, Charles. *In Our Image and Likeness:* Humanity and Divinity in Italian Humanist Thought, volume 1. London: Constable, 1970.

Tudor, Philippa. "Protestant Books in London in Mary Tudor's Reign." *London Journal* 15 (1990): 15–28.

Wabuda, Susan. *Preaching During the English Reformation*. Cambridge: Cambridge University Press, 2002.

_____. "Bishops and the Provision of Homilies, 1520 to 1547." *Sixteenth Century Journal* 25.3 (1994): 551–66.

_____. "Equivocation and Recantation During the English Reformation: The 'Subtle Shadows' of Dr. Edward Crome." *The Journal of Ecclesiastical History* 44.2 (1993): 224–43.

_____. "Ridley, Nicholas (c. 1502–1555)," *Oxford Dictionary of National Biography*. Oxford: Oxford University Press, 2004. http://www.oxforddnb.com/view/article/23631, accessed 23 February 2006.

_____. "Crome, Edward (d. 1562)," *Oxford Dictionary of National Biography*. Oxford: Oxford University Press, 2004. http://www.oxforddnb.com/view/article/6749, accessed 23 February 2006.

_____. "Bell, John (d. 1556)," *Oxford Dictionary of National Biography*. Oxford: Oxford University Press, 2004. http://www.oxforddnb.com/view/article/2010, accessed 24 Feb 2006.

_____. "The Woman with the Rock: The Controversies on Women and Bible Reading." In *Belief and Practice in Reformation England: A Tribute to Patrick Collinson from His Students*, edited by Susan Wabuda and Caroline Litzenberger. Aldershot: Ashgate, 1998.

Wall, Sarah E. "Editing Anne Askew's *Examinations*: John Bale, Foxe,

John. and Early Modern Textual Practices." In *John Foxe and his World*, edited by Christopher Highley and John N. King. Burlington, Vermont: Ashgate, 2002.

Watt, Diane. "Askew, Anne (*c.*1521–1546)," *Oxford Dictionary of National Biography*. Oxford: Oxford University Press, 2004. http://www.oxforddnb.com. /view/article/798, accessed 13 August 2007.

Wizeman, William, S.J. *The Theology and Spirituality of Mary Tudor's Church*. Burlington, Vermont: Ashgate, 2006.

_____. "Harpsfield, John (1516–1578)," *Oxford Dictionary of National Biography.* Oxford: Oxford University Press, 2004. http://www.oxforddnb.com/view/article/12368, accessed 1 Feb 2007.

Wooding, L. E. C. "Pendleton, Henry (d. 1557)," *Oxford Dictionary of National Biography.* Oxford: Oxford University Press, 2004. http://www.oxforddnb.com/view/article/21863, accessed 1 Feb 2007.

_____. "Peryn, William (d. 1558)," *Oxford Dictionary of National Biography.* Oxford: Oxford University Press, 2004. http://www.oxforddnb.com/view/article/22007, accessed 1 Feb 2007.

Woolfson, Jonathan. "Croke, Richard (1489–1558)," *Oxford Dictionary of National Biography.* Oxford: Oxford University Press, 2004. http://www.oxforddnb.com/view/article/6734, accessed 30 May 2006.

Timeline of Major Events

October 28, 1466
Gerrit Gerritszoon, later known as Desiderius Erasmus, Humanist scholar, is born in Rotterdam.

January 1467
John Colet, later a Humanist scholar, Oxford theologian, and Dean of St. Paul's Cathedral, is born in London.

c. 1485
Thomas Cromwell, later chief minister to Henry VIII, architect of Henry's break with Rome and the dissolution of the monasteries, is born in Putney, Surrey.

August 22, 1485
Harri Tudur becomes King of England by defeating Richard III at the Battle of Bosworth Field. Harri becomes Henry VII and establishes the Tudor dynasty.

July 2, 1489
Thomas Cranmer, later Archbishop of Canterbury, is born in Aslockton, Nottinghamshire.

June 28, 1491
Henry Tudor, later King Henry VIII, is born at Greenwich Palace in London.

1493–1496
John Colet studies in France and Italy, becoming a devotee of Italian Humanism.

c. 1498

Edmund Bonner, later Bishop of Hereford and London, is born in Hanley, Worcestershire.

1498

Erasmus visits England for the first time. His friendship and conversations with John Colet, Humanist scholar and Oxford theologian, inspire Erasmus to study the scriptures critically, as historical source texts. Erasmus' arguments with Colet about the correct interpretation of key passages of scripture presage the Reformation controversies concerning the Bible and what it prescribes for ecclesiastical life and lay devotion.

c. 1500

Nicholas Ridley, later Bishop of Rochester and London, is born near Tynedale in the North of England.

November 14, 1501

Henry VII's oldest son, Arthur, Prince of Wales, is married to Catherine of Aragon.

April 2, 1502

Arthur, Prince of Wales and oldest son of Henry VII, dies at the age of 16. The succession passes to Arthur's younger brother, Henry.

August–December 1503

Henry VII and his eldest surviving son petition the pope for a dispensation to permit young Henry to marry his brother's widow, Catherine of Aragon. The dispensation is granted in December 1503, the accompanying Bull arrives in England in 1504, but Henry VII nevertheless delays the marriage.

1505

John Colet, Humanist scholar, becomes Dean of St. Paul's Cathedral.

c. 1508

John Colet re-founds St. Paul's as a Humanist grammar school, modeled on classical ideals of education.

April 21, 1509

Henry VII dies, and his oldest surviving son succeeds to the throne as Henry VIII.

June 11, 1509

Henry VIII marries Catherine of Aragon, one of his first acts as king. He was not quite 18; Catherine was 23. Catherine was the first of Henry's six wives.

c. 1512

Edmund Bonner enters Broadgates Hall, later Pembroke College, Oxford.

February 18, 1516

Mary Tudor, later Queen Mary I, is born in London. Mary becomes the only surviving child of Henry VIII's marriage to Catherine of Aragon.

March 1, 1516

Erasmus publishes his *Novum Instrumentum*, which includes the Greek text of the New Testament and a revision to the text of the Latin Vulgate scriptures, at Basle.

c. 1518

Nicholas Ridley enters Pembroke College, Cambridge.

1519

Erasmus publishes the second edition of his Greek New Testament, now called the *Novum Testamentum*. Replacing the text of the Vulgate with his own Latin translation, he renders the Prologue of John's Gospel to declare that Christ is the "Speech" (*sermo*) of God.

September 10, 1519

John Colet, Humanist scholar and Dean of St. Paul's Cathedral, dies.

1525–1532

Henry VIII becomes increasingly worried and frustrated that his marriage to Catherine of Aragon has not produced a male heir to the throne. He begins a campaign to petition the Pope to annul his marriage to Catherine.

October 1, 1532

Thomas Cranmer is appointed Archbishop of Canterbury by Henry VIII. Cranmer is already sympathetic to many Lutheran ideas about the Church and the sacraments by this date.

1532–1533

Henry determines to carry out his threat to break with Rome so that he can remarry. He works with Thomas Cromwell to press Parliament to grant the king new powers over the Church. Henry gives official support to some Protestant reforms down through the 1530s, to obtain the aid of Cromwell and reformist clergy like Thomas Cranmer, Archbishop of Canterbury, in reorganizing the English Church.

January 25, 1533

Henry VIII is married to Anne Boleyn, the second of six wives, in a secret ceremony conducted by Thomas Cranmer.

May 23, 1533

Thomas Cranmer declares the marriage of Henry VIII to Catherine of Aragon to be null and void.

September 7, 1533

Elizabeth Tudor, later Queen Elizabeth I, is born in London. Elizabeth becomes the only surviving child of Henry VIII's marriage to Anne Boleyn.

1534

Parliament passes the Act of Supremacy, declaring Henry VIII to be the head of the Church in England.

1536

Henry VIII, with the aid of his chief minister, Thomas Cromwell, begins a campaign to dissolve the monasteries of England and seize their property for the crown. By winter, the Pilgrimage of Grace, a series of religious uprisings in the North of England, is underway. The pilgrims protest, among other things, the suppression of religious houses.

May 30, 1536
Henry VIII is married to Jane Seymour, his third of six wives.

July 12, 1536
Desiderius Erasmus, Humanist Scholar, dies at Basle.

October 12, 1537
Edward Tudor, later King Edward VI, is born at Hampton Court. Edward becomes the only surviving child of Henry VIII's marriage to Jane Seymour.

November 27, 1538
Edmund Bonner is promoted to the episcopate, being named Bishop of Hereford.

1539
Edmund Bonner is instrumental in having the "Great Bible," an English translation of the Old and New Testaments, imprinted at Paris. After French authorities seize some of the printed sheets, the work is completed in London. Bonner gives copies of the completed English New Testament to friends as gifts.

1539
Parliament passes the *Act of Six Articles*, marking the end of official doctrinal reform under Henry VIII. Reflecting Henry's will in ecclesiastical practices, the Act affirmed, among other points of traditional doctrine, transubstantiation, clerical celibacy, private masses for departed souls, and lay confession to priests for the absolution of sins. Passage of the Act and its subsequent enforcement, were viewed by leading reformist clergy, as a major reversal.

April 4, 1540
Edmund Bonner is consecrated Bishop of London under Henry VIII.

July 28, 1540
Thomas Cromwell, chief minister to Henry VIII, architect of Henry's break with Rome and the dissolution of the monasteries, is beheaded on Tower Hill. Cromwell was indicted on charges of corruption, heresy, and treason. Henry later expresses regret for having Cromwell executed.

1541
The dissolution of the monasteries is completed, and the crown appropriates the estates and wealth of the religious houses.

January 28, 1547
Henry VIII dies. His son Edward succeeds to the throne as King Edward VI. Under Edward, the government is decidedly Protestant, ushering in major reforms of the Church. The First and Second *Books of Common Prayer* were issued by Thomas Cranmer during Edward's reign.

July 1547
The Injunctions of Edward VI are promulgated, calling for every cleric to obtain at their own expense, copies of the New Testament in Latin and English, and the *Paraphrases* of Erasmus on the books of the New Testament. The injunctions specify that every cleric is to study the scriptures by comparing the biblical text with Erasmus' works. The new religious settlement also establishes the ritual of the Poor Men's Chest as a part of Communion.

September 1547
Nicholas Ridley is promoted to the episcopate by Thomas Cranmer, becoming Bishop of Rochester. Ridley persuades Cranmer in 1546 or 1547 to embrace the idea that Christ is hypostatically present, through his divinity only, in the Eucharist.

December 1547
At the invitation of Thomas Cranmer, Peter Martyr Vermigli arrives in England and befriends Nicholas Ridley.

April 25, 1549
At the invitation of Thomas Cranmer, Martin Bucer, reformer of the Strasbourg church, arrives in England.

June 1549
Nicholas Ridley pronounces against Transubstantiation in a debate on the Eucharist at Cambridge.

October 1, 1549
Edmund Bonner is deprived of the bishopric of London by Thomas Cranmer, Nicholas Ridley, and other authorities who wanted to better establish Protestantism in the capital. Bonner is imprisoned for the rest of Edward's reign.

1550
Nicholas Ridley is translated to the see of London, recently made vacant by Edmund Bonner's trial and imprisonment.

April 1550–March 1551
The Vestment Controversy ensues between John Hooper (c.1497–1555), bishop-elect of Gloucester, and Nicholas Ridley, Bishop of London.

July 6, 1553
King Edward VI dies, and an attempt is made to place Jane Grey on the throne.

July 9, 1553
Nicholas Ridley preaches a sermon at Paul's Cross in London, declaring princesses Mary and Elizabeth to be ineligible, as bastards of Henry VIII, to rule. Mary Tudor succeeds to the throne ten days later as Queen Mary I, and on 26 July, orders that Ridley be committed to the Tower of London.

August 5, 1553
Edmund Bonner pardoned by Mary I, under the Great Seal of England. Bonner returned to his former livings at St. Paul's that same day.

September 3, 1554
Edmund Bonner launches his episcopal visitation, or formal review, of the Diocese of London under Mary I. The visitation opens with the official publication of his injunction articles, the standards of review for faith and morals in the diocese.

July 1555
Edmund Bonner, Bishop of London, issued *A profitable and necessarye doctrine* in 1555, which was modeled closely on the *King's Book* of 1536.

September 1555
Edmund Bonner, Bishop of London, publishes a book of sermons entitled *Homelies*. The format of the volume closely follows that of Thomas Cranmer's 1547 *Book of Homilies*.

October 16, 1555
Nicholas Ridley is burnt at the stake under Mary I for heresy. Hugh Latimer is executed with Ridley just outside the city wall of Oxford.

March 21, 1556
Thomas Cranmer is burnt at the stake under Mary I for heresy. Like Ridley and Latimer, he is executed just outside the city wall of Oxford.

November 17, 1558
Queen Mary I dies and Elizabeth Tudor succeeds to the throne as Queen Elizabeth I.

April 20, 1560
Edmund Bonner is imprisoned under Elizabeth I.

September 5, 1569
Edmund Bonner dies in prison. For fear of riots, he is buried at midnight in the churchyard of St. George's Southwark. His body is later removed to St. Michael's Church, Copford, Essex.

Glossary of Key Terms and Concepts

abrenunciation — a swearing off or abjuration. From ancient times, Baptism in the Church involved a three-fold abjuration of "Satan and all his works."

Actes and Monuments *(of these Latter and Perillous Days, Touching Matters of the Church)* — the official title of John Foxe's *Book of Martyrs*, a sixteenth-century chronicle of early English Protestant martyrs.

Act of Six Articles — passed by Parliament in 1539, this legislation defined the terms of religious doctrine and practice under Henry VIII until his death. Reflecting Henry's will in ecclesiastical practices, the Act affirmed, among other points of traditional doctrine, transubstantiation, clerical celibacy, private masses for departed souls, and lay confession to priests for the absolution of sins. Passage of the Act and its subsequent enforcement, were viewed by leading reformist clergy, such as Thomas Cranmer, Archbishop of Canterbury under Henry VIII, as a major reversal.

adiaphora — literally, "indifferent things" in Greek, refers to church teachings that are deemed to be nonessential, because they do not touch directly on moral or doctrinal issues. Nicholas Ridley, Bishop of London under Edward VI, described the times for Christian worship, for example, as *adiaphora*.

bead roll — a list of people to be prayed for, by their special request. In medieval Europe, a person's last will and testament might provide for a stipend or benefice to clergy for saying public or private prayers for the soul of the deceased.

benefice — an ecclesiastical stipend for a permanent appointment, often accompanied by a grant of property.

Bishops' Book — the unofficial title of Thomas Cranmer's *The Institution of a Christian Man* from the time of its publication in 1536. Henry VIII annotated and revised Cranmer's work, issuing the much more traditional *King's Book* in 1543. In 1555, Edmund Bonner, Bishop of London under Mary I, issued *A profitable and necessarye doctrine*, which was modeled closely on the *King's Book*.

Book of Homilies — published by Thomas Cranmer in 1547, these sermons were part of an effort to provide for the dissemination of Protestant doctrine, especially justification by faith alone, from Edwardine pulpits. The sermons were to be preached throughout the realm on appointed Sundays. In 1555, Edmund Bonner, Bishop of London under Mary I, issued his *Homelies*, which included two sermons originally issued in Cranmer's *Book of Homilies* in 1547.

collation (of a minister) — the official appointment of a cleric to office. A prebend, or ecclesiastical stipend, was often provided to medieval cathedral clergy, following such an appointment.

colophon — a publisher's ornamental imprint, often appearing on the title page of early printed books.

cure — a cleric's pastoral responsibility for a parish or region. An episcopal cure or see refers to a bishop's pastoral duties for a diocese.

chrismation or **chrysmation** — the anointing with holy oil that accompanies confirmation.

Definition of Chalcedon — the official proclamation of the Church, gathered in an Ecumenical Council in 451 A.D., that Christ is one person in two natures, fully human, and fully divine. The Definition states that these two natures are not to be conceived of as conflated, nor contrasted with respect to place. It also states that Christ's humanity is not subsumed into His divinity.

deliberative rhetoric — one of the basic forms of classical oratory, it describes speech or writing that is aimed at inducing an audience to take action, or to persuade an audience not to take an action suggested by another speaker or an event. Erasmian Humanism is characterized by an adherence to this form of classical oratory, resulting in a model for biblical exegesis where primary importance is placed in the words of Christ in the New Testament as the "Speech" of God to man.

deprivation (of a cleric) — official removal from ecclesiastical office. Under Edward VI, Edmund Bonner, Bishop of London, was removed from or deprived of his see on October 1, 1549 by religious authorities who wanted to better establish Protestantism in the capital.

dirige — medieval and early modern term for a Church service commemorating departed souls. The English word "dirge" is derived from this term and practice.

epideictic rhetoric — one of the basic forms of classical oratory, it describes speech or writing that is aimed at ascribing praise or blame. Italian Humanism is characterized by an adherence to this form of classical oratory, resulting in a model of biblical exegesis that presents the whole of scripture, the Old Testament and the New, as a single, comprehensive narrative of Salvation History, the monumental acts of God in the process of His redemption of man.

exegesis — the interpretation or explication of a text, especially scripture.

ecclesiology — the branch of Theology concerned with the nature and role of the Church.

ecclesiological — of or pertaining to the church.

Foxe's *Book of Martyrs* — the unofficial title of John Foxe's *Actes and Monuments of these Latter and Perillous Days, Touching Matters of the Church*, his chronicle of the lives and deaths of early Protestant martyrs.

Humanism (or Renaissance Humanism) — a general description of currents in the intellectual life and scholarship of Europe and England emerging at the end of the late-medieval period. Characterized by a renewal of interest in ancient Roman and Greek ideas and texts, this intellectual movement became dominant by the early part of the sixteenth century. Scholars associated with this movement promoted classical ideas about education and the training of the mind, as part of the revival of ancient Rhetoric.

installation (of a bishop) — the first diocesan appointment of anyone ordained as a bishop. If a bishop is transferred to another diocese, he is "translated" to the new see, not installed.

King's Book — promulgated in 1543, this was the official primer or catechism of Henrician England. It contained sections on the Nicene Creed, the Ten Commandments, the Lord's Prayer, the Hail Mary, and prayers for departed souls. It represents Henry VIII's revision of Thomas Cranmer's *The Institution of a Christian Man* (1536). Cranmer's work, known informally as *The Bishops' Book* from its publication in 1536, was much more reformist than Henry's. Edmund Bonner, Bishop of London, issued *A profitable and necessarye doctrine* in 1555, which was modeled closely on the *King's Book* of 1536.

month's mind — a requiem mass celebrated a month after a person's death, for the benefit of his or her soul.

neo-Platonism — a philosophical theory about the origin of the universe based on the works of Plotinus (c. 205–270 A.D.). Plotinus and his followers believed that humans must transcend the world of material creation, which they characterized as ontologically deficient, noting that the physical world is subject to change and decay. The human mental ascent above the material was understood as contemplation of the eternal Universal Good. Neo-Platonic dualisms are characteristic of Erasmus' *philosophia Christi*, his description of the teachings of Jesus.

philology — the study of languages and the changes in words and word forms as found in historical texts. Such studies enabled Renaissance Humanists to deduce the relative date and origins of various writings, including the canonical scriptures.

Pilgrimage of Grace —a collective term for the series of uprisings originating in the North of England that were prompted by Henry VIII's break with Rome and suppression of religious houses. Thomas Cranmer and Thomas Cromwell were the targets of many of the rioters' fury. About 180 leaders were executed by hanging and/or drawing and quartering in the wake of these rebellions.

prebend — an ecclesiastical stipend, often provided to a member of a cathedral chapter, following official appointment to office, or collation.

Sacramentarians — sixteenth-century Protestants who wholly rejected the doctrine of the Christ's True Presence in the Eucharist. Those who subscribed to such views, which were characteristic of several strands of Swiss Protestantism, were attacked by both Catholic and Lutheran apologists alike.

translation (of a bishop) — the transfer of a bishop from one diocese to another diocese. Persons newly ordained to the episcopate are "installed" in their first episcopal cure, but "translated" to a new diocese if they are subsequently assigned to another see.

trental — a common Church practice in the late medieval period, where thirty Requiem masses are offered, one each day, for thirty consecutive days, for a departed soul.

visitation — in Canon Law, the official inspection of a cleric of his cure upon assuming office. On September 3, 1554, Edmund Bonner launched his episcopal visitation of the Diocese of London after being set at liberty by Queen Mary I in July of 1553. In September of 1554, he was then resuming his see after being removed and imprisoned under Edward VI.

Biographical Index of Main Persons

Anne Askew (c. 1520–1546) — Early English Protestant who distributed Bibles and gave public lectures on the scriptures in 1540s London. Although married to Thomas Kyme when she was fifteen, Anne refused to adopt his surname and later sought a divorce from her husband, arguing that he was not a believer. She was arrested twice on suspicion of heresy, once in 1545 and again in 1546. Both Edmund Bonner and Nicholas Ridley were among those who examined Askew. Anne was interrogated repeatedly and even placed upon the rack, in an effort to induce her to name some of the other persons in her Protestant circle, which may have included both the Duchess of Suffolk (c. 1520–1580) and Queen Catherine Parr (1512–1548), Henry's sixth and last wife. Anne was eventually convicted of heresy, and burnt at the stake.

St. Athanasius of Alexandria (c. 297–373) — Early Church Father and Patriarch of Alexandria. He attended the council of Nicea in 325, where he led the effort to combat the Arian heresy.

Anne Boleyn (c. 1503–1536) — Queen consort of England and second wife of Henry VIII. Henry's early desire for Anne, and her refusal to be seduced by him, prompted Henry to seek annulment of his marriage with Catherine of Aragon (1485–1536). Henry hoped that his marriage to Anne would bring forth the long-sought legitimate male heir necessary to stabilize the succession. The only child to survive from Anne's marriage to Henry, however, was Elizabeth Tudor, who reigned as Elizabeth I from 1558–1603.

Edmund Bonner (c. 1498–1569) — Bishop of London under Henry VIII and Mary I. Bonner studied civil and canon law at Oxford, and served as a commissioner for Thomas Wolsey (1473–1530), and, in the last 18 months of the Cardinal's life, served as his personal secretary. Bonner was an ambassador to France and Italy for King Henry VIII under the direction of Thomas Cromwell (c. 1485–1540), and worked to advance Henry's divorce suit. Bonner probably became acquainted with the ideas of the Italian Humanists during his delegations abroad. Bonner was deprived of his see and imprisoned in 1549, where he remained until the death of Edward VI in July of 1553. Restored to his episcopal cure under Mary, Bonner became a leader in the re-establishment of Catholicism in the realm, editing and publishing orthodox sermons and catechisms for the lay faithful. Bonner was committed to the Marshalsea prison under Elizabeth, where he died in 1569 for refusing the Oath of Supremacy. For fear of riots, Bonner's body was buried at midnight in the churchyard of St. George's Southwark, adjacent to the Marshalsea prison. At some later point, Bonner's body was removed to St. Michael's, Copford, in Colchester, and placed under the floor on the north side of the altar.

Antonio Bonvisi (d. 1558) — Successful banker and wool trader whose Italian family resided in England from before his birth. A very successful businessman, Bonvisi counted Cardinal Thomas Wolsey (1473–1530) among his chief patrons. Bonvisi was a close friend of and patron to many Humanists, especially Thomas More (1478–1535). Bonvisi maintained close ties with his Italian relatives and friends, enabling many promising, young English scholars to study in Italy, where they became acquainted with several leading Italian Humanists and their ideas. After Thomas More's execution in 1535, many of the Catholics that would play a prominent role in the re-establishment of English Catholicism under Mary I, gathered around Bonvisi and were part of his household. This pattern continued even after Bonvisi left England in 1550, during the reign of Edward VI. Taking up residence in Louvain, Bonvisi's house guests in 1550 included Nicholas Harpsfield (1519–1575), later Archdeacon of Canterbury under Mary I.

Martin Bucer (1491–1551) — Protestant reformer of the Church of Strasbourg, educated at Heidelberg and Mainz. Bucer entered the

Dominican order in his youth, but after meeting Martin Luther (1483–1546) in 1518, embraced the ideas of the Wittenberg reformer. Bucer succeeded in having his religious vows annulled in 1521. Bucer took up residence in Strasbourg in 1523, and worked for many years, unsuccessfully, to reconcile Luther and Zwingli (1484–1531) on the question of the Eucharist. Bucer advocated for Protestant unity to such an extent that he was sometimes ridiculed for what many other Protestant theologians took to be his overly conciliatory positions. In 1549, Bucer accepted Thomas Cranmer's (1489–1556) invitation to seek asylum in England, as the reformation in Strasbourg underwent a major reversal. Cranmer appointed Bucer Regius Professor of Divinity at Cambridge. Although Cranmer consulted Bucer for the revision of the 1549 *Book of Common Prayer*, Bucer did not play a direct role in the reformation of the English church, since he died in less than two years after arriving in England, and was very ill for much of this time.

Heinrich Bullinger (1504–1575) — Swiss reformer, the disciple and successor of Huldrych Zwingli (1484–1531) as head of the Zurich church. From the 1550s, Bullinger's work enjoyed a wide distribution in England, especially during the reign of Edward VI. Bullinger was a prolific correspondent, frequently exchanging letters with many of the English reformers both before and during the reign of Mary I.

John Calvin (1509–1564) — French reformer of the Church of Geneva. A leading figure of the Protestant Reformation, his major work, *The Institutes of the Christian Religion* were deeply influential as a kind of Protestant *summa* for many later reformers. Calvin came to prominence in Geneva after 1539 when the city council asked him to respond to a letter from Cardinal Sadoleto (1477–1547), Italian Humanist and bishop of Carpentras. Sadoleto's letter invited the Genevans to return to the Catholic faith. Although Calvin had been expelled from Geneva the previous year, and was then living in Strasbourg, the Genevans still asked Calvin to write a response to Sadoleto. Calvin accepted the invitation, which led to his being asked to return and lead the church in Geneva. Calvin was an admirer of Luther's ideas, but was a more systematic thinker, and advanced a more symbolic view of Christ's presence in the

Eucharist than did the Wittenberg reformer. Calvin organized the very strict ecclesiastical government of sixteenth-century Geneva, attempting to ensure that its citizens conformed to his understanding of the scriptural ideals of a Christian society.

Catherine of Aragon (1485–1536) — The first of his six wives, Catherine was married to Henry VIII on June 11, 1509, in one of Henry's first acts as king. He was not quite 18, and Catherine was 23. Catherine was unable to bear Henry a male heir to the throne, and by the latter 1520s, Henry determined this circumstance suggested that his marriage to Catherine was invalid, and that God was displeased because Henry had married his brother's widow. Catherine appealed her case to Rome, and Henry eventually broke with Rome to avoid sentence against him in his divorce suit. Henry appointed Thomas Cranmer (1489–1556) to declare the king's marriage to Catherine to be null and void, on May 23, 1533, some five months after the king was married to Anne Boleyn, in a secret ceremony that had been conducted by Cranmer himself.

St. John Chrysostom (344–407) — Early Church Father and Archbishop of Constantinople. Renowned for his preaching and bold denunciation of sin, he was banished multiple times by powerful and profligate enemies.

John Colet (1467–1519) — English Humanist and Dean of St. Paul's Cathedral in London. Colet was educated at Oxford, and travelled to the Continent in 1493 to further his studies in Paris and Italy, where he became the friend and admirer of a number of Italian Humanists. Colet returned to England in 1496, and lectured at Oxford on the epistles of St. Paul. Colet's lectures focused on the historical context of Paul and his writings, an innovative approach at that time that brought a stir of interest in Colet and his work. Colet met and befriended Erasmus at Oxford in 1498. His friendship with Colet inspired Erasmus to study the scriptures critically, as historical source texts. Colet was appointed Dean of St. Paul's Cathedral in 1505, and in London, became the friend and spiritual director of Thomas More. In 1509, Colet began re-founding St. Paul's School, establishing it along classical lines, which reflected his Humanist ideals.

Thomas Cranmer (1489–1556) — Archbishop of Canterbury under Henry VIII. Suggested that the universities should determine the validity of Henry's marriage to Catherine of Aragon. Ecclesiastical leader for advancing Protestantism in England, Cranmer coordinated and contributed the greater part of the work for the 1549 and 1552 *Books of Common Prayer*. He was burnt at the stake for heresy during the reign of Mary I.

Thomas Cromwell (c. 1485–1540) — English politician and chief minister of Henry VIII. A brilliant legal and administrative strategist, Cromwell engineered and organized Henry's break with Rome and the annulment of the King's marriage to Catherine of Aragon (1485–1536). Cromwell was a leading supporter of early Protestant clergy in the 1530s, and directed the Parliamentary campaign that led to the dissolution of the monasteries. Ironically, Henry VIII's marital troubles brought Cromwell into prominence, but were also his undoing. In 1540, Cromwell arranged for Henry to be married to Anne of Cleves (1515–1557), as a way to cement relations with Lutheran forces on the Continent. Henry had a great aversion to Anne's physical appearance, and blamed Cromwell for the unfortunate match. In the King's resentment, Cromwell's enemies found their opportunity to destroy Henry's chief minister, who was arrested in June of 1540 and imprisoned in the Tower. Cromwell was beheaded on 28 July 1540.

Edward VI (1537–1553) — Son of King Henry VIII by Jane Seymour, Henry's third wife. Edward's reign was marked by sweeping Protestant reforms of the English Church, led by Thomas Cranmer (1489–1556), Archbishop of Canterbury and Nicholas Ridley (c. 1500–1555), Bishop of London. Edward's uncle, the Duke of Somerset (c. 1506–1552), held substantial power as Lord Protector of England in the early part of Edward's reign. After Somerset's fall from power in 1549, the Duke of Northumberland (1504–1553), became the President of Edward's Council, implementing religious reforms favored by the King and his advisors.

Elizabeth I (1533–1603) — Queen regnant of England and Ireland from November 1558 until her death. Elizabeth was the sole surviving child of Henry VIII's marriage with his second wife, Anne Boleyn. Following the short reign of her Catholic half-sister, Mary I (1516–1558), Elizabeth worked to stabilize the realm by fostering a distinctly English Protestant national identity, which was at first slow to form. Especially after Pope Pius V excommunicated Elizabeth in 1570, Catholic worship was illegal, and Catholic clergy were sought out and destroyed. By the end of the second decade of her reign, England was very much a Protestant nation.

Desiderius Erasmus (1466–1536) — Dutch Humanist, scholar of Greek, and biblical translator. Erasmus did more than any other Renaissance scholar to promote the study of Greek and to revive classical philosophy, education, and rhetoric. Born Gerrit Gerritszoon in Rotterdam, he attended the school of the "Brothers of the Common Life" at Deventer. Erasmus was an Augustinian friar and priest when in 1492, he came to the attention of the Bishop of Cambrai, who made Erasmus his private secretary. The bishop sent Erasmus to study at the Collège de Montaigu in Paris. Living in Paris and supporting himself as a tutor to a number of English scholars, he made his first visit to England in 1498. His friendship with John Colet inspired Erasmus to study the scriptures critically, as historical source texts. Erasmus befriended Thomas More on his second visit to England in 1506, the same year that Erasmus made his first visit to Italy. In 1509, Erasmus visited England for the third time, and was appointed Lady Margaret Professor of Greek at Cambridge. Erasmus published a critical edition of the Greek New Testament in 1516, entitled the *Novum Instrumentum*. The second edition followed in 1519, under the title *Novum Testamentum*, and featured Erasmus' own Latin translation of the Greek text. In this version, Erasmus rendered the Prologue of John's Gospel to declare that Christ is the "Speech" (*sermo*) of God.

St. John Fisher (d. June 22, 1535) — Bishop of Rochester under Henry VIII and Catholic apologist. Educated at Cambridge in the 1580s, Fisher's mentor, William Melton, was one of the earliest exponents of Humanist learning at the University. Fisher was chaplain and confessor of Lady Margaret Beaufort (1433–1509), mother of Henry VII. As Vice-Chancellor of Cambridge, Fisher managed, through the patronage of

Lady Margaret, to attract leading scholars to the University, and to establish two colleges. Fisher was made Bishop of Rochester in 1504 at the personal insistence of Henry VII. Fisher was as pure in his living as he was nimble of mind, and many of his friends and visitors marveled at the austere life that Fisher maintained at Rochester. When Henry VIII began the process of seeking an annulment of his marriage to Catherine of Aragon (1485–1536), Fisher became the Queen's staunchest defender, writing several treatises that demolished the arguments assembled by Henry's supporters. The astounding range of Fisher's knowledge is on full display in these works. Fisher's public support of Queen Catherine, formalized in his refusal to sign the Oath of Succession, were the real grounds for Fisher's imprisonment in the Tower in 1534. The official pretext for Fisher's arrest, however, was his association with the so-called Holy Maid of Kent, Elizabeth Barton, an alleged mystic and prophetess who proclaimed that Henry VIII would soon die if he did not repent of his intent to divorce Catherine. Committed to the Tower in April of 1534, Fisher endured the adversities of prison with calm resignation. Fisher was first sentenced to be hanged, drawn, and quartered, but Henry VIII feared that Fisher would live to the feast of John the Baptist (June 24), to whom many Londoners were comparing Fisher at the time. The King therefore commuted Fisher's punishment to beheading, which was carried out on June 22, 1535.

John Frith (1503–1533) — Early English Protestant polemicist, and friend of William Tyndale (c. 1494 – 1536), the pioneering translator of the scriptures into early modern English. Frith was a disciple of Oecolampadius' (1482–1531) and Huldrych Zwingli's (1484–1531) views on purgatory and the Eucharist, arguing that the sacrament was a memorial of Christ, who was not present in the consecrated elements. Educated at Cambridge, Frith was imprisoned when, in the course of advancing his studies at Oxford, he and nine companions were found to possess several Protestant books. Frith fled to the continent on his release in 1525, where he wrote several polemical attacks on purgatory and transubstantiation. Frith's Protestant writings elicited several replies in print from Thomas More (1478–1535) and John Fisher (d. June 22, 1535). In 1532, Frith returned to England, and was arrested under a warrant issued by Thomas

More, then Lord Chancellor. More and several others examined Frith, who continued to publish his views from prison. For this reason, and for denying purgatory and the Real Presence of Christ in the Eucharist, Frith was burnt at the stake in 1533.

Stephen Gardiner (d. 1555) — Henrician Bishop of Winchester and Lord Chancellor of England during the reign of Mary I. In his youth, Gardiner distinguished himself in the study of Greek at Trinity Hall, Cambridge, and also studied for a time in Paris, where he met Erasmus briefly. Gardiner proceeded Doctor of Civil Law in 1520, and Doctor of Canon Law in 1521, earning both degrees at Cambridge. Like Edmund Bonner, Gardiner's impressive legal skill brought him to the attention of Cardinal Thomas Wolsey (1473–1530). Gardiner served with Thomas More on a delegation to the French in 1527, and Henry VIII made Gardiner his personal secretary. Gardiner labored to further Henry's "Great Matter," playing a leading role in having Cambridge officially pronounce against Henry's marriage to Catherine of Aragon (1485–1536). Gardiner also pressed the pope and his curia on behalf of Henry's annulment suit, and, when these efforts failed, was an ardent exponent of the Royal Supremacy, writing *De vera obedientia* in 1535, a tract defending Henry's headship of the English Church. Edmund Bonner (c.1498–1569) collaborated with Gardiner in this effort, and wrote a preface for the work. Despite working with Bonner on this treatise, Bonner and Gardiner seem to have been greatly at odds with each other until after the fall of Thomas Cromwell (c. 1485–1540) in 1540. In the latter 1530s and early 1540s, Gardiner became a favorite target of frustrated Protestants, who could not attack Henry VIII's conservative religious views directly, and so derided Gardiner as "Wily Winchester," since the Bishop was stalwart in writing against Protestant conceptions of the Eucharist. During the reign of Edward VI, Gardiner was, like Bonner, deprived of his see and imprisoned. Gardiner was not only restored to his diocese under Mary, but became Lord Chancellor. He presided at the marriage of Mary and Phillip II of Spain in Winchester Cathedral on July 25, 1554.

Nicholas? Grimbold (d. 1563?) — Chaplain to Nicholas Ridley (c. 1500–1555), Edwardine Bishop of London. Grimbold betrayed Ridley and Ridley's brother-in-law, George Shipside, in December 1554 or January 1555 by turning several manuscripts of Ridley's clandestine prison writings over to the Marian authorities. The result was that Ridley was, for a time, monitored more closely and denied access to any writing materials.

John Harpsfield (1516–1578) — Catholic Humanist and priest. Educated at Oxford, John became in 1541, the first Regius Professor of Greek for the University. Like his brother Nicholas, John was a leader in the restoration of Catholicism under Mary I. John wrote nine of the thirteen sermons Edmund Bonner published under the title *Homelies*, in 1555. John and Nicholas were both committed to the Fleet prison during Elizabeth's reign, for refusing the Oath of Supremacy, remaining there until 1574. Until his death in 1578, John continued to be harassed by leading members of Elizabeth's Council.

Nicholas Harpsfield (1519–1575) — Catholic apologist and priest, educated at Oxford, where he became close with the friends and relations of Thomas More, especially William Roper (c. 1496–1578), More's son-in-law. Although he underwent a self-imposed exile in 1550, Nicholas returned to England in 1553 at the accession of Mary I. Nicholas was appointed Archdeacon of Canterbury, where he was one of the leading commissioners for Cardinal Reginald Pole (1500–1558) in the administration of the diocese. Nicholas coordinated many of the heresy trials against lay Protestants in London. He also assisted Edmund Bonner, Bishop of London, in writing and publishing the *Homelies*, a collection of Catholic sermons, in 1555. Nicholas and his brother John were both committed to the Fleet prison during Elizabeth's reign, for refusing the Oath of Supremacy. They remained there until 1574, just sixteen months before Nicholas' death.

Henry VII (1457–1509) — King of England from August 22, 1485 until his death. Defeated Richard III at the Battle of Bosworth Field, founding the Tudor dynasty. Gifted in economic administration, Henry helped to stabilize the realm after the Wars of the Roses. Working to establish strong international relations, Henry succeeded in marrying his oldest son, Arthur Tudor, to the princess of Spain, Catherine of Aragon (1485–1536), in November of 1501. When Arthur died five months later, the succession devolved upon Henry's eldest surviving son, later Henry VIII. In December 1503, Henry VII succeeded in securing a dispensation from the pope for his second son to marry Catherine.

Henry VIII (1491–1547) — King of England and Ireland from 1509 until his death, Henry was a well-educated Renaissance prince, whose early reign was characterized by the promotion of Humanist scholarship and ideals. The impediments, however, to his producing a legitimate male heir led Henry to seek annulment of his first marriage with Catherine of Aragon (1485–1536), which in time ushered in the first era of Protestant reform of the Church in England. Although staunchly traditional in his personal views of ecclesiastical practice and doctrine, Henry collaborated with men of Protestant conviction in order to advance his consolidation of power over the English Church, as codified in the *Act of Supremacy* of 1534. These efforts culminated in the dissolution of the monasteries and the appropriation of Church wealth and lands for the crown. Tellingly, Henry's tacit encouragement of early Protestant ideals for the English Church was withdrawn as the spoliation of the monasteries came to a close. The *Act of Six Articles* (1539), a very conservative reaffirmation of traditional Church teachings on transubstantiation, clerical celibacy, and the need of auricular confession to a priest, were the final Henrician formulation for religious practice, and carried the death penalty for many of the offenses related to the violation of the articles. The administratively talented men of Protestant sympathies that Henry gathered around him in the middle portion of his reign, however, virtually ensured that Protestantism would advance swiftly under the reign of his son, Edward Tudor (1537–1533), the only surviving child from Henry's marriage to his third wife, Jane Seymour.

John Hooper (c. 1497–1555) — Early English Protestant, and Bishop of Gloucester and Worcester, Hooper underwent two periods of self-imposed exile in the 1540s, becoming a disciple of Zwingli's (1484–1531) and Bullinger's (1504–1575) views on ecclesial practice and the sacraments. Hooper was chaplain to both the Duke of Somerset and the Duke of Northumberland during the reign of Edward VI. In Lent of 1550, Hooper became embroiled in a lengthy controversy on traditional church vestments with Nicholas Ridley (c.1550–1555), which was not resolved until March of 1551. Hooper was executed under Mary I, even though he opposed Northumberland's plan to place Jane Grey on the throne following the death of Edward VI.

St. Irenaeus of Lyons (2nd century–c. 202) — Early Church Father and apologist. His greatest work, *Adversus Haereses* (c. 180) was a detailed explication and refutation of Gnosticism. Irenaeus argued that Church authorities, as heirs of the apostolic succession and under the guiding presence of the Holy Spirit, possessed the authoritative interpretation of scripture. He also argued that Church tradition, like scripture, was both inspired and authoritative for Church practice. Irenaeus asserted that even if the scriptures had not been written at all, the Church would still, through tradition, possess an authoritative guide to ecclesial practice and religious life.

Jan Laski (1499–1560) — Polish Protestant reformer, and head pastor of the so called "Stranger Church" in London during the reign of Edward VI (1537–1533). Laski's congregation was comprised of continental Protestants, whom Nicholas Ridley (c. 1550–1555), then Bishop of London, compelled to worship in ways that were in keeping with the *Book of Common Prayer*. Laski lived in Basel in the 1520s, where he became a close friend of Zwingli (1484–1531) and Erasmus (1566–1536). Living in England between 1543 and 1555, Laski was a correspondent and supporter of John Hooper in the Edwardine vestments controversy.

Hugh Latimer (c. 1487–1555) — Early English Protestant, and Bishop of Worcester under Henry VIII. Latimer was educated at Cambridge, and became a powerful Protestant preacher by the mid 1530s. Latimer was forced to resign his see in 1539 for his opposition to the *Act of Six Articles* and the sudden conservative turn in Henry's religious policies. Latimer was imprisoned twice in Henry's reign for preaching against doctrines associated with the *Six Articles*. As court preacher under Edward VI, Latimer railed against greedy courtiers who appropriated the monies and land of monastic foundations for the augmentation of their own vast wealth, rather than for the succor of the poor and indigent. Latimer's scathing sermons earned him some scorn among leading members of Edward VI's Council, because some of them were among the chief offenders. However, Latimer suffered his worst fate as a prisoner under Mary. After more than two years in prison, Latimer and Nicholas Ridley (c. 1500–1555) were burnt at the stake together, on October 16, 1555, just outside the city wall of Oxford.

Martin Luther (1483–1546) — German theologian, priest, and father of the Protestant Reformation. A former Augustinian friar, Luther challenged a number of points of doctrine concerning purgatory and papal authority in 1517. Luther's famous Theses were partially prompted by abuses associated with the sale of indulgences. As Luther's writings circulated into England, Henry VIII (1491–1547), John Fisher (d. 1535) and Thomas More (1478–1535) all wrote against the Wittenberg reformer's ideas. Many of Luther's books circulated at the universities, particularly at Cambridge, in the 1520s and 1530s.

Mary I (1516–1558) — Queen regnant of England and Ireland from July 1553 to her death in November 1558. She labored to restore Catholicism in England following the reign of her Protestant half-brother, Edward VI (1537–1547). Edmund Bonner (c. 1498–1569) was restored as Bishop of London under Mary.

St. Thomas More (1478–1535) — Renaissance Humanist and Lord Chancellor of England under Henry VIII. Educated at Oxford, More studied Greek and Latin literature, and translated the Latin biography of the Italian humanist Pico della Mirandola into English in 1499. More studied civil law in London and lived for a time among Carthusian monks, but eventually determined that he did not have a vocation to monastic life. More married Jane Colt, his first wife, in 1504. Although More became a close friend of Desiderius Erasmus, they differed in their theological outlook and understanding of Church authority. More began to write *Utopia* while on a delegation to Flanders to resolve disputes related to the English wool trade in the Low Countries. A favorite of Henry

VIII, More was knighted in 1521, and became a member of the Privy Council. As Luther's early works circulated into England, More was immediately engaged in Catholic apologetics, and probably wrote portions of Henry VIII's *Defence of the Seven Sacraments.* Despite his opposition to Henry's divorce from Catherine of Aragon, the King made More Lord Chancellor in 1529. As Chancellor, More examined and prosecuted a handful of early English Protestants, including John Frith (1503–1533), whom More had arrested, for disseminating heresy, in 1532. More resigned his post as Chancellor that same year, in the face of Henry's efforts to consolidate power over the English Church. Like Fisher, More refused to swear to the Act of Succession and the Oath of Supremacy in 1534, and was committed to the Tower of London on April 17. He was convicted of treason on the perjury of Richard Rich, and was beheaded on July 6, 1535 at Tower Hill.

Duke of Northumberland, John Dudley (1504–1553) — Lord President of the King's Council in the latter part of Edward VI's reign, and one of the sixteen executors that Henry VIII (1491–1547) left in place to share power until young Edward Tudor could rule in his own right. Northumberland, having considerable military skill and experience as both a general and an admiral, succeeded where Somerset failed, in restoring order after several popular uprisings in 1548 and 1549. In the wake of the Duke of Somerset's fall from power in 1549, resulting in large part from Seymour's failure to deal effectively with the rebels, Northumberland emerged as the leading power behind the throne until Edward's death in 1553. Dudley tried, unsuccessfully, to place Jane Grey on the throne after the young king died. For this effort, Northumberland was executed by Mary after she succeeded to the throne in the summer of 1553.

Johannes Oecolampadius (1482–1531) — German Protestant theologian and reformer. Wrote a controversial interpretation of the Last Supper in 1525, to which John Fisher (d. June 22, 1535) responded, defending the orthodox understanding of the Real Presence of Christ in the Eucharist. Oecolampadius' denial of transubstantiation and purgatory inspired several early English Protestants, including John Frith

(1503–1533), whom Thomas More (1478–1535) arranged to have arrested, for disseminating heresy, in 1532.

Henry Pendleton (d. 1557) — Homilist and Professor of Theology, educated at Oxford, where he earned the degree of Doctor of Divinity in 1552. Pendleton embraced Protestantism in the reign of Edward VI, but was re-converted to Catholicism under Mary I. Serving as chaplain to Edmund Bonner, Bishop of London, he wrote two of the sermons in the collection Bonner published in 1555 under the title, *Homelies*.

William Peryn (d. 1558) — Homilist, educated in the Dominican house at Oxford. Entering the Dominican order early in life, Peryn was an excellent and orthodox preacher, deft at refuting Protestant ideas from the pulpit. He published *Thre godly and notable Sermons of the moost honorable and blessed sacrament of the Aulter* in 1546, dedicating them to Edmund Bonner (c. 1498–1569), then Bishop of London. Peryn fled England in 1534 after Parliament passed the First Act of Supremacy. Returning to England in 1543, he left again at the accession of Edward VI. Peryn returned to England in 1553. He was made prior of the Dominican House of St. Bartholomew in Smithfield, the first religious house to be restored under Mary. Peryn assisted Bonner in writing the *Homelies*, a collection of Catholic sermons, published in 1555.

Cardinal Reginald Pole (1500–1558) — Humanist and Catholic archbishop. Pole was educated in the classics at Oxford, and studied in Italy during his youth. He was high in favor during the early part of Henry VIII's reign. Pole was, however, opposed to Henry on the question of the royal divorce, and embarked on a self-imposed exile in France and Italy in 1532, where he renewed and expanded his acquaintances among leading Italian Humanists. Against his wishes, Pole was made a cardinal by Pope Paul III in 1536. Pole returned to England in 1554 as Papal Legate, and during the reign of Mary I, became one of her chief advisors and Archbishop of Canterbury.

Ratramnus of Corbie (d. c. 870) — Frankish monk and Carolingian theologian who wrote on the Eucharist and predestination. Nicholas

Ridley (c.1550–1555), Bishop of London under Edward VI, claimed to have been converted from a more realist view of the sacrament of the altar by reading Ratramnus' treatise, *De corpora et sanguine Domini*. Ridley may have learned of this work by reading a 1527 book written by John Fisher (d. June 22, 1535), wherein the Bishop of Rochester cites Ratramnus' work, in response to Oecolampadius' (1482–1531) controversial treatise on the Last Supper.

Johann Reuchlin (1455–1522) — German Humanist, scholar of Greek and Hebrew. He was a friend and correspondent of many of the leading Humanists of his day, including Pico della Mirandola (1463–1494) and other Italian scholars, and Desiderius Erasmus (1466–1536). In 1517, Erasmus sent a copy of one of Reuchlin's cabbalistic works to John Colet (1467–1519) and John Fisher (d. 1536).

Nicholas Ridley (c. 1500–1555) — Bishop of London under Edward VI, Ridley studied Greek at Cambridge, and served as chaplain to Thomas Cranmer (1489–1556) and Henry VIII. Ridley was slow to embrace the Protestant "new learning" but was gradually converted to it, starting in the early 1540s. By the latter 1540s, however, Ridley was zealous in his new convictions, and removed altars from the churches of the Diocese of Rochester shortly after being elected bishop in 1547. Ridley publicly pronounced against the Real Presence of Christ in the Eucharist at Cambridge in 1549. In 1550, Ridley became Bishop of London, after playing a prominent role in the prosecution and removal of his predecessor, Edmund Bonner (c. 1498–1569). As he did at Rochester, Ridley had the altars removed from London churches and destroyed. At the death of Edward VI in July of 1553, Ridley was one of the leaders of the plan to place Jane Grey on the throne. Three days after Edward's death, Ridley delivered a sermon at Paul's Cross in London, reiterating Henry VIII's early orders of succession, which declared both Mary and Elizabeth to be bastards, and therefore ineligible to inherit the throne. For these activities, and for his well-known Protestant views and labors, Mary I imprisoned Ridley. Ridley continued to write from prison, and the bulk of his extant writings are from this period of his life. Ridley was burnt at the stake together with Hugh Latimer on October 16, 1555, just outside the city wall of Oxford.

Jacopo Sadoleto (1477–1547) — Italian Humanist and Catholic Bishop of Carpentras. An accomplished neo-Latin poet, Pope Leo X chose Sadoleto to be his secretary and appointed him bishop of Carpentras in 1517. Sadoleto was an irenic personality, and served the papacy as an arbiter. In 1539 he wrote a letter to the people of Geneva, inviting them to return to the Catholic faith. Although John Calvin (1509–1564) had been expelled from Geneva the previous year, and was then living in Strasbourg, the Genevans still asked Calvin to write a response to Sadoleto. Calvin accepted the invitation and wrote a reply to Sadoleto's letter, explicating several disputed points of doctrine concerning the sacraments and purgatory.

Jane Seymour (c. 1508–1537) — Queen consort of England and third wife of Henry VIII. She died two weeks after giving birth to Edward Tudor, later King Edward VI. She was the only one of Henry's six wives to receive a queen's funeral. At his own request, Henry was buried next to her when he died in 1547.

Duke of Somerset, Edward Seymour (c. 1506–1552) — Uncle of Edward VI, Somerset was Lord Protector and the *de facto* ruler of England for the early portion of Edward's short reign, as the young king was only ten at the death of his father, Henry VIII (1491–1547). Following a series of rebellions in 1548 and 1549, many resulting from religious unrest in the wake of Thomas Cranmer's imposition of Church services in English and the first *Book of Common Prayer*, Somerset lost power. Ineffective in combating the uprisings, the other members of the king's Council had Somerset briefly imprisoned. Although later released and restored to the king's Council, Somerset was executed in 1552 for attempting to take power once more.

Theophylact of Achrida (1055–1107) — Byzantine biblical scholar and Archbishop of Achrida (the area known today as Ohrid, Bulgaria). Well known for his commentaries on the books of the New Testament, which influenced the later writings of the Renaissance scholar, Desiderius Erasmus (1466–1536). Erasmus' *Novum Instrumentum* and *Annotationes* introduced several of the leading English divines, such as Thomas Cranmer (1489–1556) and Nicholas Ridley (c. 1500–1555), to Theophylact's works.

Peter Martyr Vermigli (1499–1562) — Italian Protestant theologian, educated at the University of Padua, where he proceeded Doctor of Divinity in 1527. After this time, he studied Greek and Hebrew, becoming proficient in both languages. While still an Augustinian monk, Vermigli began to read the works of the Strasbourg reformer, Martin Bucer (1491–1551), and those of Huldrych Zwingli (1484–1531). Vermigli spent much of the 1540s fleeing church and government authorities in various Italian and Swiss cities, to avoid persecution for his Protestant views. In 1547, Martyr fled to England. Thomas Cranmer (1489–1556) extended a warm welcome to Martyr, appointing him Regius Professor of Divinity at Oxford. Martyr became a close friend of Nicholas Ridley (c. 1500–1555), participating in the debate on the Eucharist at Cambridge in 1549. Many aspects of Ridley's sacramental theology appear to have been influenced by Martyr, despite their very different emphases in scriptural interpretation. Martyr left England and returned to Strasbourg at the accession of Mary I.

Thomas Wolsey (1473–1530) — Archbishop of York, Cardinal, and chief minister of Henry VIII. Educated in theology at Oxford, Wolsey served as royal chaplain to Henry VII, and rose in prominence to become the most powerful servant of the English crown. He was a dominant figure in the first half of the reign of Henry VIII. While Wolsey succeeded brilliantly at a number of domestic initiatives, including major reforms of the realm's legal system and taxation, he was unable to obtain Henry's long-sought Church annulment of his marriage to Catherine of Aragon (1485–1536). Wolsey worked desperately for Henry's "Great Matter," but since the Emperor Charles V was Catherine's nephew, and the pope feared Charles, Wolsey's efforts were in vain. Endowed with a vanity equal to his administrative gifts, Wolsey was deeply resented and envied for the pomp of his retinue, his lavish wealth, and extensive holdings.

Wolsey's legacy included a number of key diplomatic alliances, and he was a great judge of talent, discovering and promoting some of the most gifted legal and administrative minds of his day, including Thomas More (1478–1535) and Thomas Cromwell (c. 1485–1540). Wolsey's failure to obtain an annulment for Henry also earned the ire of Anne Boleyn and her powerful supporters, and was therefore the Cardinal's downfall. Facing a trumped charge of treason, Wolsey made his way to London in November of 1530. Accompanied by his personal chaplain, Edmund Bonner (c.1498–1569), Wolsey narrowly escaped the wrath of the King through a natural death on November 29, 1530.

Huldrych Zwingli (1484–1531) — A leading Protestant reformer among the Swiss, and head of the Zurich church. By the early 1520s, Zwingli called for an end of fasting in Lent, and the repeal of clerical celibacy. He advanced a view of the Eucharist as a memorial of Christ's death, wholly repudiating the idea of the Real Presence. His sacramental views could not be reconciled with those of Martin Luther (1483–1546), however, despite repeated efforts among their followers to bring the two leaders into a doctrinal alliance. Zwingli's calls for ecclesiastical property to be taken over by the government, to be converted into hospitals and schools, inspired many reformation-era campaigns to dissolve monastic foundations.